The Search for My Abandoned Grandmother

The Search for My Abandoned Grandmother

A history of family blessings

by Mary Ames Mitchell

Peach Plum Press
San Rafael, California

First Edition - July 2012

Most of the information, names, characters, places and events are the product of the author's memory or the memories of her friends and family and are represented to the best of their abilities. Some names have been changed to protect privacy and security. The order of some of the events has been changed for literary purposes.

ISBN: 978-0-9850530-1-7

Library of Congress Control Number: 2012908956

2012 Peach Plum Press
San Rafael, California
Printed in the United States of America
For more information: www.PeachPlumPress.com

This story was written for my mother,
Eileen Mary Hopkins Ames,
and her brother, Peter Hopkins.

"The effect of her being on those around her was incalculably diffusive: for the growing good of the world is partly dependent on unhistoric acts; and that things are not so ill with you and me as they might have been, is half owing to the number who lived faithfully a hidden life, and rest in unvisited tombs."

— George Eliot, *Middlemarch*

Contents

Eileen Maude Thomas' Family

- **George Thomas + Victoria Bissell**
  - Harold "Webster" Bissell-Thomas + Joyce "Joy"
    - Jill Bissell-Thomas + John
      - Philippa + Peter
        - Josh
        - Georgia
      - Adam
      - Candida + Tim
        - Thomas
        - Harriett
        - Eleanor
    - Jeffray Bissell-Thomas + Ann
      - Charles "Jungle Eyes"
      - Sarah + Bob
        - Fleurie
        - Zephir
      - Harriett + Urs
        - Sorrel
      - James + Rosey
        - Helior
    - Camilla Bissell-Thomas + Archie + Rodney
      - Cynthia + Rodney
        - Rebecca
        - Laura
        - Charles
  - **Eileen Maude Thomas** + Pryns Hopkins + No. 2 Fay Cartledge + Vernon Armitage
    - Peter Hopkins (Adopted)*
    - Eileen "**Betty May**" Hopkins + Thomas Ames
      - **Mary Ames** + Ex-One + Ex-Two + Ex-Three
        - Amy
        - Jonathan
      - Tom Ames*
      - Charles Ames*
    - Jennifer Hopkins*
    - David Hopkins*
  - Peggy Thomas + Mr. Pope
    - Pat Pope*
    - June Pope*
  - + Jack Abbott
    - Frank "Jon" Abbott + Katherine + Catherine
      - Louise
  - Eric Thomas*
  - Liala Victoria Thomas*
  - William "Billie" Thomas*
  - Daisy Thomas + Lionel "Jack" Turner
    - Lionel Turner Jr. + Dorothy
      - Michael + Claire
        - Oliver*
        - Zoë
        - Duncan*
        - Romilly
      - David*
      - Jason + Ioana
        - Sophie
    - Helen Turner*
    - Veronica Turner*
    - Anthony Turner*
  - Marie Louise Thomas*

Fay Cartledge's Family (Stepmother to Betty May and step-grandmother to author.)

- Mr. Cartledge + Dorret "Gaga"
  - Fay Cartledge (Wife No.2 of Pryns Hopkins, see above)
  - Marcus Cartledge*
    - Paul + Judy
      - Gabriel
  - Audrey Cartledge* +David
    - Carolyn + Ex-One
      - Verity
      - Jessica
  - Brother*
  - Brother*

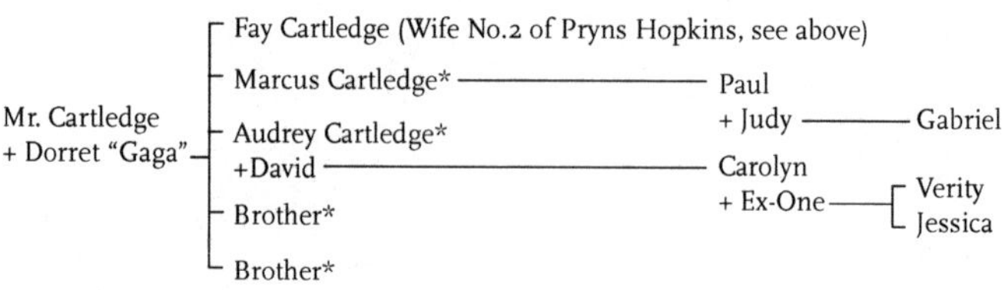

*Rest of family information not relevent to this story.

Firth of Forth
Glasgow
Edinburgh
Ayr
SCOTLAND
Dumfries
N
W
E
S
Salford
Manchester
ENGLAND
Wolverhampton
Northampton
Worcester
Cambridge
Banbury
London
Wokingham
Kew
Newbury
Herne Hill
Chichester
Yapton (Berri Court)
Southampton
Worthing
Poole
Bogner Regis
Ryde
Isle of Wight
Ostend
BELGIUM
English Channel
Guernsey
Jersey
FRANCE
Chateau de Bures
Paris
Dinard
Mont Saint Michel

Betty May, Eileen Maude, Pryns and Peter – December 1925.

Chapter 1

Departure

As conductor whistles shrieked, passengers hustled and brakes hissed from behind the anxious wheels of the boat-train about to leave for France from London's St. Pancras station, seven-year-old Betty May stood on the tips of her toes to kiss her mother good-bye. Eileen Maude straightened the soft round collar of her daughter's traveling suit. "Be a good girl, darling." Her brown eyes moistened and her glossy red lips quivered. "Chin up, we'll be together again in two months."

Betty May's older brother, Peter, age nine, waited anxiously at the top of the train platform with their father, Pryns Hopkins, and governess, Popsy. Peter reached down to help his sister up the steps.

Still holding her hand, Peter turned Betty May around to face their mother as the conductor latched the safety gate, tucking them in. The train jerked and lunged forward. Peter gave his sister's fingers a squeeze. They could see Eileen Maude recede through the lattice. Her flowered silk dress fluttered in the steam clouds left behind by the train. Her broad straw sunhat would have blown away, had she not held it down, and as she waved her white handkerchief with the other hand, she became smaller and smaller. Little did Peter and Betty May know this image would be their last of maternal love.

Pryns ushered his children to their seats. As Betty May cuddled up next to him, she asked, "Why was Mummy crying?" These partings for summer holidays had become customary since her parents divorced three years earlier.

Pryns had also noticed the difference in his ex-wife's behavior. He recorded in his journal that night, "She was seized with the conviction that it was the last time ever she would see her children, and she broke down in tears."

Eileen Maude and her new husband, Vernon Armitage, would be driving in the opposite direction from the train. They planned to tour the Lake District on their way through to Ayrshire, Scotland, where they would holiday with Eileen's favorite sister, Peggy, who married a Scot.

Betty May was my mother. She lived, until the day before her eighty-fifth birthday, in a retirement home called Villa Marin in San Rafael, California, about three miles north of me. She passed away in November of 2010. During her last few years, her perceptions of day-to-day activities became muddy. However, she recalled details of events that happened decades earlier surprisingly clearly, particularly dramatic and emotional ones such as this parting image.

"My mother faded into the distance of the cavernous tunnel as the train left St. Pancras Station," she described. "I remember her shrinking until even her large hat ceased to exist."

I had asked Mom to repeat this story back in 2006 on a Sunday morning as we ate brunch at Villa Marin, as we did almost every Sunday. She called Sundays "Family Day," because that's what her father called them when he visited her at St. Michael's boarding school. I had just published a book about my father's family and was on a new quest to learn more about hers. I hoped by knowing more about my grandmother,

I might understand my own mother better. She kept her emotions as well hidden as her mother's pearls.

"My mother had rheumatic fever as a child," Mom reminded me, "and as a result, suffered from heart disease. While she was in Scotland, she got sick and died."

"Did you see her when she was sick?" I asked.

"No."

"How long was she ill?"

"I don't know."

"Did she die in Scotland or was she taken back to London?"

"I'm not sure."

"Where is she buried?"

"I have no idea."

"Didn't you go to a funeral or anything?"

"No."

"So you don't even know if there is a grave?"

"No."

"Or if she was cremated, or if there is a plaque with her name on it somewhere?"

"No, dear, nothing!"

"What year was it?"

"Still 1933, I believe."

"How long after she got sick did she die?"

"I have no idea." Mom seemed frustrated with my questions, or maybe frustrated with herself for not remembering the answers to them. She continued anyway. "I don't even know when she died exactly, the date or the month."

"Does it bother you not to know where your mother was buried?"

"Yes, very much so. I'm sorry there is no longer anyone alive whom I can ask. Everyone who would have been around then, my grandparents, aunts and uncles, my old governess, Popsy, they are all gone. I just never thought to ask anyone and now it's too late."

Even further back, in 1975, when I was twenty-four, Mom took my brothers and me to London to meet some of these relatives. My grandmother, *nee* Eileen Maude Thomas, had been the second of eight children, giving my mother loads of cousins and me loads of second-cousins. My mother's Auntie Joy was by then the matriarch of the family, and the only one left who may have known this information. She had been married to my grandmother's older brother, Harold, by then deceased.

When I met Auntie Joy, I wasn't interested in asking about the whereabouts of my grandmother's remains. Joy and Harold's daughters, Jill and Camilla, gave a dinner party in our honor during that visit. Twenty or more members of the Thomas family mingled and prattled in Jill's living room when my mother, my two brothers and I arrived. I'd been in the room perhaps ten minutes—a little overwhelmed by meeting so many new people—when a very tall and distinguished looking woman motioned toward the sofa and beckoned me to sit with her.

"It's amazing, Mary, you look just like your Grandmother Eileen," she said after telling me she was Auntie Joy.

That pleased me immensely.

I don't recall all we chatted about, but it must have included the relationship of our relatives, because together we created a diagram of the Thomas Family Tree as Auntie Joy knew it. I remember drawing lines and boxes and filling in names as she dictated. She'd nod in the direction of the person she was talking about because "it wasn't polite to point." The tree only went back in time to the generation of her in-laws, my mother's grandparents George and Victoria Bissell Thomas. But by 2006, when I was ready to investigate that diagram further, I couldn't find it.

I remember two other things about that family gathering: my introduction to white bread sauce served as a garnish with roast chicken, and my introduction to the phrase *F-H-B*.

As we lined up for the buffet, my second-cousin Philippa moved to the back of the line, saying to me, "F-H-B you know."

I must have looked puzzled.

"Family hold back," she explained cheerily. "Just in case there isn't enough food." I glanced at the chicken to see how big it was.

Ever since learning about our resemblance—though I didn't see it at all—I've had a soft spot for this grandmother I could never know. I have many photographs of her, including the one of her wedding to my Grandpa Pryns that graces the cover of this book. I also had the embroidered silk veil she wore in that wedding, but I just sent it to my daughter, Amy, in New York to wear for her wedding in June. The large rectangle of ninety-year-old silk mesh with its embroidered edge is so delicate it's weightless, like holding a spider web.

Mom also gave me Eileen Maude's elegant red evening coat, an art deco masterpiece encrusted with gold embroidery. There is no label, but Mom believed it came from the House of Worth. The art deco pattern on the silk lining reminds me of drawings I saw in art history classes by the nineteenth-century Scottish designer Charles Renee Mackintosh.[1] A white fox collar surrounds the neck, complete with tiny fox heads, one peeking down from each shoulder with eerily realistic glass eyes.

I've pressed my nose to the inside of the coat, wondering if the scent is of my Gram. In my imagination, the red silk holds the memory of a glorious time when she must have been one of the most fashionably dressed women in London. There is a wine stain on the front. I cherish that as well, for maybe it is a drop of claret she was drinking one evening with my grandfather back in the 1920s.

I've only worn the coat once, to a New Year's Eve Venetian ball. My mother used to wear it for New Year's Eve parties, too, but she stopped attending parties after she divorced my father in the mid-1960s, when I was thirteen. She claimed she didn't like parties. I think she didn't like making small talk.

After questioning Mom about Eileen Maude that Sunday in 2006, I decided to take a trip to England to research the Thomas family and to search for my grandmother's grave. What if she were buried under a

---

1. 1868-1928

beautiful headstone somewhere? I pictured her spirit, still covered in that wedding veil, waiting all those years for her children to visit.

That may seem peculiar to many people in the United States, but there is an Italian cemetery near a place I often go to in Tuscany, where the town-folk visit the memorials of their ancestors on a weekly, sometimes daily, basis! Neither my Uncle Peter nor my mom could have honored Eileen Maude in that way, because they didn't know where she was. What if no one ever visited her? Would she wait alone throughout eternity? Was she reaching out to me now and asking me to find her, as I believe my father did after he died?

Some people claim there is no connection between the physical world and the spiritual one, but when I close my eyes I often feel that I enter the spiritual world myself and that the spirits of my loved ones who have passed on are there with me. They have joined God's host, his army of angels, like those so often mentioned in the Old Testament. Some people think angels are God's ideas. That would mean God was reaching out to me.

I started researching my family history twenty years ago to help my son, Jonathan, whose American history teacher gave the assignment to create a family tree. I already had a lot of information about my father's side of the family from a great aunt who spent her entire adult life researching. All I had to do was extract the box filled with the papers she'd sent me from under my bed. Jon's task—probably the motive of the history teacher—was to sort it out and make the charts.

Though Eileen Maude was English, my mother's father, Pryns Hopkins, had been born and raised in California. He'd traveled to England after World War I and met and married my grandmother there. We soon learned his American family was well documented, since Pryns descended from one of the 102 passengers on the 1620 voyage of the *Mayflower*. The Mayflower Society has been researching the Hopkins family for over a hundred years. They've published a thick book with a silver cover containing the information they've found.

I've uncovered voluminous information about other family lines as well. The chart that started out as four pages has blossomed to over seventy. Filling in the missing blanks has been as much fun as going on treasure hunts or solving murder mysteries.

While doing all this charting, I discovered many delightful characters and interesting migration trends. This inspired me to read books about the time periods in which my forebears lived.

I wanted to know why they came to America, what religions they followed and why they risked their lives and left their cultures to move from their homelands? And how did my religious beliefs relate or not relate with theirs? I've been searching for a feeling of foundation in my religious practices since learning Bible stories when I was five.

I uncovered over a hundred and eighty great-great...grandparents who sailed to America during one of the periods known as the Great Migration, 1620 to 1640. My father never knew he was my mother's thirteenth cousin. Two of his three *Mayflower* ancestors were the same as two of Mom's eleven *Mayflower* ancestors. I've followed the migration stories of the descendants of these Colonial Americans through thirteen, fourteen and sometimes fifteen generations. I've gone in search of gravestones around the country, from Santa Barbara, California, to Shelter Island at the eastern tip of Long Island in New York. Recently I found a four-hundred-year-old ancestor grave in Aberdeen, Scotland. I've walked the trails my ancestors William Dawes, Henry Knox and Thomas Knowlton trod during the American Revolution. Visiting tombs and the places where my ancestors lived and breathed has given me an amazing sense of connection to my heritage.

For example, Pryns' seventh great-grandfather and my ninth great-grandfather, Edmund Freeman, is buried on a mound in Sandwich at the northwest corner of Cape Cod, where his house used to sit over 370 years ago. I read about it when I was researching Edmund in the genealogy library of the Mayflower Society in Plymouth, Massachusetts. The directions in the *Freeman Genealogy* to the site were vague, so it took me three days to find it. When I did, it was dark. Fortunately the inn where I stayed provided me with a flashlight. I followed a narrow path through a small quiet wood to a ten-foot square clearing surrounded by a wood rail fence. There in the middle of the clearing, cemented into a large piece of granite close to the ground, was the brass plaque marker donated by one of Edmund's numerous descendants.

As I sat on the cold stone and smelled the damp leaves, I looked up at the stars and imagined old Edmund there with the other angels—wearing a beard, perhaps—looking down on me fondly and patting me on the shoulder, proud of me for paying him some respect. He lived hundreds of years ago, yet he led a life as significant as the life I'm leading now. Because of that grave marker, and because his descendants researched and recorded his life, he hasn't been forgotten.

I wonder if it's a common trait among genealogists to worry about being forgotten. I worry about it. I want to leave a legacy. I will leave two children, the book about my dad and this book about my grandmother. That will do for starts. They confirm that my time on Earth has been worthwhile.

When I began my research in preparation for my trip to England, I knew of only two sources for information about my grandmother and her family besides my mother. A third source existed once, but it had been lost.

The first source was my grandfather's autobiography written in 1962 and titled *Both Hands Before the Fire*. I'd read my copy some thirty-five years earlier after Grandpa passed away in 1970. He was eighty-five, the same age my mother almost was when she died. I was certain Grandpa's autobiography didn't contain any information about where my grandmother was buried, but I thought a second reading might uncover some clues I'd missed in the first go-round.

Grandpa also left an extensive set of personal journals—one for every two to four years of his life. That's close to the number of scrapbooks I've made of my life so far. I'd heard my aunt and uncle talk about the journals, but I'd never seen them. Grandpa willed them to the care of my Aunt Jennifer, my mother's younger half-sister by twelve years. She kept them in a storage locker near her home in Seattle, which meant they weren't within easy reach. I wondered how I could obtain the journal covering 1933.

The third source of information that once existed was a large scrapbook of the correspondence of my grandmother to my grandfather during their life together. I ran across it while I was visiting my grandfather on a Thanksgiving or Christmas holiday during my high school years in the late 1960s, after my parents' divorce. By then Grandpa lived in a modern, mostly glass home built by an award-winning architect in Santa Barbara, California, about two hours north of the home where I, my brothers and our mother lived in Pasadena.

I was looking through my grandfather's books one afternoon, having nothing else to do. I was often on my own since I was the oldest grandchild (age sixteenish) and the only girl. My two younger brothers were off playing with our even younger cousin, Jennifer's son Thayer. As I perused my grandfather's extensive library, I spotted the wide volume under a pile of oversized art books stacked sideways on the bottom shelf.

Who can resist looking at a scrapbook, especially one that you've discovered in your grandfather's house? Instead of photos pasted to pages, there were personal letters, often with their envelopes, and a collection of small blue sheets on which had been written short poems. I scrolled through some four or five pages before it dawned on me that the author of the letters and poems was my grandmother, Eileen Maude. Once this realization occurred, I felt as guilty as I'd felt the day I looked through my mother's wallet to see how much money she had.

My grandmother was never mentioned in my grandfather's house. I knew the reason for that, but not because anyone told me. It was the same reason my mother never learned the whereabouts of her own mother's grave. My grandfather's second wife, Fay, was an extremely jealous woman.

Blonde, beautiful, brilliant and manipulative Fay married my grandfather in London the same year my brunette grandmother died. By that time Grandpa had been living in England as a U.S. ex-patriot for thirteen years. Jennifer, his daughter with Fay, was born a couple of years after their marriage. In 1940 Pryns shipped Fay and Jennifer, as well as my then fourteen-year-old mother, to his home in America. He wanted to get them out of harm's way far from the German attacks. Peter, on the other hand, then sixteen, stayed behind. My mother always told me it was under the pretense he was eligible for the service, but that the real reason was because his new stepmother didn't want him around. I would learn that wasn't quite true. Nonetheless, Mom didn't see her brother again for ten years and lost touch with her maternal grandparents completely. The only people who kept in reliable contact with her were a schoolmate from St. Michaels, Rosemary, and two cousins, Jill and Camilla.

Fay was twenty years my grandfather's junior. When she was forty-three, she divorced him. Grandpa never remarried. Fay went on to have four more husbands. Still, she continued to attend Christmas and Thanksgiving holidays at the Santa Barbara house, sometimes with her current spouse. My grandfather remained under her spell until the day he died and bequeathed her one-fourth of his good-sized fortune. No matter what the legal papers may have said, Fay remained the queen of his roost. My mother kept in the shadows like Cinderella in her presence.

Knowing all this, the scrapbook surprised me. Why had my grandfather gone to so much trouble to have my grandmother's letters bound into a book so carefully and lovingly? Since no one ever spoke about my grandmother around me, it hadn't occurred to me that my grandfather truly loved her. I held in my lap the history of their love affair, something I'd never even acknowledged before. And to my joy, like so many people in my family, my grandmother wrote poetry!

One poem in particular caught my attention. In rhyme, Eileen Maude told Pryns she loved him very much, but it made her sad that he spent so much time away from her with his activities and social causes. I think this poem affected me deeply because one of the reasons my own parents got divorced was my father's obsession over *his* social causes. They distanced him from us, the family who really needed him.

I read through the letters and poems for only fifteen or twenty minutes before I heard some of my relatives coming up the stairs close to where I sat. Fearing that Fay would be among them, I quickly closed the scrapbook and stowed it back into the bookshelf. However, in my haste I placed it on top of the art books instead of underneath. When I returned to look for it again, it was gone.

The scrapbook resurfaced when my grandfather died a few years later while I was in college. He'd left it to my mother, naturally, but in a reaction that I knew to be typical of her—she didn't deal with emotional issues—Mom refused to look at the book.

"I was so afraid to open up the painful memories that I asked Jennifer to destroy it," Mom told me.

When I asked Jennifer about it, hoping she had secretly rescued the scrapbook and was hiding it somewhere, she said, "I remember when your mother did that. Your Uncle David and I couldn't believe she wanted us to throw the scrapbook away. Today I wish we hadn't."

I was angry with my mother. Why didn't she think about me and that I wanted that scrapbook? I was devastated I would never have the chance to read the rest of the poems. But I didn't tell my mother that. I'd learned early in life to keep a cork on my feelings around her. If I did show emotion, she became uncomfortable, told me to calm down and then quickly changed the subject.

That left me, in 2006, with *Both Hands Before the Fire* and the journals. Even those overshadowed the nothing I thought I had from my grandmother. My grandfather left behind other books about religion, philosophy, his travels and his other causes. I have eleven of them in my library. But he didn't mention my grandmother in any of them.

As I worked on my trip itinerary, I began rereading the sections of the autobiography having to do with Grandpa's early life leading up to the moment he met my grandmother. This was the first step toward getting to know Eileen Maude and my English family.

Prince Charles Hopkins – c1925.

Chapter 2

Prince / Pryns / Prynce / Prence

Prince Charles Hopkins was born on the fifth day of March 1885 in Oakland, California, into a life that was never ordinary. He spent much of that life traveling far and wide and challenging the status quo. When he died eighty-five years later, his obituary in the *Santa Barbara News Press* stated he'd traveled to every country in the world—an exaggeration maybe, but not by much.

His parents named him *Prince* after his paternal great-grandfathers, Prince Hopkins and Prince Hawes. His middle name, Charles, came from his father. Our ancestor Stephen Hopkins carried his surname to America eight generations earlier when he first sailed to Jamestown via Bermuda in 1610, and then finally to Plymouth on the *Mayflower* in 1620. In other words, he made two trips and stayed put on the second. Descendants of other *Mayflower* passengers William Brewster, Edward Doty, John Howland, Francis Cooke and John Tilly intermarried to create my grandfather, but he wasn't named after them.

The name Prince, first spelled *Prence,* sailed to America attached to our patriarch Thomas Prence, a twenty-one-year-old carriage maker from London. Prence sailed on the *Fortune,* the second ship that sailed to Plymouth, also filled with religious Separatists. He arrived the year after the *Mayflower*'s landing.

Thomas Prence married Patience Brewster, daughter of the aforementioned William Brewster, the religious leader of the colony, in August 1624. Theirs was the ninth wedding recorded in Plymouth Colony. Eventually Prence became Governor of the colony[1] and served several terms. Because of that, hundreds of Prence's descendants named their sons Prence or Prince in his honor.

My grandfather became the fifth Prince Hopkins in his family line. However, from rereading *Both Hands Before the Fire,* I don't think he knew the history of his name. In the course of Grandpa's life he spelled his name *Prince, Prnys* and *Prynce* but never *Prence.* For simplicity sake, I will employ *Pryns,* the spelling he used when married to my grandmother, except when discussing his early life, when he signed his name *Prince.* This is in spite of the fact that when I was growing up and knew him, Grandpa spelled his name *Prynce.* He made the change shortly after marrying his second wife, Fay. In short, this spelling bit has been a biographer's nightmare.

My family's cluster of Pilgrim ancestors settled on Cape Cod and lived there from 1630 to the end of the Revolutionary War—174 years. The first family member christened Prence Hopkins[2] was born in 1731 in Harwich, just west of the elbow. The Pilgrims didn't use Roman numerals to label descendants, but for clarity I will add them. Prence I changed the spelling when he named his own son *Prince* in 1768. Prince II, also born in Harwich, worked as a whaler, a common occupation for Cape Cod residents at the time. According to family lore, he barely survived a shipwreck on one of his voyages. Because of that his wife, Phoebe,

1. Plymouth only had six governors before it merged with the Massachusetts Bay Colony in 1690.

2. Prince I was the great-grandson of Stephen Hopkins and Thomas Prence.

determined to move to a place where her sons wouldn't go to sea. When the Revolutionary War ended and new lands opened up for settling in Maine and upstate New York, Prince II and Phoebe moved off the Cape. By that time both sets of their parents had died, which may have made the transition easier. This was the fifth generation from that which arrived on the *Mayflower* and *Fortune*.

Prince II and Phoebe Hopkins arrived in New Sharon, Maine, in 1804 where Prince II became a farmer. Six years later he and Phoebe named their seventh child *Prince*. He would be my grandfather's grandfather.

Panning for ancestors often turns up lovely gold nuggets. During my genealogical research, I connected with a Hopkins sixth-cousin named Helen who lives in Redding, about four hours away from me. She shares my Hopkins ancestry from Stephen all the way to Prince and Phoebe. She informed me that according to *her* family lore, Prince's and Phoebe's home in New Sharon was "marked by a tangle of damask roses that had come from the Cape." Helen did some investigating and discovered that roses from the same plant still decorated the garden of the Joshua Hopkins House on Cape Cod Hill Road, also in New Sharon. Helen contacted the current owner of Joshua's home, and he sent, from Maine to Redding, a cutting of the rose. It flourishes so well in Helen's garden that she has to cut it back frequently to keep it from overflowing its allotted plot.

I stopped by Helen's house this summer on my way home from a trip to Oregon, whereupon she presented me with my own cutting of the damask rose. I planted it in a sunny and safe corner of my garden as soon as I got home to San Rafael. Though it is still a wee plant, and I haven't inherited either my mother's or my father's green thumb, it seems to be as happy as it was in Maine and Massachusetts over the last several hundred years.

Before the birth of Prince IV, Prince III moved to the newly formed milltown of North Vassalboro, Maine, twenty-one miles northwest of New Sharon—an easy day-trip in a horse and buggy. There he married

Betsy Hawes. Betsy's parents, Prince and Betsy Hawes, had also moved from Cape Cod. They'd left Yarmouth in 1802, two years before Prince Hopkins II moved his family to New Sharon. Most likely the families knew each other well before they settled in Maine. Prince Hawes served as an elder in the Congregational Church and helped found Vassalboro's new congregation there.

By 1850, Prince III had helped establish a hardware store and successful tannery business with a fellow named Jacob Southwick, under the company name Southwick & Hopkins. It stood on Getchel's Corner, named after another man who had moved to town from Cape Cod. *The Illustrated History of Kennebec County, Maine*[3] stated that the tannery was the "life of North Vassalboro."

Prince III and Olive produced five children that we know of. Their first, born in 1837, became my great-grandfather, Charles Harris Hopkins. Not until their fourth child (third son) did they choose the name Prince [IV]. That was in 1842. Middle names became popular about that time in family trees, and the Hopkins tree was no exception. Prince's middle name was Leroy.

Sadly, Prince Leroy died at the age of four in 1849, but his first name didn't go to waste. His parents used it as a middle name for their fifth child born in 1853, George Prince, named after Olive's brother, George Hawes. George Prince[4] never married and therefore had no heirs, but his older brother Charles Harris Hopkins, at the age of forty-eight, named his one and only surviving son Prince, making my grandfather Prince V.

---

3. *Illustrated History of Kennebec County, Maine*. ed. Henry D. Kingsbury, Simeon L. Deyo. New York: H. W. Blake & Company, 1892.

4. Since Prince was George's middle name, I'm not giving him a Roman numeral. This is confusing enough as it is.

Charles Hopkins' Family

Cousins married in at least four cases. So, ancestors on the right side often repeat.

*Traveled to New England on the *Mayflower* in 1620.

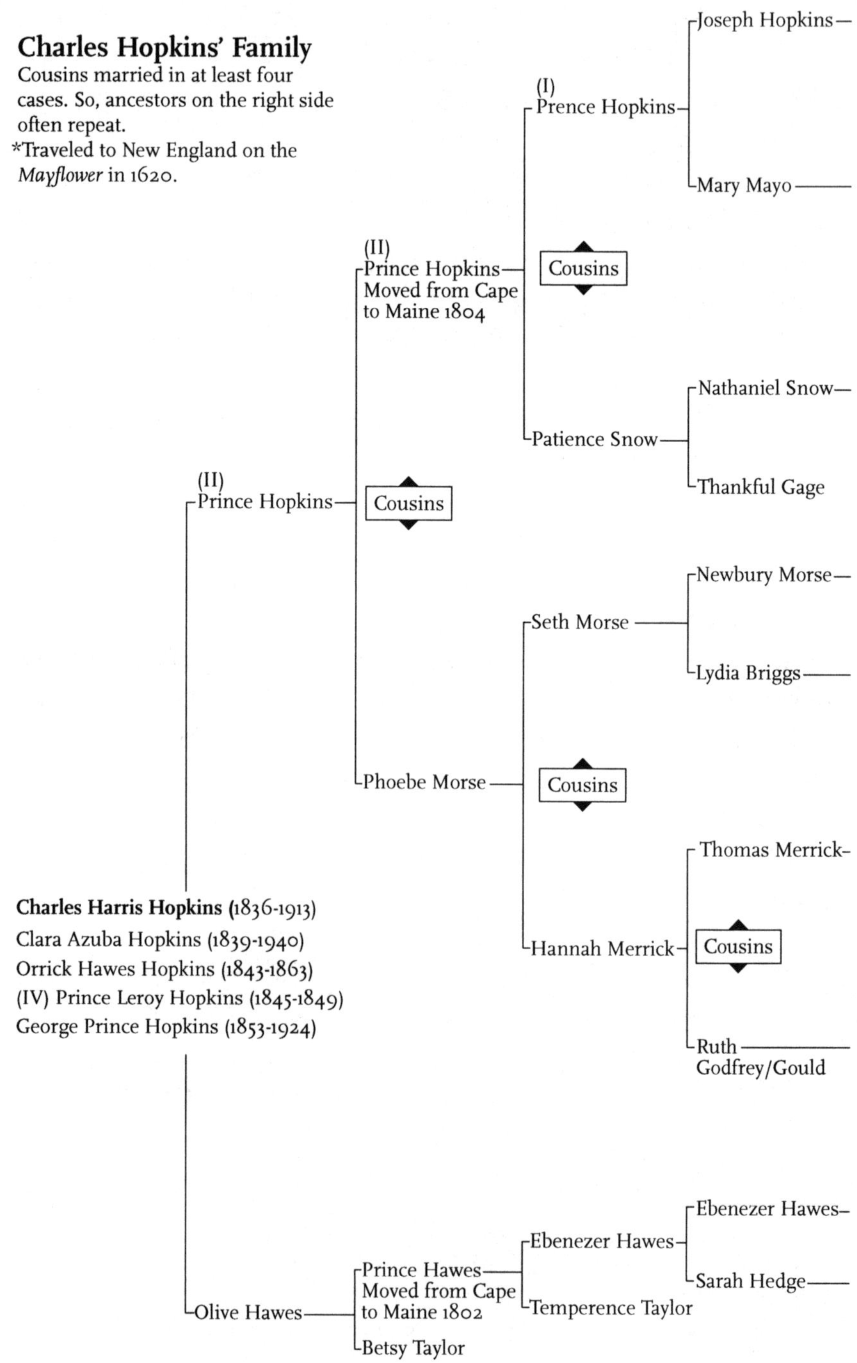

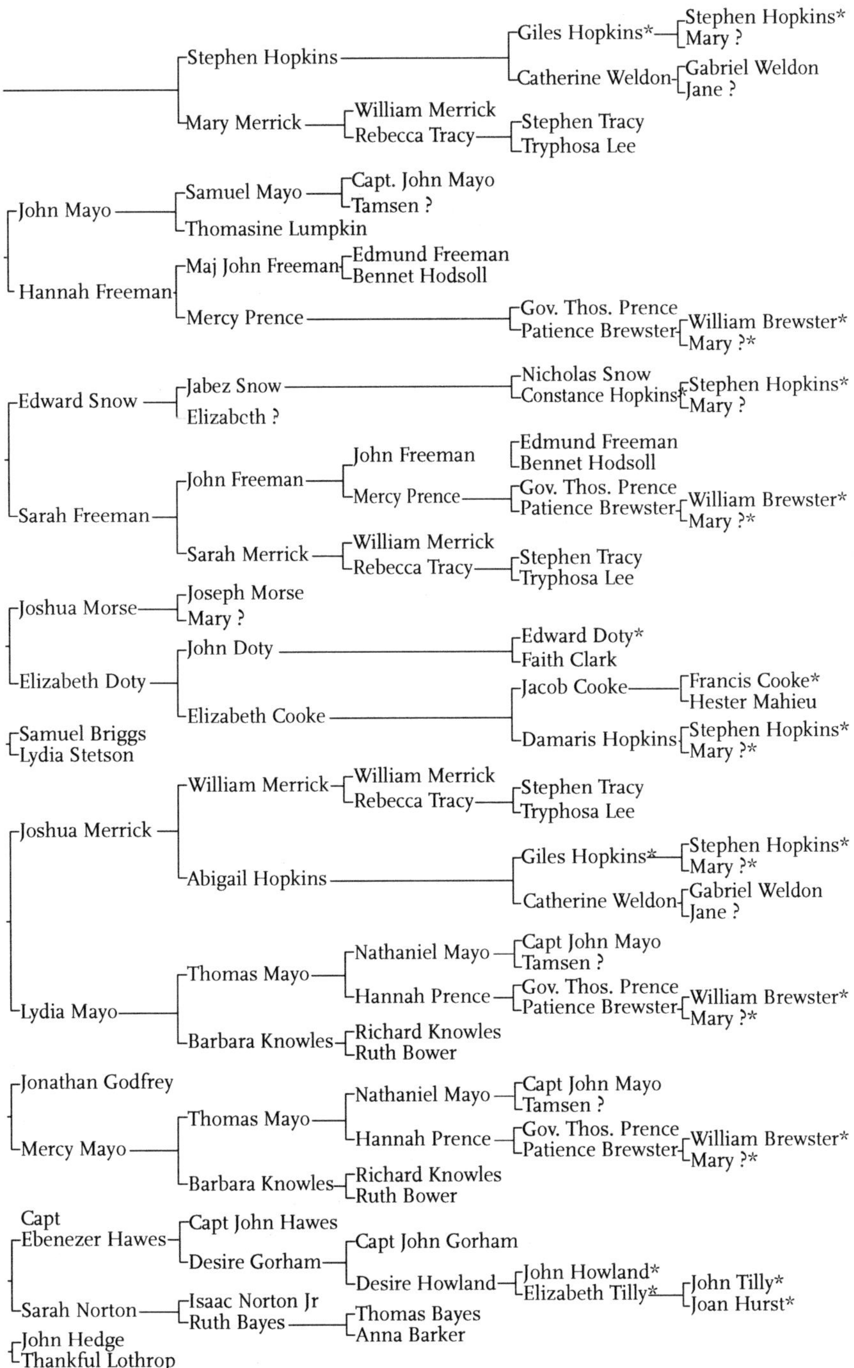
Stephen Hopkins
Giles Hopkins*
Stephen Hopkins*
Mary ?
Catherine Weldon
Gabriel Weldon
Jane ?
Mary Merrick
William Merrick
Rebecca Tracy
Stephen Tracy
Tryphosa Lee
John Mayo
Samuel Mayo
Capt. John Mayo
Tamsen ?
Thomasine Lumpkin
Hannah Freeman
Maj John Freeman
Edmund Freeman
Bennet Hodsoll
Mercy Prence
Gov. Thos. Prence
Patience Brewster
William Brewster*
Mary ?*
Edward Snow
Jabez Snow
Nicholas Snow
Constance Hopkins
Stephen Hopkins*
Mary ?
Elizabeth ?
Sarah Freeman
John Freeman
John Freeman
Edmund Freeman
Bennet Hodsoll
Mercy Prence
Gov. Thos. Prence
Patience Brewster
William Brewster*
Mary ?*
Sarah Merrick
William Merrick
Rebecca Tracy
Stephen Tracy
Tryphosa Lee
Joshua Morse
Joseph Morse
Mary ?
Elizabeth Doty
John Doty
Edward Doty*
Faith Clark
Elizabeth Cooke
Jacob Cooke
Francis Cooke*
Hester Mahieu
Damaris Hopkins
Stephen Hopkins*
Mary ?*
Samuel Briggs
Lydia Stetson
Joshua Merrick
William Merrick
William Merrick
Rebecca Tracy
Stephen Tracy
Tryphosa Lee
Abigail Hopkins
Giles Hopkins*
Stephen Hopkins*
Mary ?*
Catherine Weldon
Gabriel Weldon
Jane ?
Lydia Mayo
Thomas Mayo
Nathaniel Mayo
Capt John Mayo
Tamsen ?
Hannah Prence
Gov. Thos. Prence
Patience Brewster
William Brewster*
Mary ?*
Barbara Knowles
Richard Knowles
Ruth Bower
Jonathan Godfrey
Mercy Mayo
Thomas Mayo
Nathaniel Mayo
Capt John Mayo
Tamsen ?
Hannah Prence
Gov. Thos. Prence
Patience Brewster
William Brewster*
Mary ?*
Barbara Knowles
Richard Knowles
Ruth Bower
Capt
Ebenezer Hawes
Capt John Hawes
Desire Gorham
Capt John Gorham
Desire Howland
John Howland*
Elizabeth Tilly*
John Tilly*
Joan Hurst*
Sarah Norton
Isaac Norton Jr
Ruth Bayes
Thomas Bayes
Anna Barker
John Hedge
Thankful Lothrop

The author's mother and Lenny – 2005.

Chapter 3

Planning My Trip

In May of 2006, I saw an approaching break in my work schedule during July and August—long enough to allow for a three-week trip to England and Scotland. That gave me two months to organize, a particularly short time since my passport had expired and the normal turnaround time for renewal took eight weeks.

I had accumulated enough free miles for my airfare. Mom offered to fund the rest. I asked her if she wanted to go with me.

"I don't think I can make it, dear. I worry about all the walking, and going up and down steps. You go ahead. I'll hear all about it when you get back." Stepping up onto a curb for my mother was as intimidating as climbing Mt. Everest to me.

"Crippled people travel in wheelchairs, you know," I pointed out.

"Yes, I know. Maybe someday. Bring me back a bottle of Marmite." She grinned, knowing I found Marmite revolting.

Marmite is a bitter, sticky brown goo that comes in a small oval jar and tastes similar to the beef extract we Americans use to season stews and soups. It is made from yeast and the British love it spread on toast. An American friend of mine thinks it tastes like ground cockroaches.

While I worked out the details of my travel plans, I continued my research. Three weeks wouldn't give me enough time to scour every cemetery in England or Scotland. I needed to whittle down the prospects.

A few days later I happened across an article in the *San Francisco Chronicle*'s Sunday travel section on Highgate Cemetery in London. Buried within Highgate's thirty-seven acres are George Eliot, Karl Marx, the poet Christina Rosetti and Charles Dickens' younger brother Alfred, among other notables. As the article described, "it is London's most famous dead end," with tens of thousands of graves.

Highgate situated near to "62 Ellsworthy Road." That's how my mother referred to the home where her family (Mom, Peter, Eileen Maude and stepfather Vernon Armitage) resided during the time right before Eileen Maude died. That recommended Highgate as a likely place to find Eileen Maude's grave. I assumed Vernon had enough money to provide his wife with a proper burial because my mother's childhood memories of 62 Ellsworthy Road included "an upstairs maid, an Irish downstairs maid the age of Peter, a cook, a nanny, and a chauffeured Bentley."

I noted Highgate's street address and web site and read the instructions on how to request a search for someone buried there. This led to my first hurdle. Like most ancestral research requests, Highgate required a search fee and a self-addressed stamped envelope. But all my previous research had been within the United States. How was I supposed to obtain and send £10 sterling? And how was I going to obtain English stamps to stick on a return envelope to the United States?

A clerk at the San Rafael Post Office informed me of the proper procedure for the latter problem. To obtain return postage from another country, one must purchase an international postal coupon. Unfortunately, the coupons available at his branch were out of date and unusable. He suggested I try another branch.

I told Mom about Highgate the following Sunday, and then tried to encourage her to tell me more about life on Ellsworthy Road. She sat back in her chair to think a minute, and then sat up suddenly, her eyes flashing like a bright-idea meter.

"Why don't you call my brother, Peter?" she said, almost excitedly. "Maybe *he* knows what happened to our mother."

Peter moved to Canada after World War II and worked as a controller for a number of hotels. He's been retired for years and now lives with his wife, Josée—only five years older than I am—near Quebec. They've been married for forty years. Though Peter has a couple of children from a couple of previous wives, he and Josée have no children together. I've only seen him three or four times in my life. One year I drove to visit him from Wheaton (the college I attended in Massachusetts) during a Thanksgiving holiday, though it wasn't Thanksgiving for him.

Peter and Josée visited Mom in Pasadena while I was still living there. I moved to the Bay area only in 1995, and Mom joined me when she moved to Villa Marin in 2003. Before Mom died, they called each other every birthday. I think their bond grew stronger as their health grew weaker, knowing one might not be around by the next phone call. Mom's death upset Peter. He didn't like being the last one left.

Five years ago, however, when my mother had her inspiration, Peter had more pep. I'd always found him warm, friendly and compassionate. I sent him an email with my questions. In spite of being quite competent on the Internet, he responded with a phone call.

"You know," he said, with the same trace of a British accent as my mother, "I'm amazed to realize that not only do I not have any idea where our mother is buried, but I don't even know what year she died. You'd think I'd know that, wouldn't you?"

I was aware he was frail and probably forgetful, however I suspected that he, like my mother, was blotting out a painful time in their past. I didn't obtain any more information, but at least I learned I wasn't going to waste a trip to England and Scotland. Besides, the call was a good excuse for us to catch up with each other. Peter's biggest interest was his garden.

That same afternoon I called Aunt Jennifer in Seattle to ask her if she would sift through Grandpa's journals for clues to where my grandmother died and was buried. She willingly agreed. But since she had to fetch the books from their box in her storage unit, and because like everyone else she was very busy, I didn't expect to hear from her for a couple of weeks.

The following Sunday I hit pay dirt[1]. I asked my mother if I could sift through her own scrapbooks for clues, and she agreed. She sat, as usual, molded to her old wing chair facing the blaring television. The side arms of the chair were like waterfalls of thread, a sculpture made by her cat, Lenny, who liked to exercise his claws on them. I sat on the carpet by Mom's feet, flipping through the yellowed crumbling pages of the old books. Suddenly she gasped. Afraid something was wrong, I looked up.

"Go into my closet," she said gruffly.

"What?"

"Look for a tin file box on the upper shelf." She waved to the closet behind her as if she were waving away a gnat.

I put the scrapbook aside, stood up and did as I was told. At the far left end of her closet shelf, in near darkness, I spied a gray-green metal container that looked more like a large lunch-pail than a file box. Someone many years ago hand-painted the words "Betty May" on the outer side in perfect grade school letters. I carried the box to the living room and placed it on the floor in front of Mom.

"Well," she said, looking at me as if I'd forgotten to tie my shoes. "Open it!"

I knelt back down on the carpet, pushed in the small clasp and lifted the lid. Two books fit neatly inside as if the box had been made for them. One, bound in yellowed linen, looked at first like a ledger. A label with my grandfather's handwriting, "Photos of about 1930, Pryns Hopkins," had been pasted to the spine.

I looked back at Mom. She smiled a Cheshire cat grin that meant to me, "I know I am giving you a very big present, but you'd better not get too used to getting presents because you don't deserve them."

The other book was clearly intended to be a scrapbook—about four

1. An English cousin disapproved of this expression from California's gold mining days.

inches thick, eight inches tall and ten inches wide with a *landscape* orientation, the brown leather binding worn so thin it was as if people had been looking through the book every day since it was put together. As I extracted the book from the tin box, the spine broke off and fell to the floor along with a shower of leather dust. I glanced at Mom to see if it bothered her that her book was falling apart in my hands. She shrugged her shoulders as if to say, "That's what old books do."

Nothing on the cover of the second book identified it. Three embossed fleur-de-lis decorated the leather. I opened to the first page to see two photographs of my grandparents' wedding day pasted side by side. The photos matched the one I already had of the wedding, both in size and tone, so obviously taken by the same photographer. In the left image, Eileen Maude, dressed in her wedding dress and veil, sat in the middle of a circle of beautifully dressed bridesmaids. It must have been taken before the wedding, whereas the second image was taken after. Pryns and Eileen Maude stood flanked by two of the bridesmaids—probably two of Eileen's four sisters. That photo was taken only moments after the photo I already had. The newlyweds had moved some ten feet farther from the church entrance gate since the first photo.

In the latter, Eileen speaks to her new husband with a half smile, as if she is making a joke or wanting him to notice something. He listens attentively, enjoying himself. My combined impression from the three images is that my grandparents' wedding day was a happy time. They appeared confident, calm and content.

I thought about my own three wedding days and shivered. Though I was happy to be marrying each man—I loved and respected them at the time—I had doubts in all three cases that the marriages were going to be happy. The courtships had been full of drama. I was under the delusion that marriage would stabilize things. I felt none of the peace I saw in my grandparents' faces. To be fair, I don't think I'd ever felt that peace, so I didn't know I was going to be missing anything.

This gold mine, my grandmother's own scrapbook, was her collection of photos of her wedding in 1921, her honeymoon through Europe and a trip she and Grandpa took to America the following year. I concluded that the story line of the book ended when Eileen and Pryns were in Los Angeles before returning to England in 1922, because the last pages showed images of Spanish architecture, palm trees and oil rigs. There were no dates written.

Eileen Maude took most of the photographs during the trips herself. On the first twenty or so pages, she carefully described each event with captions. Sometimes I had difficulty deciphering her handwriting. However, she quit doing that in the second half of the book. That left me wondering who was in each scene and where it had been taken. To add to my frustration, many of the prints of her were missing, replaced by penciled notes in my grandfather's hand describing what they had been. "Eileen on Pryns' knee," "Eileen and Pryns side by side," "Eileen at El Nido[2]." I suspected Grandpa had removed those pictures and pasted them into the scrapbook my mother threw away. *Ugh!*

The second scrapbook from the tin box had been put together by my grandfather during the year or so directly after Eileen Maude's death. It held photographs of his friends, and the children when they were eight and ten years old.

"What else are you hiding from me?" I asked Mom, still kneeling on her carpet.

"There's my baby book. Would you like to see that?"

I gave her a stern look. *Come on, what do you think? Do I have to beg?*

"It's there among the scrapbooks." She jutted her jaw in the direction of the farthest shelf. "Look at the end of the row."

I pulled out a sweet, cloth-covered book about six by nine inches, not very thick, illustrated with watercolor flowers and nannies and little children in the style of its 1923 copyright. Eileen Maude had faithfully filled in most blanks including her daughter's weight records, first tooth, hair "jet black," hands "Pryns' nails white as snow," baptism records, first short clothes, vaccinations and first word "a-goo." There was a note from "Grandma" to "My dear little Blossom" for Mom's first birthday. And to my joy, a blue piece of paper like the blue papers that had been in the scrapbook Mom destroyed was tucked in between the pages—one of Eileen's poems! It was written the year after my mother's birth in 1925.

---

2. El Nido was Mary and Charles Hopkins' home in Santa Barbara. More on it later.

May 1926

Carnations! A little house for these
Sheltered and warm from a too hurried breeze
Blooms of every shade and hue May grows
Arranged in little pop row after row
Dear Heart where ever I may be,
Tend them well, in memory of me.
—*Eileen Hopkins*

She didn't need to be remembered until eight years later.

Another bit of good fortune came my way via a phone call from a psychiatrist/amateur historian named Dr. Ronald R. Koegler. Dr. Koegler found me on the Internet, where I had posted information about the book I wrote about my father, *The Man in the Purple Cow House.* Dr. Koegler was a member of the Santa Barbara Historical Museum, which, he informed me, was researching my grandfather's life because the Hopkins family helped settle Santa Barbara. Dr. Koegler became personally interested in Grandpa many years earlier, when Koegler purchased his home in the hills just north of town. The title search revealed the land's original owners of record after the native Indians and Spanish dons. On June 2, 1913, Prince C. Hopkins was granted title to the land Bishop of Monterey and Los Angeles. The Roman Catholic Church had been deeded the parcel on March 18, 1865 under an act passed by President Abraham Lincoln[3].

The good doctor became even more interested when he learned that the reason young Prince purchased the land was to build a progressive school that ultimately adopted Montessori-like ideals, an interest the doctor shared.

I was able to give Dr. Koegler some family history, and he shared his research about the school and other aspects of my grandfather's life with me.

3. *Noticias,* Journal of the Santa Barbara Historical Museum. "A Renaissance Prince: Prynce Hopkins," Koegler, Ronald R. M.D., The Santa Barbara Historical Museum, 2008. p 139

Memorial to Prince and Olive Hopkins – Vassalboro, Maine.

Chapter 4

The Path to Riches

Every time I talk about my grandfather, I am inevitably asked, "Where did the money come from?" So I will go back in time to where the money trail began.

Prince's father, Charles, was born in Vassalboro in 1837. He'd reached his twelfth birthday in 1849 when news of gold in California reached Maine, and when his father, Prince III, ran the hardware store and tannery business, Southwick & Hopkins. When Southwick died in 1855, Prince III sold the tannery to the people who owned the new thriving woolen mills, placed his brother-in-law George Hawes in charge of the hardware store and started a new business: a "house of entertainment to accommodate the great influx of strangers to Vassalboro at the time." In those days, apparently, "house of entertainment" just meant a place for a traveler to find room and board. Today's image of scantly clothed women dancing on bars surrounded by roaring men (perpetuated by the movie industry), became a natural by-product. The 1860 census indicated Prince Hopkins as an "Inn Holder,"[1] and an 1864 map of Vassalboro marked the spot for the P. Hopkins Hotel. The value of Prince's estate, as noted on the 1860 census, was $1900. Prince's son Charles would take none of that with him when he moved to California that year, but the education and experience he received from his father helped him become one of the wealthiest men in California by the time he died at the age of seventy-seven in 1913.

My grandfather described his own grandparents, Prince and Olive, in his autobiography, *Both Hands Before the Fire.* He'd visited them from Oakland as a small boy, traveling to Vassalboro by train with his parents around 1893.

> Olive Hawes Hopkins was always adorned with a bonnet with strings tied under her chin...

...except for when she gave birth to her four children—the last when she was forty-four—in her simple brick farmhouse.

> The home consisted of a kitchen, a dining room, a parlor and some bedrooms. There was no barn, just a long shed built at the side of the kitchen. Olive worked an iron hand pump for water.

Watermelon—a fruit Prince claims not to have seen or tasted in California—strawberries and pumpkins grew in the garden by the kitchen.

> Split-rail fences were overburdened with thick brambles of raspberry and blackberry vines ... goldenrod and purple astor. Apples, potatoes, onions and what not were stored in a cool cellar down a long dark stairway reached through a trap door in the kitchen floor.

One of my brothers, Tom Ames, took a pilgrimage to North Vassalboro

---

1. *Prince and Olive,* personal manuscript by Thomas Winter Ames, Jr, Norwich, Vermont, October 23, 1982.

from his home in Vermont to find out what he could about our great-great-grandparents, Prince and Olive.[2] Of the farm and hotel he could find no trace. However, he did come across the large tombstone for Prince and Olive in the Vassalboro cemetery. The smaller stone for their four-year-old son Prince Leroy Hopkins (Prince IV) peeked up from the ground nearby. It read:

Short was my stay
But lonely my rest;
Christ called me home.
He thought it best.

As I read the poem, I wondered if Prince and Olive were the last generation in this family line to trust their fate to the hands of God. How many people in today's world would be comforted knowing Christ thought it best to take their young toddler? Today our lives are shattered by the death of even one child. In Prince and Olive's day, families often lost many children.

Charles waited until he was twenty-three to travel to San Francisco to see what the golden fuss was all about. He wrote on his application to the California Mayflower Society—for which he was the twenty-fourth Founding Member—he came to California "by sea." He had probably traveled to the nearest port by carriage (Portland, Maine, perhaps), and then sailed south along the eastern coast by steamer, stopping port to port along the way. We don't know if he debarked in Panama, crossed the hot and dangerous isthmus to the Pacific and then sailed north to San Francisco, or if he sailed all the way around Cape Horn. One personal account of a trip during those days stated that in order to take advantage of the trade winds (or currents), the ship sailed from the North American coast to the African Coast and *then* west under the Horn.[3]

Arriving with "only a few dollars left in his pocket," Charles obtained his first job as a clerk in a San Francisco clothing store. He then went

2. Ibid.

3. Haskins, C.W. *The Argonauts of California, By a Pioneer*, 1890.

to work for the newly established Mint. From this job, and by being "Puritanically frugal," he saved enough cash during the next five years to purchase a return fare—the transcontinental railway was not yet completed—to Maine in 1865, or thereabouts, to ask his childhood sweetheart, Lizzie Cullis, to marry him. Lizzie consented. However, within a year of their marriage, she died giving birth to a son, who also died.

Charles returned to San Francisco, where he married on February 30, 1868, his second wife, Ruth Merritt Mathews Singer, one of the inventor Isaac Merritt Singer's twenty-two children (some say he had twenty-four). Ruth, named after her paternal grandmother, had moved to San Francisco with her mother and four siblings in 1860 (the same year Charles moved there) to escape a family scandal in New York City.

It turns out that Ruth's father's wizardry for developing a practical sewing machine had been paralleled by his ability to secretly maintain four complete households, one legitimate and three illegitimate. Isaac's legal wife, Catherine, lived on Long Island and owned the Singer name.[4] The three mistresses were given homes in New York City. Isaac lived publicly with Mary Ann Sponsler at 14 Fifth Avenue with their ten children. Under the name of Mr. Merritt, Isaac provided a home for Mary Walters and their one child at 225 West Twenty-seventh Street. And he provided a fourth home for Mary McGonigal, an Irish woman, and their five children at 70 Christopher Street under the surname Mathews.

Ruth Mathews was the oldest of the latter. Her mother, an employee of Singer, had been in a relationship with him for nearly ten years before the truth came out. One day, already suspecting something was amiss, Mary Ann Sponsler saw Isaac and Mary McGonigal riding in a carriage together along Fifth Avenue. Some say Mary Ann's screams were heard across the Hudson.

Ruth was born in 1852 about the time her father founded his company. She'd turned eight by the time she moved to San Francisco, and was but sixteen when she married Charles Harris Hopkins. Dear

---

4. *A Capitalist Romance, Singer and the Sewing Machine*. Ruth Brandon, J.B. Lippincott Company, Philadelphia and New York, 1977.

Ruth is not my ancestor, and her bloodline doesn't matter to me, but since her money affected my family and my life tremendously, I feel I owe her a great deal of gratitude and respect. Her inheritance paid for my upbringing, for my college and for the down payment on my first house. It still provides pocket change.

It's difficult to piece together how Charles gathered his estate. What we do know is that in 1863 Isaac Singer and his partner Edward Clark incorporated the Singer Manufacturing Company in New York with twenty-two patents and $550,000 in capital assets. The company annually produced 20,000 home model sewing machines. In 1874 Charles Hopkins purchased a seat on the San Francisco Stock and Bond Exchange, founded ten years earlier, "To maintain a free and open market wherein the investor could convert his cash into securities and his securities into cash at will, at a fair and honest price."[5] The following year Isaac Singer died leaving a substantial estate of $14 million. Of the portion left to his children, Ruth received two "parts", totaling $21,975. The next year Charles sold his seat on the exchange.

Ruth did not enjoy this money for long. In 1878 she, too, died while trying to give birth to a son for Charles. He, on the other hand, enjoyed the inheritance immensely. Either by investing wisely or by purchasing stock from Ruth's siblings, Charles became, so one source stated, Singer Manufacturing Company's largest stockholder. My grandfather wrote that, for the first time, his father began living with a little style.

> Adding dash to his carriage, ... he purchased a pair of high-stepping bays, and was considered quite a catch for any girl at Saratoga Springs and other smart resorts of the time.

By this time the transcontinental railroad had been completed. I wondered if Charles holidayed in Saratoga Springs often.

The young lady who made the conquest lived in San Francisco, an eighteen-year-old "pretty, golden-haired" woman named Mary Isabel Booth. Charles had befriended her father, Samuel Booth, while they were both working at the Mint in San Francisco.

---

5. "History of the Pacific Exchange." www.pacificx.com.

Samuel, a "kindly English jeweler," also wrote poems. He was particularly noted for the lyrics he wrote to support political candidates. Joanna, his Irish Catholic wife, gave birth to their daughter Mary in Boston before Samuel moved the family to San Francisco. Records of that birth are missing from the Massachusetts Archives. An article in the *San Francisco Call* stated Samuel moved directly to the Mission District and owned one of the first homes there. His listing in the *1863-64 San Francisco Directory* gives his address at "dw1 [dwelling number 1] Shotwell Street." By the 1890 directory, Dwelling Number 1 was given the proper address number of 512 Shotwell Street. That is where Samuel and Joanna's grandson Prince remembered visiting them.

According to a San Francisco map of areas devastated by fire after the 1906 earthquake, 512 Shotwell Street was lost. In 1907 we find Samuel and Johanna celebrating their fiftieth anniversary at 825 Fell Street. The building still stands and has recently been renovated. The 1907 *Call* article about their anniversary stated,

> There are probably few men in San Francisco as well known and universally liked as Mr. Booth.

The photo with the article shows Samuel wearing a short white beard and white bow tie. Joanna has her hair piled on top of her head. The tender poem Samuel wrote, as the headline in the *Call* stated, "Tells in Verses of Half Century of Married Life:"

> A half a hundred years are gone, of sun and stormy weather,
> Since on that long departed day we plighted troth together.
> Since in the joy of youthful prime we blithely went homesteading.
> And lo! The swift remorseless years have brought our Golden Wedding.
>
> Through varying fortunes, good and ill, each others' burdens bearing,
> Facing the world with right good will and never once despairing.
> O'er oceans wide, and continents, no toil nor hardship dreading,
> Until we come to this good day, that sees our Golden Wedding.
>
> May He who guides the spheres, and all that unto them pertaineth,

Still have us in His keeping for the little that remaineth.
And when we reach the Pearly Gates, the Golden pavement treading,
May it be one long Honey-moon to this, our Golden Wedding.

Mary Booth, nicknamed May, was twenty-eight years younger than her groom when she married him in 1883. The couple set up housekeeping in Oakland, considered at that time a fashionable suburb. Only the *hoodlums* lived in San Francisco, some said. Charles commuted to the city...

... riding his horse-drawn carriage on the paddle-wheel ferry that connected him to the Embarcadero before the Bay Bridge was built.

Within two years May safely gave birth to Prince.

Charles had already developed health problems, suffering terrible chronic pains in his kidney and bladder.

"He was an alcoholic," said my mother, though she never met her grandfather. He died thirteen years before she was born. "At least that was always implied by my grandmother," she added.

Seeking specialists and remedies for his ailments, Charles and May traveled to health spas all over the United States, Europe and "every part of the world," circling the globe at least twice. Sometimes little Prince went with them. But during the school months, his parents left him behind with "Tant Lucy and Uncle Dick Anthony,"[6,7] friends in Oakland. Lucy's sister, Miss Sarah Horton, who ran one of the finest schools in the Bay Area, joined them for dinners served by the Chinese servant and cook. After dinner, the men retired to one parlor to drink claret and smoke cigars while the women teachers and students retired to the other parlor to prepare for the following day's lessons.

On weekends, Prince alternately visited his parents in San Francisco, who resided at the Hotel Pleasanton when they weren't traveling, and his mother's parents, Grandpa and Grandma Booth, in the Mission District.

---

6. *Noticas,* "Prynce Hopkins," Koegler.

7. A note to genealogy buffs: the Anthony family came to America on the *Fortune* in 1621 with Thomas Prence. Is it possible the Anthonys and the Hopkins stuck together for 300 years from the Cape to Maine and then all the way to California?

In 1893, his Booth aunts (Amy, Lena, Edith and/or Ella), took eight-year-old Prince to Chicago to see the Columbian Exposition. Prince probably rode on the world's first Ferris Wheel. When he turned nine, his parents took him along on a trip that lasted over a year. They traveled first to Denver, then Europe and Cairo. Prince remembered being sent to a school in Austria to learn German. He also remembered his mother riding on a bicycle with Lady Randolph Churchill in Cairo, "clad in billowy bloomers."

Prince and May nearly died in Egypt when they came down with diphtheria. But a serum antitoxin had been recently developed in France and samples arrived in Cairo only three days before mother and son went into the hospital. Recovery was slow, but they could finally continue to Greece, Rome and Paris before returning to Oakland.

When Prince was only ten, Charles and May sent him to board at Thatcher School in Ojai, California, then still run by its founder Sherman Thatcher. Prince was the youngest child in the school. A letter from Thatcher to Miss Horton said he was a "charming little boy... always happy." "Nothing seemed to disconcert him." He was a "moral force" among the students.[8]

However, Prince remembered a lonely childhood. Later, after becoming a psychoanalyst, he wrote,

> Of course, so much shuttling between parents and various foster parents was not good; it accounts for most of the insecurity and depression that have dogged my life.

At first Charles and May traveled down from San Francisco to visit, staying in the Arlington Hotel in Santa Barbara about a half-hour drive from Ojai.

In 1897, three years before Charles took fifteen-year-old Prince to see the latest engineering feats at the Paris International Exposition, Charles and May built a grand Victorian house in Santa Barbara to retreat from San Francisco's fog. Prince wrote,

---

8. *Noticias*, "Prynce Hopkins," Koegler, p 144, quote from Stella Haverland Rouse, "Olden Days: The Story of Boyland's Rise, Fall." *Santa Barbara News Press*, 1 June 1975.

El Nido, 1900 Garden Street, Santa Barbara, California.

> Most of my vacations now, of course, were spent in our new home. Santa Barbara's population then numbered only 12,000 and it was a delightfully small, half Mexican, town. ... A street car ran down the main street ... drawn by a mule.

In those days,

> If a lady had a bit of shopping to do ... the obliging conductor would wait for her to do it and get aboard again.

The house, designed by Francis Wilson[9], still stands as an historical landmark a few blocks south of the Santa Barbara Mission at 1900 Garden Street. The round castle-like tower once contained Prince's bedroom, but May modified the original three-floor structure in 1931, removing the tower's top floor. They named the mansion *El Nido,* the Spanish word for *the nest,* and that is where they were living in 1906 when the earthquake hit San Francisco, keeping them safely out of harm's way.

---

9. From an article written for the Santa Barbara Historical Museum by Michael Redmon.

Photo from Eileen Hopkins Ames' Scrapbook.

Standing: Betty May. Seated left to right: Jennifer, Prynce, Fay and David.
Campaign photo from when Prynce ran for
California's 47th Assembly District – Pasadena, May 1946.

Chapter 5

Talking to the Dead

Only a week after I called my Aunt Jennifer about the journals, she called me. It was about 10:00 at night, and I was in the kitchen fetching a glass of water before snuggling up in bed with a good book. I almost didn't answer because of the hour, but fearing it might be my mother or my children, I did.

Jennifer had already begun reading her father's journals and was anxious to tell me about the information she had found so far.

"I'm afraid I don't have very good news," she said.

"What is that?" I asked, while searching around my kitchen for paper and pen. The only paper available was a square stack of yellow sticky notes. I sat down at my kitchen table, poised to begin writing as Jennifer continued.

"I got out two of Daddy's journals, the one for 1933 and the other for 1934. I've got them here on my lap. The first one starts on October 4,

1933, when your grandmother Eileen is still alive but very sick. He talks about the happy time he'd had on his trip with Betty May and Peter in France. He writes that he'd asked Eileen to come along on the trip, but his mother, my grandmother Mary[1], discouraged it. He writes that Eileen is very sick, but he doesn't say where he is. Only that he has to return to London."

"Then for sure my grandmother didn't die in London," I said. "It's interesting that she is still alive in October. I thought she died during the summer."

"Well, here is the bad part. From here all the way through most of February of the next year, 1934, the pages have been cut out. My mother must have hacked them all out from jealousy. Can you believe it? I don't know how she could have gotten to these journals. They were locked up in the case in which I received them after Daddy died. Even I didn't open that case for years and for a long time had no idea what was in there."

"Maybe Grandpa cut out those pages to put in the scrapbook he'd made of my grandmother's letters," I suggested.

"Well, that's possible, I suppose. But I assume it was my mother. She's executed similar attacks on documents in the past. Who else would have done such a thing? But this is horrible. Every page from November through the first part of January is gone."

I was extremely disappointed. That meant that during two crucial months, Grandpa had written something that Fay didn't want kept for posterity. I was sure I would have wanted to read what had been on those pages and that they would have revealed many answers to my questions.

I tried to look at the bright side. "At least we can narrow down the dates when my grandmother died."

"I'm almost certain that Daddy's marriage to my mother was at the end of December of 1933, and that it was shortly after the death of your grandmother. Eileen must have died in November, after the nineteenth I think. But there's more, and this is what I found so interesting. Several months after Eileen's death, he wrote about going to a séance to try to

---

1. My great-grandmother May.

communicate with her."

"Can you photocopy that part for me?"

"Oh, of course, I'm going to scan all these pages. That's all I've read so far. I just had to tell you about the séance. I'll call you again if I come across anything more exciting."

We said good-bye. I organized my sticky notes, hoping my scribbles would make sense in the morning, and went into my studio to place them by my computer. As I headed to my bedroom, the phone rang again.

"I have to tell you what else I found," Jennifer said excitedly. "There is a second visit to the medium, a different one I think. This is what she told him. 'There are a lady and a gentleman. The lady is young, looks about thirty. She has an oval face, brown hair, is not very stout. The gentleman is between fifty and seventy-five, nearly bald, hair otherwise grey, has a slight stoop.' I think my father is talking about himself."

"That's amazing!" I said. "He really thought he could talk to the dead!"

I thought about old movies from the 30s, and the popularity of fortune telling and séances at the time. I pictured my grandmother as a mummy, rising out of her coffin.

"Well, I'm off to bed," said Jennifer, "but I'll continue tomorrow."

Though intrigued, I would have to wait for the rest of the story. It made me happy Jennifer enjoyed the mystery and had become a companion in my quest. I had a similar experience of connecting with relatives when I researched my book about my father.

Prince Hopkins, age twenty-six – 1911.

Chapter 6

Prince's Formative Years

By the year "ought-six", as my grandfather would have called it, he had finished Thatcher School, done two years at the Hill Preparatory School in Pennsylvania and received a degree in mechanical engineering from Yale College in Connecticut.

All photos of my grandfather as a young adult show him as slim and fit as I knew him in his old age. I remember him always neatly and fashionably dressed in impeccably tailored clothing of fine cloth. He stood about six feet tall, and had thin gray hair, but wasn't bald anywhere. I hated it when he tried to kiss my cheek because he had a bristly little mustache that looked like Hitler's. He wasn't a cuddly grandfather. He acted formally—he more than once corrected me for saying "Yea" instead of "Yes," stood erect like royalty and was almost shy. Though he wrote a lot, he didn't speak much. I think of myself watching him more than talking to him.

From what my mother told me, Grandpa played tennis until he was seventy. Never golf. But by the time my memories kick in, he had even stopped driving.

Everything about Grandpa's life was orderly and on a rigid time schedule—meals, travel, work and play. I grew up under several assumptions set by him. I was to get a good education and get it at the best school possible. My uncle went to Harvard, as did his three daughters. Jennifer attended Wellesley. My brother Tom went to Dartmouth, as did Jennifer's daughter Maia. My mother attended Scripps in California, then she got her law degree when she was fifty-two. Wheaton wasn't Ivy League, but it was good enough. It was assumed we would give back to society somehow, no matter what careers we chose. And we were all encouraged to travel.

For a graduation present after Yale, Prince's father gave him a "handsome" check to take a solo trip to Europe. Prince set sail for France on the *Aquitania*, the first of many voyages on that ocean liner. In France he rented one of the relatively new motorcycles and noisily explored the cities and countryside into Switzerland.

He returned to America at the end of the summer to begin a program at Boston Tech, now called the Massachusetts Institute of Technology. "Needing lodging," he moved in with his father's bachelor brother, Uncle George, who'd moved from Maine to Boston many years earlier.

Prince's studies in engineering "bore fruit." On August 29, 1911, he applied for and received patent No. 1,000,849 for the design of a "flying machine." To me it looks like a ski resort gondola hanging from a wire frame structure resembling a helicopter tail. Prince proudly presented his patent to his father. Instead of giving the admiration and building funds Prince desperately wanted, his father said, "If man were meant to fly, God would have given him wings." Charles continued "his stern lecture" by quoting the figures of a mathematician who claimed "to keep a human being suspended in the air would require power equal to that of a locomotive."

My grandfather was devastated. He'd had his heart set on achieving something in the field of aeronautics ever since he'd visited the

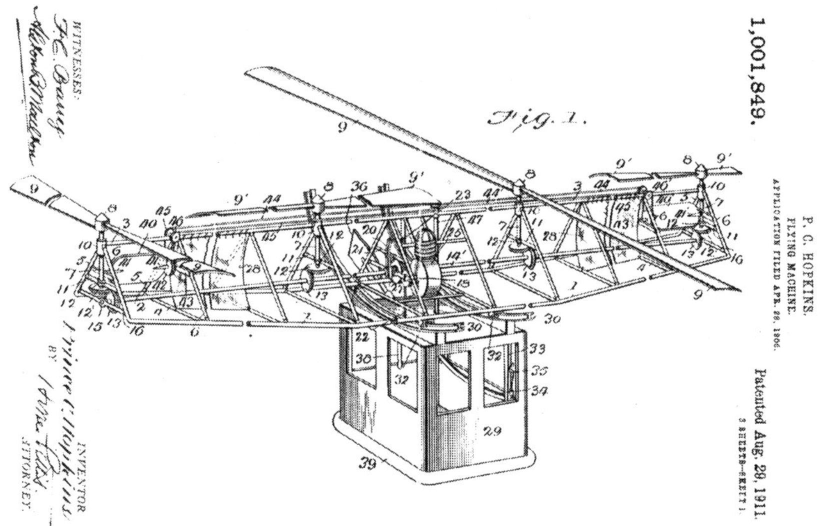

Illustration of Prince's patented helicopter, 1911.

aeronautics display at the Paris Exposition. Even at Thatcher School he'd made several attempts to build rockets. He never liked confrontations, least of all with his father. Instead of standing up for his idea, he turned "inwards." The bitterness he'd had for the old man who was seldom around, never affectionate and possibly often drunk, grew to be a bigger grudge.

Trying to figure out what to do next, Prince spent several weeks trudging pathetically from classroom to classroom at Boston Tech, hoping to find another subject that interested him. He called his depression, which lasted several months, a "nervous breakdown." Finally he decided to obtain a Masters in Educational Psychology and moved to New York City to begin studies at Columbia University.

This was 1912, two years after the death of Leo Tolstoy and five years before the Russian Revolution. While Prince studied at Columbia, he enthusiastically attended speeches on anarchism and socialism by Emma Goldman and "other radicals." He claimed in his autobiography that these speeches had more of an influence on him than his studies of educational psychology. However, a setback prevented him from rushing off to save the oppressed peasants of Russia and other countries.

He'd been living in the apartment of his mother's best friends, Mr.

and Mrs. Charles Meyer, while he looked around New York City for a more permanent apartment. The Meyers lived in The Dakota, a large apartment building on West Seventy-second Street across from Central Park—where John Lennon later lived and was shot and killed. Coincidentally, the Dakota had been built in the 1870s by Edward Clark, Isaac Merritt Singer's partner in the Singer Sewing Machine Company, who invested heavily in Manhattan real estate. Mr. Meyer worked as president of the New York Standard Oil Company. His wife, "Aunt Myra," had grown up in San Francisco and known Prince's mother, May, since they were girls. Her father, Arnold Comstock, a cousin of Henry Comstock who discovered the largest silver lode in Nevada, had moved to San Francisco as a miner in 1849. Charles was Myra's second husband and apparently neither of them had any children.[1]

One night Prince collapsed at dinner. He'd been feeling faint for quite a while, "but had attributed it to the intensity of the university program."

The Meyers immediately called in their family physician, who diagnosed Prince's condition as tuberculosis. The doctor told him to withdraw temporarily from his studies and relocate to a place with warmer weather for the lengthy period of recuperation.

The Meyers relayed the news to Charles and May in California, and they arranged for Prince to enter a sanatorium in Monrovia under the care of a Dr. Pottenger. Monrovia is a small town just east of Pasadena. Ironically, it is now known for having the worst air pollution in the state. But in its day it was a popular place for sanatoriums, and thousands of residents in Southern California migrated there because of it.

The sanatorium required Prince to stay in bed all the time. So he spent the endless hours reading, particularly about the class struggles in Czarist Russia and other parts of Europe. He devoured the works of Ibsen; Kropotkin, a proponent of anarchist communism; and especially Tolstoy. It was *War and Peace,* he claimed, that influenced him the most and converted him from "a seventh-regiment conservative into a critic of our social order and convinced pacifist."

---

1. Email to author from Jim Comstock, great nephew of Myra. Myra's mother was Sarah Bigelow. http://bigelowsociety.com/rod/sar75572.htm.

He also kept busy publishing a tiny newspaper titled the *Pottenger Pulse*, a combination of his writing and the illustrations of another patient who was a caricature artist. This would be the first of many publications on his part.

When released with a good bill of health, he returned to Columbia for the last few months it took to finish his courses. He next schemed to establish an experimental school for boys using new techniques he'd studied at university, many developed by Marie Montessori when she started her school in Rome in 1907. This time Prince's father showed more support and gave him the fourteen acres of land in Santa Barbara mentioned earlier. There Prince began to build Boyland.

It took a year to pull the school together. Unfortunately, Charles felt too ill to assist, and May was too busy taking care of Charles to assist either. Just as the first term was about to begin, Charles entered what would be "the last stages of his illness." Hoping a doctor in San Francisco could help, Charles and May traveled there for treatment. It was no use. Two months later, on November 11, 1913, Charles passed away in his suite at the Fairmont Hotel.

My mother frequently told me that her grandmother, Mary—Mom never referred to her as *May*, abhorred anything ostentatious. This is clear when one reads the announcement in the *San Francisco Chronicle* about Charles' death, probably written by May herself. Titled "Charles Hopkins Is Dead," as if everyone knew who Charles Hopkins was, it stated,

> Charles H. Hopkins, capitalist, formerly a resident of San Francisco, but for the last twelve years living in Santa Barbara, passed away at the Fairmont Hotel in this city yesterday evening shortly after 6 o'clock, after a lingering illness. He is survived by a widow.

There is no mention of what he had done for a living, how he'd made his millions, who he had been or that he had a son named Prince. Yet five months later the same paper revealed,

> May 10, the heirs of Charles H. Hopkins today paid what is believed to be the largest single inheritance tax ever paid in this State.

This isn't as grand as it sounds. I read recently California had only instituted its inheritance tax that year or the year before. The inheritance left to Prince and his mother amounted to about $3 million dollars (that's about $65 million today). It wasn't nearly what Singer had left, but Charles left fewer children to divide it. I still found no details of how Charles obtained all that money.

"I felt no sorrow," wrote Prince about the passing of his father. Twenty-one at the time, Prince had felt estranged from Charles through "his teenage and young adult struggles." He confided his bitterness to a close friend soon after the death, telling her he was gratified, because he could finally put his father's wealth to good use. The friend took him aback by replying:

> Prince, the money will never bring you any happiness.

Prince reflected,

> Her prophecy has come very near to fulfillment. It is a universal illusion that happiness depends chiefly on "things." It depends more on physical health such as my father did not have, and more so still on mental health.

Prince built a school building in the style of a Swiss chalet and surrounded it by a working miniature railway. Initially, Boyland carried out a successful program. Play was as important as class work. Classes were only held from 6 a.m. to 11 a.m, and then the children were encouraged to pursue outdoor activities, such as tending gardens and playing sports. The school took field trips to Mexico (about five hours away), San Diego and San Francisco.

The enrollment grew so fast Prince purchased a second piece of property in 1915, thirty-acres above an area now known as Oak Park. This time he built the school in a Persian architectural style. He added riding stables, a fully equipped gymnasium and more gardens. But his pride and joy was the pool, an artificial lake in the shape of a world map. Rivers ran on the continents and volcanoes belched smoke. There were boats for the students to paddle from the Pacific to the San Francisco Bay and from New York to the Mediterranean. There were even shipping lanes marked out with wire.[2]

Dr. Koegler quoted a letter from one of Prince's former students, Nilla Cook, in his *Noticias* article that I found particularly moving:

> ... your map of the world taught me to dance on continents, to know that no journey is impossible ... I once possessed the world, danced from North to South America in less than a minute, passed over frontiers, boundaries, barriers, prejudices, racial categories ...
>
> But what made Boyland an Arabian palace was Prince Hopkins himself. It was sitting on the floor of the stage [in his theater] opening to the mountains that he read us the *Arabian Nights*[3] in the evenings ...
>
> You took a special interest in nursing [my brother] out of the inferiority complex his bossy big sister had instilled! ... you are the image to which we return whenever we pass through experiences which demand an honest stock-taking of ourselves. For, to have before us in the impressionable years a man who did not spare himself, but punished himself for the shortcomings of others—breathed into us, as it were, a higher level of truth. You set out to serve your fellow man, your world, through work for children, and not an iota of your effort has been lost ... You were utterly right ... To have seen a man stand for the ideal meant more than to have read a thousand books ...[4]

Nilla was the child of one of the staff members, but most of the students came from fatherless families in the Santa Barbara area or had no parents at all. Unlike some church and traditional schools based on religious rules for obedience—"Be good or you will go to hell," Boyland was based on scientific and technological studies of human behavior.

There was to be no physical punishment. Prince encouraged his students to talk out their problems with him. Sometimes he even took on the punishment he'd given to a student[5]—not just to prove it was humane, but also to show that anyone with a little bravery could survive

---

2. *Noticias*, "Prynce Hopkins," Koegler.

3. My grandfather gave me a copy of *One Thousand and One Nights* (often referred to as *Arabian Nights*) one Christmas when I was small, along with books containing the Greek and Roman myths and Aesop's Fables.

4. *Noticias*, "Prynce Hopkins," Koegler p 177

5. *Noticias*, "Prynce Hopkins," Koegler.

a bit of reprimanding. He wanted to instill a mode of teamwork.

Nilla wrote,

> ... when he sent me away from the table for smearing butter on Johnny Doeg's nose, he left the table himself and went without dinner. On one such occasion he joined me down in my vegetable garden and ate some of my onions. ...

Prince encouraged plenty of exercise and intellectual challenges, as Sherman Thatcher had encouraged his students in Ojai. Then in 1917, Prince hired Mollie Price Cook and Rose Travis, graduates of the Montessori method, after he'd attended a training session by Dr. Maria Montessori in San Diego. Their work at Boyland helped introduce the method to the West Coast.[6]

According to Prince, "the school served a need in the community and gave a few educators the chance to experiment with modern educational theories.[7]" Unfortunately, some of his other passions were about to cause the school to close before it could become a profitable organization.

---

6. Noticias, "Prynce Hopkins," Koegler. p 148-149

7. *Both Hands Before the Fire*

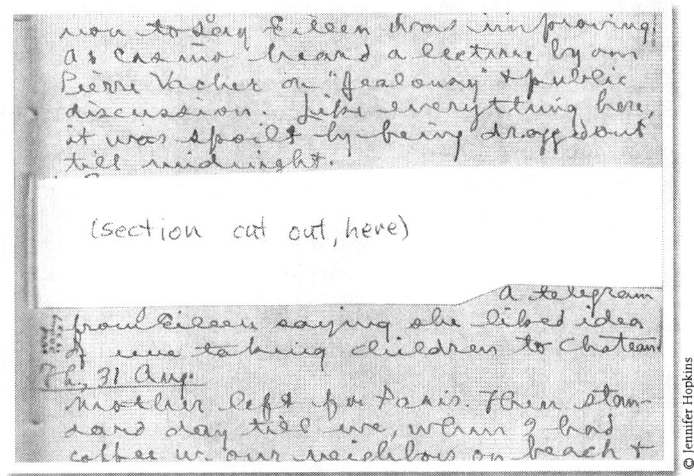
[illegible] today Eileen [illegible]; at casino heard a lecture by one Pierre Vachet on "Jealousy" & public discussion. Like everything here, it was spoilt by being dragged out till midnight.

(section cut out, here)

a telegram from Eileen saying she liked idea of me taking children to Chateau

Th, 31 Aug.

Mother left for Paris. Then standard day till [illegible], when I had coffee w. our neighbors on beach +

One of Pryns' sliced up journal pages.

Chapter 7

Internet Search

The evening after Aunt Jennifer called, she rang again to tell me she'd solved the mystery of the missing pages. She'd come to a section where Grandpa described discovering his violated journals with the pages cut out, and how, a while later, he'd received some of the missing bits in the mail.

"He knew my mother had done it!" Jennifer said. "He wrote 'she flew off the handle.' He must have charged her with the crime. I'm scanning the pages, and I'll start sending them in emails to you tonight."

Eighteen emails with perfectly scanned journal pages attached greeted me the next morning. Even though I was extremely anxious to read them, a week passed before I had time to do so.

Late Saturday night, June 3, I printed out the last scan and bound the pages with a comb binder to keep them in order and allow for easier reading to my mother the following day.

Meanwhile, I'd been making headway with my Internet research, thanks to a National Genealogical Society article I'd dug up about accessing data from the newly released 1901 census through the British National Archives (NationalArchives.gov.edu). Every ten years, genealogists look forward to a new set of data. To protect the identity of the living, census data isn't released to the public until a hundred years after it is collected.[1]

I accessed the web site and easily found an electronic search form for the census. Looking for a record page that had Eileen Maude and her parents on it, I ran into another snag. I didn't know I had mistyped the date of her birth on my family tree! Teachers in school used to scold me for not proofreading! Thinking her birth date to be 1898, making her three years old for the 1901 census, I typed that into the birth data field. A pull-down menu allowed for plus or minus three years. Next I was supposed to type in the *district*, what we in America call a *county*. I had to do a bit more research to find Eileen's birth city of Wolverhampton in Staffordshire, an area of England known as the West Midlands. I typed that in but still didn't receive any matches for Eileen Maude Thomas or her father George Thomas. I'd run against my first *brick wall*.

Then I noticed the option of searching for a census record by an address, rather than a person. My mother had given me that information: 17 Tettenhall Road. Voila! I found a 17 Tettenhall Street, but no Thomas family living there in 1901. I learned this information was not correct. Don't believe everything the Internet tells you! 17 Tettenhall Street remained standing and occupied. It pleased me to know the home hadn't been bulldozed to make way for a parking lot or strip mall. Then I wondered if they had strip malls in England?

---

1. In the USA the time is shorter. The 1940 census records have just been released.

Mary Booth Hopkins holding the author – garden patio at El Nido, Santa Barbara, 1951.

Chapter 8

Civil Disobedience

My great-grandmother May lived to the ripe old age of ninety-three, but was only fifty-one when she lost her husband. She never remarried, even though, according to my mother, "plenty of men lingered around her place." I was forty-five when I last got divorced. If I live to ninety-three without getting married again, I will have been single longer than she was. That's a lot of evenings and holidays by myself. *How depressing!*

In describing his mother, Prince wrote:

> She took a walk every morning with an erectness of carriage, which distinguished her. She insisted on obedience, kindness to animals, avoiding lewd associations, loyalty to family and church, a sense of duty and generosity.

"My grandmother was very involved in her church, St. Mary's

Catholic," Mom told me. "She was very strict and standoffish." I got the impression at a young age that all Catholics were strict and standoffish.

My mother's Booth cousins held very different memories of their great-aunt, whom they called *Queen May,* or *Maisie.* They were the grandchildren of May's brother, Frank Booth, who, with his wife, owned the apartment under May on Laguna Street where the cousins frequently visited. One cousin told me, "She was warm and cozy, always letting us, her nieces, snuggle up in bed with her." Another cousin said, "She liked giving dinner parties and wrote rhymes on the place cards." I wondered if that legacy came from May's poet-father Samuel.

Samuel and his wife, Joanna, passed away in 1909, at ages seventy-seven and seventy-three respectively, four years before the death of Charles. Prince wrote:

> [Samuel] had been such a devoted husband that when his wife came down with what would clearly be her last illness, he, unable to endure the thought of life without her, took to his bed and in three days was dead before her.

By Christmas of 1913, Prince's immediate family consisted simply of his mother. As a young bachelor, he didn't see much of his aunts, uncles and cousins in San Francisco. He seldom mentioned them in his autobiography, and I didn't meet them until I sought them out as an adult long after his death. They told me that when he was older, he visited them in San Francisco almost once a year. In preparation for each visit, he called the elderly widow of one of the cousins, told her he was coming to town, asked her to make reservations for all the cousins and their families at a fancy dinner place and then claimed the check.

Prince got "bored" with running Boyland by the summer of 1915. I suspect he enjoyed starting, creating and initiating projects more than he did maintaining them. He didn't hesitate when the Meyers invited him to tag along on a business trip to Asia. The Meyers traveled there often, especially around 1893 when Charles Meyer managed Standard Oil's Bombay, India, office.

After hiring a manager to oversee the school, Prince was on his way. Together, he and the Meyers toured Japan, India, Ceylon, Hong Kong, Canton and Shanghai by boat. One news article stated that the fleet of "boats" available to Mr. Meyer through Standard Oil included "thirty-eight ocean going tankers, five river steamers, ninety-six lighters and barges, sixty-eight tugs and launches, and one hundred thirty-four junks!"

Then Prince continued on his own to Russia via the Trans-Siberian Express hauled by a wood-burning locomotive. There he "experienced the political fires that would soon ignite the Russian Revolution."

He returned westward via Helsinki, Finland and Western Europe, with a short stay in London. He finally arrived home to Santa Barbara in the spring of 1916, right before the United States declared war on Germany.

By this time Prince firmly opposed violence. He refused to join the battles raging in Europe, believing a rational argument would be more productive. To promote and support his point of view, he began a second publishing enterprise with a kindred spirit, the Reverend Greenfield of Santa Barbara. They produced twin pamphlets titled *The Ethics of Murder* on why violence wasn't the answer to the world's disagreements—one from the secular point of view and the other from a religious point of view.

In 1918 Prince wrote and self-published another book, this one titled *More Prussian than Prussia*. It criticized the lack of support for the constitutional rights of Americans. Many conservative government authorities considered the book an act of civil disobedience and accused it of being unpatriotic. When word got around that a shipment of books was due to arrive in Los Angeles, they convinced the port authorities to seize it. But Prince learned of the threat and immediately drove the two hours from Santa Barbara to prevent the action.

While in Los Angeles, he attended a meeting of a militantly leftist organization known as the International Workers of the World Union, aka I.W.W. or *Wobblies*, to speak about the book's subject. As he walked out of the meeting, an undercover policeman addressed him.

"Are you Mr. Hopkins?"

"Yes."

"I have a warrant for your arrest for violating the Espionage Act!"[1]

The man quietly escorted Prince to the city jail a few blocks away and lodged him in a cell for the night with a criminal forger. Prince wrote that the humiliation wasn't too bad, for the jailor received him as a distinguished guest. What did cause humiliation was that Prince's friends back in Santa Barbara were arrested the same night. An article written from Los Angeles appeared in the *San Francisco Examiner*:

> Four Arraigned for L.A. Espionage Plot – LOS ANGELES – April 10, Mrs. Mollie Price Cook, Mr. and Mrs. Frederick K. Burkhardt and the Rev. George H. Greenfield, arrested at Santa Barbara yesterday under the Espionage Act, were arraigned here to-day and held under bail of $10,000. Prince Hopkins, wealthy Santa Barbara educator, alleged author of "More Prussian Than Prussia," arrested here Monday night in the same case, remained in jail, having failed to furnish bail of $25,000. The Rev. Floyd Hardin of Modesto, the sixth person named in the Government's complaint will be brought here. April 19 was set for preliminary hearing on the charges, which included the alleged circulation of the book Hopkins was said to have written.

To make matters worse, the Secret Service raided Boyland in search of evidence of espionage. Prince commented later,

> The first thing you learn in a situation like this is who your real friends are.

The Secret Service found nothing of consequence, but the publicity scared away the students' families. Prince had to close Boyland down.

My grandfather wouldn't return to Santa Barbara as a permanent resident for many years. Eventually, his Uncle Frank and the financial managers leased the building to a company that converted it to a hotel named the Samarkand. The Persian-style building remained standing until a few years ago and the hillside neighborhood still

1. *Both Hands Before the Fire.*

bears the Samarkand name.[2] But, of course, in April of 1918, Prince didn't know his life would take the turns it did.

Photo from *Both Hands Before the Fire.*

Prince's socialist friends: Upton Sinclair and Gaylord Wilshire.

After he was released on bail, Prince decided to stay in the Los Angeles area while he waited for things to cool down in Santa Barbara. He looked up a friend he'd made in London, another Socialist named Wilshire, who had since moved to Pasadena with his wife, Mary. Gay was twenty-four years older than Prince. Born in Ohio, he'd moved to Los Angeles as a small boy. In 1895 he began developing thirty-five acres of land stretching from downtown Los Angeles toward the beach. In 1900, he was arrested in the park for public speaking on Socialist issues, and though the judge dismissed the charges, he moved to New York and then London. While in London, he published a Socialist magazine. Like Prince, he hopped back and forth between London and California several times in his life. He ran for several political offices both in London and in California, but lost. Shortly after returning to California, he gave up on his Wilshire Boulevard venture before the property increased in value. He sold the strip for "a very low sum" to the city of Los Angeles.

He then took this "low sum," which, according to my grandfather,

2. Article for the Santa Barbara Historical Museum by Michael Redmon.

would have been a large sum had he waited just two more years, and invested in a gold mine near Bishop, California. This didn't "bear fruit" either, so he settled into a scholarly life in Altadena, a nonincorporated residential area just north of Pasadena, itself a suburb of Los Angeles.

Prince stayed at Gay and Mary's house as his trial proceeded, and while there took advantage of a service Mary offered. She worked as a self-taught psycho-analyst[3] in the shed behind their house, treating people for five dollars an hour.

Psychoanalysis ultimately became a key part of my grandfather's life. The procedure wasn't new in 1918 Europe, but it still met with suspicion in Southern California. Dr. Sigmund Freud introduced the concept to Austria in 1899 in his book *Interpretation of Dreams,* written in German. Carl Jung, of Zurich, corresponded with Freud in 1906 and met him in 1907. In 1908, Freud connected with Sándor Ferenczi, of Budapest, Hungary, and Ernest Jones of London[4]. Jones, trained by Ferenczi, introduced psychoanalysis to Canada, the United States and England and was one of the few gentiles in the resulting clique[5]. Jones also become Freud's official biographer.

Jones moved temporarily to Canada that same year, where he worked for the Toronto Asylum, the University of Toronto and the Toronto General Hospital. He was there when the *American Journal of Psychology* published his article "The Oedipus Complex as an Explanation of Hamlet's Mystery." When invited to Boston to discuss recent developments in psychology, Jones encouraged Dr. James J. Putnam, professor of neurology at Harvard, to organize an American symposium on psychotherapy. When Jones wrote to Freud about it, he mentioned that in America, he had to "dilute my sex articles with articles on other subjects."

Freud first lectured in America in September 1909. He, Ferenczi and Jung met up with Jones at Clark University in Worcester, Massachusetts, where Freud spoke. Soon after, Freud's associates founded the

---

3. This was the preferred spelling of psychoanalyst in those days.

4. Wikipedia, "Ernest Jones"

5. Grosskurth, Phyllis. *Melanie Klein, Her World and Her Work.* Harvard University Press, Cambridge, Massachusetts, 1986.

International Psycho-Analytic Association at a congress in Nuremberg, Germany. They were keen there being an American branch. In 1911, the American Psycho-Analytic Association formed with Dr. Putnam as President and Jones as secretary-treasurer. Jones held that post until he returned to England in 1913, the same year Macmillan published an English version of Freud's *Dreams*. Also in 1913, Ferenczi founded the Hungarian Psycho-Analytical Society while Jones and friends founded the London Psycho-Analytical Society. Phyllis Grosskurth, in her book about Jones' associate Melanie Klein (whom we will get to a bit later), wrote, "this group got together almost like the early Christians in the catacombs."[6] They would also quarrel about particular theories just like early Protestants quarreled about Christian doctrine.

The movement was interrupted by World War I, though it was very popular with Austrian, German and Hungarian governments interested in treating veterans for war neuroses. That German association caused negative feelings in England for a while. Not until 1919 did Ernest Jones found the British Psycho-Analytical Society at a meeting at his house.

Mary Wilshire must have known Jones and his associates in London. Though self-taught, her knowledge of the craft was probably extremely advanced for Pasadena, California, in 1918.

Finally, on May 4, 1918, news came from the trial. *The Examiner* in San Francisco reported:

> 2 Women, 2 Ministers, Millionaire Indicted – By International News Service – Los Angeles, May 3 – Charged with a conspiracy to violate the Espionage Act, Prince Hopkins, millionaire owner of a boys school at Santa Barbara; Mrs. Mollie Price Cook, principal of the school; the Rev. Floyd Hardin, Christian pacifist, who has been sentenced to serve six months in the city jail; the Rev. George H. Miller, a minister of Santa Barbara, and Mrs. Carrie Eddy Sheffler, wealthy resident of Eagle Rock City, to-day were indicted by the United States grand jury. The five men and women named in the charge, all of whom are well known in Southern California, were arrested several weeks ago by

6. Grosskurth, *Melanie Klein.*

> Federal officers on complaint which charges that they conspired to circulate two alleged seditious books written and published by Hopkins.

Two months later, the *San Francisco Chronicle* related:

> Four Given Heavy Sedition Fines – $502 to $27,000 Penalties Imposed in South. LOS ANGELES August 30 – Prince Hopkins, the Rev. George H. Greenfield, The Rev. Floyd Harden and Carl K. Broneer, who were indicted by a Federal Grand Jury some months ago on charges of violating the espionage act, pleaded guilty here today to the three counts returned against each of them. Hopkins was fined $25,000 on the first count of the indictment and $1000 on each of the two remaining counts. Greenfield and Harden were each fined $6000 on the first count and $1 on each of the other counts.
>
> Before sentence was pronounced the attorney for the defendants read a statement, signed by all four, in which they admitted that they had aided in circulating a book entitled *The Ethics of Murder* and certain other publications which the Federal Government classes as seditious matter. The defendants said, however, that they circulated the matter without pro-German intent.

Prince considered his punishment lighter than it could have been, since at one point he was threatened with a twenty-year prison sentence. Still, $27,000 could have bought him two or more substantial houses in Pasadena at that time.

On September 20, 1918, the *San Francisco Chronicle* reported the fines were paid, ending the article with,

> They presented a signed statement that they would refrain from further circulation of such books and would maintain a patriotic attitude.

This incident reminded me of a story I read about our ancestor William Brewster, who got in trouble with the law when he carried out his own act of civil disobedience. During the time King James ascended to the throne in 1603, thirty-seven-year-old Brewster served as one of the religious leaders of a group of religious reformists. This group believed the established Church of England, headed by King James, to be hopelessly corrupt—so corrupt that Brewster's group, known as Separatists, held their own church services in Brewster's home. When King James and his loyal bishops found out about the Separatists' secret and illegal meetings, he declared, "Conform or harry them out of the land." So in 1608 and 1609, rather than conform to King James' wishes, Brewster and his group of some 100 Separatists fled to Holland and settled in the Protestant university town of Leyden.

While in Leyden, Brewster, who'd gained legal training at Peterhouse College in Cambridge before working as a secretary to a secretary of Queen Elizabeth, set up a printing press to publish Separatist literature. Sometime around 1618 or 1619, King James learned that Brewster's press was behind the publication and circulation of anti-Church of England pamphlets. Since the King considered the Church *his* Church, he took the comments personally and as an affront to his country. He sent his soldiers across the channel to capture Brewster and transport him back to England, where Brewster was to be tried for sedition. It was assumed Brewster would be found guilty and hung. Luckily, he was able to hide from the King's men until 1620, when he snuck aboard the *Mayflower* with his wife and two younger children and fled to America.

My grandfather traveled in the opposite direction as his forefather to resist oppression. Once his trial was over, he applied for a passport so he could leave Southern California and return to London. Since the war had not yet ended, and since he'd been convicted of espionage, the government denied his application. Hoping the war would end soon, he traveled by train to Massachusetts and bided his time taking psychology and writing classes at Harvard University.

Let's put some perspective on how fortunate Grandpa was to be able to move around the world as he did. Jack London, another Socialist, wrote during this same period. In 1913, he stated in his book *The Valley of the Moon* that the working class was "starving, struggling with union breakers and fighting over jobs like dogs fight over bones."

When World War I ended, Prince reapplied to the United States government for a passport. This time he received it. However, the English government did not want him in *their* country, so refused to grant him a visa. France, on the other hand, didn't object. With a French visa in hand, Prince boarded the *Aquitania* for a second time. After spending a while in Paris, he continued on to Constantinople[7], still occupied by armies of the allied nations. He then toured through Bucharest and the rest of Romania and on into Austria, where he had "high hopes" of obtaining psychoanalysis from Dr. Sigmund Freud. Prince felt he'd learned a lot about himself from the little bit of analysis he'd received from Mary Wilshire. Now he wanted "something more complete."

Grandpa never obsessed drinking alcohol or overeating, and he had such abhorrence for tobacco that he had round stickers printed up that said "Cancer is good for you" and left them in ashtrays wherever he went. But he did have an addiction and that was psychoanalysis.

The great Dr. Freud granted him one meeting. Afterwards, he told Prince he wouldn't take him as a regular patient, gave him a list of referrals for psychoanalysts in London and closed the door. Dejected and discouraged, Prince traveled back to Paris. Fortunately, he only had to wait a few more months before some friends were able to help him obtain the visa required to cross the English Channel.

7. Constantinople was renamed Istanbul in 1930.

Photo from Eileen H. Ames' scrapbook.

Eileen Maude walking with Peter and Betty May and probably the nanny – Cannes, France, c1926.

Chapter 9

Updating My Mother

On Sunday morning, June 4, I took my booklet of twenty-five journal pages with me to see Mom. Villa Marin is a snake-like building that lines the top of a ridge with views of the San Francisco Bay on one side and the Marin hills on the other. A tidy vineyard stripes the hill outside my mother's third story window. The community dining room on the ground floor has the same view. My plan that day was for my mother and me to eat brunch in the dining room, then return to her condo where I would read the journal pages out loud. I was anxious to hear Mom's impressions, but I feared her father's words might sadden her.

I was wrong. Reading the excerpts made her very happy. She particularly liked hearing the bits her father had written about her in an endearing way. They were disappointingly few.

Before I started reading, I asked her, "Is the Marie that Grandpa refers to in the journal your old governess, Popsy?"

"Yes. Popsy's real name was Marie Popendieck."

"What do you remember about her?"

"She was in her seventies, and she piled her hair up on top of her head. In fact, she had a separate coil of hair she added to the pile. She didn't want me to see that it was a separate piece, but I suspected it for some reason. I could never catch her in the act of putting it on, even though I was bound and determined to do it. Finally, either she stopped hiding the coil, or I finally caught her in the act, which is how I knew. She spoke German and French. Maybe she grew up in Germany."

"Did she have an accent?" I asked.

"No, not that I recall. She helped teach Peter and me to speak French and German—mostly French. She also played the piano, and that is how I was supposed to learn to play the piano that you have now. Popsy came to live with us when I was around five, before my parents divorced. Maybe I was younger. Before her, Peter and I had a real nanny, or nurse. Popsy was more of a governess, hired to instruct."

"Did she stay with you when your mother remarried?"

"Yes, and she moved with us to Sussex when my mother died. She stayed about a year until I boarded at St. Michael's school in Bogner Regis [at age nine]. By that time Peter already attended boarding school, and I guess my father realized Popsy didn't have enough to do."

"It looks like your mother died on November 18, 1933. You would have just had your eighth birthday eight days earlier. Are you ready for me to read these journal pages to you?"

"Yes, please do," she said eagerly.

As I'd suspected and hoped, my reading joggled loose other memories for her, and I encouraged her to tell them to me so I could write them down. Her comments are included in the final transcription in Chapter 26.

Somewhere during my reading of the fifteenth or sixteenth page, I glanced up and saw she'd closed her eyes. "Mom," I whispered. She didn't respond.

"Mom," I said a little more loudly. "I can see you are sleepy. Shall I stop?"

She opened her eyes and tried to wake herself. "Oh, no, I don't want you to stop."

"Mom, you fell asleep. Why don't I finish later?"

"Oh all right, dear, I understand." She closed her eyes again with her head leaning against the side of her chair. Her chair faced the television, beyond which was her view of the Marin hillside. Her fat tabby cat, Lenny, slept curled on the sofa opposite.

I quietly gathered my papers and my handbag and rose to leave. I leaned over and kissed her soft wrinkly cheek before letting myself out of her condo. I took the elevator, which still smelled like split-pea soup, down to the expansive empty lobby, and walked out the main entrance to a sparkling sunny day. Mom kept the heat turned on high and the windows closed. I was always glad to be out in the freedom of the fresh air after my visits with her.

Once home I returned to researching Eileen Maude's birth and death on the Internet. Using the Ancestry.com web site, I typed her name into the search field without restricting it to the birth date, which I still didn't realize was incorrect. Lo and behold, this time I got a match! An Eileen Maude Thomas was listed with the birth date of 1892, not 1898. *Of course*, I thought. *Grandpa stated in his journal she was forty-two when she died*. Since that matched up, I felt assured I'd found the right person and corrected my family tree. Eileen was around thirty-five years old when she gave birth to my mother in 1925. Grandpa, born in 1885, would have been forty—five years older than his wife. *Not much.*

From the birth certificate, I hoped to find out more details about Eileen's parents, such as where they had been born. I noted the volume and page number in the birth index listed on Ancestry.com because I thought it would help me obtain a copy of the original certificate from the records office in Wolverhampton. I didn't yet know that in England vital records are obtained from a central national office, not from the local county offices as they are in America. I also still didn't know how to send a self-addressed stamped envelope. A friend of mine through the Mayflower Society told me of a genealogy center in San Rafael run by the Mormon Church. *Maybe they can help me.*

Meanwhile, I needed to take care of my expired passport. I hoped to leave for England in seven weeks. I paid the extra $60 required to have the process *expedited* to three weeks and trusted in God and the spirits of my ancestors to work things out.

Eileen Maude Thomas on the eve of her wedding – January 1921.

Chapter 10

Prince Meets Eileen

Several months after Prince landed in London, he learned from a former typist in the American Embassy—a woman who would later attend his wedding—that the British officials were determined to refuse him admission to the country. After he *did* get into the country, the typist overheard one of the officials grumble,

> 'In spite of all our precautions, that fellow Hopkins has entered.' The American ambassador, on the other hand, enjoyed a good laugh when he learned that the wealthy Socialist had outwitted His Majesty's government.

Prince Hopkins considered London his primary residence for most of the next twenty years. He chose his first abode on Gower Street, where, as if in a Bohemian salon, he surrounded himself with philosophers and psychologists, spending hours discussing such subjects as psychoanalysis, dream analysis, socialism, Marxism, pacifism, capitalism, pragmatism and transcendentalism. He filled many pages in his autobiography with details about this period illustrating how passionately he and his friends debated these subjects during the days after the Russian Revolution.

They even discussed vegetarianism. Grandpa only ate vegetarian food during the time I knew him, which was before menus advertised vegetarian meals. He took the family to fancy restaurants, ordered a steak with plenty of vegetables and asked the waiter to leave the steak in the kitchen.

He met many of these new people through letters of introduction he'd brought with him from friends back home, particularly Gay and Mary Wilshire. One letter granted Prince an audience with George Bernard Shaw at his house near Trafalgar Square. Emma Goldman's letter provided an audience with the anarchist Prince Peter Kropotkin. On the other hand, a letter from the Wilshires to H.G. Wells returned "with regret."

Prince was thankful to find so many people in England sharing his radical views and pleasantly surprised to be accepted in social and academic circles that he believed would have excluded him back home. He wrote that in America such "circles formed a sort of under world." By that I believe he meant people with radical points of view felt inhibited about discussing their opinions in public places, because conservative organizations, such as the Ku Klux Klan—which flourished in the 1920s, were harassing people who wanted these changes.

Things were working out well.

> With all these interesting new acquaintances, I did not fail to renew my friendship with the Harrises [friends from an earlier trip]. Edna introduced me to some young people of her set, but expressed the regret that the only girl she knew whom I would find really attractive was then out of town. Finally the night came when the Harrises were giving a dance, and I met a gentle girl of pretty complexion and chestnut brown hair, intelligent, with a vivacious, perky mien, Eileen Thomas, together with her three brothers; Harold, Eric and Bill, with whom she was staying. She had a job in London as accountant at the Midland Bank's Knightsbridge branch. As I danced

> with her that night, I realized that for the first time in my life I was in love. I arranged to see her as much as possible after that and, one night, I told her of my love and asked if she reciprocated it. She answered that while she was very fond of me as a friend, she had not as yet gone beyond that.

"My mother was still in love with someone else," Mom told me. "Before the 'war to end all wars' she had been engaged to an English chap, but he went off to fight the Germans and was killed. I doubt she was capable of loving anyone else just yet."

After refusing Prince that night, Eileen Maude went home to the flat she shared with her older brother, Harold, and his wife, Joy. As it happened, her younger brothers Bill and Eric were also there. Over dinner, knowing nothing about the proposal she'd received that afternoon, her brothers pulled her into a discussion about marriage and scolded her for having recently discouraged two or three good suitors. Prince wrote:

> This goaded her to boast that she had that very afternoon received and turned down another proposal, namely mine. Harold was infuriated and treated her to a verbal barrage regarding her ingratitude to himself and his wife. After all, they'd brought her to London and given her advantages. He went on to excoriate her wicked neglect of her duty to marry and become able to help support their [four] younger sisters and the old parents and ended by the flat assertion that he did not believe that I had proposed. In this tirade, he was supported by his two brothers.

The following morning, in the presence of all three brothers, Eileen Maude called Prince on the phone.

> "Prince, do you still feel about me as you did yesterday afternoon?"
>
> "Of course, my darling, my feelings haven't changed in the slightest."
>
> "I've thought it over, and as I told you, I'm not in love with you, however, I believe if you would take a chance on me learning to love you in time, my answer is yes."

Prince wrote that he was "elated." He wouldn't know for several years that her brothers had been standing by her side during that phone call.

> Now came all the excitement of planning our honeymoon, buying a trousseau and making other preparations for our nuptials. Eileen's brother Harold had been engaged in diamond mining in West Africa, so I took him along to give me expert advice on the purchase of a ring worthy of my pretty bride. In the midst of it all, Christmas drew near and I went up to Eileen's town of origin, Wolverhampton [about two hours slightly northwest of London by train], to meet and spend the holiday with the rest of the family. Eileen was very apprehensive about this visit because her people were very poor and she feared that their condition might make a bad impression on me.
>
> It was a large family—[George] Thomas, the father, a real estate man; Victoria (Bissell) Thomas, the mother; the three brothers whom I have already named; and [Eileen's four] sisters—Peggy, Liala, Daisy and Marie. They were a jolly lot and we had a truly merry Christmas.

As a prelude to what their marriage would be like, Prince left town the week before the wedding to attend a philosophical lecture in Fontainebleau-Avon. The marriage was scheduled to occur immediately upon his return. From an invitation I found in my mother's papers (addressed to Vernon Armitage), I learned that the ceremony took place on January 12, 1921—in the middle of winter—in St. Peter's Church in Cranley Gardens, London, SW1, near Kensington.

Photo from Eileen Hopkins Ames' Collection.

Eileen Maude Thomas as a bride – 1921.

Photo from Eileen Maude's scrapbook.

Eileen and her bridesmaids.

This brings us to the photo on the cover of this book taken after the ceremony as the newlyweds exited the church. Don't my grandparents look happy? Flower petals swirl around them like snowflakes and dot the sidewalk. One sits like a feather right on top of my grandfather's head. Prince is well groomed in a dark jacket with tails and holds his top hat down at his side, allowing us to see his slick brown hair parted near the middle. Unfortunately, we are unable to see how blue his eyes were.

Eileen is laughing and looking straight into the camera. When I stare at the photo, I feel she is looking directly at me. Her dress is simply designed of luxurious silk organdy that reaches down to midcalf. White satin slippers with organdy bows peek out from under her hem, and a soft bouquet of white carnations, her favorite flower, flows out of her hands like a fountain. She is draped in her silky veil in the style of a Madonna. Lady Elizabeth Bowes-Lyon, who wed Prince Albert, the future King George VI of England, two years later, wore a similar veil.

Reports of the wedding crossed under the Atlantic and over the continent of the United States via telegraph wires. One report appeared the following day in the *San Francisco Examiner*:

Prince Hopkins Weds Briton – LONDON – Jan. 12 – Special Cable Dispatch – 'We do not agree in our social ideas, but we love each other and it won't take long to convert my wife,' said Prince Hopkins of California at a reception in a London hotel, after his wedding to a beautiful English girl, Miss Eileen Thomas.

The ceremony was featured here as one of the biggest Anglo-American alliances, and many columns were devoted to Hopkins' record as a socialist millionaire. Hopkins gave out the details of his wooing of the handsome English girl, saying, 'I was pursuing sociological studies in London when I met Eileen. She at first violently opposed my views, but in my case it was love at first sight. Five weeks later I proposed to her. She refused me, but the next morning telephoned that she had changed her mind. That was five weeks ago. Now we are married and I believe she will soon join me in the uplift movement, although I admit a wife is not bound to agree with all her husband's social theories.'

Sketching his philosophy, Hopkins said: 'I want to democratize industry. It is along industrial lines future society will be best founded and not merely political and geographical lines.'

'What will American girls say when you return to California with an English bride?' he was asked by reporters.

'What can they say? My mother has tried to lure me into an American alliance before now. There are always a lot of pretty American girls around our home, but they must give me the liberty of saying at least one British girl is more charming.'

Prince Hopkins achieved considerable notoriety in California several years ago when he established Boyland in Santa Barbara, a set off section of land in which he allowed boys freedom of expression of their opinions and settlement of disputes by themselves as a system of training.

During the war Prince Hopkins became involved with Uncle Sam when his books 'More Prussian than Prussia' and 'The Ethics of Murder,' were ruled by the Government as being seditious.

Last year he went abroad, touring through the devastated war regions of Europe.

Eileen's death certificate.

Chapter 11

The Family History Center

Family History Centers are sprinkled across the globe so anyone can research their genealogy locally. They are sponsored and run by the Mormon Church (aka Church of Latter-day Saints). The main library containing records, mostly in the form of microfilms and microfiche, resides in Salt Lake City, Utah. But local history centers can check records out for you from the main library. In other words, if there is a film of something you want to view, the local center will send for it and you can see it on the local library's viewing machine.

When I went to the Family History Center in San Rafael, I hoped to find someone who would show me how to find genealogical information on the Internet. The Mormons have an extremely helpful web site of their own that is also available to the public (www.familysearch.org). And at the time of my visit in 2006, they offered free access to Ancestry.com.

It is my understanding that the Mormons are interested in genealogy because every member of the church is required to research his or her ancestors back at least four generations. They believe souls never die, so a deceased person's soul can be baptized and redeemed posthumously. There are many Bible stories in which descendants must pay for the sins of past generations. Most specifically, the commandment about not bowing down to other gods ends with, "I punish the children for the sins of the fathers to the third and fourth generations of those who hate me."[1] All Mormons are required to donate two years of their life to some sort of mission or service. One of the choices for that service is to help at one of the Family History Centers. Their help and the use of their center are free. That is an amazingly generous gift to the amateur genealogist!

On Wednesday, June 7, I visited my local branch behind the San Rafael Civic Center. I hauled in a large canvas tote bag filled with my family tree workbook, a notebook containing my records so far, a yellow-lined note pad and several freshly sharpened pencils.

I found the center in a one-story extension on the north side of the main church. There was plenty of parking. I entered a modest-sized room off the main hallway and found two to three computer stations placed against each wall. Humans filled most of the seats in front of the computers, concentrating hard on the screens in front of them. A kind gentleman standing in the room asked if I needed help and set me up at an open terminal. After he gave me a short lesson on how to access Ancestry.com on the strange computer—it was Windows-based and I was used to a Macintosh, I knew what to do.

I typed "Eileen Maude Thomas" into the search field and received the same reference to the index list I'd found at home. There were other Eileens, other Maudes, and other Thomases, but only the one match to her full name. I have since learned that indexes only tell you the volume and page on which to find the actual certificate in the often-ancient books held by the General Register Office in Southport, England. That's by Liverpool, 175 miles northwest from London. Obtaining copies of those certificates once you know where to find

1. Exodus 20:5, The New English Bible.

them requires contacting the General Registrar Office. Instructions are on their web site (www.gro.gov.uk/gro/content/certificates). But in 2006, this process wasn't available online. I hoped for a button to push that would provide me with a certificate and there was none.

Frustrated, I decided to look for her death record instead. I typed in "Eileen Maude Armitage," born and died in England. Nothing.

Next I tried the same name, born in England, died in Scotland. Nothing.

I typed in "Eileen Armitage," "Aileen Armitage," "Eileen Hopkins," every combination I could think of, adding the variables of England or Scotland to the mix. Nothing.

Then a young lady wearing a name tag that said "Cheryl" heard my frustrated sighs and asked me what I was trying to do. I explained, "I'm looking for my grandmother. My mother was only eight when she died and her wicked stepmother tried to obliterate her rival's memory. Now we don't know where my grandmother died or was buried."

"That's a classic genealogical story," she said. "Try typing in her name in every way it could possibly be spelled. Also try just E. Armitage."

No luck there either.

Cheryl guided me through some other channels for finding vital records of birth, death or marriage. Nothing. We then tried searching through the census records with all the varieties of spellings for Eileen's name. After fifteen more minutes I was very discouraged.

"If she died in England," said Cheryl, who had told me she was a professional genealogist, "she should have come up at the top of the matches. She probably died in Scotland. Let's try Scotspeople.org."

Google helped us find www.scotlandspeople.gov.uk. When we arrived there, much to my glee, we immediately found a match in the death records for Eileen Maude Armitage. However, the Family History Center didn't have a membership for that web site. Each record required a separate payment. That meant that before I was able to view the original of the transcript, I had to register with ScotlandsPeople, which I did using a credit card.

For about $6, I could finally view a scan of my grandmother's actual death certificate. This was extremely exciting. I wanted to shout out to everyone in the room, but when I glanced around, I could see they were all engrossed in their own searches and probably didn't want to be disturbed. As Cheryl helped me decipher the Scottish handwriting, the fascinating information about my grandmother's death revealed itself. We printed out the scanned document that stated the following:

Page title: 1933 Deaths in the District of Ayr in the County of Ayr
Name and Surname: Eileen Maude Armitage (Married to 1st Pryns Hopkins, University Lecturer, 2nd Vernon Hay Armitage, Horticulturist.)
When and Where Died: 1933 November Eighteen 0 hr 20 min AM
29 Racecourse Road, Ayr (Usual Residence 62 Ellsworthy Road, London, N.W.3)
Sex: F
Age: 41 years
Name, surname and rank or profession of father: George Thomas: Insurance Broker
Name and maiden surname of mother: Victoria Thomas M.S. [maiden surname] Bissell
Cause of death, duration of disease and medical attendant by whom certified: Valvular disease of heart, many years, heart failure, Was Cert. By Y.S. Geikie [Yeirie?] M.D.
Signature and Qualifications of Informant and Residence if out of the house in which the death occurred: Vernon H. Armitage, Witness, 62 Ellsworthy Road, London N.W. 3
When and where registered and signature of registrar: 1933 November 19th at AM Edward Pow [Row?] Registrar.

I left the Center knowing with certainty where my grandmother died, but not where she was buried. Still, this information would help me search the cemeteries. Via the Internet, I'd already found another cemetery possibility in London near 62 Ellsworthy Road. When I got home I emailed them the specifics about my grandmother's death.

The following Sunday, June 11, I dined with my mother and brought Eileen's death certificate to show her. It relieved Mom to hear it confirmed her mother died in Scotland. I had more questions.

"What does it mean Vernon was a horticulturist?" I asked. "You told me he liked to garden but I thought it was just a hobby."

"Well, he grew tomatoes!"

"You told me that before, too."

She looked at me silently for a moment, with a slight smirk. She liked holding information and making me work to pull it out of her.

"For money," she finally added. When I looked frustrated, her smirk widened into a triumphant smile.

"I see," I said, sitting back in my chair and crossing my arms to sulk. I didn't like her game. It reminded me of begging for my allowance. I thought mothers were supposed to be loving and helpful. Finally, she softened and spoke.

"I think 29 Racecourse Road might be the residence for my Uncle Jack Abbott and Aunt Peggy," she said. "She must have died at their house."

"Was it their permanent home? Or was it a second home, like a beach cottage?"

"It was their permanent home."

"How did your Aunt Peggy meet someone who lived in Scotland?"

"I don't know. Peggy was first married to a man with the last name of Pope."

Then, changing the subject, she said, "I'm surprised that 'Cause of death' didn't list pneumonia, only the heart failure. From Daddy's book, I thought it was pneumonia that killed her. She'd had rheumatic fever when she was a child. That's why she wasn't supposed to have any children."

"But she had you," I said softly.

"Yes, she did!" Mom smiled proudly.

"How old was she when she had rheumatic fever?"

"I don't know."

"What do you know of your mother's childhood?"

"Not much. I know she was the oldest daughter, but that Peggy was always the ringleader. So there was the usual sibling rivalry."

"Well then, what do you remember about living with your mother?"

She thought about it for a couple of minutes and didn't come up with an answer.

"Did you have any pets?" I prompted.

Her eyes lit up. "Yes, we had a dog. It was a wire-haired terrier named Jackie Coogan after a child star of the time." (Coogan was a contemporary of Charlie Chaplin, I found out later on the Internet.) "He wasn't a properly trained dog for he used to run away every time he got off the leash. I grew up thinking that all dogs do that as soon as they got the chance."

I thought of my faithful Welsh corgi, Annie, equally untrained.

"Vernon had an Airedale," Mom was saying. "Can't remember his name. I don't remember if Jackie was in the house with my father around. My father never really liked dogs."

He liked cats, though. For as long as I could remember, Grandpa had a shiny, completely black cat named Sooty. Sooty sat at the corner of Grandpa's desk while he wrote, which he did a good part of the day. Sometimes she curled up in a flat wooden file box Grandpa kept at one side of the desk. I was never sure if the box was put there for Sooty or for the outgoing mail. Occasionally, she prowled around my grandfather's garden. I often tried to befriend her, but she was never interested.

"Don't you remember doing anything special with your mother?" I tried again.

"I recall getting ready for bed and her teaching me to pray. 'Gentle Jesus, meek and mild, look upon a little child. Pity my simplicity, suffer me to come to thee.'

I had never seen or heard my mother pray. I looked at her in amazement.

Enjoying my surprise, she grinned.

"Would you get down on your knees?" I asked, after I got my breath back.

Mom said nothing for a moment. It occurred to me she didn't want to tell me the answer to such an intimate question. "Yes, I think so," she said finally.

"What about meals?"

"I remember that blue china," she said, pointing to the cupboard behind her in which the full set of blue and white Woods Ware dishes, soup tureens, pitchers and platters was displayed. "When Vernon remarried, a woman named Katherine, he wanted that china, but I told him, 'No,' which was probably the only time I ever stuck up for myself."

My family ate on that china for formal meals when I was growing up.

"We used that all the time, even for simple meals," Mom said. "Often Peter and I had our meals served in the nursery with Popsy.

"What did you eat?"

"Porridge."

"Didn't you have eggs?"

"Yes, poached eggs and toast and jam."

"What about tea?"

"Yes, we always had tea time. Even in boarding school."

Her eyes turned dreamy as she wondered off to her days at her English boarding school, which she attended until she was fourteen years old.

"In the dining room were several long rows of tables with chairs on each side," she said, as if in a trance. "Whether it was for breakfast, lunch, tea or dinner, we ate there. We'd all stand by the chairs and wait to sit down."

I thought of the dining hall in the Harry Potter movie.

"Did you say grace?"

"Someone did. Probably the headmistress." Mom's eyes widened again as she remembered, "Bless us, oh Lord, and these thy gifts which by thy bounty we are about to receive."

She enjoyed another look of surprise on my part, then continued.

"Then we pulled out our chairs and all sat down. We were never allowed to ask for something. We were supposed to watch out for the person on either side of us." Mom looked to her left, as if there were someone sitting there. "'Sally, do you want some pepper?' I'd have to say to Sally if I wanted some pepper. That was how I could get Sally to notice that *I* wanted some pepper."

"Did you have dishes of food placed in front of you or were platters of food placed on the table."

"Neither. The platters of food were placed in front of someone at the head of the table, and then she put the food on each plate and passed it down the long row to each person. We couldn't eat until the headmistress picked up her fork."

"What foods did you like the most?" I asked

"I remember what I didn't like," She stopped talking and stared at me, waiting for me to guess what that was.

"And what was that?" I relented, realizing she'd entangled me in the guessing game again.

"Cod."

"Every Friday?"

"Yes, and during Lent it was every Friday and every Wednesday."

"But then you went home every weekend to see Vernon, right?"

"Yes. My friend Rosemary went home to her house, too. There were several girls who left on weekends."

"Did Vernon take care of you by himself, or was Popsy there on the weekends?"

"Neither. Vernon's sister lived with us."

"Tell me about her."

"Gwendolyn Twistleton Wykham Fiennes."

"That's a mouthful. You certainly had no trouble remembering that!"

"We called her Auntie Gwen. My father called her Mrs. Fiennes. She was a remarkable woman. Peter and I were horrible to her. She certainly was no substitute for our mother. But, she tried, poor woman. She was a widow and had five sons. She used to spend hours writing to them and copying their letters in longhand with carbon copies for each son, so she could send them all the same letter and keep them all happy. That was a pretty nice thing I thought."

"Did she lose her husband in the First World War?"

"I don't know. The sons were all grown except one, David, I think. He was still in college. They called him Buz for short. And one of the sons had a baby. I can remember being home for the weekend while the baby was staying and being absolutely in love with it.

"Gwen was very active in the church—St. Johns, eleventh century—and the Ladies' Aid. When I was home and not in uniform, I wore skirts and sweaters handmade by the Ladies' Aid, which were a bit dowdy. I don't know where she went when Vernon remarried and we came to America."

I turned the conversation back to my Grandmother Eileen. "Do you remember shopping with your mother?"

"Yes, we went to Selfridges, Jaegers, Harrods and Marks & Spencer, which was kind of like a J.C. Penny."

"What about Liberty of London? You used to talk about that store to me." I had a photo of Mom and Peter when they were perhaps four and six years old, in which Mom wore a Liberty's dress with the characteristic smocking.

"Yes, we went to Liberty, but we wore uniforms to school, so we didn't buy much. Clothes for Sunday perhaps."

"How did you get around? Did you have a car?"

"Yes, we had a car. A Sunbeam. And a chauffeur. After my mother died, Vernon purchased a Bentley."

"Do you remember the chauffeur's name?"

"Nope."

"Did you go to church?"

"My mother took us now and then. There was a little church in Yapton, Sussex, where we lived after she died. Vernon and Auntie Gwen went every Sunday, but I refused to go. I just stayed home."

"You were probably pretty mad at God around then."

"Yes, I imagine I was." I let that sad comment float for a moment.

"What do you remember about your mother with your father?"

"Her brothers were quite often at our house, and they would go out together in the evenings, to the theater."

"Do you remember her wearing that beautiful Worth coat?"

"No. In my father's book he talks about how poor the Thomases were, but I don't remember them being poor. The men were educated after all. Harold was an engineer. Billy was a mining engineer in Africa."

I could tell she was getting tired. I had to gather up my questions and save them for another day.

Photo from Eileen Maude's scrapbook.

Prince and Eileen Hopkins –
Klosters, Switzerland.

Chapter 12

The Honeymoon Grand Tour, 1921

My newlywed grandparents remained in London for their wedding night. Neither Prince nor the newspapers mentioned where. However, they did not linger with breakfast in bed the following morning because they had to get up early to catch the "fast" train for Paris.

A funny thing happened when they reached their hotel on the Place Vendome, a story my grandfather frequently told his grandchildren, and which explained why he changed the spelling of his name.

The busboy showed them to their suite. Prince had asked for a special room, but was surprised to find the accommodations even grander than he'd expected.

> The hotel, misinterpreting my first name as a title, had reserved for us the royal suite. When I protested that we had no need of anything so lavish, the management apologized, but said we might remain in the suite at no

> greater charge than for an ordinary room. ... The staff continued the charade by addressing Eileen as 'the Little Princess.'

When Prince requested the maid telephone for dinner reservations that night, he overheard her say "Monsieur et Madame le Prince et la Princess Opkins," in spite of his protestations they stick to "Mr. and Mrs." He relented when he realized that "the staff found pleasure and pride in this illusion that royalty were staying among them." He did, however, change the spelling of his name to *Pryns* soon afterward.

So began an event-filled and often dramatic honeymoon. Prince knew he had to be careful with his wife's health because the rheumatic fever had permanently weakened her heart. The doctors specifically warned him not to get her pregnant. He was also to limit her exercise. This meant he must stick to a slower pace than he was used to. Nonetheless, he optimistically believed that through a regimen of diet and exercise he could improve the situation. Sadly, he pushed too far.

They traveled from Paris to Klosters, Switzerland, where, it being the end of January, Prince enjoyed the skiing. In his autobiography, Prince said Eileen only watched, claiming that since she had never been out of England, she was content appreciating the crisp, cold air and the beauty of the mountains and snow. But Eileen's scrapbook tells us otherwise. There is a photo of her on skis about to go down the mountain ahead of her new husband.

As they moved on to Nice on the French Riviera, tension arose between them.

> One day, we had a rendezvous at the Bank Nationale. Now, I was in those days extremely unconventional and Bohemian. It was all Eileen could do to make me shave daily and dress in other than my oldest clothes. I reached the bank tired and perspiring and thought nothing of squatting unceremoniously on the pavement in the portico to await my bride. When she, who was very dainty and a trifle conventional, arrived and saw me so, she was utterly horrified and treated me to a real curtain lecture.

In contrast, Prince also wrote:

> I had an inner experience as we started on our way, which I can still distinctly remember. It suddenly flashed upon me, 'This is no longer Eileen and Prince who are taking this drive together, it is we, the Hopkinses.'

From Nice they traveled to Cannes and then on to Marseilles, where they caught a boat for Algiers. Prince liked showing the world to his wife. He found her discoveries and observations enchanting. He quoted her as saying,

> 'Here is a whole continent full of people whose ways are completely un-English, and yet who are just as sure that their ways are natural and right as we that our ways are!'

It interested me to see what Eileen fancied by the photos she took. She snapped two of the sheep market in Algiers, several of the nomads on an oasis in the Sahara called Bou Saada; images of elephants and donkeys in a small caravan; women washing laundry in the creeks; as well as one of her husband dressed in a stiff-collared shirt and suit riding on a small donkey. He was so tall his feet dragged on the ground. There is a photo someone else must have taken of Prince and Eileen riding a camel. As evidenced by the titles on later pages in her album, the couple also visited BisKra and Sidi Okba, also in Algeria.

Prince wrote of falsely accusing his wife one night of hearing unreal noises. She claimed lions and tigers roared outside their tent. Thinking her fears absurd, Prince spent the entire night trying to calm her down. He learned the following day a traveling circus had passed them during the night.

> Would that we had had no more serious disputations than this—it will be recalled, however, that I never had any sisters and had been raised in the belief that I was a great catch for any girl, so that I had always rather avoided them as dangerous and had little understanding of them. Ours was therefore a marriage of one and that one was I. Additionally, I held in a cocksure manner many theories, which went squarely contrary to what

> Eileen had been taught to believe. I had naively assumed that I needed only to recommend to Eileen the reading of certain books to have her see that my views were correct—imagine my consternation when she declined to read them on the score that they might convert her to my horrid outlook!

On one occasion Prince took a side trip to Kairoan on his own, because no women were allowed in the mosques filled with whirling dervishes. When he returned, he and Eileen Maude continued on to Constantine, Tunis, Carthage, and finally Italy. His wife seemed to be glad they were heading toward home. She was slowing down and complaining of being tired. Prince wrote:

> Our hotel in Naples [Eileen included the post card from Hotel Bertolini in her book] was high above that city's picturesquely dirty and swarming streets, and was pleasant to retire to after a day's sightseeing. As at Algiers, the region round about merited excursions. The one we were most impatient to take was up Mount Vesuvius, which was in a very mild eruption. [Eileen took photos of this, too.] We took a funicular railway nearly to the rim, but had to walk the remainder of the way. Eileen was indisposed to do so, pleading her heart condition. I charged her with laziness and failure to appreciate the wonderful trip on which I had brought her.
>
> The injustice of this accusation was made clear when we reached our next point of call, Rome, for a medical examination showed that despite precautions we had taken, Eileen was pregnant. I put her in the hands of a doctor recommended by the Embassy. This physician's examination confirmed that of our English doctor at the time of our marriage—that Eileen's heart condition would not stand the strain of childbirth, and that a curettage was indicated. The emotional effect upon Eileen of this report was deeply depressant. She had been taught to believe that a wife's primary function was to bear children to her husband, and this dramatic confirmation of her incapacity to do so was a blow from which it took her some years to recover. On me, the effect was chiefly to arouse sympathy.

Reading this account brought forth many memories for me. First, I recalled the time my own family ascended to the top of Mount Vesuvius on that same funicular thirty years later when I was seven. I took a similar photo with my Brownie camera looking down into the crater of the volcano where molten lava bubbled below.

But more emotionally, it brought back the memory of my own abortion—the worst memory of my life. I looked up *curettage* to make sure it meant what I suspected it did: "a surgical scraping of the uterus by a scooped shaped instrument." My situation was very different from my grandmother's. An amniocentesis test indicated that the baby I was carrying wasn't perfect. The operation was carried out in my fifth month of pregnancy at the recommendations of my geneticist and gynecologist who claimed the little girl would be retarded and uncoordinated. Neither doctor, I learned seven years later, knew what they were talking about. My husband and I were either incredibly ignorant or unwilling to learn about the horrible, brutal procedure I had chosen to undergo to have the completely formed baby taken out of me. Our marriage therapist told us later that few marriages survived the death of a child. Ours didn't make it either.

My grandmother was lucky to have her situation attended to early in her pregnancy, and apparently the Italians didn't treat the procedure as an atrocious, illegal act. There were three photos in her scrapbook of the event: one of the nursing home, labeled "Villa Rosie;" one of Eileen Maude standing between two young nurses, all three smiling; and a third, labeled "Dr Block," of a kindly looking man in a white lab coat. Eileen Maude appears to have been well cared for.

I wondered about the crisp way my grandfather described her emotional recovery. Did my grandparents discuss the spiritual implications of what they were doing? Did either of them believe that the doctor was destroying a life or preventing one? My grandfather had to decide between his wife's life or the baby's. No one should have to make such a decision. I'm sure, even though Eileen smiled for the camera, she went through extreme emotional trauma.

Prince and Eileen moved on to the seaside resort of Rapallo on the Italian Riviera after the operation, so Eileen could rest and recuperate.

> In this picturesque and unsophisticated little seaside town we experienced

> the greatest harmony we had so far known. The period of pain was past; we were on our way home; in the improved emotional atmosphere we managed to suspend our bickerings... So, back to England, where of course, there was a round of parties for us by our friends.

The newlyweds then faced the decision about where to set up their home, incredibly privileged with the financial freedom to settle anywhere in the world they wanted. Eileen stipulated only one condition. She wanted to live close to the security of relatives. Prince wrote that tax considerations ruled out his new English relatives. However, since Eileen had become an American citizen via her marriage, no hurdles prevented the couple from moving to California to be near Prince's relatives, in other words, May. Eileen agreed. Reservations were made on the *Aquitania*, and they sailed for their next port of call, New York City in the United States of America.

Photo from Eileen H. Ames' scrapbook.

Camilla and Archie – Italy, 1959.

Chapter 13

Reaching out to My Relatives

On Monday, June 12, the day after I took Eileen Maude's death certificate to show my mother, I wrote an email to Mom's first cousin, Camilla. I hoped to visit her during my trip to England to interview her about the Thomas family. Twelve years younger than my mother, around sixty-eight, she was the only living member of my mother's generation besides Mom that I knew and the last surviving child of Harold, my grandmother's older brother. I hoped Camilla would know if more of Mom's cousins still lived.

I first met Camilla in Italy in 1959 when I was seven. My family was at the beginning of the six-month trip through Europe during which I went to the top of Mount Vesuvius. At the time my family spotted Camilla, we were sitting in a café in the tiny cove town of Portofino on the Italian Riviera. By sheer coincidence, she and her brand-new husband, Archie, walked by in front of us. They were there on their honeymoon. My mother screamed out in surprise. Camilla, equally astonished, ran to greet my mother. The newlyweds hung out with my family for a few days, which I only know because my mother took photos of the combined group in several places. Then Archie and Camilla returned to their home near Dumfries in southern Scotland, while we continued our stay in Italy. During the last two months of our trip, we traveled through Europe and ended up in Scotland, where we visited Camilla and Archie. They lived in one of several cottages on the manor estate called Arbigland owned by Archie's family.

Ten years later, the summer I graduated from college, I visited Camilla and Archie again. Archie's parents had died, and since Archie was the eldest son and heir, he and Camilla had moved into the manor home, which was well over 200 years old and like the lordly estates in Jane Austin books. Camilla, who reminded me of the actress Grace Kelly, served high tea by the grass tennis court. I watched her bake two cakes and the expected scones and serve all with toast, clotted cream, jams and fresh strawberries from a farm nearby—possibly their own.

They had a darling daughter named Cynthia, who must have been nine at the time, with brown pigtails. One morning I walked with Archie and Cynthia on their private beach by the sea as Archie threw sticks of driftwood for their shiny black Labradors.

That evening at dinner, in the long, dark wood-paneled dining room surrounded by subtly lit portraits of Archie's ancestors, Archie explained the laws of the salmon rights on the rivers he owned. When dinner was over, a servant brought in a tray on which stood a bottle of port and several cut crystal glasses. Archie took the bottle off the tray very gently, setting it down on the mahogany table as if it were made of eggshells. "One must be very careful not to upset the sediment settled at the bottom of an old port," he said. "It is customary that one always slide the bottle toward you and off the table, never lift it up directly. Furthermore, it is customary to pass the bottle to the left around the table, not to the right."

I wondered how many other things one must learn to be the laird of a Scottish manor.

Archie and Camilla lived in that beautiful manor house for only twenty months. Not long after my visit, Archie, a "keen fisherman and shot," drowned "while wildfowling with a punt gun on the River Esk estuary," as Camilla would later describe it. His younger brother inherited the estate. Camilla and Cynthia moved to London to be near Camilla's older sister, Jill. I thought it very unfair at the time that a wife and child had to be displaced by another family because of heredity laws, but my mother insisted that, especially today, it must be that way or the estate would be divided up so quickly it would soon vanish.

A few years later, in 1975, when I was twenty-four and married, my mother took my brothers, my husband and me to England to see her relatives again. At first we stayed in a shabby hotel my mother's travel agent had booked for us. When Mom's cousin Jill discovered the state of our accommodations, she rescued us and took us to her home in Chelsea, Greater London, not far from where Camilla lived. Jill awed me with her friendliness, ushering us out of the taxi like a mother hen, gushing over us about being comfortable and making ourselves at home. I recall her roundness—round body, round face with unusual cat-like eyes and thin lips. She had two daughters and a son at home: Philippa, Candida and Adam, who were a bit younger than my brothers and me and all as welcoming as their mother.

It was on the second night of our stay at Jill's that she and Camilla held the small reception of Thomas family members—the time I chatted with Jill's and Camilla's mother, Joy, and created my first draft of the Thomas Family Tree. Jill and my mother, who were the same age, had always stayed in close contact, though it's surprising Jill never told my mother that Camilla was going to be in Italy at the same time as our family. Maybe Archie's honeymoon plans had been a secret. Jill's and Camilla's brother, Jeffray, who was two years younger than Jill and ten years older than Camilla, was probably at the party with his wife Ann and four children, however I don't remember meeting them. I learned later Jeffray was as unusual as the way he spelled his name.

I saw Camilla a third time about fifteen or twenty years later when she came alone to California to visit my mother. Cynthia was married. Jill had passed away after seven years of living with Alzheimer's. I still lived in Pasadena, a few miles down the road from Mom. When I joined Mom and Camilla for dinner one night, I was struck by how pretty and elegant she was—just as graceful as she had been as the mistress of Arbigland.

True to her Jane Austin persona, Camilla painted with watercolors and drew with colored pencils. She and Mom spent one of their days together in Death Valley. While Camilla sketched the desert, Mom, an accomplished amateur photographer, who had built a darkroom off her bathroom and published many travel articles in the local newspapers, busied herself with her camera. I couldn't imagine spending a day drawing sand, but evidently it was a novelty to my English cousin-once-removed.

By the time I emailed Camilla about my upcoming trip to search for my grandmother, she'd remarried, after many years of being single, to Rodney, a widower from a prominent English family. I'd been keeping up with her through our annual holiday cards. She sent Christmas cards to me, and I sent Valentines to her. She and Rodney had just moved to a new home in a tiny village called Birdham near Chichester, not far from England's southern coast.

When I didn't hear back from Camilla after a week, I posted a regular letter to her Birdham address. I felt squeezed for time. I needed to know Camilla's availability so I would know whether to arrange my trip to southern England at the beginning of my trip or the end. That would help me decide whether to start my grave search in Scotland or London.

I had other decisions to work out. How long was I willing to be away from Annie? I worried about keeping her in a kennel longer than two weeks. On the other hand, it seemed a shame to go so far away and not stay for at least three weeks.

I also wanted to visit my mother's school chum from St. Michael's boarding school, Squitty, who'd reverted to her real name, Rosemary. Rosemary didn't meet my mother until after Eileen Maude passed away, but I hoped she could help me learn more about my mother's life with her stepfather, Vernon. I'd gotten to know Rosemary when she visited my mother in Pasadena. She was a tiny thing, just five feet tall, and as spry as Peter Pan. I found her to be outgoing, friendly and easy to talk to. During her last visit, she was still much more agile than my mother, even though they were the same age, well into their seventies.

She lived with her husband, Graham, in Poole, Dorset, which wasn't far from Chichester. I sent her an email asking her if she'd like a visitor.

Then I sent an email to my stepcousin Carolyn, to see if I could visit her in Wokingham, Hampshire. Wokingham is about an hour west of London and an hour and a half north of Poole.

Carolyn was the daughter of Mom's stepaunt Audrey, Fay's much younger sister. Audrey had befriended my mother, who was only ten years younger than she was, and they remained close. On one adventure they took together, Mom witnessed an important event in Audrey's life. When Audrey was about twenty-one and Mom eleven, she escorted Mom on one of h er cross-Atlantic trips to America. During the voyage on the large ocean liner, Audrey found favor with the ship's surgeon, a Welshman named David, whom she married several years later.

I didn't remember meeting Audrey during our family trip in 1959, though I'm sure I did. But when I was sixteen, my mother sent me to England with my school friend, Leslie, and we stayed with Audrey and David in their quaint brick house in Kent. That's when I met Carolyn, who's our age. I stayed with the family again when Carolyn and I were in our twenties, and when in our midforties, she visited me in California with her two teenage daughters, Verity and Jessica. I felt very comfortable asking her if I could stay with her for a few days. That part of the trip would have nothing to do with my search.

Four days later, June 18, I received the following from Camilla:

> Dear Mary,
>
> Thank you for your email. We have been away a lot, and trying to catch up in between. Rodney's email has been more often than not un-functional since the January move, only made fully operational in the last week. Apologies for the delay. With regard to your research: My sister Jill, who died some time ago, and brother Jeffray, who died last year on April 7th, knew the Thomas family better than myself, who can tell you little. The Thomas family were not cohesive! The following people you should meet:
>
> Jill's daughter Philippa: married to Peter, who works from home, children Joshua and Georgia. Philippa would like you to stay with them in London.

Jill's daughter Candida: married to Tim, who works in London, children Thomas, Harriet and Eleanor (who resembles my mother Joy). Candida lives in Worcestershire near to Wolverhampton, where grandfather George Thomas lived with his wife, maiden name – Bissell, at 17 Tettenhall Road, Wolverhampton, where your grandmother would have been brought up. It is not known who owns this house now.

Our first cousin twice removed Jason Turner with his wife Ioana (Romanian), daughter Sophie, and father Lionel who is in the first stages of Alzheimer's disease, but whose long-term memory is said to be quite good.

My Aunt Peggy Thomas married Jack Abbott. Their son John died in the seventies. His sisters Pat and June (now very elderly if still alive) lived in Ayrshire near their parents.

My old address books lie somewhere in a box as yet unopened, unlikely to surface in the short term. My parents did not keep contact with other brothers and sisters, but this gives you a start.

At present August looks largely clear for us, but we could be involved with some refurbishment building operations then. We would love to have you to stay here before you move on. Is your mother able to travel still?

With love from
Camilla

I felt honored Camilla put together the family information for me and had even consulted Philippa about staying at her place in pricey London. Glad Mom had at least one more cousin alive I could meet, Lionel Turner, I felt badly he suffered the early stages of "Oldsheimers." It was disappointing John Abbott was dead since he was the son of the sister of my grandmother that she was visiting when she died. He might have remembered my grandmother's visit to his house and her death there, though he would have been very young.

A second email arrived from the clerk at the Norwood Cemetery in London I had contacted when I learned it was near to 62 Ellsworthy Road.

Dear Mary Mitchell,

There are a huge number of cemeteries in London.

Visit www.londoncemeteries.co.uk for a list.

For cemeteries in Ayr, visit www.south-ayrshire.gov.uk/community/cemeteries for info.

As we explain on our web site, the West Norwood Cemetery office is where burial, cremation and other records are kept. The burial and cremation registers run purely chronological, so it helps for searching that you have a precise date of death. The manager of the cemetery, Avril, will be able to deal with your enquiry. There may be a charge. I'm not sure.

I hope this is helpful.

Jill

Secretary

I sent queries to both of the web sites Jill listed and waited to hear from Avril. Wednesday, June 22, I received an email from my second-cousin Philippa. I'd written her after hearing from Camilla.

Dear Mary,

How nice to hear from you. I remember your 1975 visit well, but am getting a bit confused about the other people who came with you—did you come with your brothers and your mum? I am sorry, but I was only eleven or twelve and we had a wonderful summer of visits from relatives from Florida and California and then heard nothing more. I am sure the adults communicated but you know what it's like at that age—people come into your life and then 'cease to exist' until the next time! And sadly mum [Jill] is not around to get chapter verse on who came and who is related to whom.

It would be lovely to catch up on the last three decades! Do come and stay with us in London. I am around in August, but at the moment I am working so hard my holiday dates depend on when I've finished the workload. My children are 16 and 13 and they are fab—looking forward to introducing them to you.

I'll write some more when I've finished the nightmare of a week that lies ahead.

All the best, Philippa

I noted how she spelled her name—one "l" and two "p"s and hoped I would remember in the future. I looked forward to seeing her again.

I had also written to her sister Candida via the email address Camilla gave me. As Camilla intimated, maybe visiting Candida in Worcester near Wolverhampton would result in a trip to look for the graves of our mutual great-grandparents, or maybe a visit to 17 Tettenhall Road, the house where my grandmother Eileen Maude and her grandfather Harold grew up.

However, my two email attempts to reach Candida bounced back. I sent an additional email to Philippa for a more current address for her sister and then spent the rest of the morning trying to purchase my airline ticket with my free United miles.

United had established two categories for redemption. One called *saver* that required less miles but had fewer options for travel, and one called *standard* using more miles but with a more flexible schedule. Attempts to find an available ticket with the saver option failed. I found a nonstop round-trip flight using the standard category, only to discover when I was finished filling in all the information that 80,000 miles were required. I only had 74,144 in my account. After an hour with a live agent, I relinquished a precious $153 to make up for the insufficient miles. Still, I was thankful. $153 was a lot cheaper than the price of a full fare ticket to England at many thousands of dollars. The worrisome news was that I had to wait from three to five days for the extra miles I'd purchased to be posted before I could use them to buy the standard ticket. I risked the good possibility that the prices and schedules would change in the meantime.

Photo from Eileen Maude's scrapbook.

Postcard of Eileen and Pryns on the *Aquatania* – May 14, 1921.

Chapter 14

Eileen Maude in America

For Pryns'[1] third time and Eileen's first, they boarded the *Aquitania*. Grandpa wrote that it would have been a fabulous voyage had it not been peppered with frequent quarrels. A Yale classmate of his, who happened to be on board, didn't help by "showering Eileen with gentlemanly attention." Pryns went to sulk in their cabin.

> I became quite jealous. When she realized this, she gave me a convincing assurance of her affection, but the incident had prevented my being at her side to welcome her to her new homeland as we passed the Statue of Liberty.

The couple planned to spend a few months on the East Coast before heading to California. Pryns wanted to introduce his wife to his New

---

1. According to Eileen Maude's scrapbook, Pryns spelled his name this way by this time.

York friends and make sure she wouldn't prefer living near New York City or Boston than in California.

Meanwhile in Santa Barbara, Queen May worried about the same scenario. She desperately wanted her son and his bride to live near her. No sooner had Pryns and Eileen stepped off the boat in New York than they received a telegram from May's banker, a Mr. Sims, declaring there was a business matter of great urgency. They should travel to Santa Barbara immediately!

Pryns purchased a round-trip ticket to Santa Barbara for himself and deposited his wife in a "country" hotel they found in Greenwich, Connecticut. He was surprised a week later when he arrived in Santa Barbara and found his mother distraught because he hadn't brought his wife.

> When I got to the Trust Company, the business matter turned out to be of such trifling import that I at once saw that Mr. Sims must have been prevailed on to send the telegram by my mother.

Pryns returned to find Eileen enjoying herself so much in Greenwich that she asked if they could stay a while longer. He leased a cottage on Putnam Avenue close to several of his Yale friends and their families. Other friends, some from college and some made through his Socialist activities, lived in New York City. Pryns wrote that to visit them, he and Eileen drove as far as 125th Street, garaged their car and completed the trip downtown by subway. Since in other parts of the story he mentioned a chauffeur, maybe the chauffeur drove them that far and then fetched them when they were finished with their activities.

Of the friends, he listed "pacifists Roger Baldwin, John Haynes Holmes and Norman Thomas." I looked the men up on the Internet. Norman Thomas was a Princeton grad, ordained by the Presbyterian Church and four months older than my grandfather. In 1921 he was about to run for governor of New York on the Socialist ticket. During his life he ran unsuccessfully for U.S. president six times—the first time in 1928. An eloquent speaker, he often discussed the differences between his democratic Socialism and Communism. Though Pryns never formally joined the Socialist Party, he claimed to agree with most of its issues. He wrote:

> Norman's socialism was the antithesis of Communism as developed in Russia and China, being essentially ethical, democratic and freedom loving, as well as embodying a strong sense of justice and of compassion for the victims of every kind of oppression or exploitation. He was the great friend of the immigrants of all nationalities who came to our country, teaching and representing to them the finest traditions of this nation—some have named him 'the conscience of America.'

At that time Pryns felt the Socialist platform was too utopian, but he wrote thirty years later that many of the utopian ideals eventually came about.

Roger Baldwin, originally from Wellesley, Massachusetts, had just the year before founded the American Civil Liberties Union (ACLU) and was working as its first director. Only fourteen months older than Pryns, he received his bachelor's and master's degrees from Harvard University, and had a background as a probation officer. He'd vehemently opposed the United States' involvement in World War I and, rather than submit to the draft, spent a year in jail. He started the Civil Liberties Bureau in 1917 to protect conscientious objectors. It later became the National Liberties Bureau, which was then renamed the American Civil Liberties Union in 1920.

Forty-one-year-old John Haynes Holmes was a bit older than Roger, Pryns and Norman, who were thirty-six and thirty-seven at the end of 1921. Like Baldwin, Haynes had studied at Harvard, where he received a Divinity degree and became a Unitarian minister. Like the others, he was a pacifist and an antiwar activist. In 1909 he'd helped found the National Association for the Advancement of Colored People (NAACP), and in 1920 was working with Baldwin to establish the ACLU. He wrote books, hymns and a play that briefly ran on Broadway. He eventually received the Gandhi Peace Award.

Being near New York City also allowed the Hopkinses to socialize with Charles and Myra Meyer. But Pryns wrote that they took part "in a very different section of New York society." When Aunt Myra gave a fancy party for Eileen and introduced her around to her own "select" young friends, Pryns feared "that Aunt Myra would reinforce social attitudes which were in conflict with my own."

The friendship was short-lived. Aunt Myra owned and adored two chow puppies. She gave one of them to Eileen with "elaborate admonitions on its care." Eileen "cherished" the puppy and assigned the task of walking it every evening to their new chauffeur.

Photo from Eileen Maude's scrapbook.

The chauffeur with Eileen's chow puppy.

A photo in Eileen's scrapbook shows her cuddling the puppy fondly while sitting in Central Park. Another shows the puppy sitting in the chauffeur's lap, peeking out of the window of the touring car. There is even an image of my grandfather walking the fluffy chow along a boardwalk. They must have had the puppy for at least three or four months, because he grew quite large. But one evening, in spite of their "elaborate care," the puppy became terribly ill. Eileen and Pryns stayed up all night trying to nurse the "poor little creature" back to health, but nothing they or their vet did could save its life. Pryns believed Aunt Myra never forgave Eileen.

Pryns seems to have had a hard time sharing his wife with anyone. When some of his artistic and musical friends encouraged her to enroll in drawing and singing classes, he felt left out. "It seemed to me to be another thing in which I could have no share."

And yet he was busy with a project of his own in which Eileen could have no share, establishing a monthly magazine he named *Labor Age* ,with its headquarters in Manhattan. He drafted a young Hungarian named Louis Bundenz to represent the magazine at labor meetings and created a board of directors led by a Mr. Maurer, the president of the United Mine Workers.

According to Wikipedia, Louis Frances Bundenz of Indianapolis, Indiana, was first a Communist spy and then an anti-Communist spy. Age thirty in 1921, he wouldn't join the National Communist Party until the early 1930s. He was arrested twenty times before renouncing Communism in the 1940s and then testified against the party members as a paid informant for the FBI. That would all happen after his stint at *Labor Age*.

The publication espoused my grandfather's theories about creating a society supportive of the working class.

> Points on which I particularly harped were ethical dealings and relationships, the abjuration of violence and the upbuilding of an American Workers Education movement such as I had seen in England.

In spite of the political sparks he ignited, life for Pryns and Eileen was relatively calm. Pryns wrote that he settled into a "groove of normality" he had seldom known before. After an early breakfast with his wife, he traveled in a jitney to the train station with other men in the neighborhood. The 7:10 a.m. train scooted them to New York's Grand Central Station, whereupon a short subway ride got Pryns to *Labor Age*'s office by 8:30 a.m. He usually put in a normal working day, lunching with friends and business acquaintances. Board meetings were held once a week at a club at 14 West Twelfth Street, where other leftist organizations, such as the ACLU, also met, allowing the various organizations to support each other and share information.

By four in the afternoon Pryns left for home. He played a game of tennis before dinner when the weather permitted. During winter months, he stayed later in town at the Yale Club gymnasium, either in the boxing room or at the club's pool. But this latter plan caused complaint from his wife, who resented his putting his physical routine before his time with her.

The decoration of their house was to be Eileen's domain, as well as the management of their social calendar. Soon Eileen found herself lonely during the daytime. Servants helped with the housework, and she'd given up her classes because Pryns was so "miffy" about it. Even her attempts at cooking met with criticism.

> One evening she prepared most temptingly a tasty squab for my dinner, but instead of receiving from me any appreciation, all she got was a sour comment to the effect that it was not worth sacrificing a little bird's life to provide so meager a bit of nourishment.

Pryns claimed in his autobiography that Eileen didn't meet his mother until they left Connecticut. But Eileen's photo album tells a different story. May must have taken the train east to meet her new daughter-in-law, because there are photos of her on a New England beach with Myra and Eileen. Eileen holds the chow when it was tiny. There was no description about how the new in-laws got along or what they thought of each other.

Before the year ended, Pryns had had enough of normality and was growing restless. Besides, he was tired of Connecticut's winter climate. The publication of *Labor Age* would continue for five more years before being absorbed by a larger journal, but its founder moved on. In spite of Eileen's "tearful protests," he canceled their lease on the cottage, arranged for Mr. Bundenz to take over the management of *Labor Age* and purchased two train tickets to Oakland, California.

The train made several stops along the way. Eileen took photos of the Great Salt Lake, and Pryns wrote,

> We enjoyed the sensation of swimming in water that buoyed our bodies up

> as if we were corks... We were thrilled when the train speeded for miles on a trestle through the middle of the shallow lake.

Eventually, they reached the train junction in Vallejo where the Sacramento River breaks through the hills to dump into the San Francisco Bay, creating a deep channel. Since this was before the erection of the Carquinez Bridge[2], the train needed a ferry to take it across the river. In the same manner trains crossed the English Channel, the train was first broken up in sections that were "shunted alongside each other" onto the ferry. Passengers could leave their train car and ride on a high deck. From that vantage point Eileen took another photo that revealed a pilot deck of the ferry named after the local county, *Solano*. The black train cars waited quietly beneath her and the empty banks of Crocket summoned in the distance. Those banks are now covered with houses. Not long ago, at an estate sale near my house, I came across an old photo of Southern Pacific's *Solano* titled the "Largest Ferry in the World."

Photo from Eileen Maude's scrapbook.

The *Solano* crossing the Sacramento River.

Once the train was reassembled on the other side of the river, the

2. The original Carquinez bridge was designed by Robinson & Steinman and dedicated on May 21, 1927. It cost $8 million to build and was the first major bridge in the San Francisco Bay Area. "The Barrier Broken," *Vallejo Evening Chronicle*, May 21, 1927.

journey continued to the piers of the Port of Oakland, where they planned to catch another ferry to San Francisco. Pryns wrote:

> As we disembarked and looked down onto the ferryboat waiting to take us across the bay, I saw Mother standing there. It was thus that she and Eileen first beheld each other.

Pryns must have been trying to dramatize his book, because, as mentioned, they had already met. In reality, it would have been surprising that someone like May, who traveled so often and so easily, would have waited over a year to meet her new daughter-in-law.

My great-grandmother's Booth family was well represented in San Francisco. Though her parents were gone, May had two married brothers—an older one, Samuel, and a younger one, Frank. She also had four sisters, an older married one, Ella, and three younger ones: Edith was also married, while Madeleine and Amy would remain maiden aunts the rest of their lives. Madeleine, known as *Lena,* taught school. My mother remembered her Aunt Amy by her "bristly chin."

Frank acted as the family financial advisor and had been managing the Hopkins estate since Charles' death in 1913. Frank had been doing such a good job that he was probably as prosperous as Charles had been.

Frank and May were building a three-story apartment house facing Lafayette Park on the corner of Clay and Laguna Streets, due to be completed in 1926—three years later. Then May could spend her winters in San Francisco and her summers at El Nido.

Mom remembered visiting the San Francisco apartment building often after she moved to America in 1940.

"It was like a Booth Family compound. My grandmother occupied the four-bedroom flat on the top floor with her maid, Laura. It had a 360-degree view of the city. Uncle Frank, his wife and two daughters lived on the second floor with only a slightly less dramatic view. The two maiden aunts shared the ground floor. A basement garage the full size of the building sheltered their cars. In that same garage a small apartment was arranged for Jack, my grandmother's chauffeur, to rest during the day when he wasn't needed."

Once the family parties were over, and Eileen had been introduced all around, she and Pryns began scouting for a place to live. Eileen took several photographs as she toured the area. In one she sits with her mother-in-law on top of Mt. Diablo. Another shows the view of San Francisco from the top of Twin Peaks. Eileen looks like she enjoyed herself. May wore large hats and sometimes veils in her photos, making it difficult to see her face. I've never seen a photo of her smiling, so it's hard to know her opinion of her daughter-in-law's company.

Pryns' account, on the other hand, focused on looking for acreage to build another boys' school. He scoped out the Oakland and Berkeley hills, but found nothing "to his liking." He suggested to his wife they move on to Southern California where there was more available land and, of course, a warmer climate.

Photo from Eileen H. Ames' scrapbook.

The Booth/Hopkins apartment building on the southwest corner of Clay and Laguna in San Francisco. Today, a taller building on the north side blocks much of the bay view.

Photo from Eileen H. Ames' scrapbook.

Betty May, her cousin Jill and Peter – France, summer 1933.

Chapter 15

Final Preparations for My Trip

On Friday, June 23, 2006, I woke up feeling a wee bit sorry for myself. It was my fifty-fifth birthday, and I realized that as a result of spending all my time researching and writing, I'd isolated myself. I had plenty of friends and relatives scattered around the world, but not many good ones in San Rafael, where I'd been living for two years. I told the few friends I made to leave me alone so I could write. At least I had plans to eat dinner with my mother and my twenty-seven-year-old son, Jon, who lived nearby in San Francisco.

By noon I felt much better. Annie came in to cheer me up when I took a bath. She looked over the rim and dropped her tennis ball with a small splash so I would throw it, which I did. I soaked while she fetched, and I counted my blessings. I had a nice cottage to live in, a family to take me out to dinner, a daughter who had called the night before, work to do, money in the bank and projects to fulfill. I didn't live in the Middle East or in Africa where life for most citizens was wretched. And I had my health, which was much more than Eileen Maude had when she died at age forty-one.

I'd been reviewing the list of cemeteries sent to me by the lady at West Norwood Cemetery in London. It was a mile long—maybe a hundred cemeteries or so. I had my work cut out for me.

Or maybe not. I received the following email suggesting I should concentrate on Ayr rather than London. That would be a relief. Ayr was smaller and there were fewer cemeteries.

> Dear Ms Mitchell,
>
> I have checked our records but could not find Eileen Armitage buried in West Norwood Cemetery. Obviously, there are many cemeteries in London. Do you know for sure she was not buried in Scotland?
>
> Please find below the email address for the Crematorium in Ayr, Scotland. You should first contact them and ask them to check their cemetery records or contact the family records centre in Scotland to check the correct registration district. Most burials take place where the deceased is registered.
>
> I hope you are successful with your search.
>
> Regards
>
> Avril
>
> Site Manager, West Norwood Cemetery/Crematorium

She gave me an email address for a Philip to whom I wrote. I mentioned I was unable to read the name of the recorder on the death certificate. It was either Edward Pow or Edward Row. I ended with:

> Since my grandmother was on vacation in Ayr from her usual residence in London, we wonder if her body was taken back to London for burial. If you cannot find her, do you know where I might find records for where her body would have been taken? There are apparently hundreds of cemeteries in London.

Then the good fairies began working. That same day I was able to purchase my ticket, departing San Francisco Airport on Thursday, July 20 and returning August 10.

On Monday I received a reply to my inquiry to Ayr about Eileen Maude's grave:

> We have checked the Ayr Cemetery Records and unfortunately can find no record of interment in the two-month period following the recorded date of death.

I also received an email from my second-cousin Philippa saying she was slammed during July. A longer visit in August would be better. So I wrote to my stepcousin Carolyn to see if I could visit her at the beginning of my trip instead of later. I also asked if she and I could visit another stepcousin, her first-cousin Paul. Paul lived in Cambridge. Not only would it be fun to see him, but if I went to Cambridge, I could look up my real second-cousin, Jason Turner, and his aging father, Lionel Turner.

I'd come to know Paul one summer in the late 1960s. He spent his 'tween year (the year between the end of high school and beginning of college) with my grandfather in Santa Barbara. A Paul McCartney look-alike, I took a special liking to him as I madly followed the Beatles that summer. Now he is a professor at Cambridge University—I've seen him interviewed on PBS specials about Ancient Greece—and he often visits my half-uncle David here in the San Francisco Bay Area. We have remained good friends. He and David are real cousins to each other since Paul and Carolyn were Fay's nephew and niece.

The next day I received a response from the archivist in Ayr.

> Dear Ms. Mitchell,
>
> Thank you for your enquiry regarding your grandmother's death, which has been passed to us here at Ayrshire Archives.
>
> I understand the Registration and Bereavement Service has checked their records and have found no record of a burial in the two months after her death.
>
> We hold Church Records for churches within the Presbytery of Ayr, as well as Monumental Inscriptions to Ayr Cemeteries, but it is unlikely that

they would record any information—ideally you are looking for a burial record, and as such, the above service would be the main source of burial information. I checked the Burgh Minutes, but could find no mention of the event in their indexes. It may be that your grandmother was not buried in Ayrshire.

On your behalf, I checked the Directories we hold here, and one dated 1934/35, records an Edward Pow as being 'Registrar'—so it's POW that is recorded on the death certificate [not ROW].

You may want to contact the Carnegie Library in Ayr, who may be able to assist you as they hold local newspapers—the death may have been reported in the news of the time: localhistory@south-ayrshire.gov.uk.

I wish you luck with your research.

Yours sincerely,
Pamela
Archivist

I wrote to the local history contact, telling them my usual story about looking for my grandmother...

I was wondering if you could look to see if any news articles about my grandmother's death were published at the time. Hopefully they would state where she was to be buried.

[I listed the statistics for Eileen Maude's death.]

Also, she was visiting her cousins, Peggy and Jack Abbot. Their names might be mentioned in the article, for they were local residents of Ayr.

Thank you so much for your help. I plan to visit Ayr during the end of July or early part of August. If you can tell me any place else to look for records I would appreciate it. I live in California in the USA. I hope not to have to search every graveyard in Ayr and London!

This is also a silly request, I know, but can you recommend a nice place to stay in Ayr? Just me.

When Philippa sent me her sister Candida's correct email address, I replied with the following:

Hi again Philippa,

Things are firming up. I won't be at your doorstep before August.

My stepcousin Carolyn will pick me up when I get in early on the 20th of July. May I arrive to your place Aug 7 or 8, stay a couple of days and then catch my flight home?

Still very flexible. Give me your thoughts.

Love,

Mary

I received another letter from the archivist in Ayr that pointed toward finding Eileen Maude in London.

Dear Ms. Mitchell,

Perhaps you have to accept that your grandmother was buried in London. As such, a good place to start would be to confirm her address in London and contact the Family Records Centre, their web site is: www.familyrecords.gov.uk

You could also try the London Metropolitan Archives, who I would hope would give you good advice if your grandmother lived in the Greater London area.

You might find that—especially if you have an address where your grandmother was living—it might not be that difficult to locate her grave, even though London is such a big place.

Yours sincerely,

Pamela

Archivist

Then I wrote to the National Archives by mistake. I should have written to the Family Records Centre or London Metropolitan Archives listed above. But from where I was sitting in San Rafael, they all seemed the same.

Hello:

I am looking for the grave of my grandmother....[blah blah...] The very helpful archivist in Ayrshire has not been able to find a record of burial during the two months after her death. Would you please check the burial records in London. I see there are nearly a hundred cemeteries and I would like to whittle the prospects down.

I leave for London on July 20.

When I received the following auto-reply, I learned that researching in the great bog of London would be a lot more cumbersome than researching in tiny Ayr:

Thank you for contacting The National Archives (of England, Wales, and the United Kingdom). We will read the contents of your enquiry carefully, and in most cases we will respond with advice or guidance within 10 working days. However, for some queries we may need more than 10 working days to prepare a reply. This will be where we are permitted by legislation to do so, such as Freedom of Information requests (up to 20 working days) and Data Protection requests (up to 40 calendar days).

[Information about hours of operation, etc.]

Good luck with your research.

Email Service Manager

Reader Information Services Department

The National Archives, Kew, Richmond, Surrey, United Kingdom

This type of red tape is typical in the United States when trying to obtain genealogical information from large cities. Just try getting anything from Chicago or New York City!

I also received this email from Ayr. It appeared less and less likely that Eileen Maude was buried there.

Dear Ms Mitchell,

Thank you for your enquiry to South Ayrshire Libraries.

We have checked the local papers for a death notice or obituary for your grandmother but didn't find anything.

Ayr Cemetery monumental inscriptions are in the process of being recorded. There are no "Armitages" listed in the two published volumes, these mainly cover earlier gravestones. If you contact Ayr Crematorium they will be able to check for a burial record for Eileen Maude Armitage in Ayr Cemetery.

If she is not buried in Ayr and if you know where her family lived in

London it is possible that the local cemeteries in the area may be indexed. It would be worthwhile getting in touch with the library there and asking what is available.

In the 1930/31 Ayr Directory a John S Abbott, The Bungalow, 5 Ewenfield Road, Ayr is listed. I assume that would be Jack.

I hope you are successful and find where your grandmother is buried and if we can be of any further help please contact us again.

The second-to-last sentence fitted a piece into my puzzle. John Abbott lived on Ewenfield Road, not the Racecourse Drive noted on Eileen Maude's death certificate. That indicated that Eileen Maude probably died in a hospital on Racecourse Drive, not at her sister's home. All I had to do was find the name of the hospital? If it was still there, maybe I could obtain the records of where they sent Eileen Maude's body?

The next Sunday I asked Mom about the Abbotts' house in Scotland.

"Was it big or small?"

"Sort of medium sized."

"Was it as big as your house in Pasadena?"

"I remember it being all on one floor and that they referred to it as 'The Bungalow.'"

Aha! That confirmed that the house on Ewenfield was the same house where Peggy was living when her sister visited her in 1933.

When I got home, I had an email from my stepcousin Paul confirming our visit.

It's in the diaries, Mary! Fingers crossed.

Safe journey

Love,

Paul

English people use the word *diary* for what we Americans call a *calendar*.

I wrote to Camilla to update her on my findings and my itinerary, adding:

I still think I want to go up to Ayr and take a look.

I have yet to reach my mother's school chum Rosemary in Poole, but I'm hoping to visit her and you on the same excursion. How is your schedule looking now? Would it be best to visit during the week of July 24-27 or Aug 1-4? I'll go to Scotland during the other week.

Look forward to seeing you.

On June 30, twenty days before takeoff, I wrote to the London Metropolitan Archives, even though I suspected they wouldn't have time to respond to me before I departed for England.

Hello:

I received this email address from the National Archives of the UK. I'm looking for the grave of my grandmother...[rest of data]...

Her family had enough money to transport her body back to London. There are indications in my grandfather's journals that he paid for a fancy burial. His name was Pryns Hopkins (also spelled Prynce).

Any help you can give me will be greatly appreciated.

I received another automated response! Obviously I wasn't the only one looking for a relative in England!

Thank you for contacting the London Metropolitan Archives (LMA) Enquiry Team.

Your enquiry has been logged and will be answered in order of receipt, along with fax, telephone and letter enquiries. We receive more than 2500 written and telephone enquiries every month, which accounts for the strict queuing of our enquiries. We aim to answer 90% of enquiries within 14 days of receipt, and 100% within 28 days.

On Independence Day, July 4, I again had no plans. So I decided to continue my life as a hermit and paint my living room walls—two of them, that is. I had already painted one the day before, and I'd painted the fourth about a month earlier. Then I painted my front door shiny black and bought a new, equally shiny brass door handle to adorn it. The elegant door added a nice Beacon-Hill touch to my humble cottage.

The following day I received an email from my stepcousin Carolyn confirming she would meet me at Heathrow Airport upon arrival. *Wonderful news!* There is nothing more welcoming than a friendly face when you exit customs after a long international flight! And it is so much more comfortable being in the home of a relative while sleeping off jet lag than in a strange hotel.

I also heard back from Camilla.

> Dear Mary,
>
> Thank you for your update. July is not good. Can do between August 1-4.
>
> In haste,
>
> Love,
>
> Camilla

My schedule was tightening, yet I still hadn't heard from Rosemary and couldn't commit to Camilla until I did. All I knew was that I wouldn't be heading south during the first week. Needing a base of operations for my cemetery inspections, I decided to rent a tiny flat in London for the first week after my weekend with Carolyn. Her home in Wokingham was too far away for commuting. I knew when I was with her, we'd be so busy socializing, I wouldn't carry out a systemized search program.

Photo from Eileen H. Ames' collection.

Eileen Maude with her mother-in-law, May –
San Francisco, 1921.

Chapter 16

Eileen in Pasadena

Once Pryns decided to look in Southern California for a place for his boys' school, he and Eileen packed onto a train and cruised down the coast. They rented a "little white cottage" in Altadena not far from Pryns' friends Gay and Mary Wilshire.

> The outstanding feature was a large rose garden, like those in [Eileen's] own dear England, which [she] delighted to cultivate.

Pryns wanted to stay in the area for a while, even if he couldn't find any land for his school. A few months later Upton Sinclair, the author, whom Pryns befriended through the Wilshires, and of whom Eileen took several casual photographs, offered the use of his extra house. Sinclair's bestselling expose on the meat packing industry in Chicago, *The Jungle*, had been published twelve years earlier. He'd been busy since then. With the profits from his book he had started the utopian Helicon Home Colony in New Jersey. However, it burned down under "suspicious" circumstances a year later. He ran and lost as a Socialist candidate for Congress. And soon before Pryns and Eileen arrived, he and his second wife, Mary Craig, moved to Monrovia, the same town where Pryns had recovered from tuberculosis, about nine miles down the road from Altadena.

Pryns and Eileen accepted his offer for a short time before finding a comfortable cottage at the Hotel Arroyo Seco, a Spanish-style building that today houses the Ninth Circuit of the U.S. Court of Appeals. The large building perches on the edge of the ravine after which the hotel was named, the *arroyo seco*, referring to the dry riverbed running north to south that divides Pasadena east from west. Covering the north end of the valley, where the arroyo seems to flow out of the foothills, is a golf course. The southern end was landscaped with walking paths through a beautiful park. The Rose Bowl football stadium would be built in the center of the ravine five years later.

The elegant Arroyo Bridge, also built in the Spanish style, spanned the ravine near their hotel. Visitors found it remarkable at the time for the hundreds of swallows that continually swooped under its arches. Concurrently, while Pryns and Eileen had a window view of the bridge from their sitting room, there was a revival of an old Spanish love song called *La Golandrina*, meaning *The Swallow*. My grandparents embraced the song as theirs. It's a waltz. I found this English translation by M. Barnett:

> Where wilt thou go my agile little swallow?
> Thy wings wilt tire if long thy flight should be.
> If wind and storm should bring thee pain and anguish
> If seeking shelter, none be found for thee?
> Ah come to me a soft warm nest I offer
> Where all the wintry season will pass thee by
> For also I wander in regions so lonely
> Mid cold and tempest and have no wings to fly.
> Ah come to fly.
> I leave the land that is to me beloved

> That gave me birth for some great distant shore
> A poor, lone wand'rer mid sharp pain and anguish
> I leave my home and can return no more.
> Thou cherished bird, thou pilgrim well beloved,
> My heart draws near thee, o're thee a watch doth keep.
> Thy tender song falls on my ears so sadly,
> Recalls my home and alas! I only weep.
> Thou cherished weep.

I wondered what it was about the song my grandparents loved. It could have been the sweet melody. Or perhaps the fact that swallows are known for traveling far, but always coming home to the same place. Did that remind Eileen of Pryns? "Wandering in regions so lonely," was my grandmother, so far from home, terribly homesick?

Pryns, meanwhile, had resumed his psychoanalysis with Mary Wilshire and asked her to help him with his "stress-filled relationship" with his wife of over a year.

> As almost everyone does, I blamed most of my marital troubles upon my partner and hoped that she would come into analysis also. Mary wisely counseled me not to put pressure on her.

How I wish I had my grandmother's point of view on this. Pryns wrote that Eileen's feeling toward him warmed up when he took her to Santa Barbara one weekend. They stayed at El Nido with his mother and visited the former Boyland property on the nearby hillside. By then it had been converted to the elegant Hotel Samarkand, advertised on a postcard in Eileen's scrapbook as "Santa Barbara's Persian Hotel." Eileen wasn't so taken by the grandeur of the hotel as she was by the swimming pool Pryns had built in the shape of a world map located in an adjacent section of the thirty acres.

Pryns wrote:

> My prestige with Eileen had been unprecedentedly raised. I reported this advancement to Mary Wilshire, and she suggested it might be a good time to bring Eileen in on our analysis sessions. The plan was superficially

Eileen Maude's photo of the Samarkand Hotel, 1921.

> successful to the extent that Eileen acceded to my request, but was a blunder inasmuch as she remained resistant and gained little from the treatment.

Eileen must have felt as if she were being treated like a rat in a science experiment, but she consented to the meeting. Mary first suggested the couple agree on a financial arrangement that allotted funds specifically for Eileen Maude's use, funds she could count on. This required a division of Pryns' net income in halves, one earmarked for his charities and social causes, and the remainder to be divided equally between them, with Eileen receiving her share as a fixed monthly amount. Any surplus was to be invested by Pryns' uncle, Frank Booth.

> We were to chip in equally for household expenses. This greatly reduced one cause of friction between us, although Eileen never was reconciled to my reserving so much of our income for 'causes,' while refusing help to needy individuals and more especially her own family who were in such desperate straits. I bitterly regret today [1962] that I did not set the old parents up in a modest cottage in Bournemouth as she wished me to do, but at the time I felt only resentment at the intrusion of the family's affairs into our life.

Up to this point in Pryns' own life, he had not pursued a career that generated income. He claimed the tax restrictions, but his socialist outlook also factored in. He refused a salary in the name of equalizing society, living only off the income generated by his estate. The impression my mother gave me was that he didn't participate in managing money himself. He left that task to his Uncle Frank, the bankers and his mother.

Once the money issues were taken care of, Mary Wilshire concentrated on the communication between her clients. Eileen finally admitted the true account of why, over a year earlier, she'd changed her mind to marry Pryns after first telling him no. He wrote:

> Instead of antagonizing me as she had dreaded that it should, it actually relieved me, by enabling me to understand our tension.

Pryns left us with no account of how the admission affected Eileen.

They continued to live in Pasadena some eleven more months into 1923, during which time they received visits from two of Eileen's sisters, Liala and Daisy. Pryns wrote that the visit from Liala, Eileen's second youngest sibling, was a joyful time for the women, but an "irritation" for him, without going into detail why. Daisy, who considered Eileen "her favorite sister,[1]" visited from her home in Argentina.

Then something happened that cut short Pryns and Eileen's stay. It started early one morning at their little house near the Arroyo Bridge before Eileen had risen from bed. Pryns answered a knock on the door to find Upton Sinclair standing on his front stoop "in a hasty mood."

Sinclair was working on a story about the dockworkers' strike in San Pedro, the port town of the Los Angeles Harbor, a forty-five minute drive south through the city of Los Angeles. Since this story is of historical significance, I will let my grandfather tell it to you himself without paraphrasing. It begins with the conversation by the front stoop:

> Upton: 'Pryns, have you been reading the newspaper accounts of how the police of San Pedro have been arresting men without any warrant and filling all the local jails with striking dockworkers in order to break the

---

1. Daisy's daughter Veronica, one my mother's lost cousins, sister to Lionel, wrote this to me. Veronica now lives in Barcelona, Spain. She remembered Prince visiting her family in Argentina several times later in life.

shipping strike?'

[Upton] went on to relate how he had had occasion, the previous day, to be in the waiting room of Mr. Hammond of the Hammond Lumber Company and had heard him ordering Chief of Police Oaks to break up the strike in this fashion.

Uppie appealed to me to be one of several 'respectable' citizens to read aloud to the strikers assembled at the harbor the Free Speech amendment to the American Constitution. Without pausing to discuss this with Eileen, I consented to do so.

First, we called on the mayor of Los Angeles, told him of our plans, and got his promise to telephone to Chief Oaks of the Harbor Police that he should protect us in our undeniable right to read aloud the American Constitution. Next we drove to San Pedro, which is the harbor of Los Angeles, called on Chief of Police Oaks, showed him our written permission from the owner of a piece of land called Freedom Hill[2], and stated that on the morrow, we would there read aloud to whomever cared to hear, the 'free speech clause' (The First Amendment) of the American Constitution.

'No, you won't?' shouted the Chief.

'And why not?' asked someone.

'Because we'll arrest you if you do!'

I asked him, 'Chief, under what law will you arrest us?'

'We'll tell you the law when we arrest you,' thundered back the Chief.

Next day some of our crowd got cold feet and did not wish to go through with our plan, but four of us stood up to be counted. The newspapers having got hold of the story, an immense crowd had gathered at the rendezvous, but were kept off the actual piece of property by a large cordon of police. These opened their ranks, however, to let us pass. At the top of the hill was another, smaller circle of police, who likewise opened ranks to let us pass, and then closed in so that nothing but policemen should hear what we had to say.

Upton then stepped forward and read aloud, 'I am reading to you without comment from the first amendment to the Constitution of the United States; 'Congress shall pass no law abridging freedom of speech or of the press or of the people rightfully to assemble for a redress of their grievances.'

'That will do!' ordered Chief Oaks, and a big policeman collared Upton

2. Most other accounts call it Liberty Hill.

and marched him down the hill.

I think it was a young English poet who then stepped forward and read, similarly, 'I am reading without comment from the first amendment to the United States Constitution: Congress shall pass no law abridging ...'

'That will do!' commanded the Chief, and he [the poet], too, was collared and taken on down the hill.

I was the third to get up and read, 'I am reading without comment from the first amendment ...'

'That's enough!' and I was led by the collar down the hill.

Fourthly, Upton's brother-in-law, Hunter Kimbrough, likewise spoke up, 'I am reading ...' whereupon at the stereotyped order the heavy hand fell upon him likewise.

The next move on Oak's part was to load us all four into the 'black Maria' and tear through the city. We were soon aware, however, that the van was doubling on its tracks and taking a more circuitous route to parts unknown. Obviously, they were trying to put any possible pursuers off the scent. Why? It must be that they wished to hide us overnight from our families and lawyers. This surmise was confirmed on our arrival at a little one-cell country jail which had been cleared of all other prisoners for our accommodation. When we asked to be allowed to phone our families and lawyers, our request was laughed at. We guessed that the plot was to rush us into and through the court, so soon as it opened next morning, before anyone could put the bail up and then to subject us to third degree methods.

Upton was elated that the Chief had fallen into our trap and got himself into an impossible situation. I was overwhelmed with a sense of guilt, however, at not having taken Eileen into my confidence before embarking on a venture which would bring great distress to her, who had little understanding of the abstract principles for which we were contending.

In the small hours of the morning, someone's head thrust itself through a small grated window in the upper part of our cell wall, and a voice asked, 'Are Upton Sinclair and his party in here?' You can imagine our joyous affirmative. It was a newspaper man, looking for a scoop for his paper, and you can be sure we gave it to him, in return for his promise at once to notify our families and lawyers.

So, next morning, there they all were when we were brought into the courtroom. The Chief and the District Attorney—so we heard from a friendly

> policeman—had sat up nearly all night, trying to devise a proper charge against us. They wanted to make it 'Suspicion of criminal syndicalism'—the then equivalent of today's 'Communism'—but decided that the charge for reading the American Constitution could never be made to stick. So all they could think of was 'obstructing traffic.' We were remanded on bail. The whole city was now laughing at the administration. The charges were quietly dropped.

Most of the dockworkers were released the following day. A few months later—two years into Prohibition—the police forced Chief Oaks to resign when they caught him, a half naked woman and a bottle of whiskey in the back seat of his car.

Just eight years ago, in May of 2003, staff writer Cecilia Rasmussen of the *Los Angeles Times* wrote about this event in her column, accompanied by the photo and caption below.

"Sinclair, brother-in-law Hunter Kimbrough, Pryns Hopkins and Hugh Hardyman, from left, were jailed on 'suspicion of criminal syndicalism' after speaking at a 1923 rally in San Pedro."

Rasmussen explained,

> The country was already in a nervous state, afraid of bomb-flinging anarchists. *The Times* had been bombed in 1910, killing 20. J.P. Morgan's Wall Street bank was bombed in 1920: 33 died. A flurry of mail bombs in the late teens and early '20s arrived at such places as the homes of John D. Rockefeller and Oliver Wendell Holmes. The government raided suspected Communist Party offices and eventually deported 556 people. Strikes were usually denounced as communist inspired. When Los Angeles dockworkers

struck in April 1923 for better wages and benefits, the LAPD arrested them—with help from the Ku Klux Klan.[3]

A nine-foot bronze and stone pillar marks the site of the protest. Sinclair wrote a four-act play based partially on the event, titled *Singing Jailbirds* that has since been made into a musical.

Pryns summarized:

> What had been accomplished was to alert the citizens of Los Angeles to the need of 'eternal vigilance' if democratic institutions are to be preserved. Within a short period, the town changed over from being one of the least free to, for at least some years, one of the freest cities in America. A branch of the American Civil Liberties Union was established here and has developed great strength.

My grandfather humbly omitted that it was his seed money that helped Upton Sinclair, Roger Baldwin and others found California's chapter of the American Civil Liberties Union shortly after.

Events may have calmed things for the citizens of Los Angeles, but hurricane warnings were up in the household of Pryns and Eileen Hopkins.

> Unfortunately from a personal angle it also branded me as a 'radical' or what today would be called a 'leftist' or a 'red.' No one, of course, knows just what a 'red' is except that he is someone whom 'the best people' do not invite to their house to play bridge.
>
> Me, the guilty party, this troubled very little—but the social consequences were so disagreeable for Eileen that I granted her earnest plea that we return to the more liberal air of Western Europe.

Upton Sinclair would carry similar burdens, but he ultimately ended up visiting the White House and nearly won the California Governor's mansion.

---

3. Rasmussen, Cecelia. "Muckraker's Own Life as Compelling as His Writings," *Los Angeles Times*, Sunday, May 11, 2003.

Photo from Eileen H. Ames' collection.

Eileen Maude with Betty May – c1926.

Chapter 17

Setting up Cemetery Search Headquarters

There is an eight- or nine-hour time difference between London and San Rafael, depending on whether one country or the other has what we call *Daylight Savings*. On July 5, the agent I'd emailed in London about renting a flat in the Kensington District counted the time difference backwards and called me at 4:10 a.m. I woke up from a dead sleep in the daybed in my studio because my bed was piled high with the artwork from the walls of my living room due to my painting project the previous day. I ignored the ringing, assuming it to be a sales call. Annie, who had been asleep at the end of the daybed, put her head back down when she saw me do the same.

At 9:30 I retrieved the message, which was from a Johnny at the London Choice rental office. I wondering why he didn't use email. He had a thick Cockney-like accent, so I had to listen to his message five times to decipher his phone number and then spend money on a long distance call! By the time I reached him I was extremely annoyed.

"Why are you up so late!" he asked.

"I think you have the timing backwards. It's 9:30 in the morning here, nine hours earlier than it is at your end." I hoped for a "sorry, to wake you" but got none.

Though the London flat had been listed on the web for £75, he wanted £120, "It's an expensive time, you know. If I can help you, I'll call back." (To convert to dollars, I roughly multiplied everything by 1.75.) I hung up to wait things out after begging him to convert to emailed communications.

Only sixteen days remained before I departed. I still didn't have a passport. I hadn't heard from Philippa about whether I could stay with her at the end of my trip. If I couldn't, I had to arrange for a hotel. I hadn't heard a word from her sister Candida. And even though I'd sent a back-up letter via snailmail to Mom's school chum Rosemary, I hadn't heard from her either, so I couldn't complete plans for my southern England loop.

Fortunately, the travel angels woke up later that day and got back to work. I found my renewed passport waiting for me in my PO box and, upon returning to my computer, found an email from Rosemary:

> Dear Mary,
>
> Good to hear from you about your visit to England.
>
> I am really looking forward to seeing you again and hoping we can fix something up. Would you be able to come and stay here for a night from Tuesday 1st August till Wednesday 2nd August, coming over by bus from Chichester to Poole or Bournemouth?
>
> Hope Eileen is well.
>
> Love,
>
> Rosemary

> Dear Rosemary:
>
> How exciting to hear from you.
>
> Yes, August 1st to 2nd would be perfect. My mother's cousin would like to see me end of that week. I'll plan on going there after I see you. I'll probably be coming from London, or I may go see another cousin near

Wolverhampton where my great-grandparents lived. Not sure yet.

I'll give you a call (or write if I can) when I get to England about the best way to get to you. Maybe you could send me travel instructions from London in the meantime. Trains, buses, whatever. I'll be traveling "lite."

Mom is doing very well and following my travel plans closely.

By the end of the following day, July 6, things came together. I booked a small flat through LondonChoice.com near Oxford Circus and Marble Arch at approximately $150 a night. I hoped the amount I saved on food would make up for the ghastly nightly rate, which was way over my nonexistent budget. But I was happy I would have my own *pied á terre* waiting for me. I knew I would want some independence while searching through the London graveyards.

All that remained was to transfer cash into accounts I could access with an ATM card. Then I would be ready to leave. *Yipee, an adventure!*

On July 12, eight days before takeoff, I heard from Rosemary again:

Thank you for your last message on 5th July, I had a lovely phone call from your mother, which was just like old times.

The best way for you to get to us from London is to get a train from London's Waterloo Station to Poole, which takes about two hours. Let me know what time your train is due to arrive and I will meet you at the station.

And I heard this from the London Metropolitan Archives:

Thank you for your email of 03/07/2006. [That's July 3 on an American calendar!] Unfortunately there are no overall indexes of burials and finding a burial location can be a very difficult task. People are not always buried in the 'local' cemetery to where they were living at the time of their death. Various factors can influence the burial location such as, for example, religion (Roman Catholics and Jewish communities often have their own cemeteries), the wishes of next of kin or the existence of an ancestral plot/burial location. Having said that, the best place to start a search is usually in the 'local' cemeteries. The 'local' cemeteries for the Hampstead area are the following:

- Hampstead Cemetery, Fortune Green Road, London NW6 1DR. The burial registers are located at the Cemetery; our information is that you cannot search yourself and that you should phone on 0207-435-6142.

• Highgate Cemetery, Swains Lane, London N6 6PJ. The burial registers are located at Camden Local Studies Library, Holborn Library, 32-38 Theobald Road, London, WC1X 8PA (Tel: 020 7974 6342) Email: localstudies@camden.gov.uk. [Well, we already knew about that, didn't we?]

• St Pancras Cemetery, High Road, East Finchley, London N2 9AG. The burial registers are located at the Cemetery: 0208-883-1231.

We are sorry that we are unable to be of more assistance to you on this occasion.

I didn't receive the answer I wanted, but at least I'd narrowed down my list of starting points. It would be ironic to find Eileen Maude buried in Highgate. My letter to them still waited for an international return coupon and the sterling, but since I was about to leave, I would take it with me. Now that I had an email address for Highgate (the *San Francisco Chronicle* article hadn't included one), I could write and the letter might not be necessary.

Dear Sir/Madame:

I am writing from San Rafael, California, and I'm looking for the grave of my grandmother.

I obtained this email address from the London Metropolitan Archives. Since my grandmother's normal address was in Hampstead, they said it is possible she might have been buried in Highgate Cemetery.

I learned about your cemetery from an article in my local *San Francisco Chronicle* newspaper, however I'm having difficulty obtaining an international coupon to send you a self-addressed envelope and the sterling.

Is there a list you can check for me? [I gave them the standard death statistics.]

I am coming to London next week to find the grave. I hope to whittle down the possible cemeteries where it might be. If you cannot check this list without the fee, would you please tell me where to go when I get to London to see if my grandmother is on the list of people buried in Highgate. Though I like to walk, I hear it is a very large cemetery.

Arg! It shouldn't have surprised me to receive an automated response email about five minutes after sending the one above.

> Thank you for contacting the Camden Local Studies and Archives Centre. We answer letter, fax and email enquiries in the order in which they are received regardless of format. We will normally reply to email enquiries by email. We aim to answer all enquiries within 10 working days.
> London Borough of Camden
> Culture and Environment Directorate

By the way, the article I'd read in the *San Francisco Chronicle* about Highgate Cemetery reported that it was fully occupied, as are most cemeteries in London, I would learn. That meant that if I did find Eileen Maude there, my mother couldn't join her when she "moved on to the next stage," as Mom termed it. Fortunately, it didn't matter to my mother. She wanted to be, and has been, buried in the Santa Barbara Cemetery next to her father and grandparents. The Hopkins plot is some of the best real estate in Southern California. It's on a bluff overlooking the Pacific Ocean with a direct view of the Channel Islands of Anacapa and Santa Cruz. My great-grandmother purchased it for the family in 1913. She, Charles, Grandpa and Mom can enjoy it for eternity. Back in 2006, I hoped to find Eileen Maude buried in as nice a place as my grandfather and his parents.

In spite of their threat not to write me for ten days, a clerk at the Archives Centre that handled Highgate Cemetery graciously responded after two, six days before my departure date.

> I regret no success. I checked the Hampstead and Highgate Express in case they mentioned a death and where a burial might be taking place but no success. No real list of deaths, only a few obituaries. No reference in the index to Highgate Cemetery burials. I also looked at the list of tombstone memorials in Hampstead Parish Church in Church Row but no memorial was recorded, but obviously a burial might have taken place without a memorial being erected or having survived.

I would suggest that you try burials in the Hampstead Cemetery in Fortune Green Road which was the municipal cemetery for the area. The registers are accessible via the Islington and Camden Cemetery Services email www.islingtoncamdencemeteries@islington.gov.uk and as they look after a number of cemeteries, do make sure to mention that it is Hampstead Cemetery that they need to search.

I wrote to Fortune Green and made the standard request.

Five days before take-off I heard from Philippa. I had begun to worry she'd written me off as a crazy relation.

Sorry not to have replied earlier—it must be very difficult trying to organize things your end. Early August is not the best for me—I am still working up until 4th. Is there any chance you could come the following week? I hope this works out as plan B. Let me know. I'll speak to Candy today and see if you have contacted her recently.

P x

I assumed the "X" meant a kiss, since it was not her initial—*another English thing!* I responded that I would stay with her at the very end of my trip.

Forming the impression that folks in England were not as glued to their email programs as Americans, I received this message from Philippa's sister, Candy, two days later.

Hi Mary,

Lovely to hear from you. Yes, would love to see you, please come and stay if you can fit us in. Not sure how much help I can be in relly [relative] quest, but would love to see you and introduce you to family.

Have you been in touch with Jason Turner and his dad Lionel? Lionel must be your mum's first cousin. Lionel talks often about 17, Tettenhall Road in Wolverhampton, where the BT's [Bissell-Thomases] lived, and has photos. Lionel lives with Jason and family in Cambridge.

Hope that helps, so glad to hear from you, sorry I've not replied, haven't checked email for ages. Looking forward to hearing from you

Candy x

Hey Candy:

Good to hear from you, too.

I'll be heading to Chichester to see your aunt Camilla on Aug. 2 to 3 and she suggested driving me back to London via seeing [your cousin] Cynthia and you. Will you be around during that part of August?

Also, I'll be staying in a flat in London July 24 to Aug 1. How far from town are you? Is it a day trip? I have no idea about geography at this end.

Re: Jason Turner. Do you have a phone number? Or better, an email address? I'll be going up to Cambridge on Sunday, July 31.

Love,

Mary

I had two days left before I was on my way. I'd requested the mail and newspaper stopped. I'd switched money to accessible checking accounts. I had physical possession of a passport, an emailed receipt for my ticket and the promise of a stepcousin to pick me up at the airport. Annie had reservations at doggie summer camp. *What else did I need?* My plane didn't leave until the civilized hour of 1:12 p.m. I planned to wake at a normal time on Thursday morning and walk to the bus terminal to catch the Marin Airporter. Walking to the bus station, only a half-mile or less from my house, would save $8.00—quite manageable as long as I kept my suitcase light.

Photo from last page of Eileen's scrapbook, unidentified.

Chapter 18

Detour to Mexico

On the way back to England, my grandfather convinced my grandmother to take a side trip. He stated in his book that they caught a steamer from Los Angeles to Vera Cruz, Mexico, and then traveled inland by train to Guadalajara. However, that would have meant they journeyed all the way south to the bottom of Mexico, through the Panama Canal—completed nine years earlier—and then north again to Vera Cruz, which is on Mexico's *east* coast. Most likely they debarked in Las Veras, on the west coast, and continued inland eastward from there to Guadalajara, which would have been a considerably shorter route.

Either way, they stayed in Guadalajara for a few nights in a Spanish colonial hotel built around a courtyard "filled with tropical plants, a large tree and a splashing fountain." They continued on to Mexico City, where a "radical" American friend of Pryns introduced them to President Alvarez Obregon and his future successor, Plutarco Ellias

Calles. Obregon and Calles had recently led the country in a successful revolt. Pryns described the men:

> Both I recall as hearty, imposing, somewhat swarthy men. They were great heroes to the peasantry to whom they were parceling out some of the vast haciendas and embroiled in a struggle with the church which resisted their innovations. [Obregon's] great enemies now were the American oil interests, William Randolph Hearst (the newspaper magnate) and others who had received fat concessions under Diaz, the great landlord and their [American] supporter.

The trip wasn't entirely centered on politics.

> The day we went out to Lake Xochimilco was one of the most romantic we spent together. Its famous 'floating islands' originated in the days of the Aztecs, when the Indian peasants started growing vegetables on rafts covered with earth on the lake. These eventually rooted themselves at the bottom [of the lake] so that the inhabitants of Mexico City and tourists alike now enjoy boating on the miles of canals among the islands that still supply the town with vegetables and flowers.
>
> We hired a boat in which we were rowed around the lake and among these gardens. We passed many barges laden with their wares and others filled with gay holiday-makers, from which happy songs and the music of guitars floated across the waters. Other boats would pass us selling flowers, or carrying a couple like ourselves with the *caballero* strumming his guitar to his *inamorata*, or a big barge containing a party of merry-makers and an orchestra.

I wonder if the guitarists played *La Golandrina*?

Leaving Mexico City, Pryns and Eileen traveled to the Yucatan peninsula and explored the ancient Mayan temples. From there they caught one last steamer to New York City. But before Pryns could return to England, he needed to tie up loose ends at *Labor Age*. He made arrangements for Eileen to sail ahead of him on the *Aquitania*.

On the day of her departure, Pryns escorted his wife to the boat. He'd stowed a large, mysteriously shaped package in the *boot* (trunk) of their taxi when Eileen wasn't looking. When they reached the dock, the taxi driver pulled out the strange package along with Eileen's suitcases. Eileen looked at Pryns inquisitively, but he smiled and said nothing. He asked the porters to take her luggage to her stateroom, insisting on carrying the package aboard himself. Once they found Eileen's cabin and enclosed themselves privately inside, he allowed her to open her parting gift, a gramophone. He'd also bought a recording of *La Golandrina.*

> We made the mistake of putting on the record ... and both of us broke down and cried and realized that, despite all our differences, we deeply loved each other.

Beedon Hill House – near Newbury, Berkshire, 2006.

Chapter 19

Off to Meet the Rellies

My grandmother-search project would eventually encompass three trips to England and two trips to Scotland. Back in 2006, when I started my journey, I didn't know what a treat I had in store for me. I would visit three of my mother's first-cousins, eight of my second-cousins, fifteen of my second-cousins-once-removed and five stepcousins. I'd met some before, and others became new friends.

I set no alarm on the day of my departure because my plane wasn't scheduled to leave until early in the afternoon. That gave me plenty of time to do my yoga exercises and enjoy two cups of my favorite mixture: tea with soy milk and honey. I copied all the photos in my iPhoto library that might be of possible interest to my mother's relatives onto a CD and made sure it worked on my laptop.

I should have disciplined myself while packing. Marin was suffering a heat wave. I would soon learn the *whole world* was suffering a heat wave. I didn't leave enough time to call a taxi, so I had to drag my overweight bag—fifty-six pounds when I checked it at the airport—to the bus. Streaming sweat, I plopped into my seat in the air-conditioned bus and was on my way.

My first panicky situation happened upon my arrival at the International Terminal of the San Francisco Airport. I got out of the bus with the driver and watched him open the baggage compartment under the bus. There was only one bag in it, a black one. My bag was sage green. Another passenger claimed the black bag. The driver looked apologetically at me and said, "I think I took your bag off at the United domestic terminal. Get back on the bus and we'll go get it."

I imagined my bag standing like a lone soldier on the curb at the other terminal. I also imagined hearing the announcements repeated regularly at every airport, "Do not leave your bags unattended." We both worried the bag would be abducted by a security guard and whisked to a place harder to reach than the curb.

When we drove up to the United domestic terminal, there was my sage green bag just as I imagined it, standing upright alone by the curb as if it were waiting for a taxi, without another person or bag within fifteen feet.

The driver stopped in front of my suitcase and opened the bus door. I almost expected the bag to hop up the steps and onto the bus on its own. When the driver descended the steps to pick up the bag, a Sky Cap yelled at him from his counter, "We knew you'd be back."

Eventually, I reached the waiting room of Gate 99 and settled in a lounge chair. The gate was shared by the passengers for a flight to Japan in the process of boarding. A thought came to me I often have when I'm in an international terminal. *By just changing direction, I could walk onto a plane going anywhere in the world I'd like to go. That is, if I could work out the ticket.* But the only place I wanted to go on July 20, 2006, was London, England.

As I waited, I reminisced about when I was last in the UK. I went with Ex-Two in 1991. I could picture us standing in the Burberry shop in London, where he bought me an expensive red raincoat. We visited my stepcousin Paul on that trip, the professor who lived in Cambridge where I planned to go again to meet my second-cousin Jason.

My trip to England with my family in 1959 was my initial visit. I'd turned eight while we were in Italy beforehand. I recalled the boat ride from Amsterdam to England and seeing Big Ben for the first time. It was the end of six months of traveling. Six months is a sixteenth of an eight-year-old's life!

The second time was the trip I took with my school friend Leslie. We stayed a week with Aunt Audrey and Uncle David at their home called Harefield, a memorable taste of English hospitality. Larger than a country cottage, but not quite a manor home, Harefield stood down the hedgerow lane from the quaint village of Old Chelsfield, near Orpington, Kent. The town was no bigger than a corner of brick buildings—a small market on one side and a pub on the other.

Inside, Harefield was all coziness. Overstuffed sofas covered in primroses filled the living room. The kitchen smelled like roast chicken and the small red potatoes Audrey grew in her garden, the best and freshest potatoes I'd ever eaten. Few gardens had vegetable patches in California in those days. Mom referred to small kitchen gardens as "victory gardens," since they were so popular during the war effort.

Leslie and I played a game of nonbouncy tennis on Harefield's grass tennis court. Since Audrey never had a drivers license, we took a train into London for a day and she guided us to the standard tourist spots. I have photos of Leslie and me in Trafalgar Square surrounded by pigeons, some standing on our heads, some eating out of our hands.

We had flown there on one of the new nonstop flights over the North Pole and arrived on my sixteenth birthday. Audrey wanted to give me a party, but when I lay down for a nap I couldn't get up. I hadn't had to deal with jet lag in 1959, because we'd traveled to Europe by ocean liner. I could smell and see a large vase of multicolored sweet peas Audrey had left by my bed. She eventually lured me up by running a hot bath in which she dissolved a cube of lavender-scented bath salts—another first that is so commonplace to me now. When I stepped out of the tub, she handed me a towel previously warmed by the hot pipes threading through their linen closet, *a warming closet,* I think my cousin Philippa would call it.

Another novelty was walking between the hedgerows to the tiny village and carrying a reusable net bag for transporting the groceries home. Paper bags didn't exist in the Old Chelsfield market, and plastic bags were still unheard of even in America. Carolyn and some of her friends, who did drive, took us to a pub for a beer. It didn't matter to anyone that we were under twenty-one. We laughed about the differences between English and American expressions. They call *runs* in stockings *ladders*. We say *drunk driving*, they say *drink driving*. We say *sweater*, they say *jumper*. We say *bathroom*, even when there is no bathtub in it. They call the *toilet* the *loo*. They wonder if women mind being called *guys*.

By the time I was sitting in the lounge at SFO in 2006, David and Audrey had passed away and Harefield had been sold. But I was really looking forward to seeing Carolyn upon my arrival the next day.

I woke up on Thursday, July 21, about to land in jolly old England! I sighted Carolyn directly after leaving customs at Heathrow. She looked just as she had in 1993, only she sported a shorter, very becoming hair cut that made her look even more like her Aunt Fay. She was also the same height, just over five feet. After a hug, we plowed through the crowd to find the *lift* (elevator). We went up a couple floors to the parking *geeraje* (garage) and climbed into her brand-new silver *Renno* (Renault) convertible.

Carolyn put the top of the convertible down. Feeling oppressed in the hot damp air, I was glad I'd brought plenty of sleeveless outfits. It took little more than half an hour to reach her home in Wokingham, Berkshire.

I thought Carolyn's modern three-story home adorable. With daughter, Verity, spending the summer in Vancouver, B.C., and Jessie moved out of the house, I had my own bedroom. It took the two of us to lug my suitcase up the stairs, already minus the bottle of wine I'd brought for my hostess. Then we sat down for a cup of tea at her dining table, where we spread a map out and took a short survey of where we were and what we might want to visit. I wasn't going to start my grave search until I transferred to London on Monday.

By noon that first day, I still felt wide awake even though it was actually three o'clock in the morning California time. I'd noticed on previous travels that jet lag didn't hit me until the second day. Carolyn promised me a nap later anyhow. She would also be tired after three straight days of working at her physical therapy practice.

We followed Carolyn's normal day-off routine—driving to her girlfriend Lizzie's house to ride Warrior, one of the horses being boarded there. I was entranced by Lizzie's fifteenth century farmhouse—three times older than any house in California. The once-little house had been added onto many times. You could see how it was originally one room with a large hearth for cooking, and how a lean-to kitchen had been added, then two more family rooms, then the second story. During the reign of Queen Victoria, an addition of equal size to that which already existed had been added as well, giving the whole house a full-sized dining room, a large new kitchen, and a breakfast nook. Lizzie had transformed the former stable into a guesthouse and built a new stable with quarters for six horses within a stone's throw of the original one.

While Carolyn rode Warrior on the nearby bridal path, I sat in a lounge chair on the patio to read my book. Lizzie soon joined me with a tray holding two cups of tea and some *biscuits* (cookies), and I learned a bit about living in the land of horses.

The following day we drove to Newbury, about an hour west of Wokingham, to stay with Carolyn's boyfriend, Tim. Tim lived in an ultra-charming tiled-roof cottage with several knobbly brick chimneys called Beedon Hill House, straight out of a storybook, just as Lizzie's house had been.

The following morning I woke up very early because of the time difference. So I decided to stroll around the gorgeous grounds and stable. Tim enjoyed point-to-point horse racing.

On leaving the house I released the two resident dogs from their sleeping quarters, a bull terrier named Melissa and a golden lab, and wished my Annie were there to walk with us too. The dogs escorted me to the thatched-roof stable. Four of the six handsome chestnut horses came to the edge of the paddock to have their noses rubbed. I stood by the white wooden fence and gazed out over rolling green hills that reached for miles without another house in sight. I found it amazingly beautiful and felt lucky to be there.

After my walk I sat in a sunny courtyard surrounded by hanging baskets full of flowers and wrote in my journal. As I waited for Tim and Carolyn to wake up, I thought about having a cup of tea and wondered if English people ever drank it with soy milk. Tim had told us the night before he would cook us a breakfast of ham and eggs. Then Carolyn and I planned to daytrip south through Hants, which I had just learned meant Hertfordshire. *Why wasn't it spelled Herts?*

I asked Carolyn if we could add the tiny Hants village of Hursley to our itinerary. Hursley was the town my ancestor Stephen Hopkins lived in for a while back in the early 1600s. Church records show he married his first wife, Mary, there. No one knows her surname. They baptized their children Giles, Constance and Elizabeth there. And Mary, who died while Stephen was trying to reach Jamestown in 1609, was buried in Hursley. There have been many books written about Stephen's ship, the *Seaventure,* running into a hurricane on its way to Jamestown and wrecking on the island of Bermuda. All 150 passengers survived and lived nine months on the island while they built two new smaller ships that finally carried them to Jamestown. But back in England, reports spread that the *Seaventure* was lost and Mary, my nine-times-great-grandmother, died thinking she was a widow. For a while, the children thought they were orphans. Stephen learned from another ship visiting Jamestown that his wife back in England was dead, so he returned to rescue his children. He then married an Elizabeth Fisher, had a daughter with her and sailed on the *Mayflower* back to America in 1620, this time with his whole family (except the daughter Elizabeth, whose demise is unknown).

I was hoping Hursley had only one church with one graveyard so it would be easier to find Mary's grave than it was going to be to find Eileen Maude's.

Photo from Eileen Maude's scrapbook.

Eileen Maude and Pryns – London, c1923.

Chapter 20

My Grandparents Back in England

Eileen Maude enjoyed herself crossing the Atlantic on the *Aquitania* and found a number of fellow passengers "to be quite pleasant." Captain Storey "especially undertook to see that she was not neglected." Once home she kept busy visiting her family until Pryns joined her a few weeks later. Again, they had to find a suitable place to live. Since Pryns wanted to reside in London, they leased a "sunny suite" on the top floor of the old Knightsbridge Hotel. Pryns wrote,

> [The Knightsbridge Hotel] had been to Eileen, in the days when she clerked at the Midland Bank around the corner, the very symbol of gracious living, so that to reside there seemed the satisfaction of an old dream.

They settled in before Pryns faced a nagging challenge.

> I have told how much the fact that [Eileen] would be unable to bear me a child weighed upon my wife's spirits. I suggested to her that we should adopt one and she gladly fell in with this plan. We therefore visited the National Adoption Society's quarters. They had there one six-months-old, brown-haired youngster who sat up so straight and looked so handsome and intelligent that we agreed to make him our choice. The society gave us an account of his origin, which promised well, as did his intelligence tests. We therefore signed formal papers of adoption and named him Peter.

I rang Peter and asked if he knew why he'd been put up for adoption.

"Yes, yes, I do. But I didn't learn why until our father died in 1970 and your mother learned the details from his papers. My birth mother was married to a military man who was fairly high up in the British Colonial Army. They were living in India. There was a strong British colony there, you know, and this man held an important position. My birth mother had an affair and got pregnant with me." (The full name of the accomplice was on Peter's birth certificate, however we won't publish it here. The first name was also Peter.)

"My mother's husband found out about the affair. In those days that was not considered the right thing to do. I suppose it still isn't. Anyway, he told her to go back to her home in Kent, that's in southern England, to have me. If she wanted to return to India afterwards, she had to give me up. That's what she did."

My grandfather seems to digress from the facts again in the next part of the story. He wrote that he and Eileen signed formal papers to adopt Peter then and there. Yet I found this news article published in the *San Francisco Chronicle* that had been published August 10, 1938:

> SAN FRANCISCO: He Crosses Sea to Adopt Boy – For years known as a millionaire radical, Prynce[1] C. Hopkins, now a lecturer in psychology at the University of London, appeared in Superior Court yesterday with his foster son and adopted the lad. The youth, 15, is a native of England and has

1. This was after he married Fay and started spelling his name *Prynce*.

> been in the care of Hopkins since he was six months old, Presiding Judge Ward was told. Due to technicalities in the English law, it was necessary for both [Prynce and Peter] to make the trip to San Francisco for the adoption. Hopkins retains residence in California. [Prynce and the young man] plan to start the return trip today.

Not only was the article published fifteen years after the day Pryns claimed to have adopted Peter with Eileen, but five years after Eileen's death and his marriage to Fay. When I discovered the article among the microfiche files at the San Francisco Public Library, I asked Mom if she knew about it.

"Yes, that was a horrible time for Peter and me. I remember when my father and Peter were getting ready to leave England for America for the adoption. It was after our mother died. We were living at Berri Court in Sussex with our stepfather, Vernon. My father came to the house, sat us down in a room and told us Peter was adopted. Until then we had had no idea."

I asked Peter what he remembered.

"I don't recall anything about the adoption. What I do remember is visiting the large house at 1900 Garden Street in Santa Barbara [El Nido]. I was a teenager at the time. So, that was probably the visit."

After reading the article, I wondered why my grandfather went to all that trouble to have Peter adopted in America if he didn't plan on taking the young man with him if war broke out? Suspecting my mother may have exaggerated the story about Peter being abandoned in England, I questioned Peter again. "Do you think your father left you behind because Fay didn't want you around?"

"No. I was of age for the service. I was a British citizen. I couldn't go to America."

Disregarding the particulars, little Peter created a family out of Pryns and Eileen. They hired a professionally trained nanny, a nurse who had graduated from one of England's well-regarded nanny schools. Then, within weeks, the family of three and attendants set off again, this time for the French Riviera. With winter approaching, the native Californian once again wanted to spend it in a warm place. They drove, or probably were driven by a chauffeur, which meant crossing the channel on a car ferry and a 525-mile drive across France to the southern coast.

By Christmas they'd engaged a charming red *villa* in Cannes on Rue Pasteur, appropriately named *Villa Cochinella*, the Italian name for ladybug. In those days one could see directly from the villa to the beach. They also rented a garage for their car a few doors up the road. In a lovely garden behind the villa, Pryns set up a table to "hammer" on his "typewriter for a few hours daily," just as he did on the card table my mother set up for him in the garden of our home when he visited when I was a young girl. From the little balcony over their front door they had a "perfect survey" of the Carlton Hotel tennis courts, where the world's tennis champion Suzanne Lenglen often practiced and played. Pryns wrote:

> She was booed for her lack of sportsmanship; she was ugly of face; but in action on the courts she represented true poetry of motion.

Their days fell into a new routine. During the mornings, Pryns worked at his writing table in the garden. On most afternoons he played tennis at a nearby tennis club. He claimed that Eileen regretted greatly she couldn't play with him, due to her health, but possibly she preferred playing with baby Peter anyway. On other afternoons all three relaxed by the seashore.

Winter and spring marked the fashionable season for Cannes in those days. With Nanny in charge of Peter, Pryns and Eileen could spend their evenings in a number of ways. The casinos provided plenty of amusement and the abundance of restaurants boasted a delicious variety of French cuisine.

> Often have I looked back to that time and longed to return again to that care-free little villa, amid circumstance that seemed so ideal a frame for happiness. Yet the supposed power of outer things to bring joy is an illusion, and to laugh or enjoy life were foreign to me, and my over-seriousness worked upon Eileen.

One night he came out of his overseriousness:

> Some street singers strolled down our way, lending voice and guitar to a catchy Italian love-song. I was seized by the spirit of the thing, ran after them, brought them back to sing under our window, and going into the house, surprised and delighted my little wife with a new romantic ardor.

A few months later a five-foot-tall female shattered Pryns' paradise, his mother-in-law Victoria Thomas. Pryns wrote he thought Eileen had invited her to relieve her loneliness. *Why wouldn't any woman want her mother to visit her? And why wouldn't any grandmother want to visit her daughter and grandson on the French Riviera?* Pryns wrote:

> Mother Thomas was quite different in type from her daughter—a stout, obstreperously energetic old lady.

Pryns jealously watched his wife share her attentions with someone more sympathetic, yet he relented in that his mother-in-law helped with little Peter. This gave Eileen Maude more time to spend with her husband.

> I found [Mother Thomas] a bit overwhelming but she always was most agreeable and considerate.

Pryns didn't stick around to endure Victoria's company for long. When he learned a group of sociologists and geographers was planning a tour through Austria and Hungry, he signed up to join them for a few months.

Cannes' fashionable season ended in May and so did the lease on the Villa Cochinella. No sooner had Pryns returned from his excursion than the Hopkins-Thomas family packed their belongings and began their return drive to England. Not surprisingly, they chose a circuitous route. Pryns earnestly wanted Eileen to see Munich, even though she displayed a hatred for Germans since they'd killed her fiancé. Because Mother Thomas was no longer mentioned in this account, I assume Pryns escorted her to a train so she could return to England on her own.

As Pryns hoped, seeing Germany for herself dispelled some of Eileen's prejudices. One night she befriended a young German who'd been crippled during the war. She told Pryns afterward that she had "finally come to realize the Germans were as much victims of their conditions as the English had been."

Another experience gave them an ominous peek into Germany's future. After dinner one evening in Munich, they sojourned to the Hofbrau Haus beer hall and sat at one of its large community tables. The friendly Germans sitting near them joined their conversation—or perhaps Pryns joined theirs. He spoke German quite well. The combined group enjoyed themselves in a friendly manner. At one point the young men even toasted Pryns' bride. As everyone laughed heartily, Pryns felt he was being watched. He glanced across the room at another table in a far off corner and observed the atmosphere there to be palpably hostile and angry—completely opposite from that of his own.

A little man at the center of the group sporting a "tooth-brush-mustache" glowered at Pryns and spoke something to his associates. Pryns had difficulty hearing what the man said over the din of the beer hall. The only words he could make out were, "diese verdampte Amerikaner," which meant, "those damned Americans." Pryns noticed Eileen's unease after following her husband's gaze, so he escorted her out of the beer hall and back to their inn. Some time later they heard the same "paranoiac accented" voice on a radio broadcast and learned the man, who would have been four years younger than my grandfather, was named Adolph Hitler. By that time, Hitler was already chairman of the National Socialist German Workers Party (NSDAP) and famous for his speaking abilities and mesmeric stare.

Pryns complained that the return trip to England was filled with "bouts of disharmony" between husband and wife. As soon as the couple settled back into their life in Knightsbridge, he began looking for a psychoanalyst. He claimed in his autobiography he wanted to learn how to better handle his personal affairs. In truth, he was fascinated by psychoanalysis, wanted to know more about the process and get to know the people involved.

By 1924, Dr. Ernest Jones was the most powerful man in the British Society and well known for publishing the *International Journal of*

Psycho-analysis[2]. He was so strong-willed and tenacious that associates nicknamed him *Napoleon* behind his back[3]. To be admitted to the British Society a person had to be fully endorsed by him[4].

Freud had also recommended Jones to Pryns back in Vienna. Six years older than my grandfather, Ernest Jones would become an important figure in my mother's family. Pryns wrote that he "played a greater part in my life than any other except my own father." Eileen Maude would choose Jones to be her children's guardian when she wrote her will in 1933.

He was born in Wales to a father who'd worked his way up to chief accountant in the steel mills of the industrial village of Gowerton. Jones excelled as a medical student at University College Hospital in London and, early on, became interested in psychology. Shocked by the treatment of the mentally ill in institutions, he studied hypnotherapy for a while. He first learned of Freud in 1903, impressed by this doctor who "listened to every word a patient said." Jones studied German so he could read Freud's works in the original[5].

Carl Jung wrote to Freud about Jones in November 1907:

> Dr. Jones of London, an extremely gifted and active young man, was with me for the last five days chiefly to talk with me about your researches. Because of his 'splendid isolation' in London he has not yet penetrated very deeply into your problems but is convinced of the theoretical necessity of your views. He will be a staunch supporter of our cause, for besides his intellectual gifts, he is full of enthusiasm.[6]

Freud wrote back,

> I believe that once the English have become acquainted with our ideas they

---

2. Information about Ernest Jones taken from Phillis Grosskurth's *Melanie Klein*, pp 154-156.

3. Grosskurth, *Melanie Klein*. p 154-155.

4. Ibid, p 158.

5. Ibid, p 155.

6. Quoted by Grosskurth in *Melanie Klein* from *The Freud/Jung Letters: The Correspondence Between Sigmund Freud and C.G. Jung*, ed. William McGuire, tr. by Ralph Manheim and R.F.C. Hull, Bollingen Series XCIV. Princeton University Press, Princeton, New Jersey, 1974. p 101.

will never let them go.

In his autobiography, Pryns described his first appointment with Jones at his office at 81 Harley Street West:

> A butler first admitted me to a general waiting-room and then conducted me down the hall to Dr. Jones' private consulting room. The door was opened by a man of short stature, broad head and forehead, thin lips and pale but energetic appearance.
>
> I began by introducing myself as an American who had already had quite a bit of analysis from a Jungian analyst. Jones nearly shut the door in my face, saying, 'I know your type of American, who flits around from one psychiatrist to another so you can go back to America and boast how you have been analyzed by all the noted practitioners and know all their tricks.'

Realizing his blunder, Pryns tried desperately to talk himself out of the hole in which he'd put himself to convince Jones he was more serious than that. Jones finally accepted him as a patient, and they scheduled a regular hour for their daily—yes, daily—appointments.

In a large gloomy room nearly bare of furniture, Pryns spent many hours stretched out on a couch by a large fireplace, gazing at the ceiling and talking about his feelings, his dreams or whatever else occurred to him. Dr. Jones sat out of sight behind Pryns' head with his legs covered by a rug, though he, too, was near the fire. Pryns' autobiographic descriptions of these visits, I noted, were in much greater detail than his descriptions of my grandmother or his children.

He found the progress "exasperatingly slow."

> At first I talked principally about my current problems, particularly difficulties between me and Eileen and brought up instance after instance in which it seemed clear to me that she was in the wrong and I in the right, only to be shown from my own testimony, in most cases, that it was I who had acted the less reasonably.

As doctor and patient dug deeper in Pryns' past, they analyzed Pryns' political and religious beliefs. Pryns expressed very "negative" feelings toward the "propertied" or privileged classes, even though he was part of one. He expressed an equally negative attitude toward God. Jones suspected the bad feelings originated in the hostility, oftentimes hatred, Pryns felt toward his inattentive father and domineering mother.

> The progress of the analysis did not make me abandon many of my political and religious aims, but it made me appreciate more realistically the obstacles that must be overcome and talk more tolerantly to persons who opposed me more persuasively.

Pryns described this period to be fraught with mood swings as he shifted between feeling badly about himself and more positively. My impression was that Eileen Maude faced life more practically, and I wonder if she tired of his self-reflection. After a while, even Pryns wanted a break from it all. He was eager to get busy starting his new boys' school. Jones insisted he wait until they finished their analysis—*is analysis ever finished?*—claiming Pryns' analysis was the most important task in the world.

Apparently, Pryns was involved with the London Psycho-Analytical Society on another level besides being Jones' patient. Phyllis Grosskurth wrote that in 1924 the Society...

> ...had a benefactor in the figure of a wealthy American, Pryns Hopkins, who donated sufficient money for a clinic in Gloucester Place, to be used mainly for the benefit of needy patients and also as a training center for future analysts[7].

Jones encouraged Pryns to return to the University of London and study for a doctorate of psychology, personally placing Pryns under the direction of two distinguished and favorite colleagues: Charles Spearman (the first psychologist ever to be honored with membership in the Royal Academy) and Jack Flügel. Flügel, one year younger than Pryns, had helped Jones found the London Psycho-Analytical Society in 1913 and the British Psycho-Analytical Society in 1919. Like Jones,

---

7. Grosswurth, Phyllis. *Melanie Klein*, p 158.

Flügel and Spearman devoted a great deal of their lives developing Sigmund Freud's ideas. When Pryns met him, Flügel directed the psychological laboratory of the University of London and would do so for twenty years.[8]

"[Jack] Flügel was a delightful, vivacious man with a great sense of humor," wrote Pryns. He and his wife became welcome friends in my Pryns and Eileen's home. Eileen included several photos of Pryns with Jack in her album. In one, they were playing tennis together. Pryns wrote that Jack beat him frequently in spite of a club foot that caused him to limp. Jack's warmheartedness must have been a breath of fresh air to Eileen.

Meanwhile, Pryns didn't fully submit to a docile life. On January 18, 1925, he helped organize a nude parade that was to progress through London's Hyde Park. He didn't include this little bit of irreverence in his autobiography. However, it was published in the *San Francisco Chronicle* for the benefit of his mother's family back home. Described again as a "young American radical millionaire, who was a leading figure in New York red and pale pink circles," Pryns was the "angel" behind the Sun Ray Club, "composed of sunlight enthusiasts who advocate sun-bathing in perfect nudity for both sexes."

Some fifty to-be-naked volunteers organized this event, planning to lead the parade to the Serpentine, where they would then take a sunbath. The aim of the Sun Ray Club was "to substitute pride of the body for shame of the body."

Applicants for the club were required to submit a photograph. The article didn't specify if the subject of the photo was to be nude. If only one member of a married couple chose to march in the parade, he or she must provide a certificate of approval from his or her other half. The organizers chose Hyde Park as the venue because it was a royal park and thus police were prohibited from entering it. The theory behind that was that it would take the regular park-keepers a sufficient

---

8. Noel Sheehy and Wendy A Conroy. *A Biographical Dictionary of Psychology*, Published by Routledge, London, 1997 & 1999. The book states Flügel, Spearman and Jones were often associated. Flügel, born in Liverpool, England, in 1884, studied at both Balliol College, Oxford, and the University of Würzburg. Two years after this story, in 1927, Flügel testified in front of a Special Committee set up by the British Medical Association investigating and reporting on the subject of psychoanalysis. "The end report was seen as the magna carta of psychoanalysis."

amount of time to assemble, allowing the parade to finish before they could stop it.

But apparently the parade never took place because I have been unable to find any more references to it anywhere.

Meanwhile, my grandfather's interest in the fresh outdoors had helped his young wife. Since their marriage, he'd kept her on a regimented health program, including...

> ... going to bed always by half past ten, sleeping eight hours nightly, plus a little rest after lunch, eating simple foods, abstaining from tobacco and taking but little wine or coffee, walking and taking quiet forms of exercise.

Grandpa continued his regimen of exercise and food when I knew him. He insisted we drink one glass of freshly squeezed orange juice daily, as his younger chemist friend Linus Pauling advised. Grandpa insisted we chew each bite one hundred times. (I always thought that a bit ridiculous, and I don't think he really did it.) Breakfasts were formal affairs. Silver napkin rings identified our starched cloth napkins. I claimed my grandmother's ring, engraved with "Eileen" and the British flag. The cook that Grandpa hired when he had guests served him a soft-boiled egg in a porcelain egg cup, and Grandpa knew how to chop off the top of the egg shell with a clean blow of his spoon, making the scissor-like gadget unnecessary. Grandpa never allowed cereal boxes on the table. Instead, puffed rice, Grape Nuts and shredded wheat—nothing with extra sugar—were served in large glass pitchers.

Arthritis caused Grandpa to give up tennis before I was old enough to remember. But he still exercised every day. He swam laps in his pool no matter what the weather and walked to his men's club for lunch with straight-legged strides. He organized a family game of croquet before Thanksgiving and Christmas dinners that we played on a side lawn he'd built especially for such games. I never heard him complain about health once. I never saw him take any medicine.

Just a few months after Peter's first birthday, Eileen's doctor finally "proclaimed" her strong enough to bear a child, though she would have to deliver it via the caesarian procedure.

> The effect of this news upon her was electrical, and one heard more frequently again her laughter, which was always like a chime of bells.

By the end of February 1925, Eileen was pregnant with my mother. Pryns wrote that he and Eileen entered upon a period of greater harmony than they had yet known together.

They rented rooms in a large country hotel in Mill Hill, about ten miles northwest London's sooty center;. Eileen made many friends among the guests and took long walks in the country air and sunshine. Pryns must have stayed in town during the days he attended university, worked at the laboratory, or visited Dr. Jones. During the last few weeks of the pregnancy, Eileen's sister Peggy travelled the two-hour trip from her home in Bournemouth to assist her. Peggy was two years younger than Eileen, but already the mother of two small daughters, Pat and June, who had probably been left in the care of their grandmother Victoria, or perhaps one of Eileen and Peggy's three younger sisters.

The day of Eileen's appointment for the caesarian finally arrived, November 10. With Pryns and Peggy in attendance, the chauffeur drove her to the nursing home[9] at 40 Belsize Grove near Harrow Weald, about the same distance from London as Mill Hill, but four miles farther west. Nurses escorted Eileen into the surgical suite, and Pryns watched her get settled and take the anesthetic before he and Peggy went outside to wait. They paced back and forth from one end of the hospital grounds to the other. The fact that Pryns' own father had lost two wives in childbirth must have been on his mind.

> So much depended on this birth! When the announcement came that all had gone well and that a little girl had been born, Peggy says it was the first time she had ever seen me show any kind of emotion.

My mother, born at 10:15 in the morning, weighed in at six pounds, six ounces. Though her parents christened her Eileen Mary Hopkins,

---

9. The British term *nursing home* means clinic or hospital, not a home for the elderly as we use it.

Grandma May insisted she be called Betty May—"simply because she liked it," Mom claimed. My mother begrudgingly kept that nickname until 1965, when she divorced my father and announced she hated her initials "BM" and would henceforth be called Eileen.

Peter was very surprised when my mother changed her name. "I didn't even know your mother was ever named Eileen. I thought Betty May was the name on her birth certificate. Even though Betty May was a strange name, it was *her* name."

A month after Betty May's birth, Eileen Maude wrote this poem in her daughter's blue satin-covered baby book.

December 1925
Month Old Impressions
Who is it holds me nice & tight
When little pains I have to fight
My mummie
Who is it makes my body warm
When others wrap and twist & fawn
My mummie
Who is it puts my pillow right
When others seem to lack all sight
My mummie
Who is it worries frets and fears
If I should sneeze or shed some tears
My mummie
Whose happy smile upon me shows
When drowsily my eye lids close
My mummie.
—*Eileen Hopkins*

The baby book had been a present from Grandmother May along with a christening robe. She'd signed the card that came with it "Grandma H." The book was inscribed with this poem:

This little book for baby years
To follow up their growing
To let them know in future years
The seed that they've been sowing.

Peter was two and a half. After a week of rest, Eileen and Betty May were ready for visitors, and Pryns escorted Peter in to see them. Peter had seemed pleased when his parents told him he would soon have a little brother or sister.

> He rushed into her room joyously, then stood stock still in the middle of the floor. The sight of the little mite of humanity cuddled in [his mother's] arms froze him. Returning to the hospital corridor, he shouted, 'If Mummie wants to see me, she can come out here!'

A similar scenario occurred when my own son met his baby sister. Jonathan was a couple months short of two at the time of Amy's birth. Also excited about having a baby sibling to play with, he waited at our house with my mother. My husband and I drove into the driveway from the hospital with tiny Amy in the back of our Volvo station wagon. I got out of the car and greeted Jonathan with a big hug. Then, taking his hand, I walked him around to the other side of the car. We opened the door to see dreamy-eyed Amy snuggled in her car seat. Jonathan watched as I took her out and cradled her in my arms. I kneeled down at Jonathan's level, and he looked into Amy's face. At first he smiled. Then after a few seconds of wonder, he looked back up at me and calmly declared, "OK, you can take her back now."

Two godmothers and one godfather blessed little Betty May at the Christening ceremony five days before Christmas at St. Andrews Church, Totteridge, on the north side of Greater London. It was very near Mill Hill, where they'd been staying. One godmother, Dr. Ethel

Vaughan-Sawyer, was a "physician for diseases for women,[10]" as well as a fellow member of the British Psycho-Analytical Society with Dr. Jones. According to Brenda Maddox, in her recent book *Freud's Wizard: Ernest Jones and the Transformation of Psychoanalysis*:

> Dr Vaughan-Sawyer[11] was a feminist, a war widow, a surgeon who had been working at the Royal Free Hospital since 1904, and a regular speaker at Fabian Society women's groups. Her progressive views, as presented in a Fabian pamphlet, included the belief that 'artificial' (that is, bottle) feeding was just as good as breastfeeding after the first two or three months.[12, 13]

The second godmother was a beautiful Italian contessa, Carla Oddone di Feletto. Vernon Armitage served as Betty May's godfather. Like Carla, he had been friends of Eileen Maude since before she married Pryns. Their names appear often among Eileen and Pryns' social activities.

Young Peter struggled with the arrival of his sister for some time. His parents insisted to the nannies that neither child be shown favoritism, but they had a great deal of trouble enforcing the rule. The nannies preferred Betty May, who was consistently agreeable, to her brother, who was developing more and more mischievous methods for attracting attention away from the baby. If he was anything like my son, he did things like hit his sister, act finicky at meal time, or shove all his books and toys off the shelf onto a massive pile on the floor.

Pryns wrote, "We would discharge the nurse and engage a new one whom we admonished to be on her guard, but the same thing would soon happen again."

---

10. *The Lancet, A Journal of British and Foreign Medicine, Surgery, Obstetrics, Physiology, Chemistry, Pharmacology, Public Health and News*. Vol. II, Thomas Wakley, Editor, Published by the registered Proprietors at the Offices of the "The Lancet", London, 1908.

11. Her husband was Captain George Henry Vaughan-Sawyer, 34th Sikh Pioneer (fighting in India), killed in action October 27, 1914. *The Bond of Sacrifice; A Biographical Record of All British Officers Who Fell in The Great War*, Vol. I Aug-Dec 1914, Military Editor Colonel L.A. Clutterbuck, Published by the Proprietors: The Anglo-African Publishing Contractors, London, 1916.

12. Maddox, Brenda. *Freud's Wizard: Ernest Jones and the Transformation of Psychoanalysis*. Da Capo Press, Cambridge, MA, 2006.

13. *The International Journal of Psycho-Analysis*, Volume 3 by Ernest Jones, Edward Glover, Sigmund Freud, John Rickman, et al. Published by the International Psycho-Analytical Press, London, Vienna, 1922. Ernest Jones is listed as president in 1921 with his office 111 Harley Street, whereas Dr. Vaughan-Sawyer's is 131 Harley Street.

This statement is reflected in my mother's baby book, in which Eileen Maude listed the succession of the children's nurses:

> Nurse Wilkie – impossible sent off at minutes request.
>
> Nurse Webster – a darling called Lady in Pink.
>
> Nurse Coward – too superior and unhappy.
>
> Nurse Dawson – went to Bournemouth, seized suddenly ill, sent off to hospital, didn't return.
>
> Nurse Baker – a quiet, capable girl, conscientious and has my complete confidence.

Pryns soon tired of this problem and left its solution to his wife. Still anxious to start another boys' school, he began looking for a location with thirty acres in one place. He needed to step outside England because, he claimed, there would be tax difficulties there and the climate was too cold. Perhaps the southern part of Switzerland might do? Or the French Riviera, of which he'd grown so fond? Only two things held him back, his wife and his psychoanalyst, but only the latter held any power over his freedom.

Then one morning Dr. Jones' secretary rang Pryns to let him know the doctor was "assailed by a severe cold" and unable to see his patients for several days. Pryns' impatience got the better of him. He hung up the phone, walked straight to the travel bureau, purchased a ticket to the continent and returned home to pack his bag.

Only then did he call Jones' secretary back to let her know he was leaving the country. Jones, furious, took the call in spite of feeling miserable, and in spite of having instructed his secretary not to let anyone through. When Jones failed to talk Pryns out of his impulsiveness, he asked if Pryns wanted to break off his analysis. Determined to follow his plan, Pryns said yes.

Eileen also tried to change Pryns' mind, pathetically pleading with him to at least wait on his departure until after the weekend, for they had already invited guests for dinner. Pryns refused. He realized later:

> It threw my relationship with my wife into a pit and proved her fears that I would desert her and our children whenever a strong impulse came over me.

He traveled directly to Montreaux, Switzerland, but found no property suitable for his school. He then traveled to Locarno, then Geneva, then Lausanne. Finally, the American consul convinced him Switzerland was overcrowded with schools and France would be a wiser choice. Pryns followed up a possibility near Biarritz, but it, too, proved unsatisfactory.

While traveling Pryns received a telegram from his mother informing him she was visiting Europe and would presently be in Nice. Happy to have a reason to return to the Riviera, he hastened to meet her. He could follow up on some property leads while he was there. He looked around the Riviera and found something he liked very much, but just as he was about to settle on it, his mother declared she needed to return to Paris quickly, and that she wanted Pryns to go with her. Pryns implied in his autobiography that this was a manipulative move.

May and Pryns booked rooms at l'Hotel de Crillon, which would often be Pryns' home away from home when he visited Paris. Taking advantage of his stay, he surveyed the area around Tours, which is about four hours outside Paris bordering the chateaux country and relatively warm. Again, he was just about to settle on a beautiful site overlooking the Seine when a friend of his mother's from Santa Barbara "happened" to show up, a man who had previously worked with Pryns' father as a real estate agent. At first May and the agent convinced Pryns it was safer working with a known person than "with those rascally foreigners." He was later disappointed with his decision.

Within a short time, the agent guided Pryns to purchase the Chateau de Bures in the Seine et Oise *Department* (county) thirty miles northwest of Paris. Then he cast aside the lawyers Pryns had come to trust and arranged the school's incorporation himself. When Pryns tried to hire the up-and-coming architect Corbusier to build the school, the agent talked him out of it in favor of another architect. Pryns knew his mother was indirectly trying to pull the strings, but he seemed to have been too afraid to contradict her. He wrote that no harm of "financially catastrophic proportions" was done, but his pride was "severely trampled."

Meanwhile, Eileen was having troubles of her own and her only communication with her husband was via periodic telegrams. During her caesarian operation, the doctors had sewn her back together with animal gut that turned out to be infected. The incision wasn't healing, causing Eileen a great deal of pain. When Pryns finally sent for her, she had to make a decision. Her gynecologist offered to reopen the wound and stitch it back up again, but Eileen no longer trusted him. She was also afraid she didn't have the strength to undergo the operation. She decided to postpone the decision for the moment, scooped up her children, their nanny and the belongings everyone would need for the next few months, and journeyed to her new manor outside Paris.

Highgate Cemetery, 2006.

Chapter 21

Scanning the Cemeteries

Carolyn and I didn't find any evidence of Stephen or Mary Hopkins in Hursley, though it was a quaint village and worth the visit. On Monday she dropped me off at the train station in Reading, and I headed to London. I stepped off a cool train into a horribly hot station. I got drippy just standing still while I studied my Underground map to determine my route. I set off as England's heat spell worsened, weaving in and out of the tube's narrow turnstiles dragging my giant overstuffed suitcase in one hand and a large bag holding my laptop in the other. By the time I reached the tiny flat I'd booked, a humongous blister bubbled and burned in the hand that had dragged the suitcase.

My cute studio, furnished with IKEA furniture, looked as neat and tidy as one of their store displays and was equally small. I dented my leg on the corner of the bed that occupied most of the room on my way to the kitchenette. A minute bathroom (a shower room, actually) opened off the kitchenette. Quite satisfied with my accommodations, I turned on the fan and lay back on the cool cotton of the fluffy duvet covering the bed, where I spread out my arms and legs as if I were making a snow angel. Inactivity for ten minutes cooled me down slightly.

Pulling myself up into a sitting position in the middle of the bed, since there was no place else to be, I opened up my iBook and tried to connect to the wireless Internet system. No luck. I fidgeted with the computer in every way I knew how, but still no luck. Since there was no land line, and I had no cell phone, I would have to return to the apartment management office four blocks away to find out what I was doing wrong. I began to perspire again just thinking it.

It was already too late in the evening for that trip, and I was hungry. The woman at the management office, where I'd collected the key to the flat earlier, had told me to go to Covent Garden to purchase groceries. Dressed as scantily as if I'd been heading to the beach, even though it was already about 8:00 p.m, I ventured back into the smothering air.

An Indian with a bow and arrow would have worked less hard that night than I did finding food. After walking twenty minutes, I reached Oxford Circus, where all the department stores clustered. A zoo of people milled about visiting Selfridges, Marks & Spencer and the other large stores. I had to shove my way through crowds to walk forward. There were so many people, in fact, that the subways temporarily closed.

The heat pushed my energy meter to zero. I just couldn't face the final ten to twenty minutes more it would take to get to Covent Garden. I aborted my plan and headed home.

I took a different route, still hoping I would run into a market. When I came to a telephone store, I walked in. I'd been wondering how I was going to communicate with my relatives, especially without an Internet connection. I made a thrilling purchase for only £29 of a handy dandy little *mobile* phone I could fill up with minute credits with my Visa card, as if I were filling a car with gas.

Continuing on, I found myself walking along Portland Place, where I remembered my grandfather had lived first on his own and then with Fay. It was very elegant, like the street on which Professor Higgins lived in *My Fair Lady*. But it also lacked markets. I made my way to an area called Marlborough, where I finally came across a Wine and Food

Store—a quick fix. The only fresh fruits or vegetables for sale were bananas, so I bought three along with a box of tea bags, a small carton of milk, a medium box of orange juice, a can of soup, a tiny jar of honey and a very small bag of sugar for the exact amount of £20. They didn't carry soy milk.

I continued walking along Marlborough, past Madame Tussauds Wax Museum, and past the now familiar Baker Street tube station, from which I'd entered London earlier. It would be my home station for the rest of my stay. I climbed up the two flights of stairs to my tiny IKEA-filled flat. Then I plugged in my new mobile phone, ate my soup, left the windows wide open and went to bed.

I woke up the next morning at 10:00 a.m, quickly stretched, showered and dressed. My sleeping schedule still needed to work its way through the time-change confusion. I sat back down in the middle of my bed with my computer and a growing pile of research papers to plan my cemetery searching strategy. Still having no Internet access, I employed my new mobile phone to call "Patricia" at the public cemeteries office for Isselton, Hampstead and Camden. As you probably remember, these cemeteries serviced the area around Hampstead, where 62 Ellsworthy Road was located. I asked Patricia to look for Eileen Maude in the death records for 1933, but she didn't find anything. After I got off the phone, I realized Eileen probably wouldn't have been buried until several weeks later, perhaps even months after her death. It could have taken a while for Vernon and my grandfather to decide what to do with her remains and then make the arrangements to transport them to London. I figured the burial didn't occur until sometime in 1934.

When I called Patricia back to ask her to search the following year, she suggested I come to her office and look at the records myself. "Four eyes are better than two," she said.

I quickly consumed a banana and two cups of tea with milk and honey—hoping I could find some soy milk soon—and headed out with Patricia's instructions on how to reach Camden cemetery. I tucked my iBook in my handbag so I could stop by the management office and hook up to the Internet. The blazing heat was worse than the day before, and heat always makes me grumpy. The four-block walk seemed like ten. I couldn't connect to the Internet there either. Worse news, the manager admitted my apartment building wasn't online yet. So I ended up at an Internet café near the Baker Street Station, adding to my grumpiness.

With the computer still in my handbag, which would get very heavy by end of day, I set off for Hampstead. At the Baker Street Station I bought a day pass, then rode to the King's Cross Station where I transferred to the Northern Line heading for East Finchley.

This train line—blissfully cooled—happened to pass by the Highgate Station. As it approached, I asked myself, *why would my grandfather go to all that trouble to ship my grandmother down to London just to put her in a public cemetery?* Even though Highgate had written to me she wasn't there, I decided they were wrong. They had probably overlooked something. Mistakes are easily made in large organizations. I jumped off the train at the Highgate Station instead of East Finchley to prove I was right.

A man at a magazine shop, whom I'd asked for directions, showed me to a map posted on the wall near his stall. Highgate Cemetery lay a half-hour walk away. I reached the small village near the cemetery at 2:00 p.m. and decided I should eat something before grave cruising. I found a small bakery and bought a steak and kidney pie—my mother used to bake a terrific steak and kidney pie—and a citrus soda called Lilt. This looked like a feast to me after what I'd been eating during the past twenty-four hours. I sat on a park bench in the shade of a tree on the town green and enjoyed my messy pie. After discarding the garbage in a litterbin, I put on some lipstick and prepared to meet my Gram.

From the town green, I walked three minutes down a narrow road with eight-foot walls on either side, which I later determined were hiding both sections of the cemetery. I finally reached the two entrances to Highgate—one to the left and one to the right. The grand stucco gate guarding the entry to the right was locked up tightly. The smaller gate to the left was open and I could see a man through the chain-link fence sitting on a chair selling entry tickets from a ticket box on a table next to him.

I entered through the gate and explained my purpose to the man. After listening attentively to my tale, he stood up and let himself into a small building nearby to retrieve a form for me to fill out. When he came back out, I immediately recognized the form in his hand. It was just like the research request letter to Highgate I'd filled out a month and a half earlier, but never sent. My copy hid in my handbag, already filled in with the facts about Eileen Maude's death. I dug it out along with a £10 note.

By then a woman associate had joined us. I explained all the circumstances a second time.

"I'll take care of that," she said, taking my form and the £10 from my hand. Without another word, she crossed the road, let herself into the large stucco gate and disappeared. I wasn't sure whether I was meant to wait for her or leave.

I figured I might as well look around the cemetery for myself. I paid the £2 tourist entry fee to the man and started my search. The cemetery, crowded with trees as well as stone markers, was a huge mess with rows upon rows of graves. Quite a few couldn't be reached because others jammed them in. Most were surrounded by ivy, and many were covered with blackberry brambles, giving the graveyard the tangled feeling of a jungle. At least two-thirds of the gravestones were unreadable until I peeled away the ivy branches. I felt like I was letting some of the gravestones breathe after years of strangulation.

I trudged up one aisle and down the next. Other people wandered about the cemetery too, but usually I walked alone on a path. I called softly to my grandmother as I progressed, "Gram, where are you? You have to help me find you." I'd done that on other ancestor grave searches, and it worked. The most amazing instance was when I went to find my great-grandmother Adelaide on my father's side, who was buried on Shelter Island in New York. My time on the island was limited to one afternoon. There were over three thousand headstones among the two non-Catholic cemeteries. I didn't have a clue where to start. So I asked Adelaide's spirit where to begin. I looked at the face of the first headstone I came across and it was hers!

Calling upon Eileen Maude for help finding *her* tombstone didn't work as well. I don't know if it was because of the weather or the dilapidated appearance of Highgate, but after twenty minutes of hunting I started to cry. I imagined Eileen Maude's grave neglected and forgotten for all those years—hidden under a snarled mass of ivy. Maybe my mother's family was like that ivy, a snarling twisting mass of complicated individuals serving themselves over the good of the family community.

At the end of each dusty path I asked her, "Which direction should I go?" I stopped at grave marker after grave marker, yanking away the shrubbery to see what was written on the stone underneath.

An hour later I'd covered only a tiny fraction of the cemetery. It would have taken days to look at every grave, weeks perhaps. Discouraged, I returned to the gate hoping the woman had returned. An older gray-haired lady had replaced the man who'd been minding the ticket box. I plopped down on the bench next to her and said, "No luck!" She didn't respond. She had no idea what I was talking about. I asked her how many people were buried at Highgate. She didn't know that either. Then I decided that the first lady who had taken my papers had abandoned me. She would write to me in America, and I would get the letter when I got home, too late to be of any use. I needed to continue on to Camden to search the public cemeteries. I asked the ticket-taker for directions. She was helpful in that department.

Then, just as I was exiting the cemetery, I looked across the road toward the big stucco gate and saw the helpful lady coming out of it. She tried to talk to me in sign language as she waited until it was safe to cross the road, but I didn't understand what she was trying to tell me. She kept pointing to the gray-haired lady sitting by the ticket box. When she finally reached my side, she walked to the ticket table and retrieved a letter sitting on it that had my name on it. She apparently left it there while I was looking at graves, but the gray-haired lady didn't receive the memo.

As the helpful lady gave me the envelope, she said, "I finished looking for your grandmother, and I'm afraid she isn't here. I've given you some numbers to call."

I tried not to show my disappointment. Actually, I tried not to burst into hysterical tears. "Well, at least we have eliminated one possibility," I said quickly. I'm not sure how realistic my smile appeared.

She gave me directions to the public cemetery via the Archway tube station, informing me it was closer than the Highgate Station from which I'd come.

The temperature still spiked and by the time I walked through Highgate Park, entirely up hill, I was parched. I found a small shop in the dear little village and bought some peach-flavored water. While gulping, I headed toward the station. Still gulping, I caught the train. I was sure it was 120° in the sun.

Standing in the subway as we whizzed toward Camden, I noticed the headline of the newspaper my seatmate read. "Record Heat Wave!" England was having the hottest weather since weather was recorded back in the 1850s! I wasn't just being a wuss.

Two more stops on the Northern Line dropped me at the East Finchley Station. There I caught bus number 263. I asked the driver to point out the stop for the cemetery, which he did. This cemetery was tidy, no vines, just grass and a few trees. *What a contrast to Highgate! Maybe Highgate wasn't as POSH as I'd thought.* I walked five minutes through the middle of the cemetery to the office, which was in a temporary trailer with no air conditioning.

Patricia immediately lugged out two huge leather volumes from somewhere behind a wall and set them down on a table for my perusal. The first ledger listed residents of the Camden cemetery in order of burial. The second ledger listed the deceased in Hampstead Cemetery alphabetically, year by year. Since I thought it more likely that Eileen Maude was buried in Hampstead than Camden—several miles further away—I started there. I looked under Armitage, Hopkins and Thomas with no luck. I then attacked the Camden volume and searched through the entries from November 18, 1933, to the end of 1934, again with no luck.

Meanwhile, during all this walking and scanning of books, I'd been trying to figure out what my grandfather's strategy had been. In his journal, he asked Eileen's spirit through the medium, "Does she like what we have done with her grave?" Grandpa never did anything in an ordinary way. He would not have allowed my grandmother to be buried in a simple grave.

With the three Hampstead options, one private and two public, eliminated, I wondered what to do next. Did I need to travel to

Wolverhampton? That would require I give up some of the paid-for days of my flat. Or should I cancel some of my plans to see friends and relatives in southern England and head north to Ayr?

As I was about to exit the trailer, a young man dressed in black leather motorcycle gear, helmet dangling by its chinstrap from one arm, popped through the screen door of the entrance. When he saw me he said with an accent that made him hard to understand, "Are you the woman from California?"

"Yes," I said, wondering if it was so obvious.

"I just emailed you," I think he said. "My email was bounced back, sayin' you was gone for three weeks. Of course! Here you are! I wrote to you with two more suggestions."

What luck! He told me about Golder's Green Crematorium in Golder's Green and St. John's Church in Hampstead. I'd forgotten about them from earlier research. He then listed some of St. John's Cemetery's prestigious residents. He spoke too quickly for me to write them down, but I didn't recognize any of them, anyway. The important thing was that he was letting me know the cemetery at St. John's Church was special enough for Eileen Maude.

"If she was a member of the parish she could have been buried there," he said.

Sounded good to me. He gave me instructions on how to find it. I thanked him for his help.

There wasn't enough time left to visit St. John's that day. To get there from my flat, I needed to catch, once again, the Northern Line, but take a different branch of it. I could visit 62 Ellsworthy Road at the same time. I was very excited to see my mother's former house.

On my way home from Camden via the Baker Street tube stop, I popped back into the Internet café and printed a map off Multimap for 62 Ellsworthy Road.

I reached my flat at 7:30 p.m, needing a shower to wash off the salty layer of perspiration that had gathered through the day. I'd seen a nice-looking pub across the street on my way home and decided to blow my budget again and have dinner there. I hadn't had any more luck finding a market, and I was worried that if I didn't get some fresh vegetables soon, I would blow up and die from constipation.

Dinner was delicious! Even though I had a steak and kidney pie for lunch, I ordered a ground beef and onion pie for dinner. It was covered with the most delicious crust and came with a mound of creamy *mash* (mashed potatoes), covered in light, wine-flavored gravy. An even taller mound of plump fresh peas accompanied the mash. I couldn't remember the last time I'd had such fresh peas, as yummy as Aunt Audrey's fresh red potatoes.

I returned to my flat to find it warmer inside than outside. I set the fan to whirring full blast and opened the windows as wide as they could go, allowing sirens and rushing traffic noises in from the street. There were no screens, but I didn't see any gnats, moths or mosquitoes hovering, as I would have at home. I read for a while, and then put my head on the pillow hoping the second beer I had drunk at the pub would knock me out so I could get some sleep.

Photo from Eileen H. Ames' collection.

Eileen Maude, Betty May and Peter –
Chateau de Bures, 1926.

Chapter 22

Doing the Best We Can

The chateau Pryns purchased in Bures was built by a paymaster of Napoleon I. It stood in the hamlet of Bures-sur-Moranvilliers, on the highway running from Paris through St. Germain-en-laye to Dinard, popularly known as the *Route de Quarante Sous*.

Grandpa wrote, "The charming old house faced a lovely park, some of which overlooked the valley of the Seine," and from the very top of the hill on a clear day one could see the Eiffel Tower. But in spite of how pretty it was,

> Eileen began to cry when she first beheld her new home. Once again she was far from the familiar English life and family she had always preferred, and she realized there would be few friends for her here in this isolated, squalid village. She spoke little if any French.

Ignoring her painful stomach, marital tensions and feelings about her new home—in a way her daughter (my mother) learned to do, Eileen set about helping Pryns convert the chateau into a school. She still pestered him about the lavish way he spent money, even though he used his Causes Fund.

He reported later in his autobiography:

> I was so niggardly towards her desperately needy family, this must be for her an embittering contrast.

His largest project was the design of another swimming pool. A modified version of the world map he poured in concrete for Boyland in Santa Barbara, this pool outlined the Mediterranean Sea, circling the hill at the top of the land. Later Pryns leveled the lower acreage for a sports field.

When I was young, I loved hearing my mother talk about the Chateau de Bures. She was thirteen the last time she saw it before moving to America, and I don't think she laid eyes on it again until we visited France during our 1959 trip. My whole family couldn't wait to see it. We found the manor house standing empty and boarded up, appearing shabby after the elegant chateaux we had toured along the Loire River. Plants grew in the cracks of the empty pool. My brothers—six and three years old at the time—skipped with me around the concrete continents, hopping from the Italian peninsula to Greece and from Greece to Egypt.

As we progressed through the garden, my mother pointed out a tree stump, which, upon closer inspection, had also been constructed out of concrete. She suggested my brothers and I walk to the farthest side of the stump, where a short arched opening revealed a circular staircase leading downward through the center of the stump. Following the staircase like bunnies going down a bunny hole, we came out into another weedy garden, about ten feet lower than the main terrace.

I was impressed my grandparents once owned a real chateau in spite of its rundown appearance. I found a picture of the building recently on the Internet. It has been fixed up since 1959 and looks as stately as ever.

Pryns had this memory:

> This time, the period when Eileen and I were both working together in full and hearty cooperation to organize the school, was for both of us the most harmonious period in our married life. In both of my marriages, the happy periods have tended to be those where we were busy together on something, and lack of a common task or common purpose has been one of the chief causes of breakdown. Had we been obliged to plan together how to make both ends meet and leave a little over for the education of our children and the security of our old age, as do most couples, it would have been incomparably better for us.

Together they hired a professional decorator and visited the department stores of Paris. Agreeing on "French peasant style" furniture, probably what we call "French Country" today, they ordered multiple pieces custom-made to accommodate all the bedrooms and the dining hall.

One night they learned what type of impression they were making with their neighbors. While enjoying drinks in a popular basement nightspot in Paris called L'Enfer, an entertainer began singing a comic song. Pryns translated for his wife. After a couple of verses about some Americans who came over to France, fancied a castle, and embarked on extravagant constructions in reinforced concrete, it dawned on them they had become a joke to the local French. Fortunately, the ex-patriot American colony in Paris was more accepting, and so small that it wasn't long before the Hopkinses made many American friends.

The school, originally intended to educate American boys, commenced classes with five teachers and four boys, expanding to a dozen pupils within the first year. At its peak, thirty-six students enrolled, including a few sisters of some of the boys. Betty May and Peter's cousins, Pat and June, were also among the student body because their mother Peggy was busy divorcing their father, Mr. Pope. Pryns and Eileen offered to help with the girls while she got back on her feet. By the time Betty May and Peter were the required age, their mother had died, and they were living in Sussex with Vernon.

Both Pryns and Eileen traveled frequently between their home in Knightsbridge and the chateau, with Eileen and the children staying most often in Knightsbridge. Pryns still insisted the family winter at the Villa Cochinella in Cannes.

During the school's second year, Pryns hired Eileen's best friend, Carla di Feletto, to assist as housemother. She needed room and board while she studied French literature at the Sorbonne. No sooner had she joined them in Bures than she met an Australian opera baritone named John Brownlee. Brownlee, originally an accountant, was about twenty-six in 1926. Having had no singing lessons, he'd entered a vocal contest in Ballarat, Victoria, Australia, and won first prize. He accepted a series of singing engagements after that and Dame Nellie Melba, also an Australian and one of the most famous operatic sopranos at the beginning of the twentieth century, heard him perform. She was so impressed she encouraged Brownlee to travel to Paris and study with Dinh Gilly, a French-Algerian operatic baritone and teacher. Brownlee made his debut in Covent Garden June 8, 1926, right about the time he met Carla. Maybe she attended the concert. Not only was John welcomed at the chateau by his sweetheart, but by the children, to whom he sang arias at night.

Families of the Chateau de Bures students visited on Sundays. Once Carla came on board, she began organizing delicious teas for these events, with elegant sandwiches and cakes. The men wore *plus fours* (knickers), the women the slab-sided dresses and inverted bowl-shaped topes cocked to the side in the fashion of the day, which my grandfather thought, "proved that to be beautiful is not nearly so important as to be in the fashion." As a result, the chateau became the *in* place to be on Sundays for the entire American colony in Paris.

By the fall of 1927, Pryns added an extensive gymnasium and improved the student dormitory, yet he was having trouble keeping a satisfactory headmaster. On several occasions he traveled to America in search of a new one.

Eileen still suffered from her cesarean wound. She had been warned the operation was extremely dangerous because of her heart condition. Since she didn't want to "put up with Pryns' fretting about it," she chose to have it taken care of while Pryns was away on one of his headmaster searches. She found a Dr. Granger to perform the procedure in a nursing home in Bournemouth, where her sister Peggy had been living since 1921. (Peggy's daughter, Pat, was born there.)

Bournemouth is on England's coast across the channel from France. Peter and Betty May probably stayed with their aunt and cousins while Eileen had her surgery.

Pryns returned to the chateau from America expecting to be greeted by his wife. Instead, he received a telegram from her from Bournemouth. Assuring her husband that her surgery had been skillfully performed, she told him she eagerly awaited his visit at the nursing home. She wanted him to stay a week or more and then escort her back to France. Pryns crossed the channel immediately, but kept her company for only one day. He impatiently desired to return to the business of his new headmaster. Eileen's pleading for him to stay got her nowhere.

By the time she was well enough to return to France, the new headmaster was securely in place, and Pryns wanted to resume his psychoanalysis with Dr. Jones and finish his doctorate at University College. Eileen met up with him at their Knightsbridge flat, where they would spend a relatively long period.

As part of his program, Pryns lectured at the university. Psychology was quickly becoming a popular subject. He eventually became a fellow or associate of various scientific bodies, such as the British Psycho-Analytical Society with Jones, Flügel and Spearman. He also continued with his socialistic and educational interests by joining the New Education Fellowship founded by Beatrice Ensor[1] (a theosophical educationist who supported Marie Montessori); and the Fabian Society, (a British Socialist movement started at the end of the 1800s "to advance the principles of democratic socialism via gradualist and reformist, rather than revolutionary, means.[2])" From his journals, it appears he attended five to seven luncheon and dinner lectures every week for these various groups.

About this time, Brownlee proposed marriage to Carla and they asked Pryns if the wedding could take place at the chateau. He had to say no because he couldn't take the time from his activities in London. So the couple got married in Paris instead on November 29, 1928. Eileen Maude was able to join them.

---

1. Beatrice Ensor lived from 1885–1974.

2. Wikipedia.

Photo from Eileen H. Ames' collection.

Brownlee Wedding – Paris, 1928.

Mom showed me the photograph of the wedding party. Eileen sits to the bride's right, looking radiant in a patterned silk dress. Her hair still cut in a bob, she seems a little fuller than she did in her wedding picture, but not chubby. All the women wear strands of pearls—one sports three strands. My grandmother wears a single graduated version my mother later inherited. The skirts hang slightly shorter than they did in 1921 and reveal legs covered by shiny stockings of real silk—something that became unheard of after the rationing during World War II.

Just as Pryns became relaxed with the routine, he received news from Bures that the new American headmaster was making a disaster out of the school's finances. Pryns traveled forthwith to the chateau and dismissed him. While Pryns searched for a replacement, he hopped back and forth between the school and London to manage things himself. He also temporarily employed Eileen's brother Harold to straighten out the ledgers.

This went on for several months before Pryns found a competent head. By 1929 the school moved along successfully, and Pryns concentrated on his work in London, though he continued to cross the channel every third week to keep an eye on things. He remained in Bures for several days each visit.

The year 1929 also blessed Eileen's sister Peggy, when she became engaged to Jack Abbott, the wonderful Scotsman from Ayr. They'd met in Bournemouth, where Jack, who'd graduated from Pembroke College, Cambridge, with an economics degree, managed a branch of the Saxone Shoe Company. The family story is that "Peggy invited Jack to dinner, hoping he had a dinner jacket." I didn't get that joke. Did it mean Jack was a scruffy Scot and Peggy's family wasn't sure he would be presentable? Or was it sarcastic because the Abbotts were so much more refined than the Thomas Family? The Abbotts had been cofounders of the Saxone Shoe Company Kilmarnock with the Clark family. The Clark brand is still well known for shoes today.

Peggy asked Pryns and Eileen if it would be all right to hold the wedding at the chateau. This time they were able to say yes. The entire Thomas family, possibly except Daisy, who may have been living in Argentina by then, arrived at the chateau that summer and stayed as guests in the manor home. Queen May traveled from California to attend; however, she preferred the relative quiet of the Pavilion Henry IV in St. Germain. Pryns described the scene as a "blaze of glory."

Grandpa didn't even mention in his autobiography the stock crash that hit the United States in October of that year. I asked my mother if the Hopkins family suffered financially during the Great Depression.

"Not that I could tell," she said, though she'd only been four years old at the time. "At least Singer stock didn't plunge. People always need clothing."

62 Ellsworthy Road, Primrose Hill, London, 2006.

Chapter 23

Visiting the Old Homestead

I spent a long hot July 26 tramping through more graveyards. I'd slept much better the night before, though I woke up with swollen joints. A little yoga and some cold orange juice helped. Then I took a cool shower and left my hair wet. A hundred dollars wouldn't have induced me to use a blow dryer in that weather! Still, I felt sticky and drippy all day except for a few peaceful moments in a coffee shop with working A.C.

Two of my three missions that Wednesday were to visit Mom's childhood home at 62 Ellsworthy Road and seek out the nearby St. John's Church Cemetery. My first mission was to purchase some stationery so I could write a note to my mother's first-cousin June Belden, the oldest of Aunt Peggy's two daughters. I could do that on my way to Hampstead.

Mom and June exchanged Christmas cards until Mom became

too confused to run her computer's label software any longer. Mom surprised me right before I left for England by handing me a dog-eared file card with June's contact information. I copied the street address in Kensington, but the card listed no telephone number. Kensington was not far from my flat. Had I known about June earlier, I would have written ahead.

I guessed June to be in her 90s. I didn't think it would be polite to drop in on a little old lady unannounced. So I planned to drop a note by her apartment after my Hampstead trip to introduce myself. *Maybe she will call me and invite me to visit her within the remaining few days I am in London.* Since June was one of the older cousins, I felt sure she'd remember Eileen's death and know what had happened to the grandparents she shared with my mother.

After purchasing the notepaper, I continued to the Baker Street Station and set off for Hampstead. I was to get off at Swiss Cottage, the first stop on the Northern Line, and supposedly the closest station to Ellsworthy Road. When I exited the Swiss Cottage Station, I wondered if I was in the right place. The buildings around me looked relatively new and middle to poor class. I expected ritzy. By the time I reached Ellsworthy Road—taking pictures as I walked to show my mother later—the homes became grander. Later I priced houses from the neighborhood in a real estate office window. They sold for a minimum of five million dollars. I also learned that the neighborhood was technically Primrose Hill, considered even more POSH[1] than Hampstead.

As I approached 62 Ellsworthy Road, a Rolls Royce pulled out of its garage. I was too far away to see who was in it, man or woman, and I thought it a bit late in the morning for someone to be heading off to work. *Executives in Rolls Royces probably don't have to be at work at the crack of dawn like we worker bees.* Closer to the house, I heard kitchen sounds. At first I didn't have the courage to knock on the door, so I stayed near the sidewalk and took pictures of the exterior from various angles for Mom.

The two-story house, built entirely of brick with white wooden

1. My cousin Philippa told me later that POSH stands for port out, starboard in—the best seats on an ocean liner.

window details, sported a bay window on the second floor and a steep roofline. I snapped shots of the street, facing one direction and then the opposite for full effect. As I looked down the tree-lined road, I wondered if Mom and Peter had bicycles when they lived there, and if they explored the neighborhood on them as I would have when I was young?

I tried to imagine the house before World War II. *Did Mom and Peter sleep in the bedroom with the bay window?* I pictured a nursery like in Peter Pan, complete with a window seat and flowered Liberty of London's pillows. By the time I finished my photo essay, I'd gathered enough courage to announce myself. *How can it hurt? The worst case will be that I will be sent packing. I've come all the way from California. Why not try?*

A Filipino woman in maid's uniform answered the door. Halfway through my first sentence, she held her hand up in a gesture that meant, "Just a minute," and then disappeared behind the door to my left, that I assumed from the sounds of clanking pots and china to be the kitchen. She returned a few seconds later with another Filipino woman who spoke English. After explaining who I was, the second woman said, "Just a minute. I will call the lady of the house. She will probably want to talk to you."

We were standing in a large entryway with a ceiling two floors high, still decorated in the style of the 40s and painted a pale green. To my right a stairway led upstairs, where I presumed the lady of the house to be. I expected the maid to go up, but instead she walked through another door ahead of me and returned with a portable phone that she handed to me.

I said "hello" into the phone. A very distinguished elderly woman's voice on the other end asked me who I was. For a third time, I explained.

The voice introduced herself. For this book I'll call her Florence. I was pretty sure she was speaking to me from upstairs. I pictured her propped up against mounds of satin pillows in a high four-poster bed, still in her silk nightgown, possibly with some feathers around the collar. Her unfinished breakfast tray rested at her side. Maybe she didn't have her teeth in yet or her wig on. At any rate, she didn't feel presentable.

Florence told me she'd been living in the house for forty-two years. During the war, before her time, the houses in the area had been divided up to make room for people trying to escape the center of London where most of the bombing took place. The modern structure across the street that seemed out of place among the traditional houses was built after a bomb landed on the previous dwelling. Hampstead wasn't *completely* safe. After the war the homes couldn't be sold as single-family dwellings again until the people who'd occupied them during the war sold or moved out.

Before I showed up, Florence didn't know anything about who owned the house before the war. She was curious about my mother's family. I told her how Vernon and my grandmother purchased the house in 1930 and that it was the house my mother and her brother remembered best from their childhood in London, because it was where they remembered their mother. Not that Florence knew any of those people from a hot rock; she just liked the history.

After Florence said good-bye, I asked the maid if I could take some interior photos. She said yes, so I took a couple of the entryway. But since the maid didn't invite me to proceed into the other rooms, and since I didn't want to impose, I left it at that.

I also felt self-conscious because beads of perspiration dripped down my nose and the sides of my face. Before I knew it, my shirt was all wet, making me feel more nervous and out of place. I'm normally not a sweaty person. I found myself anxious to leave even though I would have loved to photograph the bedrooms and the garden.

I made my way back to the main street and headed toward the tube station to catch a train for St. John's Church in Hampstead. I'd learned from my map that I needed to depart from a different station on the Northern Line than the one from which I'd just come. The Chalk Hill Station looked to be about a twenty-minute walk.

On my way I saw a church steeple peeking above some houses not far from Ellsworthy Road. Since this church, which I soon learned was called Saint Savior's, was obviously closer to Eileen Maude's home than St. John's, it was worth investigating. However, once I reached it, I saw no cemetery nearby.

Leave no stone unturned. I tried the front door of the church. It was locked. A placard attached to the door gave me a phone number for the rector. I rang the number and he answered. He explained that residents near his church, like others in Greater London that had been built relatively recently, prohibited the church from placing a cemetery near their homes. I wasn't sure if it was because the residents didn't like the idea of having dead people buried so close by or if they simply wanted to use the land to build more houses. Whatever, the rector suggested I visit St. John's. I told him I was already on my way.

I wiggled my way back to the main road heading to the Chalk Hill Station. The quality of the neighborhoods had declined by the time I reached my destination.

The village of Hampstead, on the other hand, impressed me from the moment I stepped out of the quaint Victorian station building. Across the road I faced a lovely shopping center much like Carmel in California, complete with a Gap, Starbucks and some other American stores. Probably Carmel's charm was copied from villages like Hampstead. Equally indicative of the changing state of London, I had to ask six different people before I found someone who knew the location of St. John's Church. I was sure that back in 1933 everyone knew where his or her parish church was, and in this case, it was only a few blocks away. I walked a half block to my left, turned right onto Church Row and saw the small gray stone edifice dead ahead of me at the end of a cul-de-sac.

St. John's squat stone squared-off belfry, that I'd heard indicated a Saxon church, had none of the elegance of Saint Savior's tall, white, pointed Norman-style steeple. The cemetery lay to my left as I walked into the churchyard, surrounded by the typical black cast-iron fence with pointed spikes along the top. I saw no office. However, a large sign at the entrance displayed a phone number. I called the number, reached an answering machine and left a detailed message with Eileen Maude's death particulars. Then I proceeded to the cemetery to look around.

The yard was miniscule compared to Highgate and in much better shape, though not as tidy as Camden. There were still many graves covered by berry brambles and ivy. In one case a large tree grew right out of the center of a grave plot. Some well-meaning relative had planted it there as a memento, not foreseeing it would grow big and tall one day and obscure the plot.

I tramped up one dirt path and down the next, peering under vines to look at names and dusting off stones without success. Half an hour later I'd finished scanning the yard. I would not let myself be discouraged. I sat on a bench for a while to brainstorm and cool off. *What to do next?*

I didn't see how I'd have time to travel all the way up to Ayr, but Wolverhampton still remained a possibility. Then my stomach began grumbling for food. Hot and dripping, I decided to keep thinking about what to do while I retraced my steps down Church Row to the village for lunch.

I would not get to eat yet! As I exited the churchyard, I saw another cemetery across the walkway to my left. *How did I miss that?* A sign identified it as part of St. John's. I had more work to do.

This yard was nearly twice the size of the first. The rows lined up in an orderly fashion, allowing for a more scientific search. But I could still only decipher about eighty percent of the headstones. I consoled myself by assuming that those graves that had lost their headstones, or were marked by stones too worn to read, were probably older than seventy years. Feeling overwhelmed, I dug out my phone and tried to reach the church office again. Still no answer.

As I plodded on, frustrated with how hard it was to read many of the markers, I mentally planned the instructions I would leave for creating my own headstone. Limestone is too soft. Brass letters tarnish and become too difficult to read. Brass plaques fall off the stones and get lost. Wood is out of the question. The best are marble or granite rock stones engraved with deep Roman letters. They remain the most legible over the longest period of time. The Romans knew that. I suppose if our culture lasts as long as theirs, we will learn, too.

I passed some small statues and remembered something else my grandfather mentioned in his journal. He'd interviewed an artist about having a sculpture made. Was I looking for a gravestone when I should have been looking for a statue, or bench, or even a stained glass window like the memorial of one of my father's relatives? *It would be so like my Grandpa to have a special sculpture created.* He'd commissioned twenty busts of ancient philosophers made out of Carrara marble to be placed around his garden.

From then on I looked for unique headstones, one with an angel or other female figure. *Wouldn't it be wonderful if there was a likeness of my grandmother?* However, since there were so few graves with statues, I worried that nice statues were stolen. St. John's cemetery wasn't protected by locked gates like Highgate was.

I tramped on, feeling like a grimy drenched mop covered with dust. Finally, I reached the end of the last path. Disappointed again, I sat on a bench near the gate to rest and cool off. My stomach gave a loud roar. I reluctantly stood up and marched off to please it.

I easily found a French café that served baguette chicken sandwiches in a well-cooled room. I asked the waiter for an iced coffee to go with my sandwich, but he told me the café didn't serve iced café! I thought of telling him that all he needed to do was add ice to a glass of regular coffee, but I didn't. I was too pooped to start an argument. I ordered a normal café au lait. That put a smile on his French-looking face.

I wasn't at all excited about getting back on a tightly packed subway, yet I wanted to go to the next lead on my list, Golder's Green Crematorium. First I had to locate it. I asked the French waiter how to dial England's Information Service on my mobile phone. The answer was the number 1-1-8-2-4-7—not as easy to remember as our 4-1-1. I was happy to learn that in England, Information gave you the option of having the phone number automatically added to your mobile phone directory for free. *Very cool!*

I had no trouble reaching someone at the crematorium. I asked the woman if she would please look up my Gram. She said it would take about an hour.

While I waited I walked around Hampstead. The shopping area is only two blocks long. As I entered another stationery store, my phone rang. A lady from St. John's reported the unsurprising news that there was no Eileen Maude Armitage in her cemetery. There was a George Armitage and there were plenty of Thomases, but none with names that matched my "rellies," as my cousin Candy would have called them.

Eventually, the crematorium called back also, with equally negative news. *Now what?* I was too hot to think straight. I broke down my reserve about visiting an American chain store and went into Starbucks in search of an iced coffee. Even at the Starbucks counter I could order no such thing. I could have an iced café Americano or an iced café latte—all expensive high-end drinks. Alas, I settled for an iced café latte. While I sat to drink it, I propped my plump, swollen ankles high up on a stool to calm down their throbbing. Both the drink and rest were very satisfying.

No longer needing to find Golder's Green, I spent the time enjoying the shops in Hampstead. Then I began my trip home via Kensington High Street to drop my note off at June Belden's.

I couldn't believe how steamy the subway was! I felt like I was stepping into a damp oven. Claustrophobia kicked in as bodies dripping like human water fountains crammed next to me. I jumped out of the car early at Earl's Court Station just to breath some fresh air, even though it was also hot. Kensington High Street was still a good half-mile walk up charming Earl's Court Road. On the way I bought a dozen peach-colored roses for June, just in case she was home and invited me in.

Confusion arose as I looked for her address. I had copied it as 213 B Kensington High Street, but I found no such number on any of the buildings. A pharmacy occupied the spot where I thought the address should have been. I walked in and showed the Indian woman working behind the counter the piece of paper with the address. She confirmed I stood at 213 Kensington High Street, but she said there was no suite, unit or apartment B.

"Are you looking for the hairdresser?" she asked.

"No, I'm looking for a little old lady."

"Let me show this paper to my manager and see if he knows anything."

She walked to the back of the pharmacy as I followed on the other side of the counter. After she showed my paper to the pharmacist, he said, "Yes, there was a lady at that address. She lived with her sister, but they both moved away a few years ago. The woman had a stroke and couldn't manage the stairs any longer. She'd been there for nearly twenty years."

Mom communicated only with June. I don't think she knew Pat lived with her. The clerk had been mistaken about there being no apartment.

"After her stroke," the pharmacist was saying, "her brother, or maybe it was her son, moved her away—probably to an elderly home."

"Do you have a forwarding address?"

"No."

"Is there a management company I can call to see if they know where June went?"

After he gave me the manager's name, I sat down in one of the chairs meant for people waiting for their prescriptions and dialed the information service number again using the convenient autodial from my mobile directory. The lady who ultimately answered at the property management company told me she didn't keep addresses longer than a year. After I clicked off the phone, I heard the pharmacist chuckle. I looked up.

"Not much help, are they!" he said smiling.

"Nope." I agreed.

"All they want is their money." We both laughed.

I asked him what else he remembered about June.

He said she was very nice, that she had a family, and that her sister remained unmarried, or at least didn't seem to have a family, and that June's stroke paralyzed her on one side.

With wilting peach roses still in hand, I returned to my flat. I didn't have a vase, so I filled a drinking glass with water and plopped the roses in that.

After a nap with my feet up against a wall, I decided to visit Liberty of London, the famous fabric store. I'd been there before on previous trips. In fact, I still had some of their fabric in a drawer at home waiting to be transformed into a dress or something.

Liberty is housed in a huge elaborate Elizabethan-style building in the middle of the retail district. Everyone knew where it was. While I wandered around the fourth floor, coveting the beautiful but too expensive fabrics, my mobile phone rang. It was Jason Turner,[2] the second-cousin who lived in Cambridge, and whom I'd learned about through Camilla's and Candy's emails. I wanted to meet him, and I wanted to meet his father, Lionel, hoping that in spite of being in the

2. Reminder: Jason was the son of Lionel Turner, who was the son of Daisy Thomas, who was a younger sister of my grandmother. That meant Jason and I were second-cousins, nothing removed.

early stages of dementia, he remembered my mother. I didn't know if Lionel was older or younger than she.

I sat on a chair by a wall in the fine woolens department while Jason and I figured out a plan for getting together the following Sunday, the day I was scheduled to meet up with my stepcousins Paul and Carolyn for lunch. Jason invited me to stay the night at his house, but warned me that it would be full of other houseguests. There was a music festival in Cambridge that weekend and family and friends were attending the various events. The safest time for me to catch Lionel was early in the morning. Lionel always walked to the local parish of the Church of England by himself. Jason suggested I walk with Lionel or attend church with him. I would need to be at the house by half past eight before Lionel departed.

That plan sounded perfect to me. I'd brought a flowery skirt just for the purpose of attending an Anglican service. I attended the Episcopal church at home, which was similar. But this plan meant I had to ask Carolyn if we could drive up much earlier than we'd planned. I considered taking the train up on my own and meeting Carolyn at Paul's in Cambridge.

Jason assured me the trip would be worth it. His father, at eighty-three, was still a font of old memories, including good times of traveling with my grandfather, whom he called *Uncle Pryns*. I confided to Jason that my cemetery prospects were running out in London. He gave me the phone number for our mutual second-cousin Candy. Maybe I should visit her near Wolverhampton after all.

I finished cruising Liberty of London and returned to my flat. Before ringing Candy, I enjoyed another yummy dinner at my nearby pub—an asparagus tart that came with more fresh peas and fluffy mash.

I reached Candy as she cooked spaghetti for her family. She said she didn't mind multitasking. As she cooked, we devised a scheme for me to *train up* to Worcester on August 6 and spend the night with her. On the following day, she and I would scout out Wolverhampton, an hour or so away. We'd search for the residence of our great-grandparents at 17 Tettenhall Road as well as for their graves and that of my Gram in the nearby cemeteries.

Candy assigned me the task of asking Lionel if he had any photos of the Tettenhall house. If I could copy them with my camera, we could use them as reference as we cruised the streets in Wolverhampton. Candy also repeated a Thomas family legend Jason had already told me. The eight brothers and sisters were to have written their names on the ceiling of the basement of 17 Tettenhall Road with the soot from a candle. Candy was curious if the names were still there. It looked as if I would be knocking on a stranger's door once again.

That left me with two more days in London: Friday and Saturday. I decided to use Friday to find a library that carried old newspapers. If I could find my grandmother's obituary, it might tell me the location of her burial.

Photo from Eileen H. Ames' collection.

Vernon Armitage and Eileen Maude –
January 21, 1932.

Chapter 24

Dr. Jones and Vernon

I've often thought many people in my family are like salmon, always trying to swim against a river. Grandpa Prince fit that description. However, I suspect Eileen Maude did not. She was more like a minnow.

What happens when a minnow and a salmon live in the same pond? A zoologist from the University of Hawaii named David Greenfield wrote this about salmon and minnows for *World Book Encyclopedia:*

> "Some fish, like salmon, can adjust to the change from salt water to freshwater better than other fish. Minnows are freshwater fish. They furnish the food that allows game fish to reach a large size and thus are often used as live bait to catch larger fish."

Pryns wrote in *Both Hands Before the Fire* that even after Peggy and Jack's joyous wedding, Eileen Maude wasn't happy.

> Eileen's one ambition always had been to have the security of a pretty little home and children, a husband who cherished and guided her, among either her family or my own and a few friends with whom to visit occasionally. Instead of this, I had for nearly ten years dragged her back and forth between Europe and America, settling nowhere. I was restless and discontented, tearing up every bond we formed, niggardly and often boorish to her family ... often sermonizing her on her shortcomings but never giving her a sense that she was really needed in my life.

Hoping Dr. Jones might help, Eileen asked him if he would "take her into analysis," even though she knew he had "a fundamental rule against treating two parts of a couple." Being very fond of both of them, the doctor made an exception. The meetings allowed Eileen to reveal hidden thoughts and deeper emotions. Pryns wrote:

> She hoped, especially, to get rid of a tendency to over-sensitivity, together with deep inferiority feelings, which had always made it impossible for her to assume her rightful place among her economic, social and cultural equals, or to speak with authority to subordinates.

It sounded to me like my grandmother simply never got used to having servants.

After many months, Eileen Maude lost hope. She'd come to the conclusion she wanted to dissolve her marriage and asked Jones to be there when she confided this decision to her husband. Pryns wrote:

> She put it not as a peremptory demand, but submitted the history of our marriage in proof that we were two people, each decent and kindly, and who might well be mated happily with someone else but who never were intended to be together.
>
> 'Let us always be friends, though realizing that we must live apart, and when in future our ships pass we will hail each other with a cheery message.'
>
> I was heartbroken, but I realized that what she said was absolutely true and that the fault was overwhelmingly my own.

According the Grandpa's autobiography, Eileen asked only for a legal separation. But in spite of her newfound strength, she was still influenced by her brother Harold, who pressured her to lose no further time and marry her longtime friend Vernon Armitage.

My mother consistently told me her mother divorced her father when she was five. That would have been in 1930, and would correspond to the dates in my grandfather's autobiography. However, Eileen and Vernon's wedding date recently came into question. When my mother died, I inherited all her jewelry, including both Eileen Maude's wedding bands. From my office, I dug out a printer's loupe magnifier to read the inscriptions on the inside rims. The elegant script inside the ornately carved platinum and gold wedding band from my grandfather to my grandmother confirmed their wedding date of January 12, 1921. However, roughly scratched into the very plain platinum band from Vernon is the simple record "V.H.A. E.M. 1932." That's only one year before Eileen's death in 1933. I shuffled through my mother's papers and found a copy of the marriage license confirming the date to be January 21, 1932.

It probably took a couple of years for my grandparents to complete their divorce. Eileen didn't switch husbands within a matter of months as my grandfather recorded it. But since Eileen lived with the children at Ellsworthy Road for three years, I'm left speculating whether she lived alone with the children for the first two years and Vernon visited, or they cohabited in the disguise of a married couple.

Meanwhile, Popsy attended as governess. Mom told me, "We also had a cook named Mrs. Pratley. She was very bad tempered; hated it if we came into the kitchen. But she loved canaries and had several hanging in cages from the maids' sitting room ceiling. Whenever she was really mad at us, Peter and I went on a taming spree and bought her a new canary. It usually worked.

"My father was very good about visiting us once a week, when he was in town. He'd take us ice-skating at the Grosvenor Palace at Christmas. There was an indoor skating rink surrounded by tables. In the spring and fall we visited the London Zoo."

But Pryns was visiting his mother in California when Eileen and Vernon announced their engagement to be married near Christmas. Unable to bear being in London when the wedding took place, he purchased a flight on the maiden voyage of a British Airways plane to Khartoum. From there he traveled throughout the East for over half a year. At one point he took a slow boat ride up the Nile and another down the Volga, "lying lazily on the deck day after day in the warm August sunshine, watching the banks drift by."

Vernon Armitage was a tall, slender man with an equally thin face, and had never been married. On the marriage certificate he is listed as a bachelor, nurseryman residing at Edgeworth House, Berkhampstead, Herts. The Rank or Profession of his father, Benjamin Armitage, was "Independent Means."

Eileen Maude again married on a cold January day. I've placed the black and white photo side-by-side with the photo of her marriage to my grandfather. Both were taken as the couple exited the church, groom on the left, bride on the right. Both grooms wear white carnation boutonnieres. Eileen has the same lopsided smile—like my daughter Amy has—though Eileen looks much more innocent in the earlier shot. Vernon wears striped trousers, which I believe means the wedding took place early in the day. Men in uniform in the background indicate Vernon was either a veteran himself, or had friends who were, unlike my pacifist grandfather. Eileen didn't wear a wedding gown the second time. Her white midlength dress is covered by a dark-colored fur jacket. And instead of a veil, she covered her head with a broad-brimmed hat. I wondered if it was the same one she wore when she said good-bye to her children one year later. The pair look happy, but a sense of festivity is missing. People are smiling but not laughing. There are no petals floating about in the air.

Pryns temporarily let for himself a flat near Tottenham Court Road. After it appeared his children would stay put some years with his ex-wive and her husband on Ellsworthy road, he relocated to a new flat that had just been built at 2 Devonshire Street W1 near Portland Place.

I asked my mother what she remembered about the flat.

"It was a service flat—my father used to have his meals brought in to him, with maid service and that kind of thing. One didn't really own flats like those, they were leased from someone, but it must have been possible to buy and sell the leases.

"It was extremely modern, with simple geometric shapes and lines, a style he always preferred." Grandpa wrote that he employed the young modernistic architects Wells and Coates to work on it. Rooms were divided by shoji screens, one of which was soon "punctured by a visiting dog trying to catch up with its master on the other side." The cabinets were built in place and the workmen built a ...

> ... a panel that could be let down on hinges from one of the walls over the floor, on which was a miniature electric railway system for the amusement of Peter and Betty May when they came to visit.

When I was young, and Grandpa built his own ultramodern house in Santa Barbara, he again set up that miniature train for my brothers, cousin and me to play with. Instead of naming the little towns after Peter and Betty May, they were called Marysville, Tommysville, Charlieville and Thayerville[1]. I don't recall my mother finding much interest in it.

Eileen often accompanied her children on their visits with their father.

> We found as much congenial fun in adding a miniature village and its toy inhabitants to the electric railway as the children did in playing with the trains.

Pryns missed his marriage terribly. His new freedom gave him little consolation, and he found the return to bachelorhood disillusioning, without the joys and comforts he'd come to know while he was married.

> With no one to welcome my return from the day's work, or to keep my house in order, or to love, or to share my troubles with, or be hostess to my friends, I was full of bitter regrets and more lonely and unhappy than I had been ever before in my life. I therefore entertained a great deal in my new flat and built up quite a list of attractive girl friends—not hard to find in foggy, complexion-favoring London.

---

1. The only other grandchild Grandpa had at the time was my cousin Thayer, Jennifer's eldest. Since then, Jennifer has had four more children and David has had five.

Chateau de Bures carried on successfully. During the summers Pryns organized "quite large house parties" there.

> One ended with a trip in two cars down through the chateau country of France to the Riviera and back ... Sometimes the group included younger women for whom, at the time, I felt an attraction, but nothing really serious was yet afoot. Nor did this superficial gaiety bring me happiness. My psychoanalysis was dragging along inconclusively. Never as in those years have the skies in London been so cold and gray.

A leg operation confined him to his bed for several weeks, during which he felt particularly grim. Eileen dropped in occasionally to perk him up, as did other friends, but his spirits declined as soon as they left.

> My gaze wandered from the bare walls of my room through the window and over a sea of sooty chimney tops. My memory went back to a summer-land and happier times. I saw Eileen and me again look for a homesite as we had done on the newly subdivided Lucky Baldwin Ranch [now the city of Arcadia near Pasadena].

According to his autobiography, Pryns didn't think Eileen was happy either. He didn't elaborate why except to say that during one of the visits with the children, she and he reflected on the past together. Eileen confided that if she had been able to bear a few more years with him, perhaps a divorce would not have been necessary. In turn, Pryns told her "with belated hindsight" he wished that when she began therapy with Jones, he'd gone to Vienna to complete his analysis with Freud. Maybe they could have purchased a home in Cannes to rendezvous on holidays.

I know what I think my grandmother should have replied: "Forget those psychoanalysts! All you needed to do was pay attention to me and your children instead of your silly old causes." Instead, she told him wistfully, "I shall have made you a wonderful husband for some other woman!"

I think I made my husbands better husbands for other women. A year or so after Ex-Two and I divorced, he took me out to lunch because he wanted to tell me he realized how he'd hurt me during our marriage. He said, very sincerely, that he was sorry. That was extremely comforting to me. I said I was sorry for my part, too. After Ex-Three and I divorced, he also apologized, in his fashion. "I'm sorry I was such a butt about it," he said. Both confessions allowed me to heal. I loved both men deeply before I married them. I loved them while I was married to them. And I will love them until the day I die even if I'm not supposed to be married to them any more. They were my friends. I'm happy to know my grandparents remained friends, even if Grandpa's autobiography was a tardy apology. True friendship never dies.

George and Victoria Thomas' Golden Wedding Anniversary. Standing left to right: Peggy, Eric, "Joy" (Harold's wife), "Billie," Harold, Florence (Billie's wife), Kathleen (Eric's wife), Vernon, Marie Victoria. Sitting, left to right: Liala, George, Victoria, Eileen Maude. The eighth child, Daisy, lived in Argentina at the time of the anniversary, 1932.

In the most recent photo taken of Eileen Maude, she sits in a gathering of her family taken by a professional photographer at George and Victoria's Golden Wedding celebration in July 1932. Vernon stands directly behind Eileen Maude looking erect and serene.

I learned later that most of my second-cousins acquired copies of this image, and all copies are conveniently labeled with names on the back. It took some work to figure out the date, however. We get a good clear image of who looks like whom. Almost all the siblings have their father's oval face except Peggy, who looks more like her round-faced mother. And I can see where my mother got her eyes with the saggy upperlids—from George.

Harold stands just right of center and glares straight into the camera with the same devilish grin I often saw my mother make—as if he were scheming a joke or naughty prank. I think he resembles his father the most. The other brothers, Bill and Erik, wear the same triangular mustache as Vernon. It must have been a fashionable shape in 1932. George sports the traditional full mustache that covers his entire upper lip. He is the only one with a bow tie. A pocket watch reveals itself by a heavy chain crossing his vest. All of the women are smiling except Eric's and Billie's wives, who don't look at all happy.

Like in the Brownlee wedding photo, all women wear strands of pearls or beads and soft draped dresses that hang to midcalf. Peggy asserts herself in her bold polka-dot dress. Victoria is the only woman wearing a coat, most likely to show off a large fur collar that nearly envelopes her. Her very short hair flips around the bottom at ear length, and looks just like Peggy's and Joy's hairdos, though Joy parts hers down the middle. The other women's bobs have been set in soft waves.

My gently smiling grandmother looks just like her mother sitting next to her. In contrast to the rest of the slender family, Eileen seems to have put on a bit of weight. Plump arms extend from her sleeveless silk dress and she looks very healthy for someone who is going to die of heart disease a year and a few months later.

Eileen Maude – 1932.

Chapter 25

The Newspapers

During my conversation with my second-cousin Jason Turner, I asked him about my mother's cousin John Abbott, only son of Peggy and Jack Abbott. Jason informed me that *Jon*—spelled like my son Jonathan's nickname—not *John*, was very much alive contrary to earlier reports, and living in Northampton. So on Friday morning, before heading out to find a library, I rang Jon on the number Jason had given me. I wanted to meet him, and I wanted to ask him some questions.

Since my grandmother might have been buried near Ayr, where the Abbotts lived and where Jon grew up, I wondered if she was buried in the same place Jon's parents were later buried. I also wondered if Jon remembered the time my grandmother was sent to the hospital. He would have been very little then, but it was worth an ask.

A woman named Catherine answered the line. Jon was out at the moment. When I explained who I was, Catherine informed me she was Jon's partner. *Partner* doesn't mean *gay lover* as it does in America. When I told her what I was up to, she said she didn't know much about the family, however some of the names I spouted off were familiar to her.

"Do you know where in Ayr Jon's parents were buried?" I asked.

"They weren't buried in Ayr," she said firmly. "They were buried in the Abbott vault, which is in an abbey somewhere else."

"Well, that eliminates the possibility that my grandmother was buried near them."

"Yes, it is quite specific that only Abbotts are buried in that plot." I got the impression it bothered Catherine she would be excluded from the abbey as well.

I hung up hoping Jon would call back soon.

I then left my flat in search of the British Public Library. Oddly enough, the massive structure was not listed in my tourist book. I revisited the Internet café, found the library on Google, obtained directions and printed out a map. A convenient subway ride scooted me from the Baker Street Station to the Euston Park Station. Once I walked the surface streets, it amazed me to find that fewer people in London knew the location of their public library than Hampsteaders knew the location of their local parish church.

An imposing modern statue of Sir Isaac Newton engraving circles on a map in the concrete with a giant compass dominated the entrance of the expansive complex. I recalled my previous visit with my stepcousin Paul in Cambridge. When he toured my husband and me through Clare College's library, he showed us an original Isaac Newton manuscript. Paul even let us hold it—a book Newton had written with his own hands some three hundred years earlier!

I guessed the modern red brick buildings on the left side of the courtyard to be the new library, whereas the ornate Victorian structure flanking the right side was the original building. I wouldn't get the chance to find out for sure because when I inquired at the information desk in the new building about where to look up old newspaper articles, the clerk told me no old newspapers were kept in either of the buildings. All newspapers from around Great Britain are gathered at the British Newspapers Library in Colindale. Colindale, the third to last stop on the Northern Line, was a half-hour ride away.

The clerk warned me I would face some restrictions. Before entering the newspaper archive a visitor needs to show proper identification and proof that he/she is at least eighteen years of age. That was a problem, not the age bit, just the identification, as I'd left my passport back at the flat. If I had to return to retrieve it, I would run out of day before reaching Colindale. The library clerk kindly phoned Colindale and learned to my relief that my credit card, which I *did* have with me, would suffice as my ID.

One can see the Newspapers Library directly across the train tracks from the Colindale Station. The village of Colindale is little more than a grim strip of concrete buildings lining the train tracks, including the library, a pub and a café. Beyond the buildings are nothing but fields. I lost no time walking or getting lost. I relinquished my handbag to the guard at the entrance window, as if checking a coat. All I could carry into the second floor study room were my computer, my research notes and my moneybag. No pens were allowed, only pencils. My lack of a pencil necessitated a 50p purchase. At least they didn't require me to wear white gloves. That protection is reserved for much older documents such as those at the British National Archives in Kew.

Upstairs in the study room a librarian demonstrated how to use their computer system. She entered "Hampstead" into the search window, followed by the years "1933-1934." A list of nine newspapers in publication during that period came up on the screen.

She then instructed me to fill out a special form for each of the nine newspapers so a clerk could fetch them from their places on the archive shelves. I could only submit four forms at a time and was told the wait would be forty-five minutes per search. I finished the first two forms, to get things started, and then finished the second two. That left me with forty minutes with nothing to do but eat.

I had to exit the library building to reach the café, where I ate a quick lunch of fish, chips and canned peas. I've never liked canned peas, but they were the only roughage available.

I returned to the Newspapers Library with three hours left before the closing time of 4:30 p.m. Four huge volumes awaited me at the numbered desk designated to me. The newspapers were bound by year, the pages brown with age. I started with the *Hampstead Gazette*, a monthly publication. I had to scan through every page of every paper from November 1933 to December 1934. (Old British newspapers are all being digitized, by the way.)

It was necessary to view the *St. Pancras Gazette* and *The London Times* on microfilm. Since I had to wait for a machine to become available and then figure out how it worked, the process took even longer than skimming the physical papers. At least it wasn't necessary to check out the film for the *London Times*. I found the film boxes on a shelf near the microfilm room and helped myself to the one labeled, "Nov. 1933." But since the *Times* was a daily paper, this was a bigger job than searching through the weekly and monthly papers. The good news was that the death notices were always on the first pages of each issue and easy to find.

By the time I heard the closing bell, I'd also made it through the *Hampstead Citizen, Hampstead and Highgate Record and Chronicle, Hampstead and Highgate Express*, the *Hampstead* and *St. John's Wood and Kilburn Advisor* without finding one mention of the death of Eileen Maude Thomas Hopkins Armitage. As I prepared to leave, I wondered what Vernon had been up to all those years ago? Why didn't he make sure his wife's death was published in his local paper? I knew what my grandfather was doing at the time—he was chasing after Fay.

It was time to go back to my flat. As I stood by the isolated train tracks, with no one else around me, I felt like the youngest daughter in *Fiddler on the Roof* waiting for the train to take her off to Siberia. A blue funk came over me during my ride home, and I still felt sad as I arrived at my flat, even though I'd bought myself an ice cream cone on the walk from the subway and found that the cleaning service had freshened up my little home. Not only was I discouraged about my search, I felt badly for my Gram, upset that her death seemed to have been ignored by the whole of London society, including her husband and ex-husband. Even the poorest of my relatives back in America had nice gravestones to mark the fact that they once existed.

I lay down on my bed with my feet propped up high and fell asleep. I didn't wake until a few hours later at a half past seven. I would not have risen at all if I hadn't been trying to instill a schedule in my day.

I wasn't very hungry, so I decided to skip the pub dinner and see if I could find a can of soup at a food shop I'd noticed on my way back to my flat. It had been hard to see because it was down a small, dark alley.

The shop around the corner turned out to be a well-stocked organic grocery. I was surprised the lady at the management office, who sent me on that wild goose chase for food when I first arrived, didn't know about it. I bought some minestrone soup, a wedge of goat milk Camembert cheese, a box of Carrs crackers, fresh peaches, a plum, some cookies and, finally, a box of soy milk for my tea. There were still some bottles of beer left in my fridge from a liquor store by the Internet café. I also bought the biggest jar of Marmite I could find to take to California for *me mum.*

While I feasted on soup, cheese, crackers and beer back at my flat, I watched the cricket contest between England and Pakistan on the *telly*. Someday I must get someone to explain the dynamics of that game to me!

Philippa, who lived on the southern edge of Greater London in Herne Hill, called while I was eating. We had a fun chat. She knew less about the Thomas family than I did. We decided it would work nicely for me to visit her on August 8 after I spent time with her sister Candy in Worcester near Wolverhampton. I'd stay with Philippa through the morning of August 10, when a taxi could return me to Heathrow Airport.

I planned to return to the British Newspapers Library the following day. I wanted to double check the Ayr newspapers and look up information on Eileen Maude's parents, George and Victoria Thomas. I made a quick call to Camilla to see if she knew when and/or where they died. "They were both gone before I was born [1938]," she said. "I assume they died in Wolverhampton." That gave me an approximate gauge.

Left to right: unknown, Jill, Betty May,
Peter, Jeffray and Auntie Joy – Summer, 1933.

Chapter 26

Grandpa's Journal

As the summer of 1933 approached, Pryns and his mother planned the holiday on the continent for his children and Popsy. Pryns wanted Eileen to come along, but May wouldn't have it. At seventy-two, she followed her Catholic values and expected married couples to stick it out for better or worse. She would travel from San Francisco to meet up with her family in France. A photo in my mother's scrapbook shows May sitting on a wall overlooking the harbor there. On the back, she wrote, "Thought you might like this as a mem[ory] of Dinard. Grandma."

Pryns wrote in his autobiography,

> Our party of five stayed at the Hotel Royal and spent long days on the broad beach, Mother in her beach chair and the rest of us surf-bathing, building sand castles, climbing over the rugged rocks and collecting shells and all kinds of marine life.

They were joined "at the first part of the summer" by Peggy and Jack Abbott with daughters, June, age sixteen, and Pat, age twelve. Jon would have been four years old. My grandfather didn't mention him in the book or in the journals, and I would learn later he didn't remember being there. Perhaps he was left home with a nanny or grandparent.

Harold, Joy and their two children joined the group on August 13. They'd traveled from their home on the Channel Island of Jersey. Jill, a few months older than my mother, was already eight and Jeffray turned five that July. Camilla wasn't born yet. Pryns wrote:

> The four children had great times together. You might find Betty May leading a string of little French tots—for she had even then a motherly spirit, and her ambition was to marry and have eight children.

Photos of Peter, Betty May, Jill and Jeffray at the beach building sand castles, doing somersaults and wading in tide pools were pasted in the scrapbook Mom and I would find in the tin box.

This leads us to the pages in Grandpa's journals that Aunt Jennifer sent me. They start dated August 11, 1933. Grandpa refers to Popsy by her real name, Marie. They'd been in Dinard for a few weeks. The Abbotts must have left the continent, since we know they were in Scotland to greet Eileen and Vernon after their drive through the Lake District.

I've inserted my comments, as well as my mother's.

> Thursday, August 10: The children, Marie and I all received letters from dear Eileen. Mine was six full pages and made me happy for a while.
> Friday, August 11: Standard day spent on beach with the babes.
> In the eve, Mother and I read aloud from Upton's *American Outpost.*

Upton Sinclair had written *American Outpost*[1] the previous year, 1932.

> Sunday, August 13: Yesterday Harold and Joyce arrived and in the eve we

1. *American Outpost: A Book of Reminiscences* by Upton Sinclair, Farrar & Rinehart, Inc., New York 1932.

Photo from Eileen H. Ames' collection.

May with her grandchildren – 1933.

went to a manikin parade [a parade of life-sized dolls] and Spanish cabaret at the casino with some Standard Oil friends named Wood Turline and Mr. and Mrs. Dodge. In the morning mother had let the Thomas children and governesses drive in the car and mother and I took a walk. She had brought up the question of Eileen's duty to the children, and said she herself had stuck to her guns. I pointed out that my upbringing was no such brilliant success!

That seemed like a mean comment from my grandfather to his mother. She seemed to be saying it was her duty to stay married to Charles for her son's sake. Charles must have been a very difficult person to live with. Then her son tells her she failed anyway. *Ouch!*

To-day was spent with all the Thomases in the sea and on the rocks and the beach. This eve. Mother and I had a walk, then read from Upton's *American Outpost.* Today's big event, however, was that Betty May can't abide her rubber life-belt saying, "Daddy I'm going to swim alone"—and actually did so! Six double strokes. Later she swam eight, and shouted "Daddy I can swim! Daddy I can swim!"

Wednesday, August 16: Yesterday Betty May, Peter, Jill Thomas and Marie and I drove in Mother's car to Mont Saint-Michel. We climbed up to and went through the Abbey. Back in time for the 3rd swim.

To-day was the usual happy play with the children. On awaking Betty May said to Marie, "Popsy, are you awake? I do hope this holiday will not come to an end, it's so lovely having Daddy here."

[Part of journal sliced out here, possibly by Fay.]

Monday, August 28: A telegram has come from Vernon to say Eileen's in a nursing home far too ill to come to France. I can think of little else than that, even if the day had been other than standard. I am very worried. How terrible for us all if anything were to happen to that dear little woman! And of course I can't but think that had mother invited her to be with us, she would be now in this hot sunshine full of health. Betty May is quite well again.

Tuesday, August 29: Standard day. In the evening, thank God, a telegram from Vernon to say Eileen was improving. At casino heard a lecture by one Pierre Vacher on "Jealousy" and public discussion. Like everything here, it was spoilt by being dragged out 'til midnight.

[Part of journal sliced out.]

A telegram from Eileen saying she liked idea of me taking children to Chateau [de Bures].

Thursday, August 31: Mother left for Paris. Then standard day till eve, when I had coffee with our neighbors on beach and went with them to casino for half hour.

September 1, 1933 (Friday): Telegram from Eileen saying (a) bring children to England Wed. and (b) she won't be back for weeks. Oh, poor dear! Telegram from Vernon saying Eileen is getting on satisfactorily.

Rest of day standard. Wrote many letters this eve as well as reading aloud with Marie from DeMan on Psychology of Socialism (very good).

[Part of journal sliced out.]

Saturday, September 2: Standard day. Letter from Fay C. Tennis lesson. Marie and I read aloud. Now at 10:30, I'm going to write some letters.

"Fay C" refers to Fay Cartledge, and according to Jennifer, this is the first mention of her mother in her father's journals. I suspect some of the previously missing slices describe Pryns meeting her in Dinard, because they become engaged soon after. I asked my mother if she recalled seeing Fay while in France.

"I vaguely remember seeing her during the holiday when she returned a book she'd borrowed from my father. She was staying at the same hotel."

> Sunday, September 3: In the morning the children and I took advantage of low tide to walk to a lighthouse. They were fascinated by finds of squids, baby eels, and all manner of sea animals! Then we walked to a stranded fishing boat and were invited aboard. The deck was covered with large crabs. This afternoon, bathing and sand castles. This eve reading aloud and letters.
> Monday, September 4: Standard day of sea and air bathing with children, then tennis with a M. Rouger.
> Eve: reading aloud, letter-writing and a visit to the casino where Capt. David (gym instructor) and I watched the Cuban dancer Marian—I spoke to her afterward in the wings. I should mention that on every one of these days I also put in from 2 to 3 1/2 hours on [writing] notes and book.
> Tuesday, September 5: The children and Marie and I got the most we could out of the sunshine and sea at La Baule.

La Baule is on the other side of the Brittany peninsula from Dinard. The family must have taken day trips to other beaches.

> Wed. was showery, which suited us to drive to Dinard. There the children joined the Thomas children on the beach. Joyce dined with me. Then we boarded the boat.
> Thurs. a.m. we arrived in Southampton...

"One of the biggest seaports in the south of England," inserted Mom.

> ...Thence to London, where Vernon met us at the station. He had no recent news of Eileen. We all said "good bye," the end of our holiday together. I spent the day shopping or at the lab.

Mom added, "I suspect the reference to lab is my father's office at the University of London where he taught psychology."

> Friday, September 8 Hotel Crillon, Paris: This morning the 9 am train to Paris. Found mother well. But this hotel is haunted with memories—heartbroken thoughts of Eileen. Mother took me to a nice restaurant in

rue 29 Juillet. Dear old Mother, she loves me so much. It is hard not to let her run me into promises of all sorts. We wound up with a fine war film, 'Conflict.'
[Part of journal sliced out.]

Again, this slice could have had something to do with Fay, for it's possible Pryns returned to Paris to see her, as well as his mother.

Saturday, September 9: Spent with mother this her last day here, very pleasantly. We took Miss McMurray to Chateau de Bures for lunch. This eve mother dined with me at Café de la Cremaillere, then we walked and sat along the Champs Elysees.
[Probably] September 20, London: fearful cold. At 3, emerald-dealer [Rest of sentence cut out.]

Jennifer told me her mother's engagement ring from her father was an emerald. It appears by September 20, he was already purchasing it. But he leaves no record of his courtship, leading me to believe the cut out bits must have been about Fay, not about Eileen.

Afternoon. Back for 1 1/2 hours at lab. At 4, Marie brought the children for tea. Our happy play was clouded however by two letters in which Vernon told Marie that Eileen had been out of her mind much of the time owing to drugs given. We wish to heaven she were back in London among doctors we know.
Eve: John Bovington, whom I haven't seen in seven (maybe) years dined with me in this flat, en route from USSR to USA.
Friday, September 22: Continued bad news about dear Eileen—delirium continues. This noon the children lunched with me. Later I took Peter to catch his train back to school at Seaforth. I delivered him to his headmaster, Mr. Barkley-Hill. Spent evening at home, working headings on notes.

That was the last entry Jennifer sent me for 1933. The pages from October 1933 through February 1934 were all cut out, leaving no journal description of Eileen Maude's death, only Grandpa's description in *Both Hands Before the Fire.*

George and Victoria (Bissell) Thomas
at their Fiftieth Wedding Anniversary – 1932.

Chapter 27

British Newspapers Library

On Saturday, my last day in London, I retraced my steps to the British Newspapers Library. I began the morning by looking through the 1933 issues of the *Holborn Guardian* and *St. Pancras Chronicle*. No success. Then I found an overall index for *The London Times* I hadn't seen before that allowed me to search a name across the span of its publication. I finally had my first "hit" when I typed "Armitage" into the search field. The Friday, April 8, 1932 issue (no. 46102) of *The Times* reported Mr. and Mrs. Vernon Armitage attended the wedding of Rear-Admiral F.L. Tottenham and Mrs. H. Street. I learned nothing about Eileen's death or burial, but at least I had a confirmation Eileen existed in London before November 18, 1933. It was like winning five dollars from a lottery ticket—just enough to keep me going.

I also found other articles on Armitages written much later than 1934. One was slightly significant: a death notice on May 24, 1967 for

"Kathleen Alice May, aged 74, widow of Vernon Armitage and loved sister of Connie. Funeral at St. John's Parish Church Boldre, near Lymington, Hampshire." Kathleen was Vernon's second wife. He took her to California in about 1943 to introduce her to my mother. She had a picture of the newlyweds sitting on Queen May's garden patio in Santa Barbara. That's when Vernon tried to talk Mom out of her blue and white Woods Ware china. Kathleen outlived Vernon, so there was no way to know if he would have provided a proper grave for *her*.

I finally got around to looking at newspapers from Ayr, of which there were only two: *The Ayrshire Post*, and another I can't remember, but found nothing, confirming what the people in Ayr had already told me.

I then decided to look in the Wolverhampton newspapers. Maybe my great-grandparents posted a death announcement.

Bingo! In the Deaths column of their November 25 issue, *The Midlands County Express* for Wolverhampton published:

> ARMITAGE-At Ayr, Scotland, November 17, 1933, Eileen, dearly beloved daughter of George James and Victoria Anne Thomas, 17 Tettenhall Road, Wolverhampton.

The date was not correct, but since Eileen died a mere twenty minutes into the following day, it was understandable her parents got it wrong. I also learned George's middle name was *James*, not *William* as my mother thought. My joy at finding something after such an exhausting search was overshadowed by the fact that the article didn't mention a memorial service or burial information.

The other Wolverhampton newspaper, *The Wolverhampton Express and Star*, published the exact same article in their November 20 edition. At least my great-grandparents were efficient.

I couldn't think of any other newspaper possibilities and prepared to leave. During my Internet research from home in California, I'd noted a Family Records Centre in London. (This British government entity isn't to be confused with the Mormon Family History Centers.) I asked the librarian at the British Newspapers Library where to find it. She knew exactly what I was talking about and gave me a brochure about all the family research facilities in London, which, as it happened, clustered around the British Library where I'd been the day before. I still had enough time in the day to go there.

Hopping back on the Northern Line to London, I made one connection and ferreted my way through a maze of streets to my destination within an hour. Even though I skipped lunch, only two hours remained for research. I had my computer with me in case I needed to refer to my family tree.

The large main room on the first floor of the Centre divided into three sections. The set of shelves on the left contained row upon row of tall, leather-bound ledgers listing burial records. The center section contained marriage record ledgers, and the right section contained birth record ledgers. Similar to the ledger reference I'd found online for Eileen's birth, these books only indexed the actual records that were stored 175 miles northwest in Southport. Obtaining an actual record necessitated finding the listing in the ledger, filling out a form with its location information, standing in line at the Centre and submitting the form with a finder's fee. The most frustrating part about the process was the two weeks it would take the records office to send me the record. Since I would be home by then, they would have to send it to California, where it would be of no help to my research in England.

I first tried to locate a burial listing for Eileen Maude. A clerk directed me upstairs to a computer reference section. I found the name Eileen Thomas listed several times in their data bank, but not our Eileen Maude.

Frustrated, I decided to try something easier, just to test the system and see if it worked. I returned to the main room downstairs to search for Eileen's marriage to Prince (using the original spelling). Facing a wall of dated book spines, I noted four volumes for each year; for example, 1921 was covered by a January to March ledger, April to June ledger, July to September ledger and October to December ledger. Since my grandparents married on January 12, I pulled out the January to March ledger. Surnames were organized A-Z in each volume.

Looking for "Hopkins," I flipped through the vellum pages of real goatskin (not the fake plastic kind) covered in columns of elegant calligraphy. *What a work of art!* When I came to the beginning of the

Hopkins entries, I scanned through the first names written in fading black ink to "Prince C." *Yea!* I wrote down the volume and page number on my notepad. I flipped further in the same volume until I came to the Thomases, where I found "Eileen M" with the same volume and page number. *Yea, again!*

Next I tried to find Eileen's death certificate, hoping for a cleaner copy than the low-resolution scan I'd downloaded from the net. To my surprise, the Centre did not hold Scotland's records, only England's and Wales'.

That was all I was able to accomplish before closing time. After ordering the marriage certificate, I headed back to the Baker Street Station via another sweltering subway ride. On the walk to the flat I stopped in at the Internet Café to research Wolverhampton. Hotter even than in the enclosed subway cars, it was all I could do to concentrate on the computer while a pool of perspiration gathered at the nape of my neck and dribbled down the center of my back. Thankfully, it only took a few minutes to locate a fairly organized site at www.wolverhampton.gov.uk. I could return to it from Candy's computer in Worcester before we went on our *lookyloo* for 17 Tettenhall Road.

I felt drained completely of energy by the time I reached my flat. My body felt puffy all over. I whisked the last cold beer out of my fridge, lay down on the bed with my feet up in their favorite resting position against the wall and finished off the second half of the goat milk Camembert. I even checked my phone messages from my inverted position.

Jon Abbott had called me earlier in the day while I was in the library with my mobile phone turned off. I rang him up and reached a warm cheery voice with a thick Scottish accent. At times I had to ask him to repeat things so I could understand what he said.

"I was invigorated to hear from you," he started.

I thought of my Grandfather's description of Jon at five years old, "Jon is full of charm."

We chatted for a while and I told him about looking for his half-sister June Belden.

"It's Belbin with a "b", B-e-l-b-i-n," he said, "not Belden." I was surprised my mother, an excellent speller, never noticed that.

"I'm afraid she recently passed away," he said.

Darn!

"Pat, my other sister, is still alive, but she's living in a nursing home and not in very good condition."

I glanced at the poor wilting peach roses I'd bought, their heads slumped over the side of the glass. *Mom will not like hearing this news.*

Besides spending time at his home in Northampton, Jon often visited London where Catherine had a place. He told me it might be possible to see me while I was at Philippa's on August 8 or 9. We would talk more about that later.

After I got off the phone, I had a brainstorm. When Jon referred to Philippa's mother and aunt, he used the last name Bissell-Thomas, not Thomas. Mom told me Harold was the only sibling to adopt the surname Bissell-Thomas. When I asked her why, she said, "I suspect the Bissells were better off than the Thomases—a prestige thing. In England, class is more important than in America. I've always found it amusing that here in the United States, Billy the Kid and Annie Oakley were heroes!"

I wondered if my grandmother had sometimes been referred to as Bissell-Thomas before she married my grandfather. In other words, should I have been searching for Eileen Maude Bissell-Thomas under "B" all this time as well as in the "T" section?

I decided to return to the Family Records Centre the next day. The first thing I would do was look for Eileen under that name. And since I'd learned her father's and mother's middle names, I should be able, with some diligence, to find their death and/or birth records. I would start by searching for their marriage record some time before the birth of Harold, which I'd understood to be around 1888.

Then I headed across the street for another beer at the air-conditioned pub, thinking I might order a smallish meal, too.

Photo from Eileen H. Ames' collection.

Eileen and her children – probably Cannes, c1929.

Chapter 28

Eileen Maude's Death

As Grandpa noted in his journal, Vernon met him and the children at the station in London when they returned to England after their holiday. Since the children's stepfather had to return to attend to his wife, wherever she was, Popsy must have taken the children to Ellsworthy Road and cared for them on her own, hoping their mother would return soon.

Pryns' journal entry that he returned to Paris to see his mother differs from the entry in his book that says he stayed with his mother in Dinard for a while longer after the children returned to England. In his book, he meets Fay after the children leave. But in his journal, he is receiving a letter from Fay much earlier in time than that account implies. Since Mom remembered seeing Fay in France, Pryns must have met her before or even as he learned his ex-wife was gravely ill.

In photos of young Fay, she looks like a movie star; petite, about five foot two, maybe shorter, with a square face and short blonde hair that she kept blonde until the bitter end. A woman I met later in England, who'd met Fay in the late 1960s, described her as "mesmerizing." I, too, found her mesmerizing. I watched in awe one night, when I was twenty-three, as she captivated my fiancé. Extremely intelligent and well traveled[1], she could keep up with any topic my Harvard-educated fiancé wanted to discuss. The pair covered politics and world dynamics. As she charmed and flattered him, his head rose and his chest puffed out. He thought she was delightful. Not until she got drunk that night, ran over my grandfather's sprinkler head and blamed the resulting geyser on my fiancé, did he see the other side of Fay.

She kept fit playing tennis, but at the crucial moment she met Pryns, she was writing at a desk on the other side of the hotel's writing room. Not many hotels have those rooms any more. They housed desks with pots of ink and small drawers containing stationery monogrammed with the hotel's trademark. My grandfather entered the room "to do some correspondence" and left "with her London address in hand."

That means that at the very time Eileen was sick and approaching death in Scotland, Pryns was in a love trance. It would explain why his memory of the details regarding his children and their ailing mother appear fuzzy when he wrote his autobiography thirty-two years later. Also, Fay was still alive and a big presence in his life when he published that book.

On the other hand, Pryns was very thorough with his descriptions of his courtship and four-month engagement to Fay—an affair that moved extremely quickly by today's standards, but moderately for him. He arrived in Dinard in July—who knows when he met Fay, was engaged by the end of September, and married in December. He had married Eileen only ten weeks after meeting her.

"I can recall Daddy telling me that he was going to bring Fay to meet me," said Mom. "I remember thinking Cartledge a funny name."

Since the entries in the autobiography about this period have no dates, it is difficult for me to determine just how much time went

---

1. Besides traveling extensively with Pryns, Fay traveled frequently with her second husband. He was the right-hand man to Robert MacNamara, Secretary of Defense under President Kennedy. Through this exposure, she also learned her way around Washington politics.

by between Pryns' return to England and his receipt of a letter from Glasgow in which Vernon informed him that Eileen was dying. Fay threw such a hissy fit when Pryns told her he planned to visit Eileen on her death bed that he almost didn't go. This is what awaited him in Scotland:

> The sight which I saw froze me with horror. There on her sick bed lay, not the brown-haired, musically laughing, perky little woman whom I knew but a lusterless grey head, wan face and body shrunken to skeletal proportions. An oxygen tube sustained life but could not assuage the agonized gaping for breath of the flooded lungs. At times her hands, or her feet under the blankets threshed up and down, beating a tattoo of pain. So ended one whose life had been outstanding for daughterly devotion to her old parents, loyalty and many signal kindnesses to her friends and the many persons who sought her counsel or material help, a faithful wife and a devoted mother to two children who would now be bereft.
>
> Not even my love for Eileen braced me enough to endure to its uncertain end this harrowing scene. My thoughts turned to the fiancée I had left in London and a great fear seized me lest I lose her, too, and all she meant to me if I remained longer away. Knowing full well I should never see Eileen again, calling her by the name she had always loved, I sadly kissed her 'Good-bye' and turned away to catch the night's Flying Scotsman south.

I hadn't registered on my first reading that Pryns rode the Flying Scotsman, indicating he had to have visited his ex-wife in Scotland. Or that Vernon had sent a letter from Glasgow, the closest large city to Ayr.

I wondered how Eileen declined so quickly from the image of health in her parent's anniversary photo to the frail, sickly person described by my grandfather. If Eileen was convinced she wouldn't see her children again after bidding them good-bye at the St. Pancras station, did she already know she was dying? Yet if she did, why would she plan a vacation all the way up to Scotland? Or did she want to be near her sister while she was ill? Or did she just push herself too hard during her vacation—not resting when she felt tired or not eating properly? Was Vernon too demanding? If she was feeling badly, why didn't he take her home?

The following day Pryns made his regular visit to Dr. Jones, where a telegram from Vernon found him "stretched out on the analytic couch." Eileen had died twenty minutes past midnight that morning.

> My immediate reaction to this was of pain, as though I had been stabbed, and then of fury. I cursed and blasphemed. I ridiculed the conception that a good God ruled this world when the innocent suffer agonies and little children are deprived of the mothers they so need. Grief, anger, and the sense of the impotence which we have in the face of death were complicated by remorse. To the memory of my crudeness and failure as a husband was added the newest betrayal, that of the last night when, with her death but a few hours distant, I had not bided that brief time but had hurried off.

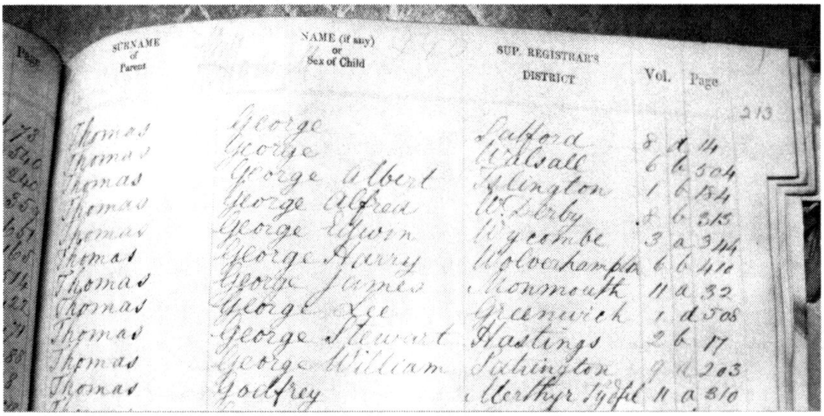

SURNAME of Parent	NAME (if any) or Sex of Child	SUP. REGISTRAR'S DISTRICT	Vol.		Page
Thomas	George	Salford	8	a	14
Thomas	George	Walsall	6	b	504
Thomas	George Albert	Islington	1	b	154
Thomas	George Alfred	W. Derby	8	b	315
Thomas	George Edwin	Wycombe	3	a	344
Thomas	George Harry	Wolverhampton	6	b	410
Thomas	George James	Monmouth	11	a	32
Thomas	George Lee	Greenwich	1	d	508
Thomas	George Stewart	Hastings	2	b	17
Thomas	George William	[illegible]	9	d	203
Thomas	Godfrey	Merthyr Tydfil	11	a	810

Ledger page in the Family Records Centre showing the George Thomases.
These are no longer available for public view.

Chapter 29

More Luck

Saturday, July 29, was a luckier day for me at the Family Records Centre. I returned early in the morning and headed straight to the marriage section in search of George James Thomas and Victoria Anne Bissell's marriage record. It would hopefully give me the names of their parents, and where they'd been living.

Beginning with the ledgers dated two years before Harold's birth in 1888, I searched through the four volumes of each year from 1886 through 1894, two years after my grandmother's birth in 1892. I've learned you need to bracket[1] just in case they had a child or two out of wedlock first. *George James Thomas* was an extremely common name in Wolverhampton, but there was no match to mine. There were no records at all for a *Victoria Anne Bissell* anywhere in England during

1. Research time both before and after the target year to allow for mistakes and missing data.

those years, spelled in any way, shape or form. I gave up that search for the moment and walked over to the birth section.

I immediately found Eileen's birth record in the second quarter of the 1892 ledger. With this in hand I searched for the birth ledgers for other babies born to Thomases in Wolverhampton. I found Eileen's sisters: Daisy Nora, Liala Victoria and Marie Louise, but not Peggy. I found no Erics, but I *did* find loads of Harolds and Williams. I just couldn't figure out which were Eileen's brothers.

As I pulled out and shoved in ledgers, I overheard some ladies next to me talking about their searches and joined their conversation. When I described my difficulties with the Thomas' wedding record, they suggested I look up the census records to help me narrow down the reliability of my data. By then I was squished for time. Only forty-five minutes remained before the Centre closed, and I still needed to stand in line and submit my order for Eileen's birth certificate. A clerk at the information station told me census records were researched through the computers upstairs. I scurried up there.

It took fifteen minutes for the staff to show me the system. First I had to type the name in the search field to bring up a list. Then I had to click on the icon for the census to give me the *piece* (reel number of the microfiche) and the page number on that piece. I came up with four possibilities for *George Thomas*, but nothing for *George James Thomas*. The helper suggested I save time by trying to find the census by the address. I typed in 17 Tettenhall Street, which I'd seen from my computer at home. Nothing. So I tried 17 Tettenhall Road.

It took me five minutes to get a hit. Contrary to the information I got on my computer at home, the address appeared on the 1901 census with the Thomases living there. This was the most recent census available in England in 2006. Since then the results of the 1911 census have been published. The next step was to reference a chart on a wall that told me which book contained the lists of streets in Wolverhampton during the 1901 census. In that book I found a list of five microfiche covering all the residences on 17 Tettenhall Road.

I needed another helper to assist me in finding the drawer containing the five microfiche and then show me how to use the viewing machine. I placed the first of the five microfiche films under the viewing glass and wiggled it around in search of Number 17. I could not find it. As I prepared to replace it with the second film, I heard an announcement over the Centre's loudspeaker. In perfect Queen's English a woman declared that the building was closing in fifteen minutes. I started to worry about ordering Eileen's birth certificate, but my helper calmly retrieved the second film and placed it into the viewer. Within seconds he'd found Number 17. There under the glass I saw, in a very fine hand, "George J. Thomas, Victoria A-wife, Harold-son, Eileen-dau, Winifred-dau, Eric-son, William-son, Liela[2] V-dau and Daisy N-dau." I was very excited. "How do I get a copy?" I asked the helper.

While he set the machine up for me to make a photocopy, I searched for the requisite 25p in my handbag. Then, voila! I had a piece of paper with the record I needed. I gathered my bag, my laptop and my pile of papers from where they had been scattered on the floor and briskly walked to the area where I was to purchase Eileen's birth certificate. The perfect voiced announcer declared the Centre was closing, but I still hadn't filled out my form. Another kind helper scooted me into the line for requesting records. "That way you will be counted as 'in line' when the building closes," she said, smiling.

While I waited, I read over the census report I'd just obtained. I wondered who Winifred was. *Was she one of the children that died? Why isn't Peggy listed?* Then I noticed that "Victoria A, wife" was born in Australia!

"Oh my gosh!" I cried out loud.

Five minutes after closing time I had made my purchase, I was in possession of an official list of Eileen's family in 1901, and I was skipping out the front door. I couldn't wait to get back to my flat and review my prizes to see if the dates from by initial searches for Eileen's siblings in the ledger books matched the data on the 1901 census report.

I still didn't know where my Gram was buried, but at least I'd broken the brick wall of her parents' genealogical line. That would allow me to research further back in time for more Thomases and more Bissells later.

---

2. This is the only place among all the Thomas family records that I saw Liala's name spelled Leila. I've chosen to use the spelling on the birth record over the census taker's spelling.

That evening I went sightseeing. I took a ride on the London Eye, a Ferris wheel with enclosed round pods the size of railroad cars. It perches on the shore of the River Thames like a waterwheel. When my pod reached the highest point, I wished my mother were with me to share the spectacular view of Big Ben and Buckingham Palace. I was beginning to feel that London Town was *my* town, too.

Photo from Eileen H. Ames' collection.

Berri Court. Photo sent by Vernon to Betty May – c1944.
Home to Betty May from 1934-1940.

Chapter 30

Missing Mummy

"How did you learn about your mother's death?" I asked Mom.

"My father came to tell me at 62 Ellsworthy Road. Peter was away at school, poor darling. I sat in my nursery. Daddy came into the room crying and said, 'You have no little mummy anymore.' Someone went to fetch me some tomato soup. I didn't like tomato soup then, but I suppose they were trying to make me feel better. I don't know how Peter found out."

I called Peter. "Do you remember your father telling you about your mother passing away?"

"No. I don't remember anyone telling me about my mother dying. I only remember being in France on vacation when they told me she was sick."

Eileen stipulated in her will that Vernon Armitage and Dr. Ernest Jones were to be the guardians of her two children. That was a wise decision considering Pryns became embroiled in his wedding plans immediately after Eileen's death. Living as wards of Vernon and Popsy, the children were discarded in Fay's wake, just as their mother had been. They didn't even get to mourn together. Mom lived alone during the week in Popsy's care, while Peter boarded at the Arnold House School a half-mile away in St. John's Woods—just the other side of Regent's Park from 62 Ellsworthy Road.

In spite of all the analysis he'd received, Pryns hired someone else to deal with his children's emotional issues. When sorting my mother's papers after her death, I came across a news article about a play based on the life of London psychologist Melanie Klein. I vaguely remembered Mom mentioning being sent to a famous woman psychologist as a child. I looked Klein up on the Internet. Not only was she a colleague of Dr. Jones, but the analyst for his wife and two children. Jones' daughter and son, born in 1921 and 1922 respectively, were only slightly older than Peter and Betty May. No doubt Jones recommended Klein to Pryns.

Melanie Klein was born in Vienna in 1882. That made her three years older than my grandfather and fifty-two in 1934. She is credited as the first psychoanalyst to use traditional Freudian practices with children, though she eventually disagreed with Freud and especially his daughter on many techniques.

The first paper Klein published discussed analysis of her son, though she didn't reveal his connection to her. She also analyzed her daughter and second son. Other early patients were mostly children of her colleagues. It was typical in those days for analysts to analyze each other's children. Grandpa's case wasn't unusual. And analysts couldn't practice until they had been analyzed themselves. Klein was analyzed by Freud's protégé, Ferenczi.

Klein employed small, nonmechanical toys in her therapy, such as wooden men and women that didn't reveal particular professions, cars, trains, animals, trees, paper, scissors and even water.

She began her career in her native Hungary, but when the country became uncomfortably anti-Semitic—Jews, including Ferenczi, were banned from the staff of the hospitals—she and many others moved to Berlin. There she came into contact with the Freud's Viennese contingent of psychoanalysts. She first confronted Freud regarding the age when children developed the Oedipal complex. Klein claimed it was years earlier than age five as Freud claimed.

Ernest Jones encouraged Klein to move to London from Berlin. It was good timing for several reasons. She was ready to leave her husband for the final time and take her youngest child with her. Melanie's husband, Arthur Klein, threatened to take custody of his children by pointing out that Melanie used them as her guinea pigs. He was deeply suspicious of psychoanalysis, as were many people during that period. One Catholic school burned books on hypnosis, claiming they were works of the devil. Another woman analyst, Hermine von Hug-Hellmuth, director of the Child Guidance Centre in Vienna, was murdered by the eighteen-year-old nephew she had analyzed.

Another reason Melanie wanted to leave Berlin was because she'd taken a stance against Anna Freud's theories. This resulted in Anna, her father and their loyal followers ostracizing Klein. About Klein's debut in London in 1925 (the year my mother was born), she wrote,

> I had the wonderful experience of speaking to an interested and appreciative audience in London. Ernest Jones asked me whether I would answer in the discussion. Although I had learnt a lot of English privately and at school, my English was still not good and I remember well that I was half guessing what I was asked, but it seemed that I could satisfy my audience that way. The three weeks that I spent in London, giving two lectures a week, were one of the happiest times of my life. I found such friendliness, hospitality and interest, and I also had an opportunity of seeing something of England and I developed a great liking for the English[1].

Being divorced and having never finished her doctorate made Melanie's ascent difficult in a male-dominated field. Still, her innovative strides in child psychology placed her in high regard. The British Psycho-Analytical Society elected her a member in October 1927. Her book, *The Psycho-Analysis of Children*, came out in November of 1932. She was well established by 1933. However, it was a traumatic year for her. Her brother and Ferenczi died, her lover moved away and her

---

1. Grosskurth, Phyllis. p 137.

daughter, Melitta Klein Schmideberg, also an analyst, turned against her. Klein may have had to deal with more grief than Peter and my mother did.

I asked my Uncle Peter, "Do you remember going to see a psychologist named Melanie Klein?"

"Absolutely! My father sent me to see her for a number of years. There is no question in my mind he sent me to the Arnold House School because it was close to where Melanie Klein lived [and worked]. I walked to see her every day. Monday to Friday."

"Are you sure you walked from the school and not Ellsworthy Road?"

"I walked from the *school.* It was a boarding school. It was after our mother died. I must have been eleven or so."

"What do you remember about her?"

"She was an older woman. She used to sit in a chair and listen to me."

Peter stalled for a second, then added, somewhat embarrassed by his failing memory, "Of course she had to sit somewhere.

"I would play with toys. I had a drawer in her chest of drawers with my name on it. That would be *my* drawer. And I would play with things in it."

"Were there dolls—people of some sort, so you could play-act?"

"No. Trains, cars, that type of thing."

"Did Mom see her?"

"I don't remember. But a long time ago your mother sent me a book she was excited for me to see. Just a minute."

We were talking on the phone. I could barely hear Peter calling to Josée from his wheelchair, asking her to fetch the book. After some scuffling around, he came back on the line.

"Here, it's called *Melanie Klein, Her World and Her Work.* By Phyllis Grosskurth." He spelled out the last name for me. "On page 153 the author talks about Mrs. Klein working with a five-year-old boy named Peter. That's me. But I wasn't five. I was much older than that. I'm sure I walked to her house by myself."

Josée sent me the book and I read everything about Klein until the 1940s. I disagree that the "Peter" Grosskurth referred to was my Uncle Peter. She was speaking about a child she'd analyzed earlier in time. Grosskurth also noted that Klein's journals from 1933 were lost, thus any information about Peter for the two months after Eileen's death. Klein had only just moved to St. John's Woods in 1933. Since our Peter went away to boarding school after Vernon moved the family to Berri Court at the end of 1934, Peter couldn't have visited with Klein for long.

What was interesting to me was how new and small the world of psychoanalysts was in those days and the significant part my grandfather played in it.

Grosskurth explained there were four principal centers of psychoanalysts during the early days of the movement: Vienna, Hungry, Berlin and London, and that "English analysts were to settle near one another in Hampstead." I wondered if 62 Ellsworthy Road was chosen because of its proximity to the psychoanalystical nest.

I also learned from Grosskurth that the aim of all analysis was to put the patient in touch with reality. Part of Klein's treatment for bringing a child to "reality" was convincing him/her there was no God, no magic, no Easter rabbit, no Father Christmas and no world of fairies. This provided "the foundations for a perfect uninhibited development of one's mind in every direction." Klein dismissed her own children's nanny when she taught that children were brought to this world by storks.

Klein is to have said, "I talk of sexual matters in the simple words best suited to their way of thought." It seemed to me she thought everything a child did or said had something to do with sex—everything natural from breast-feeding, to weaning, to toilet training, to eating. *How was a child to escape any of it and still grow up?* One aspect of the movement I found really scary was that many analysts recommended prophylactic analysis. They thought analysis should be part of every child's education. How glad I was that I was encouraged to go bicycling in the streets after school whereas Klein's children spent that time being analyzed by their mother. Since many English analysts followed Klein's theories, rather than Anna Freud's, the "English School" became known as the "Kleinian School.[2]"

2. Grosskurth, Melanie Klein. p 207

The only part of this time in his life my grandfather shared in his autobiography had to do with his new marriage to Fay. He described his "blissful honeymoon" around the continent in great detail. It lasted a month.

After their return, Pryns continued his analysis with Dr. Jones while concentrating on setting up his and Fay's new home in London. He also had the school in France to run. In his journals, however, Pryns reveals a secret side of himself Fay may never have known. The next batch of journal pages I will quote begins in March of 1934, almost five months after Eileen died, and about three months after Prince married Fay. The newlyweds are living in London.

From this point in the journal there are no missing page slices. Grandpa must have learned to keep his journals locked in a safe place.

> March 6, 1934, London: I had tea with my little daughter and Marie. Vernon gave me a present. A lovely enlargement of a snapshot of the children and their mummie bathing at Worthing.

Mom inserted, "Worthing is an English seaside town in Sussex. I met Vernon's father and sister there before Mother and Vernon married. I believe Vernon used to live there, and it was where he first kept his tomato greenhouses. Worthing was about an hour east of Berri Court, where we moved after my mother died."

> In the evening, I attended a meeting of Psychology Society. Then Ingeborg and Jack dined with us at flat and went to see Noel Coward in his latest play "Conversation Piece."

Mom added, "Flügel! Jack and Ingeborg's last name was Flügel. I remember them. He was a psychologist. They had a daughter Erica with whom I used to play. Jack was one of Dad's colleagues at the University of London."

> Wednesday, March 7 [1934]: Last evening Fay and I spent in pleasant

domesticity and reading. This noon I lunched with Betty May and Marie.
On Saturday, [March 10] I had lunch with Betty May and her little friend Leilia whom I called for at Bot. Gardens School.
Then to the annual meeting of Lord Daire's organization, The New Commonwealth. Then Fay called for me. A nice domestic eve till 9:15, when we went to the beautiful new Curzon Cinema to see a life of Schubert filmed.
Tuesday, March 20: The days have been slipping by very fast. Fay and I have lived in wonderful harmony. I see Betty May three times a week, and hear regularly from Peter [from boarding school] and Mother. All seems well among my living dear ones. My writing goes on steadily but slowly and there are occasional lectures.
Saturday Fay took Betty May and a little boy friend of hers, Mark, to Windsor Castle.

Mom interjected, "I remember Mark. His last name was Hamilton. I'm pretty sure he was a lord."

"You mean I would have been Lady Mary if you'd married him?" I joked.

Mom smiled. Royalty only marginally impressed her.

Now we get to the part my Aunt Jennifer read to me earlier.

[Another] Saturday: noon I lunched with Betty May.
At 3:30 I kept an appointment made by a young lady by phone with a spiritualist medium, Mrs. Annie Brittain of 28 St. Stephens Rd. She scored a remarkable number of "hits", also, though, of "misses." She described a spirit sitting on the arm of my chair and putting an arm around me, oval-faced, brown-haired, laughing in manner, very childlike in many ways, looking only 36 although really about 43. She had had pains in her left upper arm and right thigh. It was her heart had caused her death.
She mentioned the names Betty, Peter, Joyce, Arthur and Marie, but was vague about them except that we must look after Peter. Said I would follow her into the next world not long hence, that she loved me always, that our love was spiritual rather than physical. Said life had been very complex and full of worries for her. Mentioned she was one of five sisters and four brothers, of whom one had died (really remarkable!) [I asked] for proofs of her identity that I could verify when I phoned Peggy to-day, she said Peggy

was wearing a pendant of hers with small blue stone and a ring (wrong!); but Peggy says she has neither one, only a bracelet. Asked what Joyce has heard from Harold, she gave an impossible reply. She had no views as to what should be done with Betty May at this crisis!

We learn shortly that Pryns and Fay considered letting neighbors adopt Betty May and Peter.

She was muddled about Vernon and Fay. The medium said it seemed as if the lady had 2 husbands! She had suffered from cold feet.

I wondered if this referred to the reservations Eileen had about marrying Prince?

At the end of the séance there were so many wild shots and failures to deal with matters that would have been vital to the real Eileen that I went away unconvinced. But as I review it now, the number of hits does seem almost too many to account for by mere chance. It calms me at least to think I have tried to communicate. And curiously, it made me feel all the more affectionately toward Fay.

Did Grandpa add the last line in case Fay found the journal?

Monday, March 26: This week has passed busily and quite happily. The great excitement has been plans for getting Fay presented at court. Lady Cynthia Coleville, lady in waiting to the queen, was got by Miss Lickwell [possibly Tickwell] to offer to do so, but as an American, the request has to come through our embassy. They say they can't add any more to their list. But a Col. Egerton has told Fay he could get them to do it.
Saturday pm: Fay motored Marie and Betty May to a children's party at Marie Stope's house near Woking. We stopped en route to show Betty May her new school. She likes it but is very unhappy at leaving her present one. I'd had a long talk with her about it before noon, at Fay's wise suggestion.
To-day I was to have seen the exhibition of children's work at Betty May's school but forgot. I lunched at the flat and Fay had there her mother, whose birthday it was. Immediately afterward I remembered and went to the

> school. I then called on Betty May to be scolded. But she laughed and only talked seriously about leaving the school. Should we, after all send her to the Prior's? So thinks Marie, who called on Fay for tea (and Fay asked me to come to hear).

Mom explained, "The Priors were neighbors of Vernon's in Sussex. Their children were taken care of by one of Popsy's sisters. So, they must have known Vernon before he moved to Sussex. Mrs. Prior was very stern and Scottish, with a very strong accent. She had a son, Ian, and a daughter whose name was Maureen, I think. They also had an adopted daughter named Avril, and I think they were determined to adopt me and maybe Peter. I found out about all this later, after the negotiations were over."

"I can't imagine your father giving you up!"

"No, I don't think he would have, but that seems to have been the discussion. It's a good thing he didn't, because later Mr. Prior ended up running away with his kitchen maid or something. Actually, it wasn't a maid, but it was someone much younger. I don't know where he had found her."

> To-day's greatest event, though, was a visit to another spiritualist medium, Mrs. Mason. The appointment was made last Tuesday for me by Mr. Besterman telephoning to the London Spiritualist Alliance and mentioning my name. I went there 2:30 today for a sitting. Mrs. Mason is a very sincere-seeming woman. She commenced with some simple explanations of how Maisie, her control, liked questions asked and by telling me not to mention any names or dates but let everything be given by the spirits. My notes are as follows:
>
> Maisie (suddenly animated via Mrs. Mason who had been quiet for 5 or more minutes): There are a lady and a gentleman. The lady is young, looks about 30. She has an oval face, brown hair, is not very stout. The gentleman is between 50 and 75, nearly bald, hair otherwise grey, has a slight stoop. His recent illness was in the lower part of his body. Do you recognize either of these?
>
> I: The lady.
>
> Maisie: Her manner to you is affectionate. She passed away suddenly, though

she was in bad condition before that. It was accompanied by difficulty in breathing. There was talk of her going away just before she passed and it was cut off. She says so often you have thought if she had taken this journey she would not have died; but it would have been just the same. She thanks you for the flowers.
I: What does she feel about Fay and Vernon?
Maisie: Vernon is a small boy. You are distressed about them. You are having difficulty with them, especially Fay.

Peter is already being sent to Melanie Klein.

I: I mean, about them in the next life.
Maisie: She is smiling. Says, over there all is love. All earthly ties are gone.
I: What of my subsequent marriage?
Maisie. There is no marriage in the spiritual life. What counts is the strongest affinity. There is that link which doesn't exist with Fay and the same applies to Vernon. It has not altered her love for you. Through all eternity she says she is your wife.

Thinking that my grandfather was revealing his own thoughts during his séance, I stopped reading at this point and looked up. "Mom, do you think there is a spiritual life or an afterlife?"

"I don't know. All I know is that there is a God."

"How do you know?"

"I just know there is. But I don't think there is any communication between him and me."

"What do you mean?"

She shrugged her shoulders, as if to say, "I don't know that, either." It was also my cue to end the discussion and go back to reading.

I: What about the other [child]?
Maisie: Is it a girl?
I: No.
Maisie: A little boy. She doesn't get into communication with him so well. To him she seems simply dead. To the girl she's not so. Isn't he about 8 years?
I: Yes, about.

Maisie: About 8 or 10. He is brilliant although he doesn't show it yet. His health is better; he used to be weakly. His memory is not retentive. You have considered whether it was all right about his studies. You should alter or change his school. He is not able in this school to give full expression to himself.

Her name begins with E.

I: Yes!

Maisie: and there's a "t" in it. Sounds like Eelen, or Ellen.

I: Much like that.

Maisie: Did you call her Nell? Eelen, I get—a vibration—I give it as that.

I: What was my pet name for her, or hers for me?

Maisie: She puts a letter like P for you. Sounded like Pip. Sounds like Pin. Pinna. Something like Pinney.

I: "Pin" is quite near it. And what did I call her?

Maisie: I only get Eileen.

I: That's her real name!

Maisie: I get here a Peter. She says he's at school.

I: Yes.

Maisie: She says, "I haven't a sister."

There are four brothers.

I: Yes!

Maisie: She says, "There were five of us"—girls, that must be.

I: Yes.

Maisie: You have not been remarried long. She is glad you remarried. She is sorry for Vernon in a way, although he brought his condition on himself.

I: When shall I rejoin you?

Maisie: She cannot answer. That is in the hands of the universal spirit.

I: What did she die of?

Maisie: Intestinal condition. An operation. She couldn't get her breath. No it was her throat. She suffocated. Was she gassed?

I: No. What got her so run down? And what was it I last said to her?

Maisie: You wished her to wait for you.

I: No.

Maisie: To stay with you. Was it an operation? For it was in a nursing home. The breath! It was pneumonia. I am registering a pain in the look. There was talk of drawing fluid away. Her heart gave out.

I: Yes!

Maisie: She died of heart failure.

I: What present did I bring her?

Maisie: You put roses on her bed. You brought her scent. You brought her lilies.

I: How did you feel about my going back to London? You know how I felt?

Maisie: She didn't know she was going to die although she said she did. She was coming on drowsy. You had to get back. You thought if you had stayed you might have seen the end.

She speaks of Fay. She says she was with her mother. She talks of "Sister, sister, sister!"

I: Where do you most wish we had got a home?

Maisie: She speaks of over the water. I see only scenery. It is a hilly place. She is getting harder to hear, now. She is tired. She would rather you come again another time.

I thought the interaction between my grandfather and the medium extraordinary. It *did* seem as if the medium knew things only my grandmother's spirit could have communicated to her. Was my grandfather so in love that he would believe anything? And how could he have been so invested in this procedure while he was married to Fay?

Tuesday, March 27

Last evening—Fay and I, after dinner, had coffee chez Malinovski.[3] There we met the American Paul Robeson (Negro singer) as well as Mrs. Malinovski and others. Cyril Bunt and wife came later and we invited them to the chateau.

This morning: I phoned Vernon. He had dined last with the Priors and ascertained they still would like Betty May and Peter to come into their household so soon as Ellsworthy Road is sold.

Fay phoned; but instead of being pleased when I told her the news she went

---

3. Possibly Rodion Malinovsky, or a relation. Wikipedia: Rodion Yakovlevich Malinovsky (23 November 1898 — 31 March 1967) was a Soviet military commander in World War II and Defense Minister of the Soviet Union in the late 1950s and 1960s. He contributed to the major defeat of Nazi Germany at the Battle of Stalingrad and the Battle of Budapest. During the postwar era he made a pivotal contribution to the strengthening of the Soviet Union as a military superpower.

into a most irrational talk about my not being grateful for her interest in the children, her having already more than enough worries with the house-party, her mother's home-hunting and her own health! Only when I asked her to lunch at Jardin des Gourmets was she consoled.

Noon. – A happy lunch. Fay had felt unloved.

Wednesday, 28 March: Yesterday p.m. I had tea with Betty May. Then Fay and I went to Lady Savory's cocktail party. Fay departed early to dine with friends in the suburbs.

Friday, June 8: Yesterday I received a copy of the famous 'Ritual Murder' number of the Nazi organ Des. Lunching in the [University] staff refectory I showed it around.

After lunch Vernon and I met at Thurland's[4] and [I] went with him to the Public Trustee's office to talk about implications of my marriage settlement [child support] for Betty May.

I wondered if he settled anything on Peter.

Afterwards, I told Vernon I'd stand behind him if he purchased the house at Worthing and have confirmed in letter today.

Apparently Vernon considered purchasing a house in Worthing before he found Berri Court.

At 4:30 I consulted a medium, Mrs. Abbott, at London Spiritual Alliance. She said she saw (a) a man, whose description corresponds to no one, and (b) a lady of 40, or thereabouts though she doesn't look it. 'Her nose is well molded. She has brown hair. She smiles—a lovely smile. She has good breadth under the chin. Her face is oval.'

But the hopes this description raised were quite dashed by everything said afterwards. The medium was a complete imposter. I came away much disheartened.

I commented to my mother, "Wow, Mom! Your father must have

4. Law firm of Guscotte Wadham Thurland & Howard, Solicitors, 19, Essex Street, Strand. W.C.2. London. Francis Edward Thurland.

felt really badly about your mother's death to keep returning to the mediums behind Fay's back. I don't remember any of this being in his autobiography. He loved your mother very much."

"Yes, I guess he did."

"It was she who left the marriage, wasn't it?"

"Yes."

"I keep thinking about that poem your mother wrote about Grandpa being away all the time for his causes?"

"Yes, that's exactly the reason my mother gave me for why she left my father."

> Last night Fay and Cyril Wilson and I dined with Baron de Stempel.
> This noon Giacomo lunched with me at Jardin de Gourmets and discussed painting Eileen's portrait. I brought him back to the 'lab' to point out her best photos in the 2 albums, which I handed over to him.

I asked Mom if she knew of any portrait of her mother.

"I seem to remember that Fay learned about the commission through the artist's wife and threatened to break off her engagement to Daddy if he didn't cancel it. However, this entry is after Fay and Daddy are already married. I don't think such a painting exists.

> June 25: On Saturday we went to hear Betty May in Miss Ritz' pupil's piano recital. She did well, although she seemed nervous and said she was. That eve Fay and I went to see a play.

"Daddy took me into London to buy the piano that you now have when I was seven," said Mom, "right after my mother died. Since you've pointed out I had my eighth birthday a week after her death, perhaps the piano was my birthday present. Daddy was probably trying to make me feel better."

> Sunday we stayed abed till after noon, reading. At 3 we had a tennis party – Marcus, Prof. Spearman, the Salebys and me.

"Marcus was Fay's brother," Mom said, forgetting that I knew that.

He was my stepcousin Paul's father and I met him a couple of times.

"I also recall Professor Spearman," Mom added. "He was one of Dad's colleagues like Jack Flügel at the University of London. All those people, Spearman and Flügel, must have come around the house frequently when I was there, because I remember them well."

> Then to dine at Mother Cartledge's house.

"He's talking about Fay's mother now," said Mom. "You knew her growing up in Pasadena as *Gaga*. Her full name was Dorret Mary Cartledge. Fay's father must have passed away before we left for America."

> When we'd gone to bed Fay was sad, saying for days an old event, namely Countess Soleby and Eileen's letters, had filled her thoughts.
>
> This noon I would have lunched with Betty May but she told me she preferred to lunch with her school-mates! As I returned to college OdouPor [sic] met me and lunched with me at Escargot Bienvenue. Thence I went to London Spiritualist Alliance and had séance with Mrs. Mason and her control, Maisie.
>
> M: The lady shows a strong link with you, almost wife. I think she has not passed away very long since.
>
> I: True.
>
> M: I see the letter E. She is certainly wife, I think. She is speaking of a child, but on the earth plane. You understand?
>
> I: Yes.
>
> M: Perhaps there was an operation as there was a pain in the side

Mom interrupted again. "I wonder if Daddy was worrying about my mother's cesarean wound. I used to think it was my fault she got sick because I thought the cesarean wound had become infected again. It was nice to know from the death certificate that she died of her heart condition, not the wound."

I smiled at Mom for a second, then moved on.

> She is speaking of a little boy. She says she has seen the child's mother.

Would you understand a little girl?
I: Yes
M: She says she is so pleased regarding what you have done to the grave.

This is the mention of a grave I would cling to. *There had to be a grave somewhere!*

M: She shows me some flowers in memory of her on her home.
I: Does she like what I'm having K.L. do?
M: Is it a painting or sculpture?
I: It is!
M: It is like a sculpture and turned into a picture. She says you have only recently done it.

And this was the entry that made me wonder if my grandfather commissioned a sculpture or stained glass window.

I: What did she tell Dr. J[ones] that I have no knowledge of?
M: She's talking of her illness. She says she talked with him of an operation. She spoke to him of going away.
I: Yes, but I knew all that!
M: Also a condition of being abroad. It is only a few months since she came over.
I: Yes!
M: She says she hadn't settled down in home condition.
I: Yes.
M: She says she came the other day, but had difficulty getting through. It was not by Mrs. Mason.
I: Yes, true! What about what we're doing for the little girl?
M: She speaks of the little girl's school, and of being with her grandmother. She saw you this morning speaking to her photograph and asking her mentally to come. The letter L is connected with her, and the letter E. She has tried to make some noise to get your attention in the house. The little girl is going away.
I: How does she like the arrangements for the little girl? A girl about 7.
M: The arrangements for the holidays she likes.

I: How does she like the arrangements for the boy?

M: He is going away to school, to a larger school, to a public school. This makes him feel at home. Father in spirit world.

I: No.

M: Is it your father?

I: Yes.

M: He has been helping her to come back again. You want to believe she is living. It will help her if you think of her as living.

I was amazed my grandfather felt so guilty about his ex-wife's death and that he was so insecure about making decisions with Fay.

From here on he marked the medium's comments with a system of checks and x marks. The check marks indicated a hit, and the x marks indicated a miss.

I: I could believe if she would relate something she told Dr. Jones which I don't know but could verify from him.

M: You asked that through the other medium. [check mark]

I: Why can't she tell?

M: Because she is not a strong communicator. She was talking to him about a journey; also about the boy. He was not so strong as a little chap.

I: Will she tell what she thinks about Scotland?

M: She says you are going to Scotland and that idea is rather good. [x mark] You are going there for some time. [x mark] The house is away in the country. Go to Johann's medium. Try automatic writing.

I: How shall I get in touch with Johann's medium?

M: Ask downstairs. She sends her love to you and the children.

Here ended the séance—rather disappointing. I found that Johann's medium was a Mrs. Dowden and made an appt. for next Monday.

I think each eve this week Fay and I have been out somewhere. Thursday it was to Quaglino's Grill. I having declined the invitation of the aviatrix Peggy Solomon whom we met at a Mr. Schweder's cocktail to go to a midnight country dance. (Fay took it very sweetly.)

Betty May lunched with me Wednesday. Yesterday I'd promised to call at her school at 12:30 to take her out. I completely forgot and the poor little girlie had no lunch till 2:15. I raced over to apologize when I thought of it on way back from a tennis lesson, about 6:15.

Mom didn't remember this incident.

Monday, July 9, 1934: A week ago to-day I consulted Mrs. Dowden, Johann's medium. She gave me some hope. Her manner seemed at the start to copy Eileen's own vivacious way as she said, 'Plincikin, it is your own wife Eileen.' She started with an Ouija board. She surprised me by spelling out "MAUD" as the name of the spirit. (A man spirit 'was' also there but was dismissed.) Asked to spell her first name she gave EILEEN, and to spell Eileen's pet name for me gave PLINCIKIN, with fair speed. She also quickly spelled out Betty May's and Peter's names. Peter's relation to her as ADOPTED SON and BM's as MY OWN DAUGHTER, the last two with astonishing celerity. But the medium may easily have got cues unconsciously from my eyes glancing at expected letters or from the touch of my fingers on the back of her hand.

At the end I was not convinced Eileen's spirit had spoken to me yet my skepticism was a little shaken and I felt very comforted. I had a message to Dr. Jones which was to test it being something more than a reading of my own mind, namely that she thanked him for the help he had given her in her difficulties in getting to sleep.

Next morning I put it to Dr. Jones whether she'd been so troubled. He said in the last year it was her chief problem. Even so it is not complete proof, for sleeplessness is a thing patients often ask their doctors to help them with. That I'd known little of this is however true, and he'd helped her.

Last week was a very social one. I took most of the afternoons off.

Tuesday Fay and I went to the tennis at Wimbledon, and again Thursday.

Friday we went to the regatta at Henley. We saw Princeton and then Yale defeated by English crews.

Saturday we went to polo at Ranelagh. There I ran across the LeJeune girls who were at Biarritz. Fay at first didn't wish to meet them fearing I must have had an affair, but later she softened.

Yesterday we took Audrey [Fay's sister] swimming at the 'Lido' and then to see a beautiful English garden. We dined at their mother's house.

This afternoon I had tea with Betty May and Marie. Just afterward, Peggy and Jack Abbott arrived from Scotland bringing their little John. All looked very fat and healthy. John is full of charm.

Friday, July 27: Yesterday morning Mrs. Whimvey [my secretary] came in to my office for the last time, as she's off for her holiday. She flashed the hotel receipt 'G' had sent her for 'Mr. and Mrs. E. G. Whimvey', which gives her the long hoped for grounds for her divorce.

In the afternoon, Fay and I went to the royal garden party. She wore the same pink dress and picture-hat that she did to Ascot. We had drinks afterward at the Dorchester, then spent a quiet evening at home, very congenially.

Tuesday, July 31, 1934: This is the next-to-last entry to be made in this diary, as I shan't take it to America when we sail, day after to-morrow.

On Friday morning Fay met Peter at the station as he returned from school, and took him to Ellsworthy Road. He looked brown and healthy. His school report is bad as always—8th in a form of 9. I lunched with the children and Marie and Mrs. Fiennes and Vernon. At 4:30 Mrs. Fiennes brought them to have tea with us at the flat. Then Fay and I took them boating in the little boats in Regents Park.

Saturday morning I went to St. Pancras Station to see Marie take the children to Scotland [to visit their Aunt Peggy and Uncle Jack]. Of course I was overwhelmed with memories of the last time Marie and they and I had been at such a departure within a few days of a year ago. She of course recalled it too, and Peter, too. Betty May had repressed the memory.

In the afternoon, Fay and I drove to the Howard Park Hotel, played tennis, dined and had a chat with Mr. Howard re Samarkand.

Sunday morning we read abed.[5] At noon we drove out to Kew Gardens. It was almost new to Fay and I enjoyed showing her the big water.

The next page had two photos pasted on it: one of my mother standing in a garden with the caption "B.M. in the garden of the Prior house, Westwood" and the other of Mom and a young boy who must have been the lord, with the caption, "B.M. and Mark." This was followed by a single entry:

---

5. I love the line, "read abed"! I think of it now every time I want to stay under the covers and read on a Sunday. Grandpa and Fay were probably dressed in silk satin robes and had been served breakfast by one of their maids. I make my own tea. Occasionally, I get out a silver tray and pretend someone served it to me.

> Sunday, November 18: Our chauffeur, Wichman, ran me out to Abinger Hill. There I picked up Peter. We lunched with Betty May, Marie, Vernon and Mrs. Fiennes. We mostly did not speak of that of which this day was the terrible anniversary. When I reached London, I 'stopped in' at Cranleigh Gardens for the first time in all these years since..."

This is the reference to Cranley Gardens I would remember and wonder if it was the location of Eileen's grave.

Grandpa ended his sentence with the dot dot dot, not I. Mom didn't remember Wichman.

In *Both Hands Before the Fire,* Grandpa finished his narration about Eileen's death by saying he attempted to do two things to help keep his first wife's memory alive. One was to bind all her letters, which I would find in that scrapbook some thirty years later. The other was to commission a portrait. Mom told us what happened to that. With no scrapbook and no portrait, it appeared to be up to me to keep my grandmother's memory alive.

Lionel Turner – Cambridge, 2006.

Chapter 31

Cambridge and Lionel

On the Sunday I was scheduled to visit my second-cousin-once-removed Lionel in Cambridge, I woke up very early. The weather had finally cooled and it was a gorgeous sunny day.

I'd decided to follow Jason's advice and catch Lionel on his way to church. Thankfully, my stepcousin Carolyn agreed to meet me at Paul's house. I dressed in my flowery church skirt and headed out for the Liverpool Station to catch the train from London to Cambridge.

Knowing Jason commuted to London each weekday, I was appalled by the whopping £25 charge for my ticket. The trip took a little over an hour. The first leg whizzed me past suburban backyards of narrow brick row houses. I noted that though the neighborhoods seemed poor and run down, an impressive percentage of the yards contained healthy green kitchen gardens. In contrast, the views during the final leg of the trip reminded me of Gainsborough landscape paintings. Tall gangly trees overlooked lush riverbeds, green fields, shafts of wheat waving in the breeze and plump grazing cows. I hadn't seen any evidence of the recent epidemic of mad cow disease during my trip.

After arriving in Cambridge, I purchased a half-dozen fresh yellow roses for Jason and his wife from a chic Marks & Spencer shop in the station.

I spied a red double-decker bus across the road from the station with "Town Centre" on its placard. The driver told me he would be passing very near Trumpington Road, on which both my real cousin Jason and my stepcousin Paul lived. Trumpington Road extended from Cambridge to the smaller village of Trumpington. Paul lived at the Trumpington end, Jason at the Cambridge end. The bus driver let me off at the west edge of town and told me to continue west to find Trumpington Road. I tried calling Jason's mobile number to see if Lionel had left for church yet, but he didn't answer.

I made my way through the medieval buildings of Peterhouse College, appreciating that my ancestor William Brewster had been a student there in 1580. Then I stopped at a small magazine shop and purchased a detailed map of Cambridge. I was a little confused. I'd written Jason's address in my book as 5 Belvoir Terrace, yet he had told me on the phone he lived on Trumpington Road. From the map I could see that Belvoir Terrace was a tiny offshoot of the road. I continued on down Trumpington, but ten minutes farther realized I was no longer carrying the yellow roses. I retraced my steps to the magazine shop, where I assumed I'd left them. The shopkeeper said he'd never seen any yellow roses. It was a very small shop and I couldn't see them anywhere, either. Wishing I were a little less scatterbrained, I had to accept the fact that I'd probably left them on the bus. *Oh well, the kind driver can take them home to his wife.*

By then I was probably too late to reach Jason's house before Lionel left for church. I reasoned that Lionel would have to walk toward me on Trumpington Road, so I stared at each pedestrian as they approached me on the sidewalk. Only one person looked old enough to be Lionel, a man coming toward me on a bicycle. Knowing full well that Lionel wouldn't be riding a bicycle to church if he were in the beginning stages of Alzheimer's, I yelled, "Are you Lionel?" anyway.

The fellow looked at me peacefully, said, "Good morning" as if he hadn't heard me and continued on his way.

I finally reached Belvoir Terrace. The street didn't shoot off Trumpington at all. It wasn't even a street, like terraces are in America, but more of an alley that paralleled the real street and only eight houses long!

Only Number 6 was marked. That gave me a two-to-one chance of hitting Number 5 on either side of it. Still only nine o'clock in the morning, I didn't want to knock on any wrong doors in case non-church-going residents slept in.

I picked the nearest house, walked through its gate and up a long walkway between some tall bushes. I hoped that when I came closer to the front door, I'd find a number near it, but I didn't. The door was painted yellow like my roses. I took a chance. I grasped the lion-headed door-knocker and gave it a tap-tap.

Jason had told me his family was attending a party Saturday night as part of the music festival and would be out until the wee hours of the morning. With Lionel off to church, I wondered if Jason still slept.

I waited. Nothing happened. After a few minutes I tapped a little harder. Still nothing happened. So I sat on the steps and retrieved my mobile phone from my handbag once again. This time Jason picked up after six rings. In a very thick, sleepy, but friendly and welcoming voice he said, "Hello?"

"This is your cousin Mary. I think I'm on your doorstep."

"Well, that's good. I'm in my dressing gown. I'll come on down."

"I hope I have the right place. Do you have a yellow door?"

"All the doors are yellow," he said good-naturedly.

I looked around. "Do you have three bicycles parked against the wall leading up your front path?"

"You've said the magic words." The door opened.

Jason was just as handsome in his dressing gown as he would be in his business suit the following day, in spite of lack of sleep. He had the same oval face and brown hair as my mother. He gave me a kiss on each cheek and ushered me through the door.

I was in love with the high ceilings of the older homes in England. One could be in the smallest of places and still feel like you were in a grand palace with such a ceiling. Jason's house was very spacious. I entered a long front hall. A dining room opened to the right, and just a little farther down the hall we entered a large kitchen. I saw a good-sized neglected garden through the kitchen window as Jason filled the teakettle with water and asked me if I liked instant coffee.

I put my bags down in a corner of the dining room. The straps had been cutting a canyon through the top of my shoulder. I glanced around the casual, homey residence. Coasters scattered about the dining table, like remnants of previous conversations, indicating that when one stopped another began. Apparently, life went in and out of that dining room on a continuous basis. Chairs, left pushed away from the table by a previous resident, invited me to sit down.

I heard footsteps in the hall. Soon another handsome dark-haired man about my son's age walked into the kitchen. "This is my nephew Oliver," Jason said.

Oliver also looked a tad crumpled and blurry eyed. He helped himself to a cup and then finished making the instant coffee Jason had started but abandoned to find something in another room.

"Are you related to Jason through his father?" I asked Oliver.

"Yes."

"Then we are cousins."

"Fantastic!"

I'd noticed *fantastic* was a popular expression in England among people Oliver's age. Candy used it a lot, too, when I talked to her on the phone. I felt good when they said it, but it was a new expression to me.

With instant coffee in hand, Oliver joined me in the dining room and sat down. I took out my laptop to show him how we were related. Jason joined us, and we were reviewing what I'd explained to Oliver when another face popped through the door.

This was Ioana, Jason's wife, a petite gentle-looking woman with a round face accented by a beautiful circle of pearls that, I realized the following morning, she must always wear. She also looked as if she'd gotten up sooner than she wanted to. I felt guilty for intruding. She gave me a warm hug and kiss on each cheek.

I soon learned she had met Jason in Romania, where he'd been building a software company, and where she had grown up. Now they had a fifteen-year-old daughter named Sophie. Unfortunately, Sophie was away visiting friends for the weekend, and I wouldn't be able to meet her.

We then heard more shuffling in the hallway. Ioana left, returning on the arm of a very handsome elderly man about five-foot seven, also oval-faced like my mother, dressed in a coat and tie.

"Here's Lionel!" said Jason. (I don't think I ever heard Jason refer to his father as *Dad.*)

I was thrilled, though puzzled about the timing.

"Hi, Lionel," I said, standing up and reaching my hand out to greet him. "I'm Mary. I'm Pryns Hopkins' granddaughter, Betty May's daughter. I've come all the way from America to meet you."

Lionel broke into a delighted smile, "You are? That's wonderful!" Lionel wasn't part of the generation that said *fantastic.*

It turned out that Lionel had woken up too late for church that morning. *Lucky for me!* After he realized the hour, I expected him to go back to his room and change from his church clothes, but Ioana whispered to me, "He wears a tie all the time."

Then she disappeared into the kitchen to fix Lionel some tea. While I wished I could politely exchange my instant coffee for some of that tea, Lionel took the seat next to mine and the conversation turned to him. Lionel and I would stay in those two chairs for the next two hours, while others came and went.

Oliver was the first to run off. He had been in Cambridge to attend the music festival with his aunt and uncle and needed to return to London where he lived and worked. Not one to miss an opportunity, I quickly took my camera out of my bag to take his picture and then recorded his family information in my computer version of our family tree. Lucky Lionel had three sons. Oliver was one of four children of Lionel's oldest, Michael Turner, who was seventeen years older than Lionel's youngest, Jason. There was another brother between Michael and Jason named David whom I would never meet.

After Oliver left, leaving me with another hug and kiss on each cheek, Ioana told me that one of Oliver's sisters, Zoë, had accidently died just two years earlier on Guy Fawkes day. She had been fixing the latch on a window, damaged during a burglary on the previous year's

Guy Fawkes festivities. The rest of her friends, including her boyfriend, left for the events.

"I'll be right there," she told them.

When she didn't appear, her boyfriend returned for her, only to find that while she'd been using the power drill, she'd caught her hair and some clothing in the drill and had been strangled. Like my daughter Amy, Zoë had been a clothing designer and was just making her way into designing costumes for films. My heart felt very heavy. I'm sure the dark cloud of that tragedy will hover over Oliver's and Jason's families forever.

Jason returned to the dining room carrying two books that he put on the table in front of Lionel. Lionel pushed them in front of me. One was a bound photo-copied version of his journal from World War II. The original lived in a museum somewhere. The other book was a small horizontal album similar to one my mother had from the 1940s, with black paper pages. Like my mother, Lionel had written captions to the pictures with a fountain pen using white ink. As Lionel turned the pages, we took a trip down memory lane.

Occasionally, I snapped photos of the pictures in the scrapbook, especially those of my family members. There were no photographs of 17 Tettenhall Road to help Candy and me find it later.

Lionel grew up in South America. His parents, Daisy Thomas and Lionel Turner Senior, known as *Jack*, married right after the First World War. Jack went to South America as a trainee for what was then the Bank of London and S.A. Ltd., and is now Lloyds. Daisy followed him a few months later. They lived first in Uruguay, where Lionel was born in 1923, and then Argentina. That made Lionel two years older than my mother. His dementia was also more advanced than hers.

"I was always jealous of your mother," he said to me. "When my family came to visit England from South America, we stayed at 17 Tettenhall Road with our grandparents. Our grandmother always had little treats for Betty May, but never for my two sisters and me."

"Maybe it was because my mother had lost her mother," I suggested.

"Who is your mother?" asked Lionel

"Betty May, the lady in that photo," I reminded him. "I'm Pryns Hopkins' granddaughter."

"Oh, I was thinking you were Betty May."

"Nope, that's my mother."

"Well, it seemed that our grandmother liked Betty May better than the rest of us," he repeated.

Most of Lionel's stories were about his time in the Royal Air Force (RAF) for which he'd journeyed from South America to enlist. For a while he was stationed in Canada for training.

One funny story he told was about how he'd been sentenced to the RAF prison for twenty-eight days for taking an unqualified passenger in his plane. While he was in prison, he and his fellow inmates, who were in for the more serious crime of desertion, were guarded by four RAF policemen. One day Lionel and the other inmates were sent off to dig holes for a nearby farmer to plant some trees. When they finished, they and the guards stopped in town for a cool drink. The pub where they stopped was full of women and had a dance band playing.

"Here I was dressed in the same clothes I'd been digging in, dirt all over," recalled Lionel. "However, the girls all wanted to dance with me anyway. I danced every dance."

Pretty soon all but Lionel and another prisoner were so drunk they couldn't manage the trip home. Lionel and his partner piled them onto a cart partially filled with logs. Lionel drove the *lorry* [truck, which I assume was pulling the cart] back to prison with one of the guards propped up in the driver's seat so they could pass through the gate. Then Lionel and his fellow inmates put the guards to bed and locked themselves back into prison before morning light.

After two hours of listening to Lionel's stories, I needed to manage my trip to my stepcousin Paul's house about fifteen minutes down the road. I was scheduled to be there for lunch at noon and it was already 11:30. I excused myself from Lionel and called Carolyn. She answered from her car *enroute* from Wokingham and willingly agreed to pick me up on her way to Paul's, which she did. I left my bags at Jason's, where I would be returning to spend the night.

Pryns and Kichie, 1934.

Chapter 32
New Families

Referring in his autobiography to his new marriage to Fay, Pryns wrote it was the beginning of "twelve years of happiness." He shared no thoughts about what his children were going through in the meantime as they adjusted to life without their mother.

Fay demanded a more extensive trip for her honeymoon than Eileen's had been. So a few months after the first trip, Pryns took her on another voyage that took them around the world and lasted nearly a year. As soon as they returned, they began another project that distracted Pryns from his children even longer. Fay wanted to be presented at court. Acquiring this prized ticket by the upwardly mobile required wooing influential people. Once the event came about, the comings and goings of Dr. and Mrs. Pryns Hopkins were announced in the "Court" column of *The London Times*—as opposed to the activities of the "common sort." While perusing the overall index for *The Times*, I'd come across them in that column returning from one of their trips.

Pryns made no plans to regain his children's custody. On the contrary, he financially supported Vernon's purchase of an eighteenth-century house called Berri Court[1] in Yapton, Sussex, on property that had been owned by the Earl of Arundel back in 1415. The town is near the south coast of England, just east of Southampton Harbor and not far from Birdham, Chichester, where Camilla and Rodney lived. Betty May and Peter lived there for the next five years except for their time at boarding school. Vernon's widowed sister, Mrs. Fiennes, aka Auntie Gwen, moved in with them to help.

Mom dictated this description of the manor house and its magnificent garden to me back in 2000.

> I remember it's being redecorated before we moved in. The property was three acres. There was a walled garden for vegetables and fruit, a rose garden and a summer house, which Vernon turned into an aviary for budgerigars [parakeets/budgies]. He built three commercial greenhouses behind the house in which he raised his tomatoes, previously done in Worthing, Sussex.

---

1. I found this information about Berri Court on the Internet at www.british-history.ac.uk/report.aspx?compid=22949: "The manors, later manor, of Bercourt or Berecourt and Wildbridge were first so called in the mid 14th century, but presumably derived from fees or parts of fees mentioned at those places from c.1243. The under tenancy of the two manors was settled in 1364/5 on Edward de St. John and his wife Joan. Edward died between 1379 and 1386, and after Joan's death in 1386 the manors passed under the 1364/5 settlement to Sir John d'Arundel (d.1390). His son John, Lord Maltravers, was lord in 1412, and after his succession as earl of Arundel in 1415 the manors descended with the rape. They were considered a single manor by the early 15th century. In 1568 Henry FitzAlan, earl of Arundel, granted Bercourt and Wildbridge to John Edmunds. Thereafter it descended with the Yapton manor demesnes until at the death of Walter Edmunds in 1612 it passed to his son Christopher (d.1620), whose widow Mary married George Oglander in 1620 or 1621. In 1633 they conveyed the manor to William Madgwick; he or a namesake was dealing with it in 1662 and 1674 and Edward Madgwick in 1694. Another William owned land in Yapton in 1705. In 1771 William Madgwick sold manor and lands to Ann Billinghurst, whose relative John Billinghurst had been lessee in 1752. (fn. 69) After Ann's death 1798-1807 they were sold to James Penfold; at that date the lands totalled 131 acres. About 1840 John Boniface was owner of the farm and in 1877 Ann Boniface. The manor house, variously called Bury, Berea, and Berri Court in the 19th and 20th centuries, seems often to have been let from the 1880s. A manor house at Bercourt was mentioned in 1460. Its successor was called Berri Court in 1995. It is L-shaped, its outer walls and some re-used ceiling beams probably being 17th-century. Parts of the staircase and one door surround on the first floor suggest a late 18th-century remodelling, and there was a much more thorough one in the early 19th century, when a new wing was added between the existing ranges. At some date the south front was given a parapet, later removed, and in the late 19th century or early 20th a conservatory was built along it; after its removal a pedimented doorcase was added. The building materials include flint, brick, stucco, and Bognor rock sandstone. In 1946 there were well matured grounds containing fine specimen trees, a walled garden, a tennis lawn, and a tea lawn with lily pool. They remained notable in 1995, making ingenious use of the small site."

> Sometimes he kept chickens. There were lots of lovely lilac trees behind the house, and right across the street was a little candy store. We were between two pubs, the Black Dog and the Shoulder of Mutton and Cucumbers, which had a wonderful sign.
>
> I had one of the two large upstairs bedrooms in front of the house. Vernon had the other. A large bedroom in back was the guestroom, but it was hardly ever used. Peter slept there when he had appendicitis. Usually his room was the dressing room between Vernon's room and the large bathroom.
>
> Auntie Gwen had a small bedroom next to the guest room and a smaller bathroom, which the maids also used. They slept up on the third floor. We had an upstairs maid, downstairs maid—who was Irish and about fourteen, the same age as Peter—and our cook, Mrs. Pratley. After a year, Popsy no longer worked for us.

Pryns and Fay bought a flat at 73 Portland Place. While they'd been on their world tour, they'd purchased a small gibbon (a tiny ape) that they'd named Kichie, meaning "Little Fellow" in Malay. Since Pryns and Fay's life didn't allow for a pet full-time in their home, Kichie resided primarily at the London Zoo. They checked him out for visits and cocktail parties as if he were a library book!

Kichie's introduction to Peter went well. Peter extended his hand and they became good friends. When it was my mother's turn, she "turned shy" and withdrew. Pryns thought Kichie must have "picked up on her fear." From then on Kichie bared his teeth whenever he saw her.

"I remember the flat my father and Fay had in London after they were married," said Mom. "Daddy had an office for himself in the modern style and Fay had a boudoir more her taste. They had a car and a chauffeur who lived close by. Perhaps that was Wichman."

Peter had turned eleven before moving with his sister and Vernon to Yapton and was sent directly to the Stowe School as a boarder. It was located northwest of London about an hour by train. Pryns enrolled Betty May, by then eight, as a day student in St. Michael's in Bognor Regis, about seven miles from Yapton. When she turned nine, she became a weekly boarder and from then on returned to Yapton only on weekends.

"How did you like Vernon?" I asked Mom.

"He was a pedophile!"

"What do you mean?" I asked, horrified.

"He would touch me in a funny way when he put me to bed each night," she said, almost matter-of-factly.

"Where would he touch you?"

Mom shook her head, refusing to give me any more details. "I just thought he needed a wife," she said. "I think it was worse for Peter, who didn't like Vernon at all."

I called Peter again. "What do you remember about Berri Court?"

"It had beautiful gardens. I think it has been turned into smaller houses now."

"I have a difficult question for you. Please let me know if you don't want to answer it."

"I can't remember anything between when I was twenty-five and last week."

"Well, this question is about before you were twenty-five."

"What is it?"

"Did Vernon ever sexually abuse you?"

Peter went quiet for a short time. Then he repeated my question so Josée, who was near him in the room, could hear it. "No. What he used to do was get in bed with me. The bedrooms at Berri Court were off a hallway. Betty May had the room on the left side of the hall and Vernon had the room on the right side of the hall. Next to Vernon's room, between his bedroom and the bathroom was the dressing room. That was my room. When Vernon walked to the bathroom he would have to go through my room. He would get into bed with me, but nothing would happen. Nothing serious happened."

Josée got on the line. She must have grabbed the phone from Peter.

"Yes he did," she said with her French accent. "There was something bad going on with Vernon, but I'm not sure what. I think Peter is blocking it out."

I could hear some debate going on from Peter nearby. Josée said something back to him that I couldn't understand. Then Peter got back on the line.

"I guess something might have happened, but I don't remember. I don't think it was anything serious."

"I understand. Were you afraid of Vernon? Did he ever beat you?"

"Oh, no! Vernon was a docile individual. Looking back on those days, I wish he had been more in charge, taken better care of me, been more protective."

"Was he somewhat of a puppet to your father? To my grandfather?"

"Berri Court was a big, big house and a huge land investment. I don't think Vernon could have afforded that on his own."

I confirmed that Grandpa stated in his journal he helped Vernon finance the house.

"He must have. Vernon had a beautiful garden, and he ran a commercial nursery business about sixty miles away in Worthing. But Vernon never amounted to much. He was always being taken care of by someone else."

I thought about some photos I'd seen in my mother's scrapbook of Vernon and Katherine at Berri Court. Vernon had sent them to Mom in California, in 1944, four years after Mom left and some two or three years after Peter left. *Had Vernon been living there all that time at Pryns' expense? Was he supposed to be providing a home base for Peter?*

"I wish I had been more important to him," said Peter. "After I left for the service, Vernon seemed to disappear from my life completely. I didn't write him one letter, and he didn't write me one letter. He'd gone off with Gwen, who I didn't even realize was his sister. A long time afterward, I found out that they had gone to East Africa. My recollection was that one of Gwen's sons took the two of them to East Africa, where he lived and presumably looked after them. There was no reason for losing touch with Vernon, it wasn't as if something bad happened, or that I was bad."

My heart bled. Peter still wondered if he'd been at fault in some way. I didn't have the courage to ask him if he knew the Prior Family offered to adopt him and my mother. Therefore, I also couldn't ask him if he thought the Priors suspected Vernon's inappropriate behavior and were trying to rescue the children from it.

"Didn't you even know Vernon remarried?"

"No."

"Do you remember anything good about Vernon?" I asked Mom.

"Yes. He taught me how to press flowers."

Mom pressed flowers with me, too, when we toured the countryside of Italy, and later, with flowers from our garden at home. She purchased blotter paper from a stationery store and cut them in squares that fit inside a book. Violets were the most obliging. After laying them between two sheets of blotter paper, we weighed the book down under a stack of other books for a few days until the flowers were flat and dry.

"Vernon also helped me get my eyes fixed," Mom said. "I'd been born cross-eyed and wore glasses when I was little."

I'd seen the photos of tiny Mom in her adult-sized glasses. She peeked out of her pram looking like an owl.

"Did you have an operation?" I asked.

"No, Vernon sent me to London to see a specialist."

"What did the specialist do?"

"He gave me some sort of electric shock therapy, and I had to do some exercises."

"How old were you?"

"I think I was twelve. I took the train in from Bogner Regis to London. Maybe Auntie Gwen went with me. I didn't need glasses again until my late forties."

Pryns visited his children often and without Fay. He saw Peter at Stowe School on Saturdays, when the school held games and matches. Then on Sundays he traveled two hours southwest to Yapton. He rented horses, and he and my mother rode together in the South Downs. Afterward, he, Vernon and Auntie Gwen sometimes sat on the terrace of Berri Court for a glass of sherry.

In contrast to Fay's lack of involvement with the children, her younger sister, Audrey, became very attached to my mother. As I mentioned, there was only a ten-year age difference between them. Pryns paid for Audrey to attend art school. He'd decided he ought to help Fay's three siblings more substantially than he'd helped Eileen Maude's. When a teaching job opened up at St. Michael's, Pryns "helped" get Audrey the position. By help I assume he gave the school some financial incentive.

He wrote that "it was to Betty May's great joy."

When I asked my mother about it she declared, "I didn't like it one bit. It's not a good thing having one's family member be a teacher at your school."

By 1937 Hitler had declared himself emperor of Germany. In spite of the turbulent political landscape, Pryns planned a sketching tour through Italy with Betty May, by then twelve. Peter elected not to join them. My mother remembered this time with her father as "one of the best."

Father and daughter started in Milan, and then settled in Florence at the "homelike and delightful Pensione Consili," from which they took excursions among the "architectural, sculptural and pictorial treasures of the town." They began each morning by picking a spot where Betty May could sketch and Pryns could write on his tablet or otherwise busy himself nearby. They were "favored by sunny weather." Pryns had given my mother a copy of George Eliot's novel *Romola* that took place in Florence. After reading it with "great interest," she tried to retrace the medieval streets mentioned in the tale in the modern town. Pryns described the trip as "altogether a companionable holiday."

Both children joined Pryns—again without Fay, who was pregnant with Jennifer—for the following Easter vacation of 1938. Though he hadn't been on a bicycle since he was a child, Pryns arranged a bicycling trip through Holland. Betty May was allowed to invite her school friend Rosemary to join them, as well as one of Rosemary's four sisters. My mother remembered how one day Rosemary's sister wasn't looking where she was bicycling and plunged into a canal.

They cycled through endless fields of blooming tulips and along the flat roads lining the canals to Delft. As they continued on to Le Hague, they noticed the newspapers "ablaze" with horrific news that Hitler threatened to invade the Netherlands. All young Dutchmen were joining colors to stop him. The Hopkins party immediately returned to England, but they didn't stop bicycling. Peter, nicknamed "the great lieutenant," quickly arranged for them to continue through the tulip-growing region of northern England.

Shortly after their return, Fay gave birth to Jennifer, who quickly earned the nickname *Little Duchess.* "Fay's boudoir was turned into a night nursery," said Mom. "The nurse would sleep in the same room as the baby. The day nursery was more of a playroom."

Left to right: unidentified, Fay holding baby Jennifer, and Pryns – 1938.

Even though Pryns and Fay were only into their fifth year of "twelve years of bliss," Pryns wrote that after Jennifer's birth, "Fay stopped feeling for me as she had before."

Since he also wrote they were contemplating divorce, she must have banned him from her bedroom. They decided to wait and hope that time would "bring a happier solution." I was struck by how bleak my grandfather looked in the photo of Jennifer's Christening.

There was still no talk of reclaiming custody of Peter and Betty May. Pryns probably feared that the addition of his two teenage children to his household might tip the scales and cause Fay to leave. Peter had turned into a handsome fifteen-year-old. Though very bright, he acted out against both his stepmother and stepfather, gaining a reputation for being "a handful."

At thirteen, Betty May was also tall and beautiful. Neither child would have given Fay an advantage.

Pryns still arranged plenty of trips. The following summer, he took them to America to meet up with his mother. Fay and baby Jennifer stayed behind in England. The threesome sailed on August 4, 1938, on the *Manhattan*[2] for New York. Mom's recollection of the voyage on the ship was that "the waiter we had was miffed he'd been assigned to second class instead of first, and had to wait on us instead of the more POSH passengers."

"You didn't travel first class?" I exclaimed.

"No, my father always traveled second class. He didn't want to appear ostentatious."

I wondered if it would have been different had Fay been along.

May Hopkins hooked up with them in New York, and the whole group continued on to Canada. They spent their vacation first at Le Chateau Frontenac, then at the Murray Bay Resort on the St. Lawrence River, which Mom remembered fondly.

"I don't recall being aware of war brewing in Europe," she said, "and I certainly didn't comprehend how that war was about to change my life."

---

2. Dr. Ronald Koegler found the manifest.

Paul and Carolyn – Cambridge, 2006.

Chapter 33

Stepcousins

Carolyn showed up at Lionel's with the top of her car down, looking lovely and ready in her sundress to enjoy a sunny garden party. Three minutes later we were driving through the entry of Paul and Judy's square, two-story house that looked like an Italian villa. The gravel crunched under the Renault's tires. It was *fantastic* seeing Paul again, and since I'd never met his wife, Judy, I was thrilled to be spending the day with her. She kept busy as an attorney and commuted to London from Cambridge each day, as my cousin Jason did. *That would wear me out!*

Sitting in their patio, surrounded by colorful flowers and green shrubs, we had a delicious lunch made and served by their charming daughter, Gabrielle, who was my daughter's age, twenty-five. Gabrielle studied to be an attorney like her mum and lived in London.

After eating, Gabrielle left for home, while Judy excused herself for a nap. Carolyn, Paul and I secluded ourselves in Paul's library with coffee and reminisced about the Hopkins and Cartledge families. We, too, spent time looking at photo albums. I noticed a contrast between my stepfamily, with whom I was very familiar, and my real family, whom I'd just met.

Paul's relationship to my grandfather was exactly the same as Jason's. They were both his nephews by marriage. However, whereas Paul knew my grandfather well after spending a summer living with him and appreciating the education Pryns helped finance, Jason knew very little about his Uncle Pryns and had not benefited in any way from Ruth Singer's inheritance.

Eileen Maude may have come from a poor family compared to my grandfather's, but it appears Fay's family was even less well off. Paul and Carolyn spent a long time speculating about who Fay's father was. Fay had four siblings including Paul's father, Marcus, and Carolyn's mother, Audrey.

"When Fay died," Carolyn said wide-eyed, "My cousin Jennifer, your aunt, came across her birth certificate. It listed a Rupert Cartwright as her father! But on my mother's and Paul's father's birth certificates the father was William Cartledge!"

"How odd!" I said. "Did she have a different father?"

"Possibly," said Paul.

"I don't think so," said Carolyn. "My mother insisted that they all had the same father.

"My theory," said Paul, "is that when Fay was born, our grandfather wasn't married to our grandmother Dorret. Maybe he was married to someone else and that's why he used a fictitious name. But by the time my father, Aunt Audrey and our uncles were born, he'd gotten rid of the other woman, married our grandmother and resumed living by his real name Cartledge."

No matter what the reason for the name discrepancy, the cousins believed Fay had been born out of wedlock. That helped explain many of her social climbing tendencies, particularly her desire to be presented at court. It seemed to me there was a lot more secrecy, though probably an equal amount of drama, in the Cartledge family than there had been in the Thomas family.

I returned to the Turner household from the Cartledge household at about 5:30 that evening. Jason and Ioana had already left to attend a Reba McEntire concert, but Lionel waited for me for our dinner date. We walked to a nearby restaurant, slowly. He was fairly steady on his feet, but one of his legs got sore and sometimes he had to stop for a few seconds to rub it.

Between the walks to and from the restaurant and our dinner together, we uncovered many more war stories. It took a concerted effort to steer the subject back to my great-grandparents. One of the things Lionel remembered was that even though other houses had electric lights, his grandparents lit 17 Tettenhall Road with candles.

"There were candles everywhere," he said. "The warm feelings I had about the house might be due partly to that."

"What do you remember about your grandfather?"

"He took me drinking, and I had to keep up with him. But I never saw him drunk."

"What about your grandmother."

"She was very sweet, but she liked Betty May much better than she liked me and my sisters," he repeated again.

"Was she a big woman or a small woman?"

"She was a little tubby, but not much."

"Was she a good cook?"

"There was a woman servant who did everything. Our grandmother just showed up for meals."

"Was the house large?"

"Well, there was a room for me, one for each of my sisters, a room for my parents and rooms for my grandparents. And there were candles everywhere." (There had also been a brother, Anthony, who died in the 90s.)

His next comment surprised me. "Eileen was sick for a long time, wasn't she?"

This was the first time he'd brought up my grandmother. I thought he meant her sickness at the end of her life, so I calculated the time between when she got sick in July and died in November. "Four months," I said. "Is that a long time?" Thinking back, maybe he meant she'd had heart disease for a long time. *Was that common knowledge?* I kicked myself later for not asking him if he remembered a funeral.

"Your grandfather Pryns was a wonderful man," he said. "He came to England once a year and took all the Thomases out to a very nice dinner, usually at the Ivy Restaurant. We all appreciated that very much. And his letters to me in the RAF were very important to me."

Lionel had shown me some of those letters earlier. They were just like the letters my grandfather wrote to me, typed out by his secretary, Betty, with his signature written at the bottom in blue ink from a fountain pen. The address for the recipient was written in the lower left corner of the letter.

I saw one of my letters to my grandfather on his desk once. With that same fountain pen, he'd methodically put check marks next to the paragraphs he planned to answer when writing back to me.

Lionel talked a lot about his wife, Dorothy, who'd died just one year earlier. He met her at a party while he was in the RAF. "It was love at first sight." They danced for a bit then went into a garden to talk. "She gave me the first degree, once over, asking me about everything. I guess I passed the test." Soon after that discussion, he took Dorothy to his quarters where they "made" their first son. That was Oliver's father, Michael.

When Lionel told his family he was getting married, they refused to attend the wedding. "My father, who simply sold supplies to pubs, for all I could see, snubbed Dorothy's father, who was a machine engineer. Yet that machine engineer had a bookshelf full of every classic you could think of! And he could quote circles around my father if he'd had to. We got married in Northumberland, where Dorothy grew up. None of my family came to the wedding."

This was the same family that pressured my grandmother to marry my grandfather for his money. Lionel married for love and had a long happy marriage. My grandparents' marriage lasted nine years.

Lionel had earlier shown me a letter from my mother written from her Scripps college address in California to him in the RAF. She'd enclosed a photo and congratulated him on his marriage to Dorothy. "Someone supported your marriage!" I said.

"Who?"

"My mother, Betty May!"

He grinned. "Yes, that is probably why I kept that letter. It was very important to me."

We didn't arrive home from the restaurant until after ten, and I was ready for bed. Everyone else was still out. I planned to return to London with Jason on his commuter train the following day. So I left a message on his mobile phone, asking him to wake me.

In anticipation the next morning, I woke at five. When I couldn't get back to sleep, I got up, showered and headed downstairs, thinking I'd write in the dining room until Jason came down. No sooner had I plugged in my laptop and sat at the table than Ioana arrived. We had a great girl chat, and she told me about the translating she was doing for a Romanian author.

I found myself envious of Jason and Iaona's house and life. How wonderful to have a home from which interesting people and relations came and went. It reminded me of my grandfather's Bohemian apartment when he first lived in London. It was as unlike my hermit life as could be. My phone hardly ever rang, and I had to push myself to invite houseguests.

On the other hand, I wondered how long Jason would be able to take care of Lionel. Jason had undertaken a huge responsibility. When my mother got to the point that she couldn't live in her large house alone, I considered pooling our income and sharing a nice place with her, as Jason was doing with Lionel. It would have been less lonely for both of us. But I quickly trashed the thought because Mom and I would have spent the whole time fighting about finances.

Grandpa had similar thoughts about his older years. One of my mother's friends told me he offered to give each of his three children money to add rooms on to their houses so he could take turns staying with them. Mom told the poor man, "Daddy, you know we don't get along with you that well."

As soon as Jason came down, we dashed to catch the train and jammed ourselves into a car crowded with commuters. Jason sat awkwardly on an upturned trash bin in the middle of the aisle next to my seat, balancing his laptop on his knee to give me a demo of the impressive new software he was developing. We reached the Liverpool Station, fought our way up through the masses to the street and then kept talking as I walked with him to his workplace. Two more kisses on each cheek and we parted.

At Jason's suggestion, I headed from there to see the Tate Modern. I enjoyed the building more than its exhibit, and I enjoyed the delicious salmon and crab tart at lunch in their café more than anything else.

By one o'clock I headed back to the Family Records Centre, realizing I'd become obsessed with the place. Ex-Two would have said I was like "a pig in shit" because I loved being surrounded by other genealogy addicts. *Why wasn't I sightseeing like a normal person?* Because I had the census with me and wanted to see if I could find my great-grandparents, their birth certificates, their wedding certificates and their death certificates.

This time I felt very at home in the Centre. I checked my bags into a locker downstairs, then headed to the birth ledger section. Since Victoria was born in Australia, I didn't think I could find her record. I've since learned that some births were registered in England, even when they occurred in British colonies. In my mother's files, I have the certificate my grandparents filled out for her the year after she was born, claiming her American citizenship.

The 1901 census told me George James Thomas was forty-seven and born in Bolton, Lancaster. That meant he was born around 1854. The ledger books listed names in alphabetical columns. For example, I should have found George in one of the four 1854 volumes under T | Thomas | George | District | Volume | Page. There were dozens of George Thomases, but not mine. I found a George James Thomas born in Liverpool and another born in Monmouth, Wales, but none in Bolton, Lancaster. I tried another tack, looking for James George, but that didn't work either.

Next I tried for a second time to find the marriage certificate for George and Victoria. The 1901 census reported Harold, their eldest child, to be fifteen. That put his birth date at 1886, not 1888. I started there and went backwards. Since two, or was it three, of Victoria's children died, she could have been married long before that. I found nothing in the four volumes for 1886, 1885, 1884 or 1883. By 1882 I was about to give up.

Victoria Ann would have been a mere sixteen years old in 1882. Yet, lo and behold, that is where I found her, in the first quarter ledger! Victoria Annie Bissell married George James Thomas between January 1 and March 31 of 1882. He, at twenty-six, was ten years older than she. I marched directly to order the certificate. I wouldn't learn the exact date of their marriage or their parents' names until I received the copy of the original certificate when I returned to California. That meant I didn't have the information I needed to search further back for their parents while I was still in the Centre.

Betty May – Southern California, c1941.

Chapter 34

World War Changes

As Hitler's army threatened France, the American Colony and the students from Chateau de Bures fled Paris, causing Pryns to shut the school down. For a short time he loaned the property to the Service Civile Volontaire Internationale, and it became the home to 150 Spanish and 50 Czech refugee children.

Their little pallets lay in close-packed double rows along each sleeping porch.

Then the president of Oest Lumiere, Paris' electricity company, purchased it for a "very low price." His wife wanted a convalescent home for children of the company's employees. The last time Pryns saw his former school before the war, large dormitories had been added to accommodate 200 children, and the school was completely wired for electricity.

In the summer of 1939, Pryns still ignored Hitler's threat and rented the lovely villa Les Hortensias in Biarritz. However, Pryns kept a clause in the lease agreement that if Hitler's army came too close, he could cancel the lease. He also booked tentative accommodations on the *U.S. George Washington*, due to sail on October 20 for New York.

The family, including Fay, Peter, Betty May, Jennifer, her nanny and a cook, took the train to Biarritz where all but Jennifer and the servants played tennis, while all enjoyed the sun and had a good time. Then on August 24, as the children lay in bed, Pryns and Fay listened to the news broadcast from London and learned Stalin had made his "treacherous deal with Hitler." In other words, the day before, the Soviet's foreign minister, Vyacheslav Molotov, and Germany's foreign minister, Joachim von Ribbentrop, signed the Nonaggression Act.

Pryns claimed he and Fay weren't convinced the war would reach them in their "quiet little corner." Nonetheless, they decided to head back to England the following morning. Before going to bed, they wrote one note to their cook to have breakfast ready early and another to their nurse to have baby Jennifer prepared to travel. They also started packing. By midmorning the following day, Pryns had placed his family on the early train to Paris and purchased plane tickets for them to London. People were paying $100 for tickets that normally cost $20.

He, however, stayed in Biarritz to settle their affairs. He wrote that people were talking about the German threat in every café in town. But in general it was pretty quiet and without fear of mass exodus. Things would be different when he reached Paris where, in most areas, blue bulbs had replaced yellow ones in the stations, and street lamps were extinguished to prevent planes from seeing the city from overhead. Yet, "while most of the windows were shuttered, others were still ablaze with the normal lights."

He flew back to his family in London after only one day in Paris. He then sent Peter and Betty May back to Vernon's, even though the Sussex coast was vulnerable to German attack. People in southern England were beginning to send the women and children north out of the bombers' reach. In some cases, whole school populations were relocated in the north, some as far as Scotland. St. Michael's prepared to close down because it was so near the channel. Mom planned to move with Rosemary and her sisters to their grandmother's house in Penn, Buckinghamshire and attend a school there. Peter's school was considered safe enough, but London wasn't. Rumors spread that German planes could reach longer distances without refueling

Pryns and Fay stayed at 73 Portland Place only long enough to pack some extra clothes and close up the flat. Then they headed north to the Lodge Hill Hotel at Pulborough. They weren't the only people to find refuge there. Pryns wrote:

> Every country house had been canvassed regarding its capacity to take billetings [lodgers]. When possible, the owners were given a choice between receiving children or expectant mothers! Child evacuees began arriving on every train, half a million in just one day. Other trains whizzed past with children hanging out of the window. All trains were reserved for children, then mothers, then expectant mothers leaving London, as well as thousands of invalids trying to get to the country.

Pryns and Fay stayed in Pulborough through the "September Crises." In other words, Germany invaded Poland, and Britain, France, Australia and New Zealand declared war. British boys and young men dressed in uniform to fight.

Pryns and Fay moved to Bath for a while, thinking Pryns could commute to London, but opportunities were closing up all around him. Since he wasn't a British subject, he couldn't help with the war effort, and by this time he was forty-six years old. He proposed moving the family to America, but Fay resisted.

By January 1940, Britain imposed rationing on its citizens. In March the Germans bombed a naval base at Scapa Flow, near Scotland.

In May, the Nazis invaded France, Belgium, Luxemburg and the Netherlands, and Winston Churchill became Prime Minister. At the end of the month, the evacuation of Allied troops from Dunkirk began.

What had been occasional air raids in England became more frequent. Only Jennifer liked them because, "when everyone went into the bomb-shelters, she received mounds of attention."

"I remember experiencing a few bomb raids in shelters while I was still in England," said Mom, "but that and the bicycling trip were about the extent of the drama I experienced before coming here."

In June, the British learned of the Nazi occupation of Paris.

In July, the British learned the Germans were preparing to attack England. Fay finally consented to move to the United States.

"We were certain the Germans were going to invade," Mom said. "They'd been successful everyplace else."

According to his autobiography, Pryns purchased a ticket for his son before the authorities informed him that Peter, age sixteen and a half, was too near recruitment age to leave the country. Here was a young man who had been abandoned by his birth parents, had lost his adopted mother to heart disease and was probably suffering from abuse by his stepfather. Now he was to be abandoned by his sister and father. Pryns admitted three decades later it was an "injurious psychic blow."

Since my grandfather was an American citizen, immigration authorities required him to sail on an American steamer. He could have taken his wife and children with him, but Fay wanted to bring her mother—who would be listed on the manifest as *Mary Cartledge*—in addition to four British children of friends. The only way she could do that was by sailing on a British vessel. That meant Pryns and his family had to cross the ocean separately.

The two ships were due to sail on the same day. Pryns' ship, with large American flags painted on each side for all the world to see, left on time and sailed directly to New York Harbor, her portholes ablaze with light every night, while inside, the orchestra played dance music as loudly as it wanted.

The *Britannic*, on the other hand, departed on July 29, 1940, from Liverpool, two days after her sailing date because of a bombing raid. She then followed a zigzag course, via Iceland and Greenland, in an effort to avoid German submarine attacks.

"They covered up all the windows with black paper at night to keep the lights from being visible," Mom said. Her ship arrived in New York Harbor more than a week after her father's ship, tardy but safe.

"I never thought of myself as American," Mom told me. "Even when I was in America surrounded by American relatives, I still thought of myself as British. I suppose I always will."

I don't think of myself as English, even though I qualify in the same way my mother did. But I loved my mother's Britishness, just as I loved the Beatles and the show *Upstairs Downstairs* and tea houses that served scones with clotted cream. Mom gave me the doll house she played with as a girl, complete with one-inch scale porcelain figures—nothing plastic—including maids, a nanny, butlers, children of various sizes, a mom and a dad, all dressed in flannel doll clothes of the 1920s style. There were miniature dishes, knifes and forks made out of pewter. One plate had a model of a tiny roasted lamb stuck to it. I played with the house and its occupants often, pretending I was part of an aristocratic English family. Since my mother was the same age as Queen Elizabeth and I was nearly the same age as Prince Charles, I even had fantasies of being royal.

My mother didn't see her brother again for over ten years. She didn't remember seeing him again in England. "I may have visited him in Canada, much later, where he lives now," she said.

I asked Peter what he remembered of the time after his sister left for America. In an email he wrote that he continued at boarding school and then spent about a year at Cambridge University before being drafted. He served in the Glider Pilot Regiment as a pilot, whose job it was to be towed behind enemy lines and then released to spy around. Afterward, he was sent to Palestine as a foot soldier. He didn't remember seeing his sister again in England, but he did remember Pryns visited him nine years later in 1948 before Peter moved to Canada.

After arriving in New York, Pryns transported his family across the American continent and set up residence at the Claremont Hotel in Berkeley, California, on the opposite side of the bay from his mother. By then she lived in her fourth floor apartment at 2101 Laguna Street, at least part of every year. Pryns sent Betty May directly to board at Katherine Branson School in Marin County, north across the Golden Gate Bridge from San Francisco.

"There were two prisons in Marin," Mom often said with her devilish grin. "San Quentin and KBS. I suppose it was better than being sent to Scotland to live with a strange family. Jack, my grandmother's chauffeur, often released me on weekends and took me into the city to spend the weekend with Grandma. The Golden Gate Bridge had been built before my arrival, however I remember taking the last ferry trip from Marin to San Francisco. After shopping, my grandmother and I always stopped for a peppermint fudge soda at the Blums soda fountain on Union Square. During the summers, I'd stay with her in Santa Barbara at El Nido. She sat in the living room listening to the radio. Her favorite shows were H.V. Kaltenborne, a commentator on world affairs, and Lum and Abner, a comedy team."

After a year in Berkeley, Pryns and Fay moved to Pasadena and set up residence in one of the Huntington Hotel's *cottages*, 1375 Oak Knoll Avenue. The cottages are now independent homes that sell for millions of dollars, with four bedrooms and more. But then they were connected to the hotel by a graceful wooden walk-bridge covered in wisteria vines. It was a short walk to tennis courts and a popular pool frequented by Hollywood movie stars.

Mom said, "Maids from the hotel served Fay her breakfast in bed every morning at 8:00 sharp. We were never allowed to talk to her until she had had her egg."

My half-uncle David arrived during the second year of residence, giving Jennifer a brother five years younger and my mother a half-brother eighteen years younger. Since he is only eight years older than I, and was the same age as Ex-Three, he is often mistaken as *my* brother.

Fay divorced Pryns when David was five and Jennifer ten in 1948. Pryns immediately left for Asia to bury himself in Eastern ashrams and Buddhist retreats. Since that was the same year he visited Peter in England, he must have stopped by on his way.

At this juncture I want to give Fay credit. After her second and third marriages—to the same man—she spent a good deal of time with my grandfather and owned a home not far from him in Santa Barbara. She was a good companion in his later years, even if she wasn't sexually attracted to him. She provided stimulating conversation, shrewdly challenged him at gin rummy and accompanied him for dinners out. They shared a history that included two wonderful children and, eventually, ten beautiful and clever grandchildren. She encouraged me to get to know my grandfather in ways I wouldn't have otherwise, and advised that all good wives should learn to bake a cheese soufflé.

Pryns Hopkins' writings.

Chapter 35

Philosophies of Life

A great-aunt on my father's side, Rosemary Ames, the one who left me all the family records, used to say, "If we get to know our ancestors, we get to know ourselves." One of the things I wanted to know about myself was what religion I was. My mother went to Anglican services as a girl. Her school required it. Dad attended the Episcopal church in Chicago until he moved with his mother to Pasadena when he was twelve. Then he attended the Presbyterian Church with his grandparents. But until I was about ten, my parents sent me to a Congregational Church because it was the nearest church to our house. My folks didn't attend services themselves.

During high school I hung out with a young man who, along with his whole family, was a Baptist. So I went to a lot of Baptist services. I didn't care about the church doctrine particularly. I just liked being with my boyfriend's family on Sundays, away from my own household and my parents' radioactive divorce. I just wanted *family*.

The philosophy that first truly interested me was Transcendentalism. My high school English teacher described it when we studied Ralph Waldo Emerson and Henry David Thoreau.[1] She said Transcendentalism was like "tapping into a universal cloud of knowledge and truth."

World Book Encyclopedia included this entry:

> A philosophy that became influential during the late 1700s and 1800s... According to Transcendentalism, reality exists only in the world of the spirit. What a person observes in the physical world are only appearances, or impermanent reflections of the world of the spirit. People learn about the physical world through their senses and understanding. But they learn about the world of the spirit through another power, called reason. The Transcendentalists defined reason as the personal, independent, and intuitive capacity to know what is absolutely true.

It seemed like a good explanation for the source of creative ideas. When I write a story or a poem or solve a graphic design problem, I never know ahead of time what I am going to say or draw. And yet, something always comes to mind. Where do those inspirations come from?

When I was twenty-three, I married a Christian Scientist and delved deeper into more metaphysical ideas. For a while I studied the writings of Mary Baker Eddy, who founded that church. To me, the biggest difference between Transcendentalism and Christian Science was that the latter termed "Reason" as "Divine Mind" and based everything on Biblical teachings and examples.

Christian Scientists describe God with seven synonyms: Life, Truth, Love, Spirit, Soul, Principle and Mind. God is a combination of all things universal, good, timeless, powerful and infinite. That made sense to me. I never did think there was a bearded human pulling the power strings. Humans may be able to create cells, but how could we possibly create spirit or wisdom. Mary Baker Eddy claimed there is no devil or evil force. Evil is simply the absence of good or God. And evil

1. Louise May Alcott's father, Amos Bronson, was also a major figure in the movement.

has no power if you don't give it power. Christian Scientists don't fret about paying a price for Eve eating the apple.

After I got divorced, I attended the Episcopal church. I thought it felt more like home. I stayed there for almost thirty years. I would eventually work my way closer to Christian Science again. Was I divinely schizophrenic or just divinely confused?

All I really *knew* was that the creation of the world seemed too amazing to have been the result of a roll of the dice. There had to be a great creator of some sort, and it had to be something spiritual, not physical. Don't the terms Great Spirit, Universal Spirit, God and Good all mean the same thing? In the movie *Star Wars*, the term for the Great Powerful One is "The Force."

I had a deep desire to know what Eileen Maude believed—what all my ancestors believed. Prince and Olive Hopkins inscribed on their deceased four-year-old son's headstone "God thought it best," because they believed there was a God-blessed reason their little boy passed from this earth plane to Heaven. What else did Prince and Olive believe so strongly?

A great-great-grandfather on my father's side left behind his spiritual autobiography. It fascinated me! He became a Free-Baptist minister at age fourteen and then had an epiphany that man was born good, not bad, and switched to become a Unitarian minister.

Did Eileen Maude have a spiritual journey? Did she believe in the Universal Spirit that the spiritualist Grandpa visited mentioned? Eileen Maude only heard about the horrors of World War I, but she forgave the Germans when she realized how human they were. Would her beliefs have changed if she'd experienced the Holocaust?

On the other hand, I know a lot about my Grandfather Pryns' journey, because he wrote many books about it. In the 1940s, he taught a comparative religion class at Claremont University College (aka Claremont Graduate University). Leading up to that he'd studied Buddhism, Islam, Taoism, Animism, Shintoism, West Aryan religions, Persian Demonology, Hinduism, Protestant Christianity, Catholicism and, most importantly, the modern religion of his era, Psychoanalysis.

He started this journey on that trip to Asia after Fay divorced him in 1948. He spent a year in India, Burma and Ceylon. In the conclusion of the book he wrote about his experiences in ashrams and retreats[2], he wrote that were he to follow any of those creeds arduously for three to ten years, he could probably prove any of them to be a road to enlightenment. Like the Catholicism of his youth, all required persistent practice or prayer, confession, forgiveness and attendance. And he discovered that crucial on the road to spiritual success was the possession of a strong enough desire for enlightenment to take the steps to get there. He quoted this story:

> Once when a Hindu seeker complained of no progress, his guru held the man's head under water until the poor fellow nearly drowned. Said the guru, "when you desire Brahman as desperately as just now you fought for air, you will attain him!"

My grandfather didn't discuss Transcendentalism, but he agreed with it on one point when he wrote that the one element he found "shy" in all the theologies he studied was *Reason*. He wrote:

> The last refinement of Reason is found in Science. Until Reason has justified intuitions against possible objections and against other, rival intuitions, they remain too uncertain to build a life upon.

Pryns was a scientist. He belonged to a generation that thought man could solve everything through a process of hypothesis and experimentation. He asked,

> Could science, the tendency of which has been to destroy religion's claim that there was purpose behind the cosmos, help man now to provide himself with purpose?...Yes.

Psychology was that science. He continued,

---

2. Hopkins, Prynce. *World Invisible, A Study in Sages, Saints and Saviors,* Traversity Press, Penobscot, Maine, 1963, p 160.

> We must get our support today from psychiatry and from educational psychology.

What about faith? What about trusting the things not seen? Just because it is a cloudy day doesn't mean that the sun isn't there.

My grandfather thought one should...

> ... understand the human psyche, the conditions of its illness and health, and therapeutic procedures.

But if we spend all our time looking for faults, won't that be all that we find?

Ironically, he ended his book on his religious experience with this quote that he credits to the Austrian Dr. Alfred Adler, founder of the school of individual psychology.

> So act as to elicit the best in others, thereby eliciting the best in yourself.

Didn't Jesus say something similar two thousand years earlier?

> Love thy neighbor as thyself?

At least my grandfather had the courage to test his theories. He studied, and he discussed, and he read, and he went to lectures. He never took anything for granted. He encouraged and set up funds for his family to educate themselves, and he wanted his offspring to make educated decisions. He used to take me to a variety of churches on Sundays—Catholic, Protestant, Christian Science. I think he even planned to take me to a synagogue once.

Jesus wanted us to judge people by their acts and not by their words. I think he would have given my grandfather a very good grade.

Betty May (far left) and Rosemary (far right) –
St. Michael's School, Bognor Regis, July 1937.

Chapter 36

On to Dorset

I woke up at six-thirty Tuesday morning, July 31, ready to head to Poole, Dorset, to see my mother's school chum Rosemary. My train to Poole wasn't scheduled to leave the Waterloo Station until 10:40 a.m. However, I was so worried about missing it, I woke up too early—I had forgotten to bring my alarm clock to England with me! Since I had fallen behind on my writing, I put the tea water on to boil and booted up my laptop.

I'd been doing my yoga exercises every morning to stretch my limbs, just as I did at home. Yoga made me think more about Grandpa. He started practicing yoga when he took that trip though the Far East in 1948. He learned the yoga moves and practiced them most mornings from then on. I used to see him stretching in various poses in the cubicle he used as his bedroom and office. Even though he had a very large house, he didn't sleep in the master bedroom. My Uncle David explained to me that Grandpa was embarrassed he'd spent so much money on building his house that he never enjoyed living there. Keeping his actual living space to a minimum helped calm his guilt.

Sometimes Grandpa meditated by the side of his pool. He was very skinny and looked a lot like Mahatma Gandhi in his swimming trunks. He could sit in a perfect lotus position, which I have never been able do. My stepcousin Paul remembered catching him in a headstand pose once before breakfast.

Grandpa taught me the significance of facing the rising sun during the "sun salute" in the way Muslims face Mecca while praying. I learned that most western churches were built to face east, or toward Jerusalem, allowing for the sun to come up through the stained glass windows behind the altar during the morning service. Even Mary Baker Eddy wrote that she faced Jerusalem when she prayed three times a day.[1]

Grandpa collected many religious icons during his travels. Statues of Buddha and other Asian archetypes decorated the paths in his garden. More than twenty busts of secular and religious leaders such as Benjamin Franklin, Jesus, Mao Tse-Tung and Marcus Aurelius surrounded one courtyard. Ben and Marcus live in my garden now. The rest were bequeathed to the Thatcher School, his alma mater.

During one of his visits to the Arab world, Grandpa commissioned the making of a set of ceramic tiles for a small Muslim prayer nook. He planned to install the nook in the east wall by his swimming pool. That meant knocking out part of the existing wall to make space for the two-foot kneeling space. Grandpa then left for another trip while the nook was installed. The workmen mistakenly plastered it into the south wall. Grandpa was furious when he returned and saw the error, knowing how ridiculous it was to have a Muslim prayer nook facing south. But by then the mortar was set and the nook firmly in place. It was really pretty. It had a cobalt blue background with gold and orange swirls dancing through it. However it was useless. There wasn't even room to shade a table or chair.

I still face east every time I do the yoga sun-salute. After my exercises I sit for a minute in a cross-legged position. I don't meditate eastern-style. Instead I say or sing the *Lord's Prayer*. Afterward I sit quietly and

---

1. Eddy, Mary Baker. *Miscellaneous Writings*.

pray some more, which for me means tuning in to the Great Spirit.

"What do you want of me?" I always ask. "If thy will be done, what the heck is it?"

During that morning in England, I also tried to talk to my grandmother's spirit.

"Gram. Show me where your body is buried. I want to know what happened to you at the end of your life, so I can tell Mom. Was Vernon caring for you as he should have been?"

Then I called on Pryns. "Grandpa. Where did Vernon put her?"

I didn't want to communicate with Vernon after my mother told me he was a pedophile. When I was little, she told me he died from hiccups. I guess he got what he deserved.

I sat there listening for a while. This is what I thought I heard: "We can't tell you, Mary, but don't worry, you are doing a good thing. Look at all of the relatives whose lives you are touching and bringing together. You will make people happier even if you don't find that grave."

"That grave has to be somewhere." I answered Grandpa in my mind. "If Gram was only cremated, and if her ashes were strewn somewhere instead, wouldn't you have mentioned it in one of your journals? Besides, I've come to dead ends at the crematoriums, just as I have at the cemeteries. What about Wolverhampton? Will I find anything there?"

I had a little mishap on my way to the Waterloo Station. As I mentioned, my suitcase was large and extremely heavy. The easiest way to get it down the three flights of stairs from my London flat to the street was by letting it fall from stair to stair, bump, bump, bump. What I didn't realize was that while I was easing the strain on my back, I was putting a big strain on my suitcase's built-in aluminum handle.

I made it to the Baker Street Station and purchased my subway ticket—a single one-way to Waterloo. As I headed for the train, I reached another set of stairs. I descended with my suitcase in the same manner as I'd descended the stairs of my apartment building: bump, bump,

bump. This time I heard a loud crack from the handle. I looked down to find the handle bent at an abnormal angle. I suspected a fracture. I was right. Ten paces later the handle bent completely and broke off.

I now held a lethal looking aluminum rod, sharply torn at one end. But I couldn't find any trash bins in the subway stations anywhere. Trash bins attracted bombs. As a safety measure, they'd been removed. I continued on my way carrying my fifty-six pound suitcase by the handle in one hand and the mean-looking saber in my other. Fellow passengers looked frightened when I got on the subway. I wasn't able to get rid of the weapon until I finally reached the Waterloo station. I handed my saber off to an agent at the turnstile.

My mother returned to England in 1948 after attaining her majority. (That was the same year her father traveled to Asia, so in spite of Peter's and her memories, they must have seen each other.) She stayed with her dear school chum Rosemary while she conducted her business. Mom had to decide whether she wanted to retain her English citizenship or be an American citizen. It is my understanding she couldn't be both. She also had to claim the inheritance ("articles of household or domestic or garden use or ornament") her mother had left in trust with Vernon until she turned twenty-one. He had retained rights to their use until that time. The baby grand piano from her father needed releasing from its place in storage. When Mom returned to America, the piano and Rosemary traveled with her.

"We sailed on the *Queen Elizabeth*. Rosemary and I had a fabulous time," Mom told me.

Together, the young ladies rented a "working girls" apartment in Pasadena. I've seen photos of it. They placed two studio beds fitted with polka-dot skirted covers and matching cushions against the wall so the one room could serve as a seating area by day and bedroom at night. Mom still kept one of those studio beds in her den at Villa Marin.

Rosemary worked at odd jobs like volunteering, waitressing and dog-sitting. Mom, who had graduated with an art degree from Scripps College in Claremont, worked as a secretary to a jeweler. Near the end of that time my mother met my father and their courtship began.

Rosemary returned home before my parents' marriage in 1950.

When Rosemary visited my mother in Pasadena many years later, she told me how special that time from 1948 to 1949 had been. Their letter writing never stopped. They called each other on birthdays up to the day of my mother's death. One of Rosemary's three children, Gail, stopped by to see Mom when she was spending her 'tween year touring the United States. I met Gail then; however, I hadn't met Rosemary's husband, Graham. I was looking forward to it.

Rosemary was waiting at the station when my train arrived. She drove me through the pretty seaside town of Poole to her house on Anthonys Street—there was no apostrophe in Anthonys—where I met Graham and their elderly golden lab, Poppy. We spent the two days chatting over meals and during long walks with Poppy—one along the waterfront and another through a shady wood. I probably bored them with my recitations of all the research I'd been doing, but they at least pretended to be interested. It felt family-like, as if they were my aunt and uncle. Rosemary continued to surprise me with her youthfulness. She seemed so much younger than my mother. Graham had some knee problems, (or was it his hip? I can't remember). However, I could barely keep up with Rosemary on our walks.

She wanted to know everything about my mother—what she had been up to and how she was. Rosemary had warm memories of my grandfather, Pryns, too. She brought up the episode when he included her and her sister on the bicycle trip to Holland and the sister rode into the canal. Rosemary didn't remember anything about Vernon, leading me to believe Vernon didn't visit my mother much at boarding school. We also talked about their school days. Twice Rosemary mentioned that my mother was a more clever student than she, revealing a bit of rivalry. Mom had never mentioned anything about that.

"Your grandfather visited Betty May almost every weekend," she told me, telling the story about his renting horses and taking her riding on the South Downs. "I liked Pryns very much, he was a sweet and generous man."

From Poole I traveled via Southampton to the small town of Birdham, just outside the cathedral town of Chichester, where I stayed with Mom's cousin Camilla and her husband, Rodney, for two nights. I arrived on a Wednesday.

Rodney and Camilla had been married for six years. They'd recently bought the house they were living in and were in the process of "doing it up." It was the second home redo they'd done. They toured me past the first one, possibly the most charming house in Chichester Centre, an old parsonage.

Camilla was a fabulous cook. The first night she made a delicious chicken curry that she served with fresh carrot rounds. While dining, we laughed over the different eating customs between Americans and English people. For example, Rodney ate a soft-boiled egg served every morning in an egg cup. My mother's aide, not knowing what an egg cup was for, used one to serve my mother her morning pills. The English stack their toast in a toast rack to cool it so the butter won't melt. I butter my toast as soon as it comes out of the toaster because I *want* the butter to melt. And, of course, there is the difference in how we hold our utensils while we eat. The Brits keep their fork in their left hand and use the knife in their right to pile the food onto the tip of the fork, bringing the food to their mouth with the left hand; whereas Americans, once they've used the fork to steady the food while the knife in the right hand cuts it, put the knife down and switch the fork from the left, bringing the food to their mouth with the right hand. My stepcousin Paul's mother said to me, years back, "Using your knife properly reflects from what class you've come."

After breakfast the next morning, Rodney, a Christian Scientist, and I lingered at the table as I told him how there were many things about studying his religion thirty years earlier that had stayed with me. Rodney said something I will never forget,

"Isn't it interesting how Truth sticks to you? No matter how hard you might try to shake it off, you can't."

I pictured collecting blocks of truth along the way in my life. The Ten Commandments and the Sermon on the Mount were my foundation stones. As I added each truth-block on my wall, I tested it to see if it would fall off. Bit by bit, my wall of truth grew taller and stronger and more protective. And with each truth came faith. Once I knew two plus two equaled four, I had faith that two plus three equaled five. Once I knew one person loved me, I had faith someone else would love me, too.

On my second day, Camilla gave a small dinner party in my honor, beginning with tenderly roasted chicken and potatoes and ending with a dessert called *fool*. Fool had been a new dish to me until Carolyn's friends served a gooseberry fool the week before. It is basically just fruit, usually tart, mixed with whip cream—hence its name because it is so easy to make. Camilla used kiwi and also added an egg before whipping the cream.

I slept in a luxurious bedroom that opened to their two-acre garden, centered by a large man-made pond that kept Rodney, dressed in galoshes, busy chasing after leaks. As I lay in my bed, I remembered the guest room at my grandfather's house that also overlooked his garden and pool and what a treat it was to sleep under smooth ironed sheets. In the 1950s, the arrival of "drip dry" on the market delighted all housewives like my mother. All she had to do was hang them on a line to dry in the sun. But compared to my grandfather's sheets, they were scratchy and wrinkled.

In between our tour schedule and dinners, I extracted a few bits of information from Camilla to add to what was now an *illustrated* family tree because of the addition of photos. She added some details of births, marriages and deaths for her immediate family, and she described her father's life.

Harold was seventeen years older than Camilla's mother, Joy. Joy was twenty-two years old when Camilla's sister, Jill, was born, but thirty-five when Camilla came along.

Harold, at fifty-two, had lived a full life by then. He served first as a captain for the Royal Artillery in World War I, eventually emerging from the battlefields of the Low Countries as Lieutenant Colonel. After marrying Joyce, they lived in various places including South Africa, where among his achievements as a mineralogist, he secured the concession for the highly successful mining conglomerate

Consolidated Gold Fields. They also lived in South America and the Channel Island of Jersey. Harold served again as a captain during World War II, when he moved his wife and Camilla, who was just a toddler, to Hurlingham, London. Jill and Jeffray were in boarding school by then. After the war, in 1946, they returned to Jersey, to a house called Pendeen, where Camilla would return from her own Swiss and English boarding schools. Ten years later, Harold and Joy purchased a larger house called Chantry, where they lived out their lives.

Camilla Joy Victoria Bissell Thomas was born in London, educated at Moreton Hall in Shropshire and finished at Madame Boué's Study Home in Paris. She trained as a fashion designer at St. Martin's School of Art before marrying Archie.

Jon Abbott phoned me while I was at Camilla's with the disappointing news he would not be able to meet me in London as he'd hoped. However, since we were on the phone together—he in Northampton and I in Birdham—he offered me an interview. I grabbed my computer in preparation of taking notes.

I told him about the birth records I'd found of the Thomas siblings and the 1901 census. "Who was Winifred?" I asked.

"Winifred was my mother," he said. "Peggy was her nickname. I don't believe she was ever called Winifred."

I then asked him for his own particulars. He said he was married and divorced once with "no issue." I was accustomed to seeing that term for "no children" from my genealogy work, but I thought it funny he used it. Maybe it was a Scottish thing. He was born in 1929, four years after my mother.

"My father, Jack, adopted Pat and June Pope, the daughters from my mother's first marriage. Their father was such an awful person, they shed his name and became Abbotts." I didn't ask Jon if that qualified his half-sisters to be interred in the Abbott Family Vault.

Finally, we got to the subject of my grandmother's death.

"I was five or six at the time," he said.

I pointed out that the death occurred in 1933, and he could only have been four.

"Well, I remember it very well, as if I'd been much older. I remember the great concern when my Aunt Eileen became ill and was rushed off to Seafield Hospital. It astonished everybody when she died suddenly. Very unexpected. My mother, Peggy, protected us. She insulated us completely from her grief."

Was that the customary way to deal with emotions in the 1930s? I wondered. *Insulate oneself or one's loved ones? That would explain my mother a great deal.*

I told Jon he'd just given me the name of the nursing home, a very important clue for my search. He didn't know if it was still operational.

"Do you remember a funeral?" I asked.

"No, as I said, my mother protected us from what was going on."

"Do you remember your parents preparing to attend a funeral, dressing in black, for example? Anything that would indicate they were going to a burial in Ayr."

"No, I don't remember anything like that at all."

Jon and I reviewed the burial locations I'd already eliminated, to see if anything sounded familiar to him, but nothing did. He didn't know where else I should look, either. However he did say, "My parents belonged to the Church of Scotland. Your grandmother probably belonged to the Church of England. It's likely that if she were buried in Ayr, it wouldn't have been in the churchyard of the church my parents attended."

The Church of Scotland is like the American Presbyterian Church. The Church of England is like the American Episcopal Church. There is a big difference in their doctrines. I had not checked any churchyards in Ayr. I put that on my "To Do List."

I realized I was going to have to return to England again soon, so I could meet Jon. He sounded like a wonderful gentleman!

Harold between his children, Jill and Jeffray – c1933.

Chapter 37

Harold's Grandchildren

From Chichester I took a train to Winchester, where I stayed a few days with Ex-One's college roommate, Jonathan, and his wife, Henrietta, known as Henri. This was a short break from my family quest. On Sunday, August 6, Henri returned me and my fat suitcase to the Winchester train station to catch the 10:31 a.m. direct train to Banbury. After a two-hour train ride, I was met by my second-cousin Cynthia.

A refresher course in family structure might be helpful. My grandmother's brother, Harold, the one who pressured my grandmother to marry my grandfather, had three children: Jill, Jeffray and Camilla. This day I was spending time with two of Harold's granddaughters: Jill's daughter, Candy, and Camilla's daughter, Cynthia. Candy, with family, planned to meet us for lunch. After lunch, Candy's clan was taking me back home with them to Worcester.

Cynthia, as elegant and beautiful as her mother and with the same light brown hair, was dressed in a sleeveless, taupe linen sundress. None of the Thomas women wore blue jeans as I would have at home. So I stuck to sleeveless tops and soft skirts the rest of the trip. The climate was very comfortable.

As Cynthia drove me through the town of Banbury, she asked, "Do you remember the nursery rhyme 'Ride a cock horse to Banbury Cross, to see a fine lady upon a white horse, with rings on her fingers and bells on her toes…?'"

"She shall have music wherever she goes," I finished. Cynthia pointed out the cross in the middle of the roundabout ahead of us. I grabbed my camera in time to snap a shot of the statue of the lady on her horse as we breezed by, though we weren't close enough to inspect her fingers and toes.

Banbury is nestled among the Cotswolds, one of the most picturesque areas of all England. Charming lanes passed by ancient stone houses topped with thatched roofs. I continued snapping photos from the Land Rover's window the rest of the way to Cynthia's country home. We entered by a tree-lined drive as we discussed the meaning of "chester," as in Winchester. It means "walled city." Cynthia's home was also walled. The house dominated the right of the enclosure and the stable with stalls for six horses, but "no equine residents presently," dominated the left.

Within an hour, I met four more second-cousins and six second-cousins-once-removed, i.e. the children of second-cousins. I called the youngest generation my "mini-cousins" since "second-cousins-once-removed" was such a long phrase. Cynthia and her husband, Roddie for Roderick, an executive at Land Rover, had three darling children: Bex, seventeen, Laura, sixteen and Charlie, fourteen. They greeted me one by one—more kisses on each side of the cheek—as Cynthia and I entered the kitchen of their 250-year-old cottage. There we collected the makings for a lunch of sausages and chicken that we carried across the wide lawn to a pool area enclosed by shrubs. Roddie had his Webber fired up and ready to grill.

Candy and crew arrived from Worcester, which was a little over an hour north of Banbury. Her hubby, Tim, sixteen-year-old son, Tom, and daughters, Hattie and Ellie, fourteen and ten respectively, piled out of the car and greeted their cousins Bex, Laura and Charlie. Candy and Cynthia hadn't seen each other for over five years. Their husbands had never met. Some of the children had met before, but since it was so long ago, the introductions were like new. I was applauded for giving both families a reason for the *rendezvous.*

We spent the rest of the afternoon by the pool and watching the more adventurous drive in circles around an adjacent horse meadow in an ATV (all-terrain vehicle). I was able to coerce Laura into giving me a tour of the house. The main difference I noticed between the very old country cottages and the very old city homes was the height of the ceilings. In this country house, I had to watch my head while going under the thick dark beams crossing doorways. I was charmed.

After much chitchat, a yummy lunch, some delicious rosé wine and a few dips in the pool for some, I climbed into Candy and Tim's van, and we began the drive back to Worcester. While Tim drove, Candy, from the back seat, added more information to the story of her grandfather Harold Bissell-Thomas. I took notes in my iBook. Candy never met her grandfather. He died five years before her birth. She grew up hearing his legend from her mum, Jill, a gifted storyteller like her mum, Joy.

Joy's sister, Willa, nicknamed Harold "Webster," because he had an incredible vocabulary and because he was so smart it seemed that when anyone asked him a question, he always knew the answer. No one in his family knew why he chose to go by Bissell-Thomas rather than just Thomas. Candy agreed with Mom's speculation that the Bissells might have been of a higher class. I would find out the answer much later.

Harold attended the Cornish school of mines in Cornwall, where he met Woodrow Wilson as a fellow student of metallurgy. During the First World War, he narrowly escaped being gassed to death. The story went: one night he arrived home late to his tent. The rest of his regiment had already gone to sleep and left no room on the floor for Harold, so he had to sleep sitting up. While he was sleeping, the Germans sprayed poisonous gas into his tent. The gas, being heavier than air, sank to the floor and killed everyone asleep there. Harold woke to find that he alone survived. Candy believed that many of the health problems he suffered later were a result of this event[1].

During Harold's lifetime he made two fortunes, losing the first before making the second. Before the Russian Revolution, he worked as an engineer on the Trans-Siberian railway and learned to speak Russian in six weeks while in the court of the Czar. He then worked in South Africa, encouraging his brothers, Eric and Billie, and a brother-in-law, Ian, to join him.

Harold and Joy also lived in Brazil for a time. While they were there, Joy wrote many children's books, usually when Harold was off traveling without her. My mother had copies of *Dragon Green* and *The Amorous Baron*. For a while, Joy had a spider monkey that sat on her wrist as she wrote. "The monkey was so small he could fit into a teacup." As Candy formed her hand into a little cup shape as she narrated, I realized she inherited her grandmother's gift for storytelling as well.

Later, Harold bought a home for his family on Jersey. When their first baby, Jill, threatened arrival, Harold ferried Joy to France to the nearest hospital. (Ironically, Jill was born in Dinard.) Candy believed they would have preferred having their baby in England, but "with the boats being so slow in 1925," it was too difficult to get there in time. Jeffray and Camilla, however, *were* born in England.

Candy's dates confirmed that the Bissell-Thomas family lived on Jersey in 1933 when they left to visit Harold's former brother-in-law, Pryns Hopkins, and his children in Dinard. It came as no surprise that Candy didn't know if her grandfather visited his sister, Eileen Maude, in Scotland when she got sick, or if he attended a funeral for her after her death.

Candy told another hand-me-down story about the family evacuating the Channel Islands when Germany invaded France. The Channel Islands are right off the coast of Normandy, and to this day, gun placements and fortifications guard the waterfront around Jersey. In 1940, when Jill was fourteen, Jeffray twelve and Camilla just two, the Germans invaded France. The family quickly packed to escape on the last ship that would leave Jersey. It stopped for more passengers in the

---

1. I read up on how these gasses killed people and Harold's story doesn't make sense. However, we'll leave the family legend alone.

smaller Guernsey Island on its way to Southampton, as my mother said, the largest southern port in England. As the family stood on the ship's deck in the harbor, waiting for the new passengers to board, German fighter planes attacked the port. The ship was only a merchant ship carrying mainly women and children. It had little to defend itself except one gun at the stern. Webster, the seasoned World War I veteran, took it upon himself to grab the gun and begin firing at the Germans. Candy thought there was a famous photograph of her grandfather defending the ship.

Meanwhile, a "nice policeman" that Jeffray had just been talking to was hit and killed, and the briefcase he'd been carrying burst open. A cloud of cash (money the policeman must have been trying to take out of Guernsey to England), spilled out and bills fluttered everywhere. Amid the barrage of enemy fire, young Jeffray scurried about grabbing them and stuffing them into his pocket.

The ships that had gone ahead reported the attack to the English in Southampton. Everyone assumed the ship was lost, but not true. She cut her lights as night fell and then quietly escaped from Guernsey Harbour. As she reached Southampton, shouts of welcome greeted her from the quays with celebratory waterspouts shooting into the air from the harbor's fireboats.

Supposedly, Webster was on his second round of being a millionaire by the time he moved to England and didn't need to work any more. Whereas Camilla thought he moved his family to London, Candy thought they moved to Kent. It is likely only Jill went to Kent, since she told her daughter she was sent to a "succession of boarding schools" and watched the dog-fights in the sky as the war raged on—something many people living in Kent during the war reported.

After the war, Harold moved his family back, first to Guernsey, then to Jersey as Camilla stated, where they purchased Pendeen and then their final home, Chantry Manor. Candy believed that by that time there was a law that only English who owned property in Jersey before World War II could purchase houses again.

"And that brings us to Deedles, my mum's cat," said Candy.

Deedles had been left behind in Jersey when the family escaped to England. After the family returned to the island, Jill tried to find him.

Every time she asked a Jersey resident if they knew anything of the cat's whereabouts, they told her they didn't know, but with "a shifty look in their eyes." Jill suspected something wasn't right. She investigated further until someone finally admitted that the island residents had been so near starving to death during the war that they'd eaten all the pets.

Jill left the island for high school. "There was no airport in Jersey," said Candy, "When my mother returned home to her parents from boarding school, or later from London, the planes landed on the beach. It was such a small place that every time she arrived, it was announced in the *Jersey Evening Post.*

In 1951, when Jill was twenty-six, Jeffray twenty-three and Camilla thirteen, Webster went to his bed and basically never got up, suffering from a gastric ulcer and a resulting stomach operation in 1953. During eight sedentary years he sat in bed and read. His wife bought him three or four books per week from Boots, the general store, and he went through all of them. "He also told stories about his younger years in the jungles of South America, particularly the one about a vampire bat sitting on his toes sucking his blood," said Candy.

In 1959, while Harold still rested in bed, Camilla introduced him to her fiancé from Scotland, Archie. She said it was "a little awkward." They married that June at St. George's Church, Hanover Square, London, without Harold's presence and then traveled to Italy, where my family ran into them in the spring. Harold died the following Christmas Day.

Only two of Webster's eight grandchildren were born before his death. Candy was the last of the Bissell-Thomas grand-ducklings, born in 1964.

"Granny Joy stayed in Chantry and soon married Bob, a retired cavalry officer." Bob died in 1975, when Candy was eleven.

"What about your own father?" I asked.

"My father, Dr. John Peter Henry Moxon Rae, met my mother through her brother, Jeffray, and cousin, Jon Abbott. My father and uncle were schoolmates at Harrow on the Hill. When I was four, my father ran away with our au pair to Canada. He subsequently married her, and they had two children that we keep up with. He died young, almost twenty years ago in 1987, when I was twenty-three."

Candy, Phillipa and Adam's mother, Jill, who was left with little income, moved her children to Jersey after her stepfather, Bob, died. That would have been right after my mother, brothers and I visited Jill's and Camilla's families in Chelsea, London. With a small inheritance, Jill bought a house about a mile away from Chantry to be near her mother, Joy. "I was twelve when we went to live there," said Candy. "During the summers it was all visitors. There were also many storms. If you couldn't get off the island now and then, you went a bit stir crazy. I was sent to the same school my Aunt Camilla had attended. Granny Joy died in 1991 and my mother moved into Chantry. Eventually, Philippa left for England to attend art college and I went off to university at Exeter. My brother, Adam, never left. He still lives in Jersey."

The same year Candy's father died, Jill started showing signs of Alzheimer's disease. "Tim and I had our wedding in Jersey that year. Mum was already strange. Chantry was a complete mess. It had always been a spooky house, in particular the room where our grandfather Webster lived all those years. When I was little, I stayed in that room and had terrible nightmares—always about everyone I loved dying—traumatic and bizarre dreams! My cousin Cynthia told me she had the same dreams in that room! Really bizarre!

"Some people thought the house was haunted by the spirit of a child who died there. My brother, Adam, brought a friend to the house who was very in touch with spirits. He didn't tell her about the room. When she got to the top of the staircase, she stopped short and wouldn't go in. She turned and ran screaming from the house.

"We had to rent out Chantry to pay for my mother's nursing home, but even the renters were spooked by the house. One of their friends wouldn't sleep there. He slept in the yard instead.

"When Mum died in 1997, we had to sell the house to pay off the debts from her illness. We were told we had to disclose that the house was haunted."

By the end of Candy's tales, we had arrived safely at her home in Worcester. It was fairly late in the evening, but Candy and Tim had to go out again to rescue a fish aquarium full of fish that some friends, who were moving, wanted to unload. While Candy and Tim were out, I accepted their invitation to use their computer to research our trip to Wolverhampton scheduled for the following day.

Tettenhall Road, looking from Number 17 toward Wolverhampton Centre.

Chapter 38

Wolverhampton

On Candy's computer, I was able to re-find the Wolverhampton government web site I'd discovered that hot day in the Internet café in London. I searched for cemeteries. Even though Wolverhampton is a large city, I found the situation to be fairly simple. Only one municipal cemetery existed in 1933, Merrydale. And there were only four Churches of England in the neighborhood of 17 Tettenhall Road.

That gave me hope. I had learned that Tettenhall Road used to be called Merrydale Road. That would put the cemetery close to the home where my grandmother grew up. Since the only mention of Eileen Maude's death was in a Wolverhampton newspaper, the chances were looking better she might be buried there.

The next morning I phoned the cemetery and churches, while Candy fussed with the fish tank. Within twenty minutes I'd spoken to a woman at the Wolverhampton City Centre who checked Merrydale

Cemetery. To my disappointment, I learned it was not the current residence of my grandmother's bones. *Dash*! I then called the four churches. One phone number was no longer in service, one church gave me a negative report and the remaining two didn't answer their phones. We would have to research those two churches in person.

Candy and I left for Wolverhampton right before lunch, stopping at a roadside café for a sandwich on our way. While we drove and ate, she told me a bit about her own family. Tim sold insurance and Candy, who had just finished obtaining her teaching credential, was starting at first grade in the fall. Red-headed Tom, a high school student, played video games addictively and went sky-diving with his father. Brown-haired Hattie had many interests. Fashion and boys were at the top of the list. Not quite as red-headed as Tom, Ellie tried to keep up with Hattie.

Candy moved on to tell me about her Uncle Jeffray Bissell-Thomas' family. Jeffray had died just the year before. His wife, Ann, by then in her eighties, still lived at West Hall, a large home in Kew directly west of London on the Thames. "It stands on its own grounds in a nice part of town and even has a proper ballroom!"

The oldest of Jeffray and Ann's four children, Charles, never married and still lived at West Hall with Ann. He attended Harrow, the prestigious prep school, as his father and uncle had, and while there began cultivating the dreadlocks he still sported. However, he didn't feel at home at Harrow, and one day Ann received a phone call from the school saying that she needed to pick up her son because he had enrolled himself in another school. He went on to Sussex University, where he majored in anthropology. When he studied the great apes and orangutans, he was so taken by them that he changed his name to Jungle Eyes Love. He has been signing his name J.E. Love ever since. He also became a fruitarian—someone who eats only fruit.

"Jungle Eyes is a type of witch doctor, possibly the only one in London using Celtic, druidic rituals," said Candy. "He owns a therapeutic crystal shop, where he sells dinosaur eggs and crystal pendants. He makes the pendants himself, and Prince Charles purchased one to help with the arthritis in his shoulder."

Jungle Eyes also rented a mock medieval building, called Appley Tower, in the coastal town of Ryde on the Isle of Wight, where he ran another gem shop. The Isle of Wight lies offshore from Portsmouth and Southampton Harbours, in the direction of Jersey Island. Candy thought he still owned an orchard there, too, where he grew apples and pears. At one point, Jungle Eyes lived on oranges and avocados alone, which were "being delivered to West Hall by the crate load." But for the previous year, Charles had been confined to bed because he was ill with the nervous disease called beriberi, caused by a thiamine (vitamin B1) deficiency. He was being nursed by his elderly mother.

Jungle's story overshadowed those of his siblings.

"Sarah is the next in line," continued Candy. "She has lived with her partner for a long time. They have two children, a girl Fleurie and a boy Zephir, and live in Brighton. I think they keep busy doing up houses to sell.

"After that are the twins, Harriet and James. Harriet is the eldest by twenty minutes. She is a restaurateur, owns and runs two successful cafés in Greater London. One is right on the Thames and the other a short walk away from the first, overlooking a sweet park. They serve all vegetarian food and are only open for lunch. Harriet and her partner, who is no longer on the scene, have one daughter called Sorrel, as in the herb. She is a sweetie pie, of about eighteen now."

"James is also very creative and also a vegetarian. He's a globe maker, specializing in antique replicas. Not too long ago, Christie's mistakenly sold one of them as a real antique, which was a coup for James. He and his partner, Rosey, have one son, Helier."

Candy saw me lift my eyebrows in wonder at the name.

"Helior is the patron saint of Jersey," she said. (There was a difference in spelling.) "My Aunt Anne's family has lived there since the days of Charlemagne. Helier was named after several ancestors of the same name. It's such a tiny island everyone there is a cousin of someone else.

"James and Rosey live part of each week in the carriage house next to West Hall and the rest of the time in Ryde on the Isle of Wight. With Jungle Eyes ill, James has to help oversee the crystal shop in Ryde as well as manage his globe business. He commutes to Kew to help his mother with West Hall."

West Hall had experienced its own drama the year before my visit with Candy. One night shortly after Jeffray died, the top floor caught fire. Candy suspected it was caused by one of Jungle Eyes' crystal-making projects. Another theory was that computer wires crossed and sparked. The floor, covered in documents, quickly caught the flames and most of the third story burned. Candy thought the house had only two stories left, her Aunt Ann and Jungle Eyes living in one of them. James helped his mother with the rebuilding. Since the house was one of Kew's oldest, they were running into a tangle with English Heritage. For example, English Heritage insisted the beams be a particular type of oak, whereas the insurance company wanted a more economical solution.

"One last thing about Jeffray," said Candy. "He didn't get along with his cousin Lionel very well. One night when they were at a dinner party together, Lionel mentioned that he was part of the Lancaster Bombers. Jeffray left the room, declaring he refused to sit at the same table as a murderer."

I later looked up Lancaster Bombers on the internet. The heavy airplanes, designed to fly at night, were one of the RAF's most important vehicles. They delivered 608,612 tons of bombs in 156,000 sorties during the course of World War II.

The last person on Candy's "relly" report was Jon Abbott. The information broke my heart.

"Jon's father, Jack, owned a shoe company based in Northampton, a center for making hats and leather goods that vied with the fancy London store Dolcis. He had a daughter named Louise."

"He did?" I interrupted. "He told me he had no children."

"She apparently took her own life by jumping off a building. I'm sure he didn't want to talk about it."

I reflected on that bit. Any problems I'd dealt with in my own life suddenly seemed piddly indeed.

Candy and I arrived in Wolverhampton at about 2:00 in the afternoon. A circular road enclosed the town center. From that road, streets stretched out like spokes on a wheel. Tettenhall Road, one of those spokes, lead from the center road toward the village of Tettenhall. Number 17, as one might suspect, stood very close to the center of town. It was one of a series of typical row houses—three stories high with a basement level that probably once housed the servants' quarters. The building had been broken up into flats and numbered on the mailbox by the front door. Candy and I could see through the glass in the door to a hallway dominated by a staircase.

17 Tettenhall Road, Woverhampton, 2006.

Candy, who was braver than I about calling on strangers, rang all of the doorbells one by one, hoping to find someone at home who would show us the basement. Not one of them answered. We left a note under the doormat explaining who we were, how they could reach us and that we wanted to know if anyone knew of any names written in soot on the basement ceiling. We would never hear from anyone. Years later I read of another graffiti artist, Emperor Maximilian I[1], writing a poem on the wall of his hunting lodge, Schloss Tratzberg, with lamp black (another name for the soot of a candle or oil lamp), and that it remained there for centuries. I wondered if my grandmother and her siblings had heard that story when they wrote on their own ceiling.

Neither of us believed the house to be very grand. Candy and I grew up hearing different versions of just how wealthy or poor our great-grandparents had been. They couldn't have been as poor as my

1. 1459-1519

grandfather made them out to be, but they weren't wealthy, either. Before leaving, Candy and I took photos of each other standing next to the Tettenhall Road sign for all posterity.

Our next mission was to find the churchyards and, hopefully, Eileen's tombstone. Maybe we could find our great-grandparents' tombstones as well. We traveled a short distance down Tettenhall Road toward Tettenhall to the first church. I learned after I returned to California and received our great-grandparent's wedding certificate that it was the church where they were married. It was probably the church Eileen Maude and her seven siblings attended every Sunday growing up. But Candy and I didn't know that then. The church had no cemetery attached. We walked around the building looking at the stained glass windows, but didn't see any *in memory ofs*.

The second church, even farther from town down Tettenhall Road, had a very large and tidy cemetery. There were no vines or brambles, just grass. Candy and I split up to look through the gravestones, starting at opposite ends of the yard. As we scanned the markers, we moved toward the center. We continued like this for nearly an hour as it became cold and dark. We found nothing. We retraced our steps in a few places, but there was no hint of Eileen Maude, her parents or any of her brothers and sisters. The whole family must have been buried somewhere else.

We'd failed as sleuths. So we headed back to Worcester for an easier assignment, feeding Candy's starving children. As she pulled out a jar of Marmite from her cupboard and spread the brown paste on white bread to make sandwiches, we talked about how nice it had been to have the day together and get to know each other. Maybe the spirits of our great-grandparents were looking down upon us and blessing us for that.

The following day I took a train to London for my final destination, Philippa's house in Herne Hill, where I would stay my last nights in England, August 9 and 10.

View from the tour bus – London, 2006.

Chapter 39

End of the Road

Herne Hill is a middle-class residential area in the southern part of Greater London, though it is a bit seedy near the subway station where Philippa picked me up. We got back to her three-story row house in time for a late tea and cake, sitting on the terrace overlooking her grassy backyard. Later she made a delicious seafood couscous for dinner. I was impressed throughout my trip by what good cooks the Thomases and the Cartledges were!

Philippa was warm and bubbly, and when she laughed, her rosy cheeks twinkled. She stood shorter than her sister, like her mother, whereas Candy was tall like their Uncle Jeffray. Both sisters had the same unusual heart-shaped faces as their mother, aunt and grandmother, and the cat-like eyes.

Philippa worked as a web designer and had a boring, tedious commute each day. Her husband, Peter, wrote for advertising agencies from his office in their third floor attic. Sixteen-year-old son, Josh, attended high school and was a very accomplished musician. He gave me a copy of the music CD he and his band produced called *Mojave*. Georgia, a gorgeous thirteen-year old with long blond *plaits* (braids), told me she liked the theater, the mysteries of life and wanted to have five children. I took their snapshots in the backyard for my illustrated family tree. Georgia made me retake hers five times.

The following morning, Philippa gave me the phone number of her Aunt Ann, Jeffray's widow. I called from the sitting room, ready with a note pad and pencil since my iBook was out of gas.

Ann, a couple years younger than my mother, with a very cheery rhythmic voice that I learned was her Jersey accent, remembered "Uncle Pryns" well. "He visited England often after he moved to America. Came over nearly once a year and would gather all the Thomases together for these huge dinner parties at the Ivy. They were delightful. I got the impression he felt terribly guilty about his divorce from Eileen."

It interested me both Lionel and Ann talked about the dinners Grandpa put on. It reminded me of the dinners he provided for the Booth cousins in San Francisco. Some of them felt guilty he spent so much money on them, but I knew my grandfather enjoyed being with his family more than anything. He could afford the dinners, and he was otherwise alone and lonely. He also took my family out for nice expensive meals when he visited us when I was young.

Ann added her family's statistics to my family tree and confirmed most of what Candy had already told me about what her four children, Jungle Eyes, Sarah, Harriet and James, were up to.

"I'm afraid I can't invite you out to visit West Hall," she said. "We are living in a rubble here. I hope you'll come back soon."

"I do, too," I told her sincerely.

Then she asked me if I knew a woman named Jenny X. (For privacy, I won't publish her last name). When I told her I didn't, she said, "Well, she was a friend of your grandfather and his wife Fay. I'm not sure how they knew each other, but she is a good friend of mine. You should give her a call. I think she would be delighted to talk to you."

It wasn't clear how a friend of Fay's could tell me anything about my grandmother Eileen, but I dialed the number Ann gave me for Jenny anyway. I was only able to leave a message.

I took my written notes upstairs and left them with my charging computer. It was my last day in England, and I wanted to concentrate on other things, especially getting to know my second-cousin and my mini-cousins.

Philippa and I spent the rest of the morning sitting at her dining table. She showed me some of the books written by her Granny Joy. It struck me that Philippa was also wonderful with words like her sister, mother and grandmother. *I wonder what I inherited from my grandmother?*

We talked about Philippa's difficult schedule, my disappointing love life, what her kids were going through as teenagers, and what it had been like during the seven years her mother, Jill, declined with Alzheimer's. I wanted to know more because my mother was becoming so loopy and difficult. Mom didn't have Alzheimer's, but she couldn't do certain things anymore, like figure out a tip at a restaurant, or finish a book. She'd always loved reading.

I felt badly for Philippa and Candy because Jill had shown the same stubbornness about finances that my mother was showing. Jill had refused to let anyone help her prepare for her old age while she was in a more competent position. Ultimately, the whole house of cards, in other words Chantry, fell down.

My mother filed her bank statements by throwing them on top of a pile on her dining table. As she opened her bills, she added them, often unpaid, to the pile. The pile grew larger and messier over the weeks until there was no place to eat and the phone company or electric company called her with a "friendly reminder." Only then did she allow me to sit with her and sort things out.

Mom's identity and her government of the family were heavily based on her control of the purse strings. She obtained her law degree at age fifty-two. She worked for Legal Aid part-time while she studied for the bar, then took the California Bar exam once, but didn't pass. Before a second attempt, she married my stepfather and decided she didn't want to work full-time anyway and continued as before, living off her inheritance from my grandfather.

In contrast, when not a student, I'd worked in some capacity since I turned eighteen. And it didn't take a law degree to see Mom was leaving her accounts vulnerable to theft and mismanagement. She'd lost track of what accounts she had and where her money was. When I asked her to grant me financial power of attorney so I could speak directly to the bankers, she growled, "Over my dead body!" with a sneer that made my blood curdle. When I pointed out some dangerous mistakes the bankers had made, she told me to mind my own business.

Philippa and I spent the rest of the day sightseeing. We strolled around Buckingham Palace, took a tour on a red double-decker bus and slurped ice cream cones in Hyde Park. While I struggled with my drippy chocolate mint cone, Jenny X returned my call on my mobile phone.

I had difficulty hearing her, partly because I was in a crowded area and partly because my hearing is going to pot. I couldn't understand her when she explained how she had known Pryns and Fay. She wanted to get together for lunch, but I didn't have any more time left in my schedule. I jotted down her street address and promised to write. She wasn't yet on email.

The trip home from Heathrow to San Francisco was like an episode of the old TV show "The Twilight Zone." A huge plot to blow up planes heading from Heathrow to major airports in the United States had been uncovered the night before. The suspected bomb-carrying flights were all nonstops, very likely including mine to San Francisco.

I'd gone to bed having no idea about the discovery and awoke the following morning equally ignorant. Since my flight wasn't due to depart until 2:15 in the afternoon, I leisurely ate breakfast and as calmly took a shower. When I returned to my room from the bathroom I noticed there were two phone messages on my mobile. The first was from Carolyn.

"Mary, I've been listening to the news about the problems at Heathrow. I just wanted you to know that if your flight doesn't go out today, you can come stay here if you like."

Alarmed, I threw my bathrobe back on and headed down the stairs toward the sitting room. As I descended, I listened to the second message, which was from Jenny X. "Mary, I heard the news on the telly about the bombing plots. It doesn't look like you'll be going home today. I was thinking, maybe if you are still here we could meet up for lunch."

When I reached the bottom of the stairs I could see Philippa, still in her lounging robe, chatting with Josh. The TV across the room from them was off.

"Philippa!" I cried. "We should turn on the TV. Something has happened at Heathrow! Something about bomb threats!"

Josh flipped the switch and tuned to a broadcaster telling us about a mess at the airport, one that would take weeks, maybe months to sort out. There had been threats on up to ten planes, making it a plot three times larger than the scheme to terrorize New York on 9/11/2001. Meanwhile, news banners at the bottom of the screen proclaimed, "BAA: Outgoing travelers should stay away from the airport." I was traveling on United Airlines, not British Airlines.

If I didn't try to catch my flight and it left anyway, I would have a heck of a time booking a seat on another flight. However, if I knew for sure my plane wasn't going anywhere, then I could enjoy the day with my cousins or Jenny.

After some investigating, I decided to go to the airport. Meanwhile, Josh relayed reports that passengers were prohibited from carrying anything onto the planes except money, passports, medicine and keys. No water bottles were allowed, since the authorities suspected bombs made with fluids, and keys with remotes attached were prohibited since they might be detonating devices in disguise.

That meant I had to pack my valuable computer, smartphone, digital camera and jewelry into an unlocked suitcase. I remembered the time my son packed his computer in his suitcase. When the bag arrived at SFO it had been ransacked—the zipper broken, clothes spilling out, and the computer gone.

I had no choice. I repacked my suitcase to make room for all the things I'd planned on carrying onto the plane with me and backed up all the new data on my laptop to a small portable USB hard drive, just in case someone stole the computer. While the data copied, I purged the suitcase of superfluous matter. The worst sacrifice was my large bottle of Marmite. I knew Philippa would enjoy it because I'd seen a half-empty jar in her cupboard.

Full of electronic devices, my already obese bag grew heavier than ever and still missed its pull handle. Philippa and I set off for the subway in her car. I finally found myself on the last stretch of the Piccadilly Line, normally crammed with travelers. Only two other passengers rode in the train car with me as we approached the last stop at Heathrow, like on a ghost train! I wondered what I was getting myself into?

I got off the subway at the Heathrow stop into a deserted lobby and ascended the elevator to the departure level. Security guards hovered everywhere, but few travelers. I was relieved to find a short queue at the check-in counter and a roll of plastic bags available for my carry-on items. I made three last calls: one to Philippa, one to Carolyn and one to Jenny, to tell them I'd made it safely to the airport. Then I stuffed my little English phone into my bulging suitcase, ecstatic to be relieved of the monstrous bag and happier still to learn I wasn't to be charged an overweight fee.

As I walked away, I jangled my plastic bag through which all the world could see my money and my passport. I wasn't even allowed to carry on a tube of lipstick or a book to read. My load was light, but I felt naked. It was worse for a poor elderly lady I saw later, her plastic bag filled with adult diapers.

I walked through the door at the top of the escalator and faced an astonishingly long queue, reaching as far as I could see in either direction. I was sure I would be in line forever and had no chance of making my plane. An hour later I reached the spot at the top of the escalator where I'd entered the hall. It was two o'clock and my flight was due to leave at quarter past. A friendly-looking flight attendant assured me that if any plane was about to leave, someone from the airline would come down the line and rescue its passengers.

And that is what happened. Twenty minutes later another attendant called everyone carrying a United boarding pass to step out of line. She ushered us toward a double door. *Free sailing!* I thought until I passed through the doors and was met by another queue leading to four security check stations.

Forty-five minutes later a security guardess thoroughly frisked me while my plastic bag glided through the scanning machine. As she patted every part of my body, I watched the guards in the station next to me argue with a woman who insisted she be allowed to take her large leather handbag through security. I was surprised she had made it that far and relieved when the guards prevailed.

The nearly deserted halls ahead were lined with duty-free shops. I had a long walk through them because my gate was the farthest away. As I passed empty shop after empty shop, I felt sorry for the storekeepers. They stood helplessly alone watching their prospective customers scurry by. Not only did we not have enough time to buy anything, we were still unsure what we would be allowed to keep when we boarded our planes. As feared, there was another security checkpoint at my gate, and I was still allowed only my plastic bag.

In spite of all the delays, I stood first in line for my flight. I walked into a completely empty waiting room, sat down and wished I had a book or magazine to read. For all I knew, I could be waiting in that room for days. Happily, within forty minutes all the other passengers had been cleared to enter the room, and we boarded our plane. It left for America only half-full, at the most. The airlines treated us to one of the best airplane meals I've ever had and nonstop movies on the individual screens in front of us.

I found the huge customs area at San Francisco International Airport equally deserted. My steps echoed as I walked from one end to the other and out the double doors. *Home!* I finally relaxed and took a long breath, walked the short distance to the Marin Airporter stop at the curb and stepped onto the bus shortly afterward. As soon as I found a seat, I fell asleep, only to wake up when the bus made its first stop in Marin County after crossing the Golden Gate Bridge.

After getting off in San Rafael, a taxi took my fat suitcase and me to my front door. It seemed like I'd been gone for ages. I entered my little yellow cottage feeling blessed I have such a cozy and safe place to live, but also discouraged. My three weeks were filled with wonderful adventures, and I got to know my fantastic family, but I hadn't found what I sought. I hoped my mother wouldn't think I'd been tilting at windmills.

Eileen Maude, Peter, Pryns
and Betty May with glasses – c1928.

Chapter 40

Slim Pickin's.

From the end of August to the end of October 2006, my graphic design business slammed me. I couldn't have pursued my search for Eileen Maude even if I'd wanted to.

When the plate finally cleaned off in November, I had two leads to follow—weak ones, but a place to start. Jon Abbott had told me the name of the hospital where Eileen Maude died, Seafield Hospital in Ayr. Maybe they still had the records from 1933. And if they did, maybe the records indicated where they sent Eileen Maude's body.

I Googled Seafield Hospital and learned this from Wikipedia:

> Seafield is a southern district of Ayr, Scotland. The district is a popular retirement place with scenic views overlooking Ayr beach. The area is also home to the old racecourse of Ayr, which is now used for golfing. Seafield Children's Hospital, which served Ayr, is now closed.

I was sure a hospital wouldn't close down without sending its records somewhere. *How was I going to find out where those records went?*

My second lead was St. Peter's Church in Cranley Gardens. When I returned from England, the marriage certificate for Eileen Maude and Pryns I'd ordered from the Family Records Centre in London awaited me. It confirmed the exact name of the church where they married, but not whether or not the church had a cemetery.

Employing Google once again, I received many hits for St. Peter's Church, but nothing for St. Peter's Church, Cranley Gardens. The only one worth pursuing was a St. Peter's Church on Kensington Park Road. Unfortunately, their web site didn't list an email address. I sent the following letter regular mail:

> I am looking for the grave of my grandmother and am writing to ask you if you have a cemetery and if her grave is in it. Her name at the time of her death ...[my usual explanation.]
>
> My grandfather mentions in his journal that he visited St. Peter's in Cranley Gardens on the anniversary of her death in 1934. When my mother and I realized that her parents were married at your church on January 12, 1921, we thought it might be possible my grandfather had her buried there.
>
> It is also possible he left a different type of memorial other than a grave, such as a stained glass window, or a bench. All we have to go by is a mention in my grandfather's journal, 'I hoped she liked what I did with her grave.'
>
> Please let me know if there are any memorials to Eileen Maude Armitage anywhere in or around St. Peter's, or if you might know where else to look. I am enclosing a self-addressed envelope and what English money I have for postage. You can also send me an email at the address above.
>
> Thank you very much for your help.

I enclosed a pound coin. I didn't have anything smaller.

On November 6, four days before my mother's eighty-first birthday, I received this response via email:

> Dear Mary
>
> Thank you for your letter of 31 October, and the contribution towards postage. I am sorry that I don't think I can shed a lot of light on your hunt.

We do not have a graveyard, and though we do have some memorial tablets around the interior of the church, I have searched these but without finding one for your grandmother. The address of the church is Kensington Park Road, but it is at the junction with Stanley Gardens (not Cranley Gardens), so that would not correspond with your Grandfather's journal. You may be interested to look at our web site—www.nottinghillchurch.org.uk, which will give you some historical details of the church. I have copied below the text of our historical details, but none of this is as personal as you were hoping!

I do hope you are successful in your search.

With all good wishes,

Anne

Parish Administrator

After reading the email, I reviewed Pryns and Eileen's wedding certificate again, just to make sure it said Cranley Gardens and not Stanley Gardens. The handwriting script on those documents is often hard to decipher. Then I wrote:

Dear Anne:

Thank you so much for your detailed response to my inquiry about my grandmother and your thorough search.

I looked again on the wedding certificate and it states '1921 Marriage solemnized at St. Peters Church in the parish of St Peters Cranley Gardens in the County of London. Marriages in the Registration District of Kensington.'

Do you think that would be another church? Is Cranley Gardens a different place? Is there any possibility that the name changed?

By the next morning I'd received an email from Anne:

Dear Mary

I have done a little more hunting for you and I think this may be fruitful. I looked up Cranley Gardens and there is a Cranley Gardens in South Kensington, but no church there now. However, I then went to the nearest church and discovered that they are 'with St Peter's', which would suggest that historically they may have swallowed up an earlier parish—maybe if the church building had been bombed in the war? [She gave me the web site for the church.]

Hopefully they will be able to shed some light.

With all good wishes,

Anne

It disturbed me to learn the church where my grandparents married was bombed during the war. If it did have a cemetery, Eileen's grave was probably blown up, too. I took a look at the web site, keeping my hope lit. The web site led me to "St Mary with St Peter and St Jude," West Brompton, The Parish Office, St Mary's Church House, Contact: Gerald.

Dear Gerald:

I found your email address on the web site for St. Mary with St. Peter and St. Jude. I'm looking for the church where my grandparents were married...

Is it possible that the church I am looking for was destroyed during the war and that the parish combined with your St. Mary's?

What I'm hoping for is to find out if there is a cemetery associated with your church. We are looking for the grave ... [standard details].

Any help would be greatly appreciated.

I never heard back from Gerald, though I still receive periodic emails from the church about their socials. In the meantime, my daughter, Amy, came home from New York for Thanksgiving vacation. We joined Mom for Sunday brunch at Villa Marin.

I'd been telling Amy about my quest, and she wanted to see Eileen Maude's will. We went up to Mom's condo,where she directed us to the folder in a rusty old file cabinet across the room from her wing chair. We found the will, and to our surprise, another yellowed document in the same folder—a record of the settling of Eileen Maude's estate. Amy and I looked carefully through the old document and discovered a promising category, "Funeral Expenses," under which it read:

Wylie & Lochhead	26.14. 6
Kendal Milne & Co.	21.10. –

[That is pounds, shillings and pence, in case the reader has never read English money before.]

Wylie & Lochhead, I found via Google, is a funeral director in Glasgow, Scotland, with several branches. Glasgow is about thirty miles northeast of Ayr. The web site didn't list an email address, so I would have to write another snailmail letter.

Kendal Milne & Co. turned out to be a department store in Manchester, purchased by Harrods in 1919 and sold to Housse of Fraser in 1959. Manchester is a large city in England quite a bit south of Ayr, but only an hour or so north of Wolverhampton. Maybe some of the Wolverhampton relatives purchased some clothes or other items for Eileen Maude's burial?

Holiday activities between Thanksgiving and Christmas prevented me from writing the letter to Wylie & Lochhead until New Years' Day, when I had a quiet afternoon to myself.

Dear Sir/Madame:

I am on a search to find the grave of my grandmother. I have been working on this for nearly six months and took a fruitless trip to England last summer. Then recently her estate papers were unearthed and we found a listing under "Funeral Expenses" for your company, Wylie & Lochhead. I located this address on the Internet. I see that there are at least four or five offices of this name in Glasgow. I sincerely hope you will forward this letter to someone who can help me if I picked the wrong office.

I would like you to check the records for Eileen Maude Armitage to see if there is mention of where her body was buried. The particulars are listed below: [I gave the standard details.]

My mother was eight when her mother died and moved to America soon after. She did not attend the burial or funeral and now, at age eighty-one, would very much like to know the location of her mother's remains.

I can't tell you how much I hope you can help me. My email address is listed above.

Thank you,

Mary Mitchell

A week later, Monday, January 8, 2007, as I drove to the Lawrence Berkeley Lab across the bay to carry out some freelance graphic design work, I took a peek at my smartphone to see if I had any emails, even though I knew it wasn't a safe thing to do while driving over the steep Richmond Bridge. There were several, and one was from wylielochhead.glasgow@letsco-operate.com.

Probably another letter saying they are sorry they can't find any records of my grandmother. When I stopped in the parking lot of the lab, I opened the email, but only read this far:

> Dear Mary
>
> I was given the task of locating the last resting place of your Grandmother Eileen Maude Armitage. After some research into our old accounts I found that your grandmother was cremated at Glasgow Crematorium Maryhill on Nov 20th 1933. Your grandmother's ashes were dispersed in the Garden of Remembrance at the crematorium.

I glanced at the next paragraph, but it was about money. I needed to get into the lab or I would be late. I was already crying, overcome by a heavy sadness mixed with disbelief. I needed to pull myself together or I would enter the lab with a tear-drenched face. *I'll finish it later.* I jammed the phone down into the bottom of my handbag, furiously.

Is that it? I fumed. *Is that all that became of her? Just a sprinkling of ashes in an unfamiliar place? What was Vernon thinking? Was my grandfather no help at all?*

I needed to concentrate on my work that day and then had to dash from Berkeley to Sonoma, where my monthly book club met. That was a drive of an hour and fifteen minutes. I was so upset by what I'd read that morning that I didn't finish reading the email.

The ladies in my book club had heard plenty about my trip to England. As I settled on the sofa, one of the members asked, "Any news of your search?"

"As a matter of fact, yes. I received an important email today, but I didn't finish reading it."

"Then read it to us."

I dug my smartphone out, scrolled to the message and read it out loud. The last part said:

> If you require a photograph of the Crematorium Garden of Remembrance, I would be only too happy to take some pictures for you. Also if you require an entry in the *Book of Remembrance*, there is a charge of £50-00p for a two-line entry and £75-00p for a five-line entry and with badge or emblem £150-00p and for a copy for your own personal use a further charge of £150-00p. I hope I have given your mother and your kind self some peace of mind, and that you and she now know the last resting place of Eileen Maude Armitage. If I can be of any further assistance please do not hesitate to email me.
> Daniel
> Funeral Arranger, Wylie Lochhead

We all sat silently while I digested the information, as disappointing and pragmatic as it was. Finally someone said, "Well, the idea of a Garden of Remembrance seems nice."

I felt extremely let down, and my most materialistic self came through. *No grand tombstone. No statue with a likeness of my grandmother. No stained glass window. No bench. Not even a mention in a* Book of Remembrance*! My grandmother was just tossed into the air like a handful of fertilizer to float down on top of the ashes of all the other people who'd been scattered into oblivion, leaving no permanent record of existence.*

Why wasn't Eileen's name entered in the Book of Remembrance*?* I fidgeted in my place on the sofa, wanting to go outside and kick a trash can or something. *Was Vernon so cheap and selfish he couldn't cough up a couple hundred dollars to have his wife's name written in a ledger?*

I thought about my grandfather helping Vernon purchase Berri Court in Sussex for his tomatoes. I thought about Vernon fondling my mother inappropriately when he tucked her into bed at night. I thought about how Vernon's friends, the Priors, offered to adopt my mother and Peter. *This was turning into a very sad story indeed.*

Couldn't my grandfather have done something? Was he that thoughtless? Did he know there was no grave, no headstone, no urn and no name written permanently in a book to keep the memory of his former beloved alive? His mother had purchased an entire cemetery plot for her relatives. How much had he spent on all those séances to relieve his own conscience? And what about Eileen's parents, who hadn't even reported the correct day of her death to the newspapers? My questions were mounting up like the bills on my mother's dining room table.

On January 9 I wrote back to Wylie & Lochhead:

Dear Daniel:

On the one hand I'm glad to know the final answer, but on the other I was sad to receive this email and learn that there was no grave marker or anything to honor my grandmother's memory. Does this mean no one entered her name in the remembrance book at the time? For now, YES. Please do send us some photos. I'll be showing this email to my mother and we can talk about what we'd like to do next. What exactly is a badge or emblem? If we would like to partake of these services, can we do it online with a credit card?

Thank you so very much for your help and research.

Daniel replied two days later:

Dear Mary,

Thank you for your reply to my email. The badge or emblem can be a clan badge or military badge or a symbol of sorts, a Celtic symbol or a flower or a rose. An option to insert a name in the *Book of Remembrance* is given at the time of the arranging of the funeral, and I can only assume that the person arranging it did not hear the option due to distress of a loved one passing away. If you would like to partake in this service I will be only too glad to assist you. Yes, it can be paid by credit card. For security reasons I would advise you sending several individual emails with the credit card number, the expiration date and the last 3-digit secure numbers on the rear of the card. Please take your time and think about what you would like on the insertion of the *Book of Remembrance.* I will make the effort to go to the Garden of Remembrance on Sunday and take a picture for you.

Daniel

My grandmother was shoved aside when she was alive, then she was shoved aside when she died. I was determined that this wasn't the end of it.

Several days later, Daniel emailed me several photos of red-stone Maryhill Memorial Church and its enclosed Garden of Remembrance. I printed them out on my color printer and took them with Daniel's email to show Mom the next Sunday. I wondered if she would be as devastated as I was. I decided to paraphrase the email since I thought Daniel's phrasing a bit too business-like.

After meeting Mom in the dining room at Villa Marin, we selected our food from the buffet and settled into our seats. I waited a few moments while she put her napkin in her lap, ordered coffee from the waiter and began eating her Eggs Benedict. Then I began. "I received news about the whereabouts of your mother this week."

She looked up from cutting her soggy English muffin. Her hands were so arthritic, it was a challenge, but I knew she wouldn't let me help her. "Did you really?" she said. "And what did you hear?"

"Do you remember that listing for a Wylie & Lochhead I obtained from your mother's estate papers?"

"Not really." She wrinkled her brow.

"I wrote a letter to them and I received a reply this week."

"Yes? And what did it say?" She seemed curious but not overly eager. It was as if she didn't want to set herself up to be let down.

I took a deep breath. "It turns out that your mother was cremated at a crematorium in Glasgow. Then her ashes were scattered in a Garden of Remembrance there."

For a mere second she looked disappointed. Then she gave me a weak smile and said, "Well, now we know, don't we."

"Here, I have some photos of the garden."

I reached down to take them out of my purse, which was resting near my feet. As I handed the sheet of prints to Mom, I recalled my grandfather's comment in his journal on the anniversary of the last time his children saw their mother: "Betty May had repressed the memory." I also remembered Jon Abbott's comment, "My mother shielded us from her grief."

I said, "All along we've had the information we needed right here. We could've found your mother in our own backyard, so to speak." Then I remembered how loving and gracious Camilla and all my other cousins and their families had been. How they'd taken me into their homes, fed me and shared their secrets. My words choked in my throat, and I had difficulty getting the last sentence out. "But just think, if I hadn't gone to England, I wouldn't have had the chance to get to know all of your family."

All efforts at holding on to my emotions failed, and I started to cry, overcome by the knowledge of the loneliness my mother had gone through and by how much my grandmother had given up to be what her family wanted her to be. I knew my crying made my mother uncomfortable, so I stopped as soon as I could. Besides, we were still in the dining hall and I didn't want to embarrass both of us.

Mom put on her "cheer up" smile, reached out her hand to mine and gave it a quick pat. "Yes, it's a very good thing you went to England. Thank you, dear, for doing all this work to find my mother for me."

That made me feel good and calmed me down. When I had my voice back, I told her about the *Book of Remembrance*. "I think we should pay for the entry in the ledger. What do you think?"

"Yes. I think we should do that," she smiled.

"And maybe some day, you know, two hundred years from now, when you pass away, we can write on your tombstone in Santa Barbara, 'Daughter of Eileen Thomas Hopkins Armitage whose ashes were scattered in Scotland.' Then your descendants in California will know what happened to her."

"That would be very nice." She gave my hand another pat and returned to her muffin.

During the next week I researched what it would take for my mother and me to go to Scotland and have our own little memorial for her mother. The following Sunday I presented Mom with a plan. It included all the arrangements and challenges that would be necessary for a nearly crippled person to travel.

"Are you sure you wouldn't mind going to all that trouble?" she said.

"Of course not. You'd have to pay, though." I said, hopefully.

"Yes, of course I'll pay. I'll think about it."

While she was thinking about it, I looked into all the options.

I wanted to go to Glasgow to have a ceremony in the Garden of

Remembrance. To get from San Francisco to Glasgow, one had to travel through London. There were no nonstops. It was cheaper to buy a round-trip ticket to London and then a separate round-trip ticket between London and Glasgow than to purchase connecting flights. From Glasgow we could rent a car and drive to Ayr to see The Bungalow.

Since we were traveling through London anyway, why not stop and see the *rellies* there for a few days? If we stayed in a nice hotel, they could visit us and Mom wouldn't have to walk anywhere.

Dear Daniel:

I've discussed this with my mother. We do want to do something. In fact, I'm trying to talk her into traveling to Glasgow. Meanwhile, what is the address for the garden? I'd like to look it up on Multi-map. Is it a nice neighborhood if we book a hotel nearby?

Best regards,

Mary Mitchell

Betty May and her cousin Jon Abbott – Scotland, c1937.

Chapter 41

Planning for Glasgow

Not until July 17, 2008, did I book two sets of tickets on British Airways to London and Glasgow. That was a whole year and five months from the time I started planning the trip with my mother. By that time she felt too frail to travel. My daughter, Amy, age twenty-seven, eagerly took her place. Jon, by then thirty, wasn't interested in spending so much time with a couple of gabby girls.

We were due to leave October 1—Amy from New York City and I from San Francisco. She would arrive at ten-thirty in the morning of October 2 and I would arrive a half hour later. That left us four hours before our connecting flight to Glasgow to individually get through customs and meet up for lunch, plus a safety net in case either of our flights were delayed. We would be exhausted when we reached Glasgow at 4:00 in the evening.

I tried very hard to convince Mom to go with us. I begged and I pleaded and I showed her how she could travel with as few difficulties as possible, obtaining wheelchairs when necessary to avoid stairs and long walks. She simply didn't want to go. "I want to remember London as I last saw it. I'm afraid I wouldn't like to see how it's changed." Old people must be allowed their memories, I supposed, and there was also the issue of having a restroom close by.

During the previous year, two sets of our English relatives came to visit us. Candy and her family flew into San Francisco during the summer of 2007. We spent one day shopping on Union Square; our dollar was so low to the English pound it was like Filene's Bargain Basement to them. We spent another day paddling canoes down the Russian River in the Wine Country an hour north of my home.

Camilla and Rodney arrived in May of 2008. They stayed with Mom at Villa Marin for a couple of days, then with me for a few days more. I showed off the Sonoma Mission, the Wine Country again and the artist-haven Bolinas on the coast. While they were with me, we drafted a tentative schedule for Amy and my trip to London after Glasgow. They invited us to stay with them in their London flat. And while we were there, Camilla wanted to reunite the Thomas Family with a fork supper (what we in America call a lap supper, or buffet, as opposed to a sit-down dinner for which everyone has a place at a table).

With tickets arranged, I called Mom's cousin Jon Abbott in Northampton (he never converted to email) to see if he could join us in Glasgow or at least make it to Camilla's party so I could meet him. He was honored we wanted to visit the area of his old home in Scotland, but he suggested we skip driving to Ayr and visit Edinburgh instead. Since Camilla and Rodney strongly suggested the same thing, that is what we decided to do.

Amy planned to stay two weeks to my three. We would stop in Glasgow for a day or two to hold a "wee" memorial service for Eileen Maude at the Garden of Remembrance and have her name inscribed permanently in the *Book of Remembrance*. Jon Abbott also advised we see the architecture of the craftsman designer Charles Rennie Macintosh for which Glasgow is famous and which I'd enjoyed studying in art school.

I wrote to Daniel at Wylie & Lochhead to let him know we wanted to hold a service for Eileen Maude on Friday morning, October 3, at 10:00 a.m, right after he opened his office. That was the day after we arrived in Glasgow. I thought his office was very close to the garden, and we'd be able to finish in an hour. I was mistaken.

As part of the ceremony, I hoped to play a recording of *La Golandrina*. I downloaded a PDF of the sheet music, and my church organist digitally recorded it for me on his piano. I copied the file to a CD as well as my iPod.

The next Sunday I carried the CD with me to Villa Marin. When Mom and I returned to her condo after brunch, I slid the recording into the disk player I'd given her—a machine she'd never tried to use—and while it played, I sang. The score and the tune matched awkwardly, but my mother was not a harsh critic.

"That was very nice," she said.

"Would you like me to sing it again?" I asked sheepishly. I hadn't sung in front of my mother since I was a Brownie reciting the songs I'd learned at summer camp. But I wanted a second try at mastering the odd rhythm.

"Yes, that would be nice."

After I finished she said, "I'm sure my parents are looking down on us and smiling," My eyes filled up with tears. I looked across the room at her. Nothing on her face revealed how she was feeling, which was disappointing but not surprising. Yet her comment touched me.

I have to scratch deeply into my memory bank to find times when my mother showed emotion. I remember her leaving the room in tears once when she was married to my dad. The only other emotion I remember is her anger, usually directed at me. My brothers left for boarding school when they were thirteen and never moved back. Mom got angry for minor infractions, like coming home after curfew or riding on the back of my boyfriend's motorcycle. I was the good daughter, hoping to please her. I never did drugs. I never got drunk. I never wrecked her car. Maybe one of the reasons I was going to all the trouble to find her mother's grave was to find a way to reach my mother's soul?

My mom loved me. She was devoted to me. She made sure I was properly fed, clothed, housed and educated and that I learned a workable skill so I could be independent, like she was. She encouraged me to draw and sew, like she could. She showed pride in me when I graduated from high school, from college and from teaching school and then got a teaching job when no else could get a teaching job. She came to my graduation from professional art school fourteen years later. But did that pride reflect her or me?

She didn't ask me questions about what was going on in my life, When I asked her why, she said, "It's too hard for me to see you in pain." I often wondered if she was interested in me as an individual. Did she like Mary Ames as an unique person, or just because I was her daughter? I think Ex-Three learned more about me on our first date than my mother did during her whole life!

I wondered if maybe my mother was jealous of me. Did she think it weakness on her part to praise me? When I offered a business or legal suggestion, she popped back with, "I don't need your advice. Remember I have a law degree." She didn't want me to be pretty, lest I attract the wrong type of man. Was that because of the way Vernon treated her? I asked her once if it bothered her I didn't get A's in school like my brothers did, just B's.

"B's were fine," she said. "I didn't worry about you."

Maybe I *wanted* her to worry about me. Maybe it bothered *me* I didn't get A's.

I felt sorry for my mom as she got older and isolated. She didn't complain, but I knew she was lonely and hungry for stimulating conversation. Because of her arthritis, even the tiniest task, such as brushing her teeth, became extremely difficult. What happened as she grew older, I've since learned, is not that unusual. Her view of me changed from being that of her child to being that of her parent. She was like a rebellious teenage child. She growled at anyone who tried to assist her, "Leave me alone, I can do it myself." Losing her independence made her miserable. She was angry about growing old. I couldn't predict when she would snap at me or at someone else.

But she didn't ask for much, only that I show up for brunch on

Family Day. And we finally seemed to connect when I started writing. She wrote beautifully herself. She published many interesting travel articles in local and national papers. She helped me with the editing of my book about my father and acted proud of me when it was published. By the time I started writing this book, she no longer had the attention span to help. Nonetheless, I hoped it would give us something to talk about and that she would enjoy the attention of sharing her memories with me.

Once an older male friend told me how important it was for a father to recognize when his son had become stronger than he was. Isn't that what bar-mitzvahs are all about or becoming a brave in an Indian tribe? Women need the same thing. We need recognition from our mothers that we have joined the world of women, that we are equal to them. I wanted more from my mother than her pride in me. I wanted her respect. Like in the Biblical story of Jacob, when he wrestled with the angel and wouldn't let go until the angel blessed him, I struggled for my mother's blessing.

Four days before departure day, I received good news from Jon Abbott telling me he'd arranged to meet Amy and me in Glasgow. He was seventy-nine years old, only four years younger than my mother. The last time Mom saw Jon was when my family visited him during the 1959 trip.

He planned to stay at a Premier Inn not too far from the bed and breakfast where Amy and I were staying. He suggested we meet the night of our arrival at a restaurant he called "budget," at £39 each. *Eeegads!* That was nearly $80 a person. The trip promised to be even pricier than the one I took two years earlier.

Amy and I extended our stay in Glasgow to three nights to allow us to do more sightseeing before we trained to Edinburgh for two nights. I booked a B&B in Glasgow for $80 a night for both of us with a bathroom down the hall. The B&B in Edinburgh charged $220 per night, *ensuite*. At least they both included hearty Scottish breakfasts.

Camilla sent me the draft of her schedule for our time with her. She kindly included my stepcousins Paul and Carolyn in her guest list for the fork supper, as well as Mom's school chum Rosemary and her husband Graham. Camilla expected twenty-nine people, although I wasn't exactly sure who.

There would be no temptation to visit the Family Records Centre in London. I had recently read in a newspaper that the ledgers were transported to Siemans, a computer company in Germany contracted to digitize the data. The project halted midway, with Siemans claiming they couldn't complete the task. The ledgers were being held in a vault somewhere out of reach, with no plans for returning to England. I was extremely fortunate I'd been able to access them when I did.

Planning a simple service for Eileen Maude, I borrowed a tiny speaker from my son that plugged into the bottom of my iPod with *La Golandrina* downloaded. I sent Amy the recording and the music score so she could practice singing it too. I made copies of the two poems Eileen Maude wrote that still existed: *Month Old Impressions* and *Carnations*, and I planned to draft a poem of my own during the plane trip.

The only difficulty I encountered was that I couldn't reach the famous Willow Tea House in central Glasgow, one of Macintosh's landmarks. (Not only did he design the architecture and furniture, he designed the dishes, flatware, waitress uniforms and the typeface used on the menus.) I thought it would be a nice place to have our memorial reception. What could be better than high tea with scones, clotted cream, tea and cakes?

Jon Abbott, the author and Daniel –
Wylie & Lochhead, 2009.

Chapter 42

Great Britain Round Two

The flight to London went smoothly. Amy and I had agreed to look for each other in customs. If she didn't see me come in before she was through, she would wait at the exit. Plan C was to find the nearest set of car rental counters and meet at the Hertz Counter. Plan D, if no Hertz counter, find the rental car company with the first letter of the alphabet, Alamo, or Budget, etc., and meet there.

I didn't see Amy in customs and she wasn't waiting for me at the exit. There were no counters in the car rental section, just a curved alcove with a set of phones, and she wasn't there either. I then consulted the departures monitors and learned her plane wasn't due to arrive for another twenty minutes. I planted myself at the customs exit under the monitor where I could keep an eye on her flight status, sitting on my suitcase in between all the limo drivers holding up signs for arriving passengers.

While I waited, I wrote the memorial poem to Eileen Maude. An hour later, as I tried to write the last line, I heard my name paged. I closed my notebook with the unfinished poem, stashed it back in my bag and set off to find a service phone to answer the page. The airport agent told me Amy had stayed airside. He instructed me to go back through security and find her at the gate.

I passed through the scanner, slipped on my shoes and, as I concentrated on threading my belt through the belt loops, I felt a tap on my shoulder. There was Amy, holding a grande-sized Starbucks in her hand. She could have been standing in a New York airport and the scene would have been the same. She gave me a big hug, which felt really, really good. I hadn't seen her in a long time, and I was extremely thankful she was sharing this journey with me.

Relieved we'd left enough time for such a scenario between flights, we found some comfortable chairs in the lounge to wait for our gate to be posted for the trip to Glasgow. I'd brought forty English pounds left over from my earlier trip, so I was able to buy us some granola yogurt cups and a decaf café latté for myself. I'd cut caffeine from my diet since the previous trip. I considered converting some dollars into pounds, but since the conversion rate is usually higher at the airports than in ATM machines on the street, I decided to wait. That decision caused a big problem later.

The flight to Glasgow from Heathrow took about an hour. From there a taxi carried us through the old shipping port. Glasgow celebrated its heyday in the 1850s, when it was second only to London as Great Britain's most important shipping center. Singer Manufacturing Company built its first offshore manufacturing plant there in 1853, but slaves and tobacco were the chief commodities.

Weathered brick warehouses amid modern arenas and museums bordered the River Clyde that we crossed when we entered the old city. The town itself consisted of imposing, ornate Victorian structures crowned with turrets and decorative tableaux. Unlike London with its many modern skyscrapers, Glasgow kept a fairly low skyline, but it sat high on a hill. There were a couple of interesting towers—a church steeple and a clock tower—neither as striking as Big Ben, pardon the pun.

Our bed-and-breakfast was situated perfectly at the end of a row of inns and other B&Bs on Renfrew Street, which scored the crest of the hill. The city didn't allow parking along the narrow street. It was good we'd abandoned the idea of renting a car. Amy and I were both too chicken to drive on the wrong side of the road anyway. We were able to walk to everything in a matter of minutes.

Jon Abbott wanted us to phone as soon as we reached our B&B. His train from Northampton had been due to arrive earlier in the afternoon. I'd brought my little mobile phone with me from my last trip, even though the instructions warned that after a year of no use, my account might be closed. When Amy and I got to our room, I crossed my fingers and plugged it in. I was very excited when the Nokia logo materialized on the screen and the phone connected to the invisible cell waves. All my relatives' phone numbers were still stored inside. I didn't know if there were any minute credits left on the account, and I couldn't remember what number to dial to find out, so I left the phone on the dresser to charge and went downstairs to the front desk to see if they would ring Jon's hotel for me.

Jon was "delighted" to hear from us. Since it was already the dinner hour, he offered to make a reservation at his budget spot and come on over to our B&B to meet with us. He asked when Amy and I would be ready to go out. I said, "Now."

We figured it would take Jon five, perhaps ten minutes to reach our B&B. Amy and I freshened up and went downstairs to wait for him in the tiny lobby. It wasn't a lobby really, just a hallway with no place to sit. We perched on the steps leading to the first floor and chatted with the Indian fellow at the desk about Glasgow and how to get Amy's Blackberry to work. Ten minutes went by, then twenty, then thirty. I started to worry and decided to try calling Jon again. By that time my phone was charged. But when I reached the Premier Inn, the receptionist told me there was no Jon Abbott registered, only a Frank Abbott. "Try that," I said. No one answered. Finally, after thirty more minutes, Jon arrived. He'd gotten a wee bit lost.

At first glance I was struck by how much he reminded me of his first-cousin, Lionel Turner. He had the same body shape, face structure, demeanor, sense of humor and, like Lionel, was well dressed. He wore a checked wool blazer and Barbour cap. He gave us a happy, warm reception—as I've since found all Scots do—and we headed off in the direction of the restaurant he'd chosen.

I was thankful I'd brought my wool scarf because the fall air felt chilly. Amy wore her boots and a fluffy sweater. We descended the hill one block to Sauchiehall Street, the main drag running parallel to Renfrew Street, where we were staying, then turned left onto Sauchiehall. After a few blocks the street transformed into a mall closed to traffic. We passed everything from Boots to Marks & Spencer, and then the Willow Tea Rooms for which, after a great deal of difficulty, I'd finally managed to reserve three seats for tea for the following day.

Jon played the part of father, grandfather and charming escort for the evening. He was smart, elegant and humorous. His Scottish accent wasn't too difficult to understand—not as thick as some I would hear on the trip—but I did feel rude having to say, "Sorry, what was that?" so often. We had a lively conversation covering the shoe business his family once owned and operated, his memories of when my grandmother got sick and of his own mother, Peggy, and how close she had been to Eileen.

"They were of one mind," he said, "like twins. Along with their older brother, Harold, they broke off from the rest of the Thomas siblings somewhat. My mother may have dominated her sisters, but Harold was the real ring-leader, sometimes with an overly critical hand.

"But I do remember once that my Aunt Daisy came to visit us from her home in Argentina," he said. "She brought her two sons, Lionel and Anthony, and two daughters, Helen and Veronica. The two daughters stunned us one night with a chorus line doing the Flamenco step."

The next morning dawned the big day. Amy and I spent twenty minutes before breakfast sitting on the beds in our room practicing *La Golandrina*. We stumbled a lot. Maybe the rhythm worked better in Spanish, but that wasn't an option. The little speaker emitted a weak and scratchy sound. I hoped the Garden of Remembrance had a quiet place to sit where we could hear the music. Amy practiced for a while longer while I wrote the missing final verse for my poem.

We found Daniel's office on Pitt Street, only a few blocks from our B&B. A large wooden sign declaring Wylie & Lochhead spanned the building. We'd passed it twice the night before on our way to and from the restaurant and had pointed it out to Jon. We had also written the address down on a piece of paper for him. He was due to meet us that morning at 10:00.

Daniel greeted us at the door, a cheery, red-flush-cheeked Scot, only a little younger than my mother and Jon Abbott. Jon had arrived before us and the two of them were sharing war stories. Daniel told us a wonderful tale about a man named Willie Angus of the Highland Light Infantry, known as the "Maryland Mafia." Willie had signed up for the war at age fifteen. During one battle he risked his life to save a comrade from his hometown, who was stuck in a dangerous place. Willie did this even though his superior officer had told him not to. In spite of severe wounds, he and the comrade made it out safely, and Willie received the Victoria Cross. For the rest of Willie's life, Captain Martin, the man he'd rescued, sent him ten *bob* (shillings) and a telegram on the anniversary of the event.

This inspired Jon to tell us about our own relative, Eileen's brother Billie Thomas. Billie had also signed up at age fifteen during the First World War as part of the South STAFFS, the Staffordshire Regiment. After coming home, he wanted to sign up for a second tour of duty, but his sister Peggy, Jon's mother, notified the war office Billie was underage; she wanted to keep him safe at home. This diminished Peggy's popularity with her brother, for a while at least. Jon was proud of the fact that all the Thomas men had served in World War I. I thought about my grandmother's fiancé who never returned home.

After an hour more of stories, we took photos of ourselves with Daniel. After all, he was the man to finally discover Eileen Maude's whereabouts. Then we set off for the crematorium's office, managed by a lady named Fiona, the woman in charge of the *Book of Remembrance*. The crematorium and garden, it turned out, were several miles north of town and required a train ride.

We stayed in Fiona's office for another hour, at least. She explained that Wylie & Lochhead, founded in 1895, was one of perhaps two of the oldest funeral directors in Great Britain to record cremations. The process was legalized in 1884. "Funeral Director is the politically correct term for undertaker," she explained, "sometimes known as 'boxmen' since many FDs, even today, build their own coffins." Cremations came into vogue with the starving times of the late 1800s because throwing dead paupers into graves was found to spread disease. By 1933, cremation was more a fashion of efficiency.

With a five-line limit of fifty characters each, we decided to write the following inscription in the *Book of Remembrance*:

> Armitage, Eileen M. Thomas Hopkins
> Born 9th Feb 1892, died 18th Nov 1933
> Missed by her children Eileen and Peter
> 'Carnations! Dear Heart, where ever I may be
> Tend them well, in memory of me.'

Obviously, we'd used the poem Eileen wrote in 1926, *Carnations*, as our inspiration. Since we had the option of including a family crest or symbol of some kind next to the inscription, we chose a carnation. But what color? Red? Pink? Yellow? Fiona solved our dilemma by informing us we could have a bouquet of three carnations if we wished. Jon pointed out the line in Eileen's poem, "blooms of every shade and hue," finalizing the decision to render three carnations: one red, one pink and one yellow.

Then we hit a snag. The cost for the calligrapher to inscribe Eileen's name in the *Book of Remembrance* was £150—roughly $275. That included drawing the bouquet of carnations. Since Mom would never be able to see the book, we could purchase a card-sized version especially for her with the exact calligraphic entry and illustrated carnations. Since it was the same amount of work, just on a smaller substrate, it also cost £150. The trouble began when I took my credit card out to pay for it. Daniel had been mistaken. Fiona would only accept cash or a postal order.

Wells Fargo Bank only allowed me to take out a maximum of £165 ($300) per day using my ATM card. Had I been warned, I would have taken out £165 the day before and only needed another £135. The remaining twenty pounds in my wallet were needed for the rest of that day's expenses. I had a debit card for another account, but I wasn't sure I knew the PIN (personal identification number) for it.

Fiona invited Jon and Amy to wait in her office while I went in search of an ATM machine. I'd noticed one across the road. When I approached it I found a sign on the screen saying it was out of service. I went to look for another. The next machine was also out of service. I started to feel like a beggar going from house to house for a tuppence. Finally I found a third machine with a long queue. By the time it was my turn, a new queue had formed behind me. I extracted the first £165 from my Wells Fargo account, but the PIN I thought I knew for my second account didn't work. I tried several different numbers, but they didn't work either. Feeling the heat of the people in a hurry behind me, I cancelled out and stepped away from the machine to think about what to do next.

I found a credit office, but they couldn't help me. Neither would the bank. Worrying I'd have to give up the small version for Mom, I returned to Fiona's office without the money I needed. Luckily, Fiona assured me I could send the balance I owed her when I got home. Jon must have worked his charm on her while I was gone.

Having overstayed our welcome in Fiona's office—she was trying to leave early for a mini-holiday that weekend—we took a group photo with her and set out for the Garden of Remembrance. It closed at 4:00 p.m.

It was past noon. In spite of the gigantic Scottish breakfasts we'd all been served at our B&Bs—eggs, toast, sausages, pinto beans, baked tomatoes, cereal and tea, Jon was hungry and didn't want to wait until after our visit to the garden to eat. The Willow Tea Rooms were *sort* of on our way to the Queen's Train Station, so we asked the *maitre'd* there if we could have our tea party early and forgo the 3:30 p.m. reservations.

"Certainly," he said, before seating us in small square Macintosh-designed chairs in the upstairs tearoom. I wasn't sure I had the appetite for high tea, but that is what we ordered. Jon encouraged me to try Assam tea. Amy ordered the Willow Tea Rooms' house blend. A three-tiered platter arrived. Quartered and trimmed sandwiches filled the bottom plate and included cheddar cheese and tomato; cucumber and cream cheese; salmon with watercress; and tuna. Plump buttery scones filled the second plate, and the top tier displayed a variety of pastries we'd pre-chosen from the pastry counter. The crowning glory, a large meringue confection about four inches in diameter, bursting with clotted cream, was Amy's. I selected a brownie and Jon a ginger cake.

We managed to consume nearly all of it. By then it was 2:00. A nap would have been in order had it not been necessary to complete our mission to the Garden of Remembrance. After trips to the loo, which I only mention because I considered it a design flaw that we had to climb three flights of stairs to get there—Jon called it the "Alpine tour," we trudged toward Queen's Station on the south side of town. Jon kept up the pace during the ten-minute walk without problem, even though he struggled with a stiff knee, just like his cousin Lionel. Fortunately, we caught a train that left five minutes after our arrival. The next would have come an hour later and blown our schedule completely.

We knew from the map we were supposed to get off at Kirkintillock. However, even Jon didn't recognize the pronunciation of the name when it was announced over the loudspeaker, so we missed our stop. That meant we had to get off at the following station and find a taxi to backtrack. It thankfully delivered us right to the door of our destination.

The chapel looked like St. John's Church in Hampstead, complete with the squared Saxon tower I recognized from the pictures Daniel had sent to me via email. We gave ourselves a tour of the sanctuary. Amy and I took photographs for my mother, and Jon knelt in a pew and said a prayer. Then we exited the chapel's side door, which led to the

Jon at Maryhill Chapel. The entrance to the garden is to the right.

garden through the small room displaying the *Book of Remembrance*.

The mediaeval-looking tome was enclosed in a glass case supported by a large wooden pedestal. Each page measured ten or eleven inches wide. Opened flat, it appeared like an old Bible. The same calligrapher must have written the inscriptions for years, because every entry appeared to be in the same hand. The book opened to October 6, displaying the entries for every person who had died October 6. Had the day required more entries than the two available pages, a second book would have been opened next to it with the remaining entries.

We'd told Fiona we wanted Eileen's entry inscribed on the sixty-fifth anniversary of her death. November 18, 2008, was a month and a half away. Every November 18 afterward, her name will be on display for everyone who views the book that day. I shall remember that next time I visit Glasgow.

Happy with the book, we proceeded to the garden courtyard enclosed by a tall red-stone wall, also familiar from Daniel's photos, except large peach-colored begonias had replaced the impatiens planted in the borders. I saw no evidence of ashes.

Brass plaques covered the walls around the garden, but I'd learned the fee for those plaques must be renewed every ten years. Who knows who will be around to pay that fee in the future?

After a look around, I decided on a wooden slat bench backed up against the wall of the chapel as the venue for our ceremony. Jon sat to my left and Amy to my right. In my lap I placed my papers and

Amy looking at the *Book of Remembrance*.

The Garden of Remembrance.

my iPod. I explained to Jon what we'd planned as I plugged the tiny speaker into the iPod and scrolled to *La Golandrina*. Fortunately, we had the quiet garden to ourselves.

Amy and I sang the song through, not messing up too badly. Just for extra measure, we sang it through a second time.

"Well done," said Jon, clearly moved.

Next, I read through Eileen's two poems, first *Carnations* and second *Month Old Impressions*. I'd also brought along a copy of the Beatitudes from Matthew 5:3-10, which seemed appropriate for Eileen Maude. Especially:

> How blest are the sorrowful;
> they shall find consolation.
> How blest are those of a gentle spirit;
> they shall have the earth for their possession.

In conclusion, I read the poem I'd written to my grandmother while waiting for Amy at London's Heathrow Airport.

Ode to Eileen Maude Thomas Hopkins Armitage
October 6, 2008

We're here on this day to honor Eileen
She was Mummie to two, and more should have been.
Had she lived to a ripe age, as she should have done

She'd have met her grandchildren, so now we have come.
I wish I had known her, seen her face to face.
I'm sure that her spirit is here in this place
As well as all over, for where she is now
There are no such limits, as time or whereabouts.

She knows we've been searching, she knows she's been found.
She knows we've been traveling around and around
To answer a question that's haunted her child
Whatever happened to Eileen Maude?

We found no large headstone that shouts she was here
No shrine, no stained glass, not a mention of tears
Not so much as a sentence in the London paper
Saying that she had died, leaving some who would miss her.

But she has been missed, indeed very deeply
By her son and her daughter, whom she left so abruptly
And by those who like me have noticed the space
Where a grandma should be—it's her empty place.

The happy news is, in this search for release
We've uncovered her memory, which will bring my mom peace.
Here's to you, Eileen Maude, like the wings of the dove
You have lifted us all, and we share in your love.

With that we sat for a while quietly. The damp air smelled of pine and fresh earth. The birds chirped and the soft wind blew as we pondered on Eileen, the place, life, and I don't know what else.

"Beautiful," said Jon.

"That was really nice, Mom," said Amy.

"Yes. That was a good thing," said I.

We finally got up off our bench. Jon wandered around looking at the garden while Amy and I took more photos for Mom. When I was sure no strangers were looking, I stooped down, and with the tips of my fingers, quickly pinched a tiny bit of earth from one of the flower beds and tucked it in a plastic bag I had hidden in my handbag. I planned to put the dirt in a little container when I got home to give to Mom—a bit of the Garden of Remembrance for her to have in America.

When everyone felt we'd completed our *adieu*, we walked through the iron gate to the driveway, where we stood for a moment trying to figure out how to return to Glasgow. We found the train station we'd missed on the way out a half-block away. A long steep staircase lead down to the tracks. I was again amazed at Jon's agility and pep in keeping up. There is no way my mother could have negotiated those steps.

But I thought too soon. Upon our return to Queen's Station, Jon begged to be excused to return to his hotel for a rest. Amy and I had been walking at the pace we were used to at our home cities, where everyone was perpetually in a hurry. We'd worn Jon out.

By then it was after 5:00 p.m. Amy and I wanted to do some sightseeing. We agreed with Jon to meet up at 7:00 at "78 St. Vincent," the name as well as address of a restaurant he knew of. Jon turned right in the direction of the Premier Inn, while Amy and I walked left toward the fashionable strip of shops on West Nile Street.

I could see by Amy's shivering she felt as cold as I did. We entered a Starbucks, as common a shelter in Glasgow as in San Francisco. Sitting on their stools in the window we could see most of the buildings built in the 1850s mentioned in the guidebook we were reading. Warmed up after my decaf mocha, piled high with more clotted cream, and Amy's café latté, we set off for some of the other sites we'd noted in our book.

All the shops in Glasgow closed at 6:00 p.m. By then we'd seen most of what we wanted to. We found refuge from the cold in an interior mall and sat on a bench behind a staircase. Amy fussed with her Blackberry. She'd finally fixed it by calling Verizon on my English mobile phone. I could tell from her sighs and moans, something was amiss. Neither of us yet knew the mortgage crises had just hit the U.S. Some of the clients of Amy's fashion design company were returning their merchandise, trying to redeem their cash. Clients who had received merchandise were stalling payments, while vendors were demanding early payment. We'd been so preoccupied with our memorial we hadn't kept up with the newspapers or the telly.

While she clicked away on her mini keyboard, I watched the

shopkeepers closing up. One sat calculating his sales. Another mopped his floor. They didn't know what was about to happen to the economy either. At 6:30 we headed to the restaurant, hoping they'd seat us early.

Jon found us at our table sipping drinks and discussing Amy's correspondence. Since there was nothing she could do, she put her Blackberry away and tried to enjoy our evening with Jon, but she stayed tense and preoccupied. He understood her predicament having been in the retail business himself.

At one point I asked Jon to tell us more about his own life. He started by clarifying his first name was indeed Frank. "I went to grammar school in Scotland and then on to Harrow in England. Didn't like it much. I was too young to serve in World War II, but when the war was over, I joined the King's Dragoon Guards."

I learned from Catherine later that Jon had been a bit of a misfit. One of his friends called him "the only civilian in the British Army." For most of his young life he was in the shoe business, like his father. After retirement, Glasgow University asked him to compile *The Scottish Business Biography*, relating his experience in the shoe business. He considered himself somewhat of an expert on three other subjects: Cole Porter, sailing and wine. He smiled sheepishly when he said he'd been with Catherine for "quite some time."

Jon described his mother as a "gifted clown" and was a bit of a clown himself. He frequently threw jokes out and made us laugh, but he also said at one point, with tears in his eyes, that "we all have painful things in our lives we try to forget." I thought about his daughter Louise, whom he never mentioned. I thought of my cousin Michael losing Zoë, Camilla losing Archie, my mother losing Eileen Maude. And I thought about the tiny daughter of my own I'd let the doctors take away.

After dinner the three of us crammed into the back seat of a taxi that dropped Jon off at his inn. We said good-bye with repeated hugs. "See you at the Thomas Party in London on the eleventh."

The next morning Amy and I accepted a modified version of the Scottish breakfast served at our B&B before packing up. We spent an hour looking around the Glasgow School of Art, another Macintosh design, and then walked on to the Queen's Station. Trains heading to Edinburgh left from Glasgow every hour.

Back row left to right: Lionel, Harriett, Jason, Adam, the author, Camilla and Rodney. Front: Philippa.

Chapter 43

The Thomas Family Reunion

A charming upgrade from the Glasgow B&B, our Edinburgh quarters were conveniently located near the nicer shops and close to a fantastic pub where Amy and I ate three times. On the first day, we toured Edinburgh's eight-hundred-year-old castle on the hilltop, returning home alongside a parade of kilted bagpipers. On the second day, we rode a public bus to the small village of Cramond and ate a delicious Scottish meat pie in a small café overlooking the Firth of Fourth. We'd heard the *Queen Elizabeth II* was moored there, visiting as part of her last trip around the world before being turned into a tourist hotel at some Arabian resort. But we couldn't see her.

On Tuesday, October 7, a plane lifted us from Edinburgh, heading toward London's Gatwick airport. As we flew over the Firth of Fourth, we saw the *QEII* floating below. From our position among the clouds, it was difficult to appreciate her majesty. I thought of Mom and her friend Rosemary sailing on the first *Queen Elizabeth* so many years ago. Mom told me the last time she saw the *QEI* was in Hong Kong, her stern pointing straight up. At least the *QEII* floated properly.

In London we tubed our way to Putney. Rodney and Camilla's city flat was situated half a block from the Putney Bridge tube station, right on the Thames. It was great to see them again.

Camilla took us sightseeing during one of the few free days before the Saturday party. During another of those days, Amy met up with a friend from New York while I stayed at the flat and read *The Amorous Baron*, one of the books Camilla's mother, Joy Bissell-Thomas, had written. Joy might have had my grandfather Pryns in mind when she wrote it. Either that or my grandfather's situation was a common one. The delightfully witty story took place during the time between the wars when my grandfather lived in England and France, and when the British aristocracy had little money to support the old manor homes. A lusty English baron struggled so financially that he had to rent his manor out to a rich American couple. That reminded me of Grandpa purchasing Chateau de Bures in France and being chided for Americanizing it. It also reminded me how resentful the British were of Americans during that period, and I wondered if any of my English relatives resented my American grandfather who had no legitimate claim to British society other than his money?

Amy, meanwhile, had realized she needed to get back to New York to rescue her business. This required giving up $400 dollars to change her plane ticket to leave after the party.

Friday we prepared for the event. A painter busily touched up some construction that had been done to the kitchen and bathrooms. Camilla assigned Rodney the task of re-attaching doorknobs and towel racks, as well as typing a list of attendees and their contact information onto a spreadsheet on his computer. A very competent caterer would deliver the food the next day. I prepared additional salmon canapés and accompanied Camilla to the nearby wine store to order bubbly and rent glasses. Amy spent the afternoon as a Sloan Ranger[1], browsing

---

1. *The Official Sloan Ranger Handbook*, featuring Lady Diana Spencer on the cover, was England's answer to *The Preppy Handbook*. It was written by Peter York and Ann Barr and published in 1982. Sloan Street is a fashionable shopping street.

Harrods and the Knightsbridge shopping district on her own to purchase gifts for friends back home.

We expected twenty-nine guests on Saturday, not counting the four of us. Rodney placed a large piece of plywood over the bed Amy and I had slept on, transforming the guestroom into the caterer's workshop. We polished the rented wine glasses as well as the silver platters on which Camilla arranged a second set of salmon canapés. I prepared the illustrated family tree I had printed out for display on two large cardboard sheets. We covered the finer wood furniture pieces in cling wrap to prevent rings from abandoned glasses (a procedure I'd never seen before). The flat required a final vacuuming, especially after the caterer left. We were still setting out food when Camilla's daughter, Cynthia, and husband, Rodney, walked through the door. The merriment began.

The relatives who attended included descendants of Eileen Maude, her brother Harold and her sister Daisy. We had expected Peggy to be represented by Jon Abbott, however he'd sent a disappointing letter a few days earlier expressing regret he couldn't join us. He was recovering from his rigorous trip to Glasgow. I felt horrible we had worn him out, especially when his partner Catherine told me about a stomach condition he never mentioned. I had been looking forward to witnessing his reunion with his first-cousin Lionel, who, in spite of his fading memory, remembered Jon fondly.

Lionel, dressed again in coat and tie, and hair slicked down tidily, was still taking good care of himself, though he didn't remember *me*. He sat in one chair the whole time entranced by the recently published biographical booklet Dr. Koegler had written about my grandfather. I'd brought it from home to show around. Lionel was so entranced, in fact, that I think he read it twice. When he got up to leave at the end of the party, I caught him hiding the booklet behind his back, planning to take it with him. I explained it was the only copy I had, but he pleaded that Pryns had been very important to him and that the booklet should be his. I won the toss. However, when I looked closely at the booklet later, he'd made his claim by writing "Lionel Turner" on the front cover. I decided to order myself another one and send the first to him once I was assured there were more to be had.

Rosemary and Graham came, as did Paul and Carolyn with her two daughters, Verity and Jessica. As my grandfather would have said, "We were a jolly lot." Romilly, daughter of Lionel Turner's extremely handsome eldest son Michael, declared she had never known she had so many relatives!

Since my last visit, Candy had divorced Tim and Jason had divorced Ioana. Lionel was still living with Jason, but to help with finances, he and Lionel moved to another place. Jason brought his daughter, Sophie, who I'd been unable to meet on the previous trip.

I met Ann Bissell-Thomas for the first time—a gracious, enthusiastic and cheerful woman with a very round face and cheeks even rosier than Philippa's. She attended with two of her four children: twins James and Harriet and their grandchildren. James, distinguishable by a mop of curly brown hair, brought his son, Helier. Harriett, with the same round face as her mother and wide bright eyes, brought her daughter, Sorrel. Jungle Eyes was still in hospital. The fourth child, Sarah, couldn't make it up from Brighton, but her daughter, Fleurie, came with her cousins, Sorrell and Helier.

The party went on until the sun fully set and London's lights twinkled through Rodney and Camilla's windows. Before Ann left, she invited Amy and me to lunch at West Hall the following Monday. She explained that workmen had repaired the third floor and roof from the fire two and a half years earlier, and she could now entertain company. She also wanted me to meet her friend Jenny X.

I felt rotten declining for Amy, who at that very moment was packing her bags to leave with Carolyn, who would drop her at Heathrow on the way back to Newbury after the party. I did not want to say good-bye to my daughter. We'd had a wonderful love-filled time, and who knew how long it would be before we could have another ten days together?

The following day, after the hustle and bustle of cleaning up the flat, Rodney, Camilla and I sat in front of the telly and caught up on the financial disaster, helplessly watching stocks plunge in value. In America they were down 32 percent. In Russia, they'd plummeted to 58 percent. America was getting blamed for everything. I tried not to take it personally.

West Hall, home of Jeffray Bissell-Thomas' family – Kew, Surrey, 2011.

Chapter 44
West Hall

After Candy's description of West Hall in Kew, I really looked forward to seeing it on Monday.

Kew, just west of London along the curvy Thames, is also the home of the British National Archives packed with Britain's most ancient documents. Since I wanted to find some information there before the party at West Hall, Camilla dropped me off at 9:00 a.m. Three hours barely allowed me to figure out their filing systems, but I did get to read, and even hold (while wearing white gloves), the original contract for the Massachusetts Bay Colony from 1629! I then walked the seven minutes to West Hall. Ann had given me instructions at Camilla's party.

I expected to find the mansion missing its top and looking charred, but it was not. It looked quite respectable on the outside—stately in fact. Once through the door I saw evidence of construction, but not of fire. No charred walls. No soggy planks from the fire hoses that typically do more damage than the fire.

I arrived at the same time as another guest, Oliver, who was not a family member, but the tenant of Ann's friend Jenny X, whom I was also looking forward to meeting. Oliver carried a stack of books and papers half his size. James met us at the door and escorted us to a clothes rack parked in the entry for our coats. I thought Oliver would put his books down, but he didn't. Ann soon buoyantly descended the stairs to greet us and then guided us on a tour of the house with its typically high ceilings and beautiful ornate woodwork. A scene of tired but not forgotten dreams, much repair had been done, but there would always be more to do—surfaces to sand, spackle and paint, faded chairs to mend and worn sofas to recover. Ann talked of her remodeling plans with a sparkle in her eye. I thought of my own father and his unfulfilled dreams for the large house he bought when I was young that was much more a maintenance nightmare than West Hall.

Ann led Oliver—still carrying his books—and me upstairs to the ballroom, set up as a sitting room dominated by a huge full-length portrait of an nineteenth-century woman, an ancestor of Ann's. As she talked about the room and how it had been spared from the fire because it was separated from the rest of the house by a brick wall that had once been an outside wall, I noticed a buffet table of goodies, including a most delicious-looking salmon tart, awaiting us in a sunny room next to it. James informed me the paneled room was properly called the supper room because it was where guests retreated to rest and nibble when they tired of dancing in the ballroom.

Oliver finally unloaded his arms of the stack of books and papers when Ann ushered us to a round table placed next to a window overlooking the garden. That is when I learned Oliver had brought the documents to show *me*. Through six degrees of separation, it had been discovered Oliver was a descendant of an adopted grandchild of Isaac Singer.

As Oliver described the documents to me, Jenny X showed up. She must have been fifteen years older than I, the same age as my Aunt Jennifer. After our introduction, she explained her connection to me. Her father had been my step-grandmother Fay's boyfriend before Fay met my grandfather Pryns. Jenny thought her father might even have been *dumped* because of Pryns. Another small-world connection. When Jenny went to live in California during her 'tween year, Fay talked Grandpa into giving her a job helping him type his autobiography, *Both Hands Before the Fire.*

Jenny was under the notion that my grandfather was a blood descendant of Isaac Singer. That is why she was interested to learn that her tenant, Oliver, was sort of a descendant of Singer and why she wanted to meet me and have me meet Oliver and why Ann invited all of us for lunch at West Hall.

I felt badly popping this bubble of excitement. I corrected the information by telling them that my grandfather was only a benefactor of the Singer money, not the Singer blood. I think I also disappointed them by revealing that though my grandfather had been a wealthy man, he dispersed all his money before he died, mostly to charity. He donated his house on Santa Barbara's Riviera to the Quakers.

The arrival of Harriett Bissell-Thomas and Michael Turner meant we could start eating. The salmon tart tasted even more scrumptious than it looked, and the trifle that followed was better yet!

After lunch James showed me a file folder filled with old family documents that, like the ballroom, had managed to elude West Hall's fire. There were birth and marriage certificates of family members, including James' grandfather Harold Bissell-Thomas—whom James always referred to as Webster—and our mutual great-grandfather George James Thomas. I was interested to learn Harold had been married to someone before he married Joy. What was even more interesting was that the letter describing his divorce had been written on the letterhead of St. Peter's Church, Cranley Gardens, the very same place where Harold's sister married my grandfather a year later! Perhaps Harold needed the church's approval to get married there again. Divorce was very rare in those days, with a good deal of social stigma attached, yet my mother was the third in her family, after Harold and Peggy, to go through with it.

Another gold nugget in the folder was the copy of George James Thomas' birth certificate. From this I obtained the complete date of our mutual great-grandfather's birth and the name of our great-great-grandparents, George and his wife Hannah Turner—no relation to

Lionel Turner that I know of, but you never know for certain.

My chatting with James and his mother joggled Ann's memory. "I seem to recall that George Thomas' father was a headmaster at Eagley School in Lancaster," she said.

I scribbled the information down, planning to return to the National Archives the next day. I had learned that morning that the National Archives had gained Internet access to Great Britain's vital records. These new facts could help me find George James Thomas' birth records.

I asked James about his father, whose full name, I learned, was Jeffray James Bissell-Thomas. "He was named after his uncle, Granny Joy's twin, spelley with 'a-y' rather then 'e-y', which is more common. He actively campaigned for things in which he believed. For example, in 1966 he was very involved with Save the Whales. Brilliant, always inventing things and burying his head in scientific journals. He allowed us children to do what we wanted, which certainly gave Jungle and me the feeling that anything is possible in this life."

Ann added proudly, "We thought it was important for our children to be able to express themselves fully."

Jeffray was born in London in 1928, three years after my mother's birth. Mom had told me "he was called Duffy as a child." He attended Harrow on the Hill, and then Baliol College, Oxford. He worked first as an engineer for British coal and atomic energy companies, then for Honeywell in computers.

"For a while he taught at an East End [London] school," said James. "He so resembled the television star George Peppard that the students nicknamed him Banacek. Eventually, he went to work for the BBC as a computer specialist and continued there happily until retirement."

When the party was over, Michael Turner escorted me to Camilla and Rodney's via the tube. He was so handsome and charming I couldn't help wondering if it was permissible to have a crush on a second-cousin.

Samuel Bissell	Head
Emily E. Bissell	Wife
Tasmania Bissell	Dau
Victoria A Bissell	Dau
Josephine Bissell	Dau
Ada M Bissell	Dau
Mary L Bissell	Dau
Emily M Bissell	Dau
Eliza Richards	Servant

The Bissell Family on the 1871 English Census for Wolverhampton, Staffordshire.

Chapter 45

More Genealogical Treasures

I hoped to answer two questions upon my return to the National Archives and ended up answering three. I wanted to find out when and where my mother's grandparents died, and I wanted to find out who my great-great-grandparents were and from where they came. In the process, I also found the probable reason Harold Bissell-Thomas added Bissell to his surname.

When I'd asked my mother what happened to her grandparents George and Victoria, she said, "To my knowledge, they were still both alive when I left for America. No one told me when or where they died. I never heard from them again."

I already knew from George's and Victoria's wedding certificate that George's father's name was also George Thomas and that Victoria's father's name was Samuel Bissell. The mothers' names weren't listed on the certificate.

I'd learned from my previous trip to the Archives how to use their computer banks to find census records. The first treasure chest I uncovered was the 1871 census page for Victoria Bissell's family. That year, "Victoria A," age ten, lived with her father Samuel and mother Emily Bissell at 95 Clark Street, Athal Terrace, in the Municipal Borough of Wolverhampton in the Municipal Ward of St. Mark's in the Ecclesiastical District of St. Jude. That was very close to Tettenhall Road. The record confirmed what the 1901 census stated, and what Victoria's marriage certificate stated, that Victoria had been born in Australia.

With a little help from Google Maps, I discovered an amazing amount of information from that one piece of paper. In 1871 the family consisted of Samuel, his wife Emily (born in Ireland!), six daughters and two servants—one domestic servant and one nurse. Here was the probable reason Harold took on the name Bissell. Samuel's progeny were all girls! His surname was destined to be "daughtered out," as we say in the genealogical world. And Samuel made a name for himself that someone like Harold would logically want to retain.

Victoria was the second child, two years younger than her sister Tasinaina, a name I immediately suspected was a misspelling—a common occurrence on census records. All the other names in the family were common ones. Since Victoria was named after the place she was born—Melbourne, Victoria—I didn't think it too far afield to presume Tasinaina was a misspelling of Tasmania. The large island south of Melbourne was named that in 1856, three years before her birth. It's no surprise the census taker had never heard of it.

Tasmania, as well as the two younger sisters—Josephine age six, and Ada age five—were also born in Australia. But two-year-old Mary and one-year-old Emily were born back in Wolverhampton.

Samuel Bissell	Head	Mar	44		Commercial Traveller	Stafford W Hampton
Emily E. Bissell	Wife	Mar		35	do Wife	Ireland
Tasinaina Bissell	dau			12	Scholar	Australia
Victoria A Bissell	dau			10	Scholar	do
Josephine Bissell	dau			6	Scholar	do
Ada M Bissell	dau			5	Scholar	do
Mary L Bissell	dau			2		Stafford W Hampton
Emily M Bissell	dau			1		do do
Eliza Richards	Servant	Un		41	Domestic Servant	do Willenhall

Samuel listed himself as a "Commercial Traveller[1]." The clerk at the Archives told me that meant "traveling salesman," and I learned from a death record I found later that he was a "hardware merchant," in other words, he travelled to Australia to sell hardware.

It appeared Samuel took his family with him to Tasmania sometime before the birth of his first daughter in 1859. Before Victoria's birth in 1861, they crossed the Bass Straight to Melbourne. The family stayed in Australia for at least seven years for the birth of Ada in 1866, but no longer than ten years, because they returned to Wolverhampton before the birth of little Emily in 1869.

Samuel probably sold hardware to gold diggers. The date of Tasmania's birth was only eight years after someone discovered gold in Ballarat, about sixty-one miles northwest of Melbourne, igniting the Australian Gold Rush. As San Francisco served as the portal for California's gold diggers, Melbourne became the portal for Australia's gold diggers. Business must have been fairly good to allow Samuel to afford the passages of a family of six to return to Wolverhampton. He could have been even more successful than that. He could have owned his own ship or a fleet of ships. Wolverhampton isn't a port town, but it is within an easy commute to Bristol, then England's second largest port. Unfortunately, I didn't have time to look up the Archives' merchant records.

Samuel was forty-nine in 1871 and Emily thirty-five. Assuming Tasmania was their first child, they had children late for those days. A birth record I also found indicated Samuel was born in Tettenhall, just down the street from Wolverhampton. Maybe Samuel sailed to Australia at the beginning of the gold rush and met Irish Emily there—more research to do.

Samuel must have been influential in the Thomas children's lives. Eileen Maude and Harold grew to adulthood with him close by. I learned from Samuel's death record he died at the age of ninety in 1909 of bronchitis and heart failure. Harold was twenty-three, Eileen Maude seventeen and Peggy fifteen. I noticed on the 1901 census that I had with me that Harold, at fifteen, already worked in the building

---

1. The English spelling of the word.

trade. Perhaps he worked for his grandfather, Samuel?

My lucky streak continued with the Thomas family. The 1861 census record for George and Hannah (Turner) Thomas showed them living at 66 Temple Street. That's on the opposite side of Wolverhampton from where Samuel Bissell and family lived. Their son George must have moved to 17 Tettenhall Road to be closer to his in-laws.

My great-great grandfather George Sr., head of household, worked as an optician in 1861. He had changed his profession from schoolteacher, the job he'd held in 1852 when George James was born. George Sr. was born in Bristol sometime around 1812, making him about six to eight years younger than Samuel. My great-great-grandmother Hannah Turner was eight years younger than her husband and born around 1820 in Preston, Lancashire. Preston is a good deal north of Bristol and Wolverhampton, but maybe George Sr. met her when he took the teaching position in Lancashire.

The couple was probably married in the bride's hometown of Preston. Their oldest child, William T, who was nineteen in 1861 and working as a Printers Compositor, was born in Clitheroe, just northeast of Preston, still in Lancashire. The family stayed in Clitheroe at least two years because Sarah Jane was born there also. By the time Eleanor Ann came along a year later, they'd moved to Eagley Bridge near Bolton, in southern Lancashire where Emma, Hannah and George James were born. Who knows why the family ended up in Wolverhampton nine years later? They had no servants living with them in 1861.

Lastly, I uncovered my mother's grandparents' death records, which explained why she never heard from them again after she moved to America. Seventy-seven-year-old Victoria A. Thomas, "wife of George James Thomas retired Insurance Broker," died at 17 Tettenhall Road of myocardial degeneration and chronic bronchitis on June 8, 1940, only six months after my mother reached California.

George lasted two more years. The online ledger told me he died at the age of ninety-two sometime between January and March of 1943 in Wolverhampton. The certificate, which could have told me the cause of death, wasn't available. Because of a typo someone made when they digitized the record, the certificate may be lost in the files forever.

Victoria left this world while Mom finished her first year at Katherine

Branson School. George departed about the time Mom commenced her studies at Scripps College. Mom's cousins, aunts and uncles experienced World War II while she studied. Harold scrambled to get his family out of Jersey and seek safety in England. Peter flew glider planes over Europe. Lionel flew Lancaster Bombers over Germany. Lionel's sisters lived in Argentina. Jon Abbott studied and probably assumed his mother told my mother about their grandparents.

None of the relatives I got to know in England knew what happened to the remaining four Thomas siblings: Billie, Eric, Liala Victoria and Marie Louise. Maybe their descendants will read this book and look me up on the Internet!

Berri Court, 2011.

Chapter 46

Berri Court

I have one last, but important errand to report about England before relating how I told my mother about my trip. Camilla and Rodney consented to take me to see Berri Court in Yapton, about ten miles as the crow flew from their country home in Birdham. Traveling on the wiggly English country roads made the measurement a wee bit longer.

The village of Yapton stretched for three buildings, situated across the street from a school. The one-window Yapton Post Office hid housed within the slightly larger general store. Both the postal clerk and a shopper in the store told us we could find Berri Court a short distance down the road and that an elderly man we'll call Mr. Z owned the house.

We easily found the white wooden gate with BERRI COURT written in black letters, marking the entrance off the main road. Rodney drove slowly up the gravel drive, flanked on both sides with impressive bushes, flowers and trees of many kinds, to a white two-story Georgian house with a central entrance and gabled windows. A shallow algae-filled lily pond glistened in the middle of the front lawn.

Camilla, Rodney and I walked gingerly to the front door and knocked. A white-uniformed nurse answered and informed us Mr. Z was not at home. She explained that she took care of his wife, who suffered from being elderly, and that Mr. Z usually showed up for lunch, which, on a fine day, he ate on the front patio where we were standing. I was sure that is where my grandfather used to enjoy a glass of sherry with Vernon and Gwendolyn Twistleton Wykham Fiennes after visiting my young mother.

In the afternoons, Mr. Z worked in his garden and that might be a good time to catch up with him. The nurse wrote his phone number on a scrap of paper Rodney found in his pocket. When we rang Mr. Z that night, he granted us an appointment for a tour the following afternoon.

Fortunately, a morning that started off drizzly turned into one of England's sunnier days by the time we returned to Berri Court. As Rodney parked the car by the house, Mr. Z emerged from the bushes dressed in a polo shirt, khaki Bermuda shorts and hiking boots. Rusty cheeks and skin spots revealed how much he liked working outdoors. His tiny wife, all smiles, trailed behind him like a puppy dog.

Contrary to my Uncle Peter's report that Berri Court had been turned into a B&B or teahouse, the Zs had owned the home since 1968, for forty-three years! They brought up three children there and would probably stay another decade or two, but the grounds were becoming too much of a burden. Mr. Z mowed the countless lawn patches himself. He explained that he'd removed the massive greenhouses in front of the house after he purchased the place. Since my mother and Peter described the greenhouses at the back of the house, not the front, and since the article I found on the Internet about Berri Court described "a pedimented doorcase" added after the removal of the conservatory, I suspect the entrance was switched to the opposite side of the house after my mother and Peter lived there.

Ducking under branches, we joggled through several acres of gardens, grass and a crumbling old stable. I saw no evidence of a tennis court, but I did recognize a side garden where several photos of Peter and my mother had been taken when they were little.

Most curious to see the layout of the bedrooms, I was pleased when Mr. Z guided us upstairs. As we came up to the second floor landing, I found everything just as I had imagined it, matching both my mother and Peter's descriptions. What had been Mom's bedroom was on the left. Vernon's was on the right. And after we passed through Vernon's room, we went through the dressing room where Peter once slept. I shuddered as I stood there and imagined what it must have been like for my then-young uncle.

We climbed the narrow curving staircase to the third floor attic rooms that used to house the upstairs maid, the Irish downstairs maid Peter's age and Mrs. Pratley with her canaries.

Jar of earth from the Garden of Remembrance, 2009.

Chapter 47

Mom

I missed my plane to San Francisco. It was a foolish act. I hurriedly checked the time on my ticket and noted the hour the plane landed in San Francisco rather than when it left from Heathrow. I was shopping for gifts at Harrods when I should have been taking a subway to the airport. When I did get to the airport and innocently put my credit card into the check-in computer, the screen said my flight had left hours earlier. Like Amy, I had to pay $400 to rebook. Another flight took me home via Los Angeles. I was in bed by midnight.

I woke at 4:00 a.m. the next morning. My body thought night was day and day was night. *I might as well be useful.* I got up, unpacked, did my laundry and was ready to retrieve Annie from doggie camp at 9:00 a.m. By noon I'd fetched the mail from the post office and read through most of it. I'd even sifted through my emails and marked all those that had to be attended to right away.

That was Wednesday. I wasn't scheduled to see my mother until the following Sunday. That gave me four days to download over 600 photos, edit and put them in order, then save them as an iDVD movie. I also wanted to do something special with the pinch of soil I'd stolen from the Garden of Remembrance. I purchased a tiny glass container with a cork stopper, poured the soil into it from the plastic bag and plugged in the cork. Then I made a label for it that read:

> This is a wee bit of the Garden of Remembrance in Glasgow, Scotland, where the ashes of Eileen Maude Thomas Hopkins Armitage were scattered on the 19th of November 1933, and where her granddaughter Mary Ames Mitchell, her great-granddaughter Amy Claire McCormick and her nephew Frank Jonathan Abbott came to honor her on October 6, 2008.

I pasted the strip over the cork like a tiny jam jar label. To complete the presentation for Mom, I typed up the quotations I'd read for the service and printed them out on nice stationery.

During our brunch, I told Mom the unemotional details of the trip: where I'd been, what it was like being with Amy, who I'd been able to see, what I'd learned about her grandparents, etc. She listened quietly to everything. When she finished eating, I asked her if she wanted to go back to her condo and see the slide show I'd prepared.

"Yes, let's," she said, pushing herself away from the table. That was my cue to run around to help her stand—often a lengthy process—then fetch her bright red walker.

The slide show took about a half hour. By the time it was over, Mom had seen where Eileen Maude's ceremony took place. I recited the readings. The hardest part was the poem I'd written. I had to hold myself back from crying.

I explained how we came up with the words for the *Book of Remembrance,* and how I'd been disappointed that due to space restrictions, we'd only been able to write "Eileen M," not "Eileen Maude."

"I'm so glad," she said. "She always hated the name Maude."

Then I gave Mom the little vial of soil. She liked that the best. She kept twirling it around in her fingers saying, "That's wonderful, darling.

I feel as if you brought a little bit of England back with you."

That was just what I wanted to hear. I wasn't able to take my mother to England with me, nor could I bring my grandmother back to her. However, I was able to connect the spaces of time and place and get to know my grandmother in a deeper way. I also felt a lot closer to my mother. My missions were accomplished. I thought.

Chapter 48

The Vanishing Generation

Mid-March of 2010, I received a reply to a Valentine card I'd sent to Jon Abbott at his Blackthorn Close address in Northampton. The letter was written by his partner, Catherine. Jon had gone into hospital just before Christmas with pneumonia. He passed away a week later. I cried for days. Such a sweet man! And he'd cared so much about my mother, even though he'd seen her only a few times. I also felt for Catherine, since I knew how hard it was to find a good partner.

Eight months later I lost my mother.

I've heard that no matter what your relationship is with your parent, you are never prepared for her death.

Mom died peacefully in her own home. I thanked God for that. She was following her normal morning routine. Her Filipino aide, Morena, showed up at 8:00 a.m, put on the coffee, fed Lenny the cat—who had been waiting for her by the front door for the previous hour—and helped my mother out of bed. Mom took a minute or two to gain her balance on her walker before stepping forward. Slowly, very slowly, with Morena at her side, she shuffled across her condo to the bathroom with the walk-in shower. After her shower, Morena assisted Mom back to her bedroom to help her get dressed.

Usually, once Morena had combed my mother's hair, she helped her back to her walker and they proceeded to the dining table in the middle of the condo. Morena pulled out the chair, turned Mom around so her rump was in line with the chair, and said, "Here you are." That was the flag for Mom to fall into her seat. She always smiled in triumph once she'd made it. And more often than not, she stayed in that chair for the rest of the morning. It was getting more and more difficult to move back and forth from her wing chair. Morena turned the television on. Thank goodness for remote controls. First Mom ate breakfast, then read the paper, then opened the mail Morena fetched for her from the mail room on the first floor of Villa Marin.

But on November 9, 2009, the day before I was scheduled to take Mom to Piatti's Italian restaurant for her eighty-fifth birthday, where she would have ordered her favorite linguine with clam sauce, something started to go wrong as she reached her bedroom. It was as if an outer force began turning off all the switches to her body so her spirit could leave it behind for Heaven. Her bowels failed, her heart fluttered and she had difficulty breathing. Morena couldn't get Mom back on her bed so she lowered her to the carpet between the bed and the bathroom. Then Morena pulled her cell phone out of her pocket and called the doctor in the nursing unit downstairs.

Meanwhile, I was parked in my car in a driveway in Petaluma, about forty minutes north of them, about to go into a house where my writing group gathered. I coincidentally called the nursing unit at Villa Marin to make an arbitrary doctor's appoint for Mom, just at the time she was having trouble.

The nurse who answered the phone said, "Something's happening in your mother's condo right now. The doctor and nurse just went rushing up there."

"I'll leave my cell phone on," I said. "Please call me back when you know something."

That was at 9:58 a.m. Before I joined my group, I touched the button on my smartphone that turned the sound up. Unknowingly, I'd turned it off instead. I kept listening for my phone for the next three hours, but heard nothing. Morena informed me later what happened.

When the doctor and nurse reached Mom, they asked her if she wanted to go to the hospital.

"No, no hospital!" Mom insisted. She was having trouble breathing, but refused the oxygen mask, frantically pushing it away.

"Are you in pain?"

"No, no pain."

The doctor tried to call me around 10:15. I didn't answer. He left a message that my mother was in distress. Did I want him to send her to a hospital?

That was the second time he'd ignored her written request for no resuscitation and no hospital. The time before, Mom was sent to the hospital with a bump on her head. The doctors there pronounced she was fine but that she was unsteady on her feet. She had been unsteady on her feet for fifteen years! The doctors were worried about being sued. Medicare paid Mom's bills for her stay in the heart patient ward. There was nothing wrong with her heart. My mother hated hospitals. But not only had she refused to assign me financial power of attorney, but power for her health as well. It took three days of my yelling and screaming to get her out of the hospital and into the nursing unit at Villa Marin. Mom's stay at Hotel Marin General Hospital cost the people of California $85,000—for a bump on the head! At least the event forced Mom to give me medical power of attorney. By November 9 it was in place.

At 10:25 Mom started calling for someone, looking up at the ceiling. "Hurry, hurry. Help me," she said.

"We're right here, what do you need?" asked Morena, who knelt at Mom's side, holding her hand. But Mom didn't seem to hear her. She kept gazing at the ceiling, as if she were talking to someone there.

"Hurry," my mother said one last time. That was at 10:30.

"Then her eyes went blank," said Morena. "The spark left. Her spirit was gone."

I left my meeting at 1:05 thinking all was well because my phone had remained silent. I looked to see if I had any phone messages and discovered the sound was off. I had two messages, but before I could listen to them, Morena was calling me.

"Your mother has passed away," she sobbed.

I went through the normal stages of grief. First disbelief: *Oh, come on, this is just another false alarm. Maybe I'm dreaming. My mother couldn't really be gone. She has been there all my life. She would never leave.* Then anger: *That stupid phone. I'm sure I left the sound on. Why couldn't I have been there for my mom?*

By the time I reached Villa Marin, the doctor had signed the papers declaring my mother's death, the police had interviewed Morena and filled out their own papers, my mother's body had been taken to the funeral director's in the center of town, and they had filed her in her own refrigerator drawer.

When Morena told me about my mother's last moments, I was furious with myself. I missed the last intimate moment of my mother's life. I could understand how my grandfather felt about missing the last minutes of my grandmother's life. Mom would have called her passing "moving on to the next stage." Why wasn't I there? I prayed that it wasn't me she was wishing would hurry.

Sadness, bitterness and self-pity came over me when I let myself think I'd lost the chance to be close to my mother. She never gave me the blessing I wanted. Then I reminded myself she did the best she could. My poor mother never received a blessing from anyone. She didn't know how it was done.

Mary Baker Eddy taught to "stand portal at the door of thought." She wanted us to let good, truthful, God-given thoughts through the door of our consciousness and keep negative, destructive, evil thoughts out. I took that advice, or at least tried to. It was time to concentrate on my mother's goodness and forget the demons she reflected the last years of her life. My mother was a good woman. She meant well. Her goodness and love were expressions of God. Somewhere underneath that crusty, grumpy, but false exterior, my mother liked me, too. She knew darn well I attended Family Day more than any child of any other resident at Villa Marin.

I shooed the bitter grudges away from the door. I only let in thoughts of Mom as the reflection of the Great Spirit. She was, and still is, good, wise, loving, kind, beautiful, warm, cozy, tender, caring and oftentimes even funny.

Mom chose me, her only daughter and only child living on the West Coast, to execute her estate and act as trustee. She had already agreed to be cremated and "planted" in the Hopkins plot next to her father and grandparents in Santa Barbara. Besides sorting her tangled finances, which I'm still trying to figure out, I only needed to arrange for two funeral services: one in the local Episcopal Church in the Bay Area, and one by the graveside in Santa Barbara. About fifteen friends and family members attended each service. Brother Tom flew in from Vermont with his daughter, Camille. (Megan was in China and Emery couldn't get off work.) Brother Charles arrived from Buffalo with his wife, Paula. Their son, Colin, joined us from Paris. Amy came in from New York. Jon was already here. A sprinkling of my friends joined us in San Rafael, and several of Mom's old friends from Pasadena joined us in Santa Barbara.

I wrote the following poem and read it at both services. In San Rafael, I stood in front of the tiny group of loved ones as they sat in the dark wood pews of the Victorian church that reminded me of old churches in England. In Santa Barbara, friends and family sat in folding chairs placed on the grass about a hundred feet from the Pacific Ocean. As I stood in front of them, I looked down on the little mahogany box holding Mom's ashes, held up by two wooden supports over the hole in the ground where the box rests now. On top, in gold letters, were the words *Eileen Hopkins Ames.* I heard waves softly rushing the shore and seagulls overhead. It smelled of the eucalyptus grove nearby and reminded me of the trees in my mother's backyard in Pasadena.

Ode to My Mother

November 14, 2011

My mother was different, not one to comply,
She had a funny accent and served us kidney pie.
She liked music, and roses, her cat and TV.
But a visit on Sunday was all she wanted from me.

She had a hard time saying she loved and she cared
But deep down inside I always knew she was there.

As I was growing up, she set some high standards.
Three square meals every day and don't ever philander.
Never live on credit; brush your teeth every night
Beware of fads and fashions and don't ride motorbikes.
Speak the truth, she would say, stand up straight and tall

Keep your tummy tucked in, was a favorite of all.
But in time she gave up on such things as nutrition.
A good meal was some chocolate, became her position.

Traveling on airplanes was her favorite sport
To China, or Egypt, she went, port to port.
Tunisia, Alaska, and six months in Europe.
The cure for all ills was to take a long trip.
And while she was at it, she took lots of photos.
Her slide shows and albums were her favorite mementoes.

In spite of how wobbly she became in the end
On no wheelchair or person would she depend.
She guarded her money like an Egyptian cat
She even avoided the estate tax. We thank her for that.

Thank you, Morena, who helped her last days
You ignored all the foibles and eccentric ways.
Thanks to Lenny the cat, who made Mom's life worthwhile,
Most important of all, he made my Mom smile.

Now she'll be with God's angels, where it's peaceful and calm.
But we'll miss her down here. Fare thee well, dear old Mom.

The brass plaque that was cemented over the hole holding the box of ashes arrived a few months later. It read "Eileen Hopkins Ames, daughter of Prynce and Eileen." The cemetery didn't allow me to include the whole description of my grandmother's ashes scattered in Scotland. As it turns out, it is a good thing they didn't. There were also rules against burying the vial of earth from the Garden of Remembrance. At least future generations will know by the plaque that my mother was Eileen's daughter, not Fay's. Next to Mom rest the ashes of her father, who always loved her mother.

Armitage Family Vault, Weaste Cemetery

Chapter 47

The Twist

I have no doubt my grandparents' spirits guided me through the journeys described in this book. And, like my mother, they worked me hard.

This book was ready to go to press on May 27, 2012, six years from the beginning of my search for my grandmother's grave. I'd spent all my savings on editors who'd corrected my tenses, inserted missing commas and deleted misplaced ones. I'd posted the files to the printer's web site and ordered gift copies to send to my English relatives. I can picture Eileen and Pryns sitting in white chairs on a cloud somewhere watching me and saying to each other, "What do you think? Shall we finally let her in on our little secret?"

Within hours of clicking the button on my screen approving the files to be printed, I received an email from my Aunt Jennifer.

Mary —

Please call me if you're available — I've discovered the cut-out portion's of Dad's journal at the time of your grandmother's final days! She died in Manchester. I'd be happy to read the pages to you or send them to you immediately. I know this was something you were searching for.

Hope we'll be in contact soon.

All the best!

Affectionately,
Jennifer

Imagine my surprise. Manchester? How could that be?

I called her the following morning. She explained she'd been sorting old storage boxes preparatory to putting her house on the market. Some were dated from her father's death forty-two years earlier, including one box filled with loose papers she didn't remember seeing before. She sifted through letters to and from her father and her mother, lecture notes, old wills and trust documents before finding a clump of yellow, lined papers fastened with a rusty staple. When she realized the clump was comprised of passages cut out from Grandpa's journals, she became excited and knew she had to send them to me.

"It was Daddy who clipped the bits out of his journals," said Jennifer, "not my mother. He didn't want her to know how distraught he was about your grandmother Eileen's death, or how much he still loved his ex-wife!"

I received Jennifer's express mail package a few days later. Along with the original journal pages, Jennifer inserted three postcards from Eileen to Pryns. They were of no importance to the location of my grandmother's remains, however they reflected the schizophrenic spelling of my grandfather's name and confirmed some addresses of previously mentioned places.

Grandpa dated the postcards in pencil before saving them. The first, dated 17 July 1922, is an illustration of a steamship titled "Calais—La Malle dans les Jetees—The Mail in the Piers," addressed to "Prince Hopkins, Esq. c/o Labour Age, 41 Union Square, New York, USA." The message reads, "Just crossed rough sea, but managed not to disgrace the family—on to Lucerne. —Love Eileen."

The second card, dated 25 Aug 1926, is of "Le Mont-St-Michele-Côté Sud," addressed to "Prynce Hopkins at Chateau de Bures, Par Villenues [Villeneuve?], Seine et Oise, France. "Motored here today very interesting indeed. Do let me know how the babes are. Love Eileen."

And the third, dated "About 6 Aug., 1933" must have been sent as Eileen traveled toward Scotland with Vernon. The image is of a stone bridge spanning a river lined with scrawny trees and piles of boulders, labeled "Greta Bridge near Morritt Arms Hotel." I looked it up on the Internet and the two-star hotel that exists in the hamlet of Greta Bridge today is located in County Durham in northern England. This time Eileen addresses her ex-husband, "Pryns Hopkins Esq., Hotel Royal, Dinard, France." The numbers 411/412 are written over the address in blue pencil. Perhaps they were the room numbers of the Hopkins party at the Hotel Royal. Eileen writes, "You would love this wonderful wild scenery. The air is clean & fresh. It seems as if every one is going north. Miles of cars. Hope all is well. Eileen." This was sent twenty-two days before Grandpa learned Eileen got sick and was sent off to a nursing home.

Based on the apparent age of the rusty staples, Grandpa probably fastened the clippings together himself. In most cases, he dated each slip on the left edge in pencil, and they appear to be in chronological order. I have deciphered his handwriting below. In a few cases the reader will recognize information I have already written since it was from these notes Grandpa wrote the autobiography quoted earlier.

M 14 Nov [Monday 14 November 1933]

It's now midnight & I shall read a letter from Vernon re Eileen and retire. May it be happy news!

Wednesday, 16 Nov

The rest of what I have to write to-night is the saddest story I ever have & probably ever shall, put on paper.

Thurs. morning

Dr. Jones told me Peggy & Vernon had phone[d] from Scotland to say all hope for Eileen's life was gone! I had expected this soon, but was completely crumpled by it. As I lay sobbing Dr. Jones tried to comfort me.

I had Mrs. Whinneg phone or telegraph cancellations of all engagements & ask Fay to phone me, also to try to charter an aeroplane for Scotland (but the fog prevented). I called on Betty May at her school and took her for a few minutes' walk.

Catching the 1:30 "midday Scot" I reached Ayr 11 pm & drove straight to the nursing home. Peggy & Vernon were there. He took me into Eileen's room.

I then had the most horrible experience of my life. I had expected to see Eileen pale and ill — Peggy had warned me 3 weeks ago that the sight would distress me. But I simply could not recognize Eileen at all in the ashen woman, shrunk to the bone, with gray hair standing straight out who sat bolstered at the other end of the room moaning, sobbing and fighting for every breath.

When Vernon motioned me to come away I was trembling all over. I was simply obsessed with the utter horror for hours. Jack came and took Peggy home but I remained with Vernon and lay on the floor by the fire. But it was long before I could sleep.

At 4 am Jack returned to fetch us. We had another look at Eileen. Though still labouring for breath, she was sleeping, so we went to Jack and Peggy's house and slept.

Yesterday (Friday the 17th) we returned about 10 am. Eileen was rolling her head from side to side in agony or grief. When in greatest distress she would thresh about with her knees and thrust her right arm upward. I came close up this time, held her head or her hand, stroked her and kissed her. I spent the rest of this morning with her. I implored her to help us fight against the illness by being calm, taking a little liquid nourishment, etc. I told her she had every thing to live for and that the kiddies and all of us so loved her and wanted her. I told her Fay and I were engaged and soon she and Vernon and the children could come and visit us and everything would be so much easier. Every possible source of worry I tried to reassure her about. I called her my little Honeykins and pleaded with her whole heart. I think she understood me, but she could rarely say even "I know." Nothing was ever more pitiful than her inability to speak a word, to tell us what she suffered or wished or understood, unless it was her continued moaning and crying.

We left to have lunch.

Returning 2:30, we found her asleep. Peg and I took a long walk but she was still asleep. So also a second time. We had tea at the house & on our return found her still sleeping. But this time I remained nevertheless by her side, caressing her till 6:30.

At this time came Glekie[1], her regular doctor with Cowan, a heart specialist recommended by Ed. Glover[2], whom I induced them to send for. The verdict was that Eileen might live a few days but would succumb to the first heart attack. The weak heart had let circulation down & this had given bronchial pneumonia its chance. The feet were now swelling, a sure sign there'd be no recovery.

Returning to Eileen's room we found that she was again writhing and groaning pitifully. After an hour the others went home to dine, but I could not leave Eileen. It was the last time I should ever spend in her beloved presence, I knew. So I again caressed and pleaded with her till 9:20, when they led me away to catch my train. "Good night, dear little Honeykin!" I said for the last time in this life.

I caught the train back and arrived in London 7:30 this am. About 10, the message came through to the lab that Eileen had expired at mid-night. When the party returned from [leaving me off at] my train, she was found sleeping so they went home. This morning the nurse told them she had died quietly without ever awaking.

Sa 18 N

Of course now I am overcome with remorse that I didn't remain a few hours longer.

Sa 18 N [later]

To-day I have broken the news to Betty May, who at first cried bitterly but soon seemed to forget all about it. I had tea with her and Marie this pm also.

Upon reading this, I reflected on the description of my seven-year-

1. Glekie was the doctor noted on Eileen's death certificate.

2. Dr. Edward Glover was another member of the British Psycho-Analytical Society in London. Grosskurth claims he was the second most powerful after Jones. Glover sided with Anna Freud against Melanie Klein.

old mother hiding her emotions, and I again wondered why there was no mention of Peter? Eileen treats her children equally in her will, though I noted she described Peter as "adopted" in spite of the fact he was really a foster child.

Sa 18 Nov 1933

But for hardly a moment has Eileen's image ceased to haunt me. That that radiant creature, the living embodiment of innocent extasy [sic] in her joyous moments should have been reduced to the pitiable heart-rending sufferer on that bed, and now is snuffed out all together, is hard to grasp. I still almost tremble with fear at the gruesomeness of it. If I had in me any last tendency to believe a good god ran this universe, this terrible death of one so lovely, compassionate and innocent would be the final utter refutation.

Words cannot express my agony, I hear Eileen's bell-like voice everywhere. Whenever I enter a restaurant or a rendezvous where we used to meet, her dear little ghost will appear in its accustomed place. The whole thing is too fiendish. I seem to have woven no dream but she was in it. Even my marriage to Fay included the picture of mutual visits between the Armitages & us, and Fay & Eileen becoming sisters.

And when I think that once that dear person gave herself into my keeping and that for ten years I only antagonized and tortured her and finally drove her away to another man, I am ready to shriek out my despair.

Sunday morning, 19 Nov.

I awoke to an agony of regrets & grief, which I have vainly tried to work off in a long letter to Mother. I seem to have been so selfish all my life with Eileen, giving her all the responsibilities and taking all the pleasures.

How she did look after the dear children, leaving me only to call occasionally & play with them. What will become of them now? Fay grieved me last night with her lack of enthusiasm for assuming at once a full fledged family. Yet I realize that that is only natural. O, Eileen you are so much needed by all of us!

Undated

The Brighton pier choked me with memories of Ostend. I am resolved to live my life as Eileen would see me live it. One thing she would wish is that I should marry & be happy and not broken-hearted over the loss of her — this last will be hard. I can scarcely put my mind to anything else, the memories and joys and regrets flood in so thick.

w 23 n [Wednesday 23 November]

Tues. Joyce, Eric & Billy Thomas & I caught the 8:30 am for Manchester.

Note the brothers still lived in London and that Eileen's brother Harold is missing from the list.

At the Queen's Hotel we joined Mrs. Thomas, Peggy & Jack Abbott, Liala, Marie, Daisy & Jack [Lionel] Turner, Vernon & some cousins of his.

There was no listing of George Thomas either. The death announcement found in the Wolverhampton paper listed both parents. So, he must have been alive. Why didn't he attend his daughter's funeral?

After lunch we drove to the moratorium. So soon as the first of us stepped out of our car a man bearing a little white casket and a clergyman in untidy white led us into the chapel & commenced a service. I stopped him till Eileen's mother and Vernon should arrive. Then he recommenced. I suppose the words were very lovely and I tried to join in the responses as I felt Eileen would have liked me to do but presently they stuck in my throat, so false were they to the injustice and cruelty of her fate. I could only stare at the name "Eileen M. Armitage" printed on that little casket — Armitage, not Hopkins, and try to keep back the sobs.

Then we filed out and to the Armitage family vault. It was approximately on the top of the rolling[rounded?] hill which, thick-set with tombstones and bereft of verdure (so far as I recall) forms this gloomy cemetery overlooking the smoky brick town of Manchester. What a place for the ashes of radiant little Eileen to rest in!

As the casket was lowered few of us could restrain our sobs. Mrs. Thomas cried out in her anguish and had to be held from toppling after it into the purple-lined pit. I helped her back to a car & rode with her, but then myself quite broke down.

I told her I'd not let her suffer financially and I talked to and tried to comfort all Eileen's sisters.

I believe that having done this gave me a little surcease of my own sorrow and remorse on the return railroad journey. I asked Joyce, Billy & Eric to dine with me.

This (Wednesday) morning I met Vernon & Billy, Eileen's executors, at Thurland's office. We read her will. I was hurt to find there was not one mention of my name in the entire document. Yet I can imagine various reasons for this.

Vernon seems to take this whole affair more calmly than I'd have thought. I told him that protem [short for pro tempore, or temporarily], I'd pay 2/3 household expenses if he'd keep up 62 Ellsworthy Road for the children — say till towards end of Feb. I said we could then consider whether I felt I could afford to buy the house as I feel Eileen might wish me to.

W 23 Nov

If our engagement should be called off, I think I'd give up all idea of marriage, which I see threatens to separate me from the children and make me have to hide photos of Eileen.

Mo., 27 Nov.

All yesterday I sorted Eileen's letters to me. The earliest dates from our engagement and they continue until last summer. I believe I have every message she ever wrote to me during all our life together, thank god. At times, as from the Villa Coccinella, she wrote me almost daily. I was amazed to find not a bitter word, seldom even a reproach in all that time. Nearly all vibrate with loving feelings. As I read, I went through a hell of remorse, regrets and anguish. It was a terrible day.

W 29 Nov

This noon I lunched with B.M. & Vernon. He gave me Eileen's album with all the pictures of our life to-gether since that summer (1922?) when we were at the Lido. I am going to read it through to-night in bed. How it makes the past live again!

Th 30 Nov

A letter from [Nums/Mums/Sims?] tells of financial distress as I anticipated. Neither Vernon nor other trustees are much use, but I am glad to be able to help.

As I finished reading and typing, my heart bled for my grandfather. I felt badly I'd accused him of being so heartless and unconcerned about his ex-wife's funeral. I felt badly I'd accused Fay of vandalizing the journals, though this stack of clippings didn't include all that had been missing. I even felt badly for accusing Vernon of doing nothing.

Meanwhile, my brain jumped in chaotic circles trying to weave the new development into my existing story—without changing the page count.

After I transcribed all the handwriting to a digital format, I began, once again, looking for the exact location of Eileen's grave.

I remembered the listing for Kendal Milne & Co. on Eileen Maude's estate documents, and that at the time I read it, I wondered what the connection was between Eileen Maude's estate and Manchester. I looked the company up again on Google to see if I'd made a mistake. Maybe it was a funeral director, not a department store. Alas, all hits pointed to a department store. Why would there be a charge to a department store if my grandmother was cremated?

Next I typed "Cemeteries in Manchester England" into Google's search engine. I easily found Manchester's "gov" site, with a page on "Family History in Manchester, Cemetery Records and Monumental Inscriptions." This page linked me to "Manchester Burial Records," which connected me to another search form.

I inserted "Eileen" into the "Deceased Forename" box and "Armitage" in the "Deceased Surname" box. I left the choice of cemetery at "all" and inserted "1933, exact" where I was to specify the "Date Range."

Without a hiccup, I received the record for:

Burial Date: 17/03/1936
Deceased: Eileen Armitage
Cemetery: Southern Cemetery
Grave Number: MChurch of England 4262, Position 9

Note the wrong date!

To obtain more detailed information, I needed search credits. The next step was figuring out how to purchase those credits.

After working through the details with my VISA credit card, I returned to the burial listing again, clicked on Eileen Armitage, spent two credits and learned that this young lady was not my Gram. She was an eleven-month old baby. *Arg*!

Looking for more leads to the location of an Armitage family vault, I searched for Vernon Armitage among the burial listing. No luck. So, I tried his father, whose given name was included on Vernon and Eileen's marriage certificate: "Benjamin Armitage of independent means."

I received hits for three Benjamin Armitages. The first, a mechanic, died at age forty-seven. The second worked at something that ended with "of Business." (I couldn't decipher the handwriting to read the first word.) He died at age eighty-five and was buried "privately" (as opposed to "Single," like the first Benjamin was) in the Southern Cemetery where I'd found the baby Eileen Armitage. "Private" sounded more like a family vault than "Single," however, the second Benjamin was buried in an "Unconsecrated Part" of the cemetery. The third Ben died too early in time.

I voted for the second man and returned to Google to see if I could find an email address for Southern Cemetery. No. But I did, with some perseverance, obtain a street address. Apparently, part of Manchester is in Lancashire, or was.

Southern Cemetery
Barlow Moor Road
Chorlton-Cum-Hardy
Lancashire M21 7GL England

Experiencing *dejá vue,* I wrote the following letter and sent it snailmail on June 5, 2012.

Hello:

I am looking for the final resting place of the ashes of my grandmother. Though I was unable to locate her name on the Manchester Burial Records, I have reason to believe she is in "the Armitage family vault" in your cemetery, or another cemetery in Manchester. There was another listing for someone with her name (Eileen Armitage), but it was an eleven-month-old infant. My grandmother was forty-one when she died.

Here are the statistics on her death certificate...[the usual].

The reason I believe she was buried in Manchester is because my grandfather said so in his journal, stating that she was buried in the Armitage vault. My grandmother was probably of the Church of England.

I am inserting significant passages from my grandfather's journal.

> "... caught the 8:30 am for Manchester. At the Queen's hotel we joined ... we drove to the moratorium. So soon as the first of us stepped out of our car a man bearing a little white casket and a clergyman in untidy white led us into the chapel & commenced a service ... I could only stare at the name "Eileen M. Armitage" printed on that little casket...
>
> "Then we filed out and to the Armitage family vault. It was approximately on top of the roll[ing?] hill which, thick-set with tombstones and ... forms this ... cemetery overlooking the smoky brick town of Manchester."
>
> "... the casket was lowered ..."

Does this description match any part of your cemetery in 1933? Or does it match a location in another cemetery in Manchester that you know of? Or do you have any records of a burial corresponding to this data?

I also wrote a letter to Daniel at Wylie & Lochhead:

Hi Daniel,

Do you remember me? I visited Wylie & Lochhead to hold a service for my grandmother Eileen Maude Hopkins Armitage in 2009. You helped me find the record of her cremation.

I was just about to print my book about my experience when some more family records surfaced. My grandfather wrote in his journal that he attended a funeral for Eileen in Manchester.

I was wondering if we were mistaken about what happened to my grandmother after she was cremated at Wylie & Lochhead. Instead of her ashes being thrown in the Garden of Remembrance, might they have been poured in a box and sent to Manchester?

[I inserted the passages form Grandpa's journal again.]

Would you please recheck your records and see if there is any indication of ashes being sent to a moratorium in Manchester?

Then I found a listing for a funeral director in Manchester named Paul. I wrote him an email asking if he knew of a cemetery that matched my grandfather's description.

All I could do after that was sit back and wait for responses to my queries. I was in a bit of a quandary. I couldn't afford to return to England. I'd been receiving no income for over six months while trying to get this book finished. But I couldn't let the book go to press as it was. I pushed on.

On June 6, I dug out Eileen's will and estate papers to reinspect. There was nothing more than the two listings I'd found before. The amount paid to Wylie & Lochhead was only slightly more than the amount paid to Kendal Milne & Co. So, I decided I needed to find out more about the latter. What if Kendal Milne & Co had a subsidiary funeral director business?

I found nothing on the Internet. I returned to searching for cemeteries in Manchester. I wasn't encouraged by the notation that "the registers and most other early records of the [Manchester] Crematorium were lost when the company's office on York Street, Manchester, was destroyed during the winter blitz of 1940."

On the other hand, the Manchester Crematorium web site looked promising. I liked the photo of a pretty chapel on its home page and imagined a funeral there. The address for the crematorium was the same as the address for the Southern Cemetery, except for the town name and the last digit of the postal code. Either this address or the previous one must have been incorrectly posted.

The Manchester Crematorium Ltd.
Barlow Moor Road
Chorlton-cum-Hardy
Manchester M21 7GZ United Kingdom

Fortunately, the site gave an email address: office@manchester-crematorium.co.uk. I sent a letter similar to the snailmail letter I'd written to Southern Cemetery.

That same day, June 6, Daniel at Wylie & Lochhead responded to my letter:

> I do recall you not as clear as I would like to, due to my recent health problems...
>
> I will look into this and see what we come up with, however I think what may have happened if the ashes did go to Manchester, is the family stated they would have the ashes scattered and then changed their mind and had them interned.

I heard nothing back from Paul, the funeral director. Daniel wrote me again on June 7, but he wasn't much help.

> Looking at your grandfathers entry I have a feeling this casket was a CHILD. Two reasons: one, the casket is described as white (we use white for all children's caskets to represent innocence) and [two], he also describes it as SMALL and the name plate is Eileen M Armitage, not Eileen M H Armitage. I would check family birth records and see if any children were stillborn or died in infancy around that time. Will look into this on Tuesday when I return to work.

Daniel never wrote me back. I guess he didn't find anything more.

On Monday, June 11, I heard from the Manchester Bereavement Services.

> Good Morning Mary
>
> I have search[ed] our records for Eileen. She is not buried in any of our Manchester Cemeteries. You may have to contact Glasgow Crematorium. They should hold the records to say where the ashes went to.
>
> Kind Regards
>
> Ellen
>
> Customer Services Manager, Bereavement Services
>
> Manchester City Council

Dear Ellen,

Thank you for your prompt reply. I have been in contact with the Glasgow Crematorium for some time.

Can you tell me if there is an Armitage Family Vault?

Hi Mary

Not in any of the Manchester Cemeteries.

Kind regards

Ellen

I was stymied.

How could I end the book this way? If I returned to England, what were my chances of disproving Ellen? I suspected by the way she wrote that she was a young clerk who consulted the same database I did online? Did she know anything about the layouts of the cemeteries in Manchester? Did she know of any cemeteries on hills? Did she have any knowledge of records being destroyed during the war? Would she be able to find out where all those other Armitages that had been listed online were buried?

I also wondered if my Grandfather meant to write Glasgow rather than Manchester. If he did, wouldn't Daniel have a record of the whereabouts of the box of ashes? What about the location of Kendal Milne & Co in Manchester? There had to be a connection.

I was very tempted to cancel the trip I'd planned to Washington, D.C., the following week and go to England instead.

After a nap, I wrote back to Ellen.

Dear Ellen,

Please excuse me for being so persistent. I've been working on a book about my grandparents for over six years and spent thousands of dollars researching, including three trips from California to England and Scotland. I only just found this journal from my grandfather and it so clearly states that Eileen was buried in Manchester that I don't know where else to look. I've already been to Glasgow because their records stated that the ashes were scattered in the Garden of Remembrance there. I'm going to insert the entire description of the funeral by my grandfather into this email with hopes you might direct me where else to look—private cemeteries, old libraries?

[Grandpa's description.]

Is it possible that the records were destroyed during World War II?

Would it be worth a trip on my part to Manchester to walk around the cemeteries myself?

Here is another clue to the mystery. Under funeral expenses in my grandmother's estate papers, it lists Wylie & Lochhead (the FD in Glasgow) and Kendal Milne & Co (which, according to the Internet, was a department store in Manchester). There is some connection to Manchester.

My grandmother's family came from Wolverhampton.

I hope you love mysteries and can help me figure this out.

Ellen never responded.

Feeling down and discouraged, I wrote to my mother's dear friend Mary Faulkner in Pacific Grove, California. She'd been helping me edit this book. I sent her a copy of this last chapter so far. Bless her heart, she did a better job at searching through the Internet than I had and quickly discovered that Kendal Milne & Co was at one time in the funeral director business. She sent me two links.

The first was for an article from the *Manchester Evening News*, by Deborah Linton, dated September 23, 2010.

Kendals celebrates 175 years of trading[3]

By the close of the [nineteenth] century, there was a catalogue and the range had expanded from drapery and fashions to include cabinet-making, funeral undertaking and consumer goods.

The second link led me to the Manchester & Lancashire Family History Society web site,[4] with an article about the first cremation in Manchester titled "A Brief History of Cremation: The Manchester Experience."

---

3. http://menmedia.co.uk/manchestereveningnews/life_and_style/s/1328749_kendals_celebrates_175_years_of_trading.

4. http://www.mlfhs.org.uk/articles/37-2_cremation_history.pdf, p 1.

'The removal of the deceased from Carlisle to the Manchester Crematorium was carried out under the supervision of Messrs. Kendal Milne & Co. of this city.' (*Manchester Courier*, August 1892)

I was now convinced my grandmother's ashes were somewhere in Manchester. All I had to do was find someone who could check out the cemeteries for me. Who was willing to search for a cemetery on a hill overlooking the city?

I thought of my cousin Candy's children: Tom, Hattie and Ellie. They were old enough to drive. Maybe one of them needed a summer job. I looked up the distance between Worcester and Manchester—approximately 82 miles (132 kilometers).

Hey there Candy!

[Some small talk.]

I have a task that needs doing and was wondering if one of your children needed a summer project that offers cash!

You know that book I've been working on for SIX years now about looking for my grandmother's grave? Well, I was just about to publish it ...

I told Candy what I knew already and inserted the clip from Grandpa's journal describing the funeral.

When I didn't hear back from her after a couple of days, I conducted an Internet search for a professional genealogists in Manchester. I found this promising prospect:

Alan Smith
Genealogy Research Services
Lancashire Origins (but he also covered Manchester)

I wrote Alan an email and described what I needed.

He replied the next day and told me I should find someone more familiar with Manchester than he was. He suggested I contact a Kathryn Stout and gave me her email and URL addresses. She lived in Manchester and had been a genealogist for over 30 years.

On June 17 I wrote:

Dear Kathryn,

I live in California. I am looking for the grave of my English grandmother who was buried somewhere in Manchester. Actually, her ashes were buried there.

I understand from Alan Smith you are an accomplished genealogist, and I assume sleuth!

Would you be able to research this for me? I have been working on a book about looking for this grave for six years. I've already been to England three times. But it is too costly to go there this summer. [Besides, the Olympics are taking place in England now.]

I have already exhausted Ellen in the Bereavement Services.

[I described everything I knew and inserted Grandpa's description.]

Please let me know if you are available for this project and what your fees would be. I can easily pay you through PayPal.

Dear Mary,

Many thanks for your interesting story and, yes, I am in a position to help you. I am not sure who Alan Smith is, [but] yes, I am a genealogist, and I like to help solve mysteries when I can.

There are many cemeteries around Manchester. Most of them were open in 1933 and appear on the Manchester burial index. Although I am told this index is complete, I do have my doubts as both my grans were cremated at Blackley crematorium and both their names do not appear on the index.

There is only one crematorium that Manchester people from all over the area use. [It] was open in 1892 and is still used today. I imagine that the service for Eileen took place here and her ashes buried in the family vault at Southern Cemetery. Both the cemetery and crematorium are situated on Barlow Moor Road, but are classed as two separate places. Sometimes people do get confused over this because they are so close to one another.

So, it is my guess that Eileen's ashes are at Southern Cemetery because your grandfather's journal states, "we filed out to the Armitage family vault." He did not say, "We got back in the car and drove to the vault." So I think we can say that the vault was [with]in walking distance.

Manchester crematorium is privately owned with two chapels that can be adapted for use by a variety of denominations. The service for Eileen could have taken place in either one of them.

As there is no recorded letter for Eileen's service to have taken place, the only suitable suggestion I can say to you would be to go to Southern Cemetery in the hunt for the Armitage family vault. If you would like me to help you with this I am going to need some idea, if you know of course, who is buried in the vault?

Normally a vault would be a huge square stone. It could have the names of the people who are buried in it. It might also have Eileen's name on it to say her ashes are there. There again, it might not. Do you know where Vernon went to after her death and could his ashes be in the same place?

Sorry I do not know of a Queens Hotel. But it should not be too difficult to find.

You mentioned Kendal Milne & Co. I have access to a cremation obituaries index [in which] surnames have been extracted from various newspapers—some for the Manchester area. I had a look at this for the surname Armitage and found 16 surnames for this name, all cremated at Manchester Crematorium. Most of them used Kendal Milne & Co. Unfortunately, I did not find Eileen, not that I expected to as she did not die in Manchester. Nor did I find a reference to a Vernon Armitage, although the name of Vernon Kirk Armitage, youngest son of the late Sir Elkanah Armitage of Manchester was there, if there is any connection. Please note this list that I have does not say that the Armitage people['s] ashes were buried in a vault.

Please note that my suggestion of the Armitage vault being at Southern Cemetery is only guess work until proven.

[Kathryn gave me the rate for her services, which would include traveling to the cemeteries and taking photographs of the vault.]

Looking forward to hearing from you.

Kathryn Stout

Dear Kathryn,

Thank you very much. This information confirms the scant bit I've been able to find online.

Yes, I would like to hire you to follow up on all the leads you've mentioned.

This may include more genealogical work on the Armitage family. Since Vernon was my mother's stepfather, we don't have as much information as we would if he were my real grandfather.

> [I approved Kathryn's fee and payment method.]
>
> Please start by visiting the Barlow Moor Road location to see if you can find an Armitage vault on a hill overlooking Manchester.
>
> [I listed what I knew about Vernon as well as Eileen's vital information.]
>
> I look forward to news!

I expected Kathryn to write back directly to confirm she would take my case. Nine days went by, during which I traveled to Washington, D.C., to attend a conference for the National Society Daughters of the American Revolution. I only had my iPhone with me, but was able to receive an email from Candy telling me that Hattie was keen to help with my search. I asked Candy to have Hattie write me directly so I could fill her in on the details. But only a few hours later I heard from Kathryn again.

> Dear Mary,
>
> I can now tell you that Eileen Maude Armitage's ashes were not buried in a vault at Southern Cemetery. This cemetery is on flat ground and there are no hills of any sort anywhere in this cemetery.

Kathryn pointed out that listings for ashes put into grave plots or vaults were classified as *burials*, and that such listings would include the name of the deceased, their age, their last address and whether their cremated remains were enclosed or scattered.

> Southern cemetery's burials all now appear on line. I have checked to see if [Eileen's] name is given and I am sorry to say there is no reference to her.
>
> I have also checked ... Philips Park Cemetery. I searched both the Church of England and the Non-Conformist sections. I only looked at the page [for] 23rd November as this was the day her ashes were supposed to have been placed in the Armitage vault.
>
> I [also] looked at Cheetham Hill Wesleyan Cemetery. It was located on Thomas Street Cheetham Hill off Bury Old Road Manchester 8, [and] was used for burials from 1815-1968. Originally there was a chapel. Later a mortuary chapel was built and the burial ground extended. The cemetery closed in 1968 ... in 2004, the ground was cleared and the remains removed to another cemetery. Tesco supermarket now stands in its place.

There was no mention of Eileen M Armitage in these cemetery registers.

You mentioned ... Queens Hotel in Manchester. Upon looking at a trade directory for 1933 for Manchester I noted the following:

Queens Hotel - Bartley Dunne 391, 393 & 395 Ashton New Road, & 247 Mills Street Bradford

Queens Hotel - John McManus, 787 Rochdale Road

Queens Hotel - John Mellor, 304 Ordsall Lane, Salford

Queens Hotel - Samuel Rogers, 227 Queens Road, Miles Platting

The Queens Hotel used by Eileen's family members could have been any of the above.

The Queens Hotel on Rochdale Road is, to my knowledge, near Manchester General Cemetery (also known as Queens Park Cemetery). It is located on Queens Road Harpurhey, now off Rochdale Road Manchester 9. This cemetery was used for burials from 1837-1961. The cemetery is now closed except for existing family graves. The lower section was cleared and landscaped as a park [in] the 1960s.

[The library] only has access to burials from 1837-1905. Unfortunately, I am not sure [where the records of burials] after 1905 [are held].

Kathryn explained that the Manchester General Cemetery was in a terrible state, and that people were in the process of transcribing the readable grave markers and "doing a general tidying" which, though worth it in the end, would take some time. She wrote she would make some telephone calls to see if there were registers available after 1905, if I wanted her to. Then she went on to discuss the Queens Hotel in Salford.

The only cemetery that I can think of [near there] is Weaste Cemetery. However, it was not [with]in walking distance of Ordsall Lane. The family would have had to use a car. This cemetery is now closed except for existing family graves. Weaste was open in 1857 and is a huge cemetery. There is a charge of £16.00 at the cemetery office for a grave search to be done.

Would you have any idea who is buried in the Armitage family vault? If I had some idea of the names, it might be easier for me to locate them. In turn, it should take me to Eileen? Have you done any research on the

Armitage family in general, or do you have any names and dates of death that I could pursue that could lead me to Eileen?

You told me Eileen's second husband, Vernon Hay Armitage, may have gone to Africa to live. It would appear he came back to England.

[I found under the] *UK Incoming Passengers Lists 1878-1960*

> Vernon H Armitage, 64 yrs
> Kathleen Armitage, 59 yrs
> Port of departure: Cape Town, South Africa, Travelled First Class
> Port of arrival: Southampton
> Arrival date: 15 June 1952
> Ships name Bloem—
> Proposed address in the UK: Vernon c/o Harvey Gravel Path, retired & Kathleen, Berkhamstead, Herts, housewife
> Country of last permanent residence: Kenya (both of them)

Vernon later died in May 1958 aged 70 yrs. It would appear he left a large amount of funds to his wife.

Probate Index

Vernon Hay Armitage, died 5 May 1958

Probate date 24 July 1958 of the Savoy Hotel, West Cliff, Bournemouth, dies at 3 Owls Road, Boscombe, Bournemouth.

Probate: London 24 July to Kathleen Alice May Armitage widow and Frank Newton Battersby solicitor effects £30,636 19s 3d

Resealed: Nairobi, Kenya, 15 October 1958

I am finishing here and I look forward to your comments on the above research. Eileen's ashes could almost be anywhere. There are not many churches in the Manchester area which still did burials as late as 1933. However, if they were to open a grave/vault and place [the ashes] in, it might be a different matter.

Dear Kathryn

Wow. You have been busy.

It seems clear that the family did take a car from the Queens Hotel to the place where the service was held. I vote for paying the £16 fee to search Weaste if there is a chance there is a hill overlooking Manchester.

I am in Washington, D.C., for a week without access to my computer, just my iPhone. I gave you everything I know about Vernon's family. I sent you his age. If you would like to research him more, that's OK.

I was able to pay Kathryn's search fee using PayPal on my iPhone.

That was June 26. I was losing hope I would ever find my grandmother, at least from a distance. What was I going to do with this book? I wanted my relatives to learn about all my other research even if I didn't find the grave. Strangely, I wasn't completely discouraged. A small voice kept telling me an answer would come eventually. I just needed to be patient.

When I checked my iPhone on June 29 from my hotel room, after a long day of meetings and sightseeing in Washington in 104 degree heat—it reminded me of my time in England during their record heat spell—I received the email from Kathryn I'd been afraid to dream of.

Dear Mary,

I am pleased to inform you that I have located the Armitage vault that contains the ashes of Eileen along with 5 other Armitage graves/vaults, all in the same area, which refer to twenty plus individuals/families.

With such a find I could not help but to take a vast amount of photographs for you.

No wonder you never found any reference to Eileen in Manchester as her grave was not found in Manchester

Perhaps now you can finish your book!

Dear Kathryn,

What fantastic news. Really fantastic. When do I get to see the photos? I am still working from my phone until July 2.

Since this book is about the genealogical search process, I hope you will confide how you found the answer.

Mary,

The reason why I have not submitted [to] you a report on the cemetery visit [is because] it was late when I emailed you, and I knew that I would not have time to complete it. Plus, 106 photos were taken of Eileen's vault and other Armitage graves that were found. I intend to put them on a disc and send them to you to view on your own computer, where you have the option of enlarging the photograph. Do you want me to send a transcript of each headstone? This could take me at least three hours to do. Or would you like to do this yourself? All the headstones will be easy enough to read, apart from two where some of the lead lettering has fallen off.

I hope I did right in taking photographs of the other Armitage graves. They were Eileen's ancestral in-laws. In the meantime, I have attached four files of Eileen's vault.

I wouldn't be able to view the images until I got home. I wrote back.

Yes, you did right taking the photos, thank you. If you would please transcribe Eileen's information, I will do the rest. Is it difficult to figure out the connections?

The big question is, where were the graves?

I am so excited the puzzle has been solved and look forward to your report.

I gave her my address for sending the disk.

Dear Mary,

Eileen Armitage was buried at Weaste Cemetery, Salford, along with Vernon's family.

I will explain in more detail in my report how I came to find her in Salford. I have copied the photographs onto a disc ready for posting. Would you like my report and transcript of the vault posting with it, or do you prefer my report and transcript by email?

I asked her to send me the transcript for Eileen's grave in an email and send the rest as a hard copy with the disk.

I looked up Salford on Google Maps. It is about three and a half kilometers west of Manchester, the next town over.

When I got home from Washington, D.C., on July 2, a letter from Kathryn with four photos and the following transcription waited for

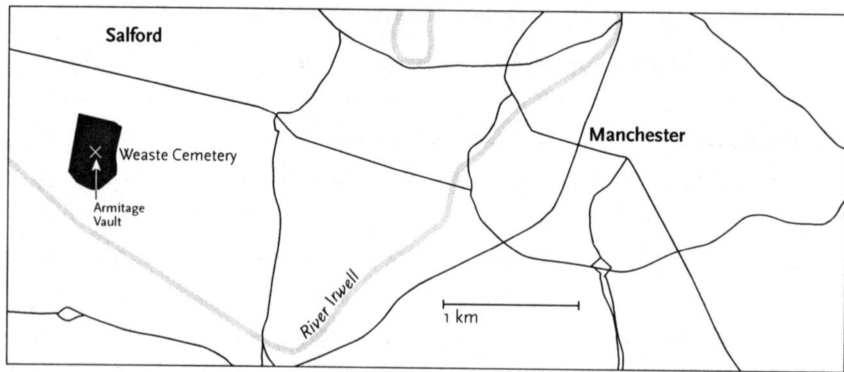

me in my email queue. Even though Grandpa described the casket being lowered into a vault, I'd been imagining an opening in a small stone building. The Armitage vault isn't like that at all. It is a large hole under the ground covered by an equally large double-tiered granite stone, like a sheet cake placed over a bigger sheet cake (see the photo at the beginning of this chapter). The stone cake sits on top of the ground surrounded by grass and regular upright headstones. The whole thing is about six feet long and three and a half feet wide. Each tier is four or five inches thick, so the cake rises eight to ten inches off the ground. The inscriptions on the top stone describe the demise of Vernon's family, beginning with his father:

IN MEMORY OF

BENJAMIN ARMITAGE,
WHO DIED DEC. 4TH 1899 AGED 76 YEARS

ELIZABETH,
WIFE OF BENJAMIN ARMITAGE
WHO DIED FEB. 11TH 1855, AGED 31 YEARS
AND WAS INTERRED AT HARPURHEY CEMETERY

ELIZABETH,
THE SECOND WIFE OF BENJAMIN ARMITAGE,
WHO DIED MARCH 5TH 1899, AGED 72 YEARS.

FREDERICK [ARMITAGE], THEIR ELDEST SON,
WHO DIED APRIL 5TH 1879, AGED 32 YEARS.

JOHN ELKANAH [ARMITAGE]
WHO DIED MARCH 19TH 1887, AGED 31 YEARS.

HAROLD JAMES [ARMITAGE],
THE SECOND SON OF FREDERICK ARMITAGE
WHO DIED FEB. 27TH 1899, AGED 23 YEARS.

JULIE HENRIETTE [ARMITAGE],
WIDOW OF FREDERICK ARMITAGE,
WHO DIED DEC. 25TH 1901, AGED 52 YEARS.

The rest of the names circle the ledge made by the bottom stone, creating a frame. Eileen Maud Armitage was on the left edge (at seven o'clock), nearest the bottom and to the left of Julie Henriette. Vernon was listed on the right (at five o'clock). It was as if he had his back to Eileen. There is still some room on the left ledge on Vernon's side in case more relatives need a final home.

Starting with Vernon and circling clockwise:

VERNON HAY ARMITAGE
5 MAY 1958 AGED 70

CHARLES SMITH, FOURTH SON OF THE LATE BENJAMIN ARMITAGE
WHO DIED 20 JULY 1904, AGED 53

EILEEN MAUD ARMITAGE
18 NOVEMBER 1933

BENJAMIN ARMITAGE
5 JAN 1936 AGED 85

KATHERINE DUVERNET ARMITAGE
21 JUNE 1927

WILLIAM HENRY, SECOND SON OF THE LATE BENJAMIN ARMITAGE
WHO DIED 21 MAY 1925, 77 YEARS

Apparently Vernon's second wife was not buried with his first. Katherine couldn't be Vernon's Kathleen because she died before Vernon and Kathleen sailed home from Africa in 1952.

Listed among a group of virtually unfamiliar relatives wasn't the grand monument I dreamed of for my grandmother. But at least her new family didn't abandoned her. She and Vernon were married for one year. We don't know if or how long she knew his family before she met and married my grandfather. It will remain a mystery why no one ever told my mother or Peter about this grave.

On July 3, Kathryn sent me her report:

> I am pleased that the grave of Eileen has at long last been found and that you can now finish your book.
>
> From the onset it was a bit like looking for a needle in a hay stack. The

clues you gave me were the key[s] to finding Eileen's grave. There were so many churches and council grave yards in Manchester in 1933, where [was] I [to] start!

I rechecked the Manchester Council-owned burial/cremation indexes. No reference was found to Eileen. I ruled out any of the city centre churches as they would not have been "overlooking the smoky brick town of Manchester."

I needed to look for somewhere on the outskirts of Manchester with a clear view of the city. Southern Cemetery should have been a favourite, however the cemetery was flat and with grass, not "bereft of verdure."

The next clue was the Queen's Hotel. Which one of the four that I found was near a cemetery? Ordsall Lane, Salford, was near Weaste Cemetery, but Weaste Cemetery was mostly flat and not part of Manchester. Did it view Manchester?

Salford is a city in its own right, which borders onto Manchester. In fact, part of it is adjacent to Manchester city centre. Salford City Council holds burial registers for their city—likewise Manchester for their city. That is why I found no reference to Eileen in Manchester.

After more investigation via Salford City Council, a reference to Eileen was found at Weaste Cemetery, Dissenters Plot A4, Eccles New Road, Salford, Greater Manchester.

Having located the grave, I found that the surrounding graves also contained [notable] members of the Armitage family. (See wilkipedia.org/wiki/elkanah-armitage.)

Photo No 186 shows a view in the direction of Manchester. If you were to take away 80 years of growth from the trees and remove the buildings, I am sure that the view would be of Manchester.

All the Armitages found at Weaste are [probably] related but more research would have to be undertaken to prove this.

Katheryn included a photo of a placard at the cemetery detailing Weaste's history. The municipal cemetery, opened in 1857, and now closed to new grave plots, is the oldest of Salford's four cemeteries. The four chapels are now gone, including the one where Eileen Maude's service took place. There are over 332,000 interments within its thirty-nine acres. Before the cemetery opened, the deceased were buried in

Photo No. 186, facing toward Manchester from Weaste Cemetery.

churchyards. But churchyards began running out of room during the Industrial Revolution when thousands migrated to the filthy cities. The placard said, "Dangerous working conditions, inadequate housing, disease and the lack of medical care meant that, for ordinary people, life expectancy was short. In the 1870s a man in Salford could expect to live to just seventeen years of age." The poor were often interred in common graves with up to twenty other people.

Weaste's web site[5] said that Victorians considered cemeteries an amenity, like a park or garden. Designer Pritchett of York intended to offer a beautiful landscaped garden where people could escape the "bustle of city life." The park provided "lungs" for city dwellers "away from the foul factory fumes."

"Weaste Cemetery was favoured by the most well-heeled Salfordians and Mancunians who chose to be buried in the 'rich man's plot.'" Gram Eileen has distinguished neighbors. Joseph Brotherton, Salford's first Member of Parliament, believed in clean living and a clean environment. He helped Salford establish a library, a museum and an art gallery and persuaded Parliament to pass the Public Libraries Act. Weaste Cemetery, Brotherton's dream, opened early especially for his funeral after his untimely death. Eileen's other neighbors included: Sir Charles Hallé,

5. http://www.salford.gov.uk/weastecemetery.htm.

who conducted and played the piano for Britain's longest-established professional symphony orchestra. Mark Addy saved fifty-three people from drowning in the River Irwell near the factory where he worked. Eddie Colman, a Busby Babe, died tragically in the Munich air disaster of 1958. Ferdinand Stanley survived the *Charge of the Light Brigade*, immortalized by Alfred Lord Tennyson.

Equally interesting were Eileen's father-in-law, grandfather-in-law, and great-grandfather-in-law, who seem to have amounted to more than Vernon did. According to Wikipedia, Vernon's father, Benjamin, who died when Eileen was seven, was a British industrialist and Liberal politician. He sat for Salford in the House of Commons from 1880 to 1886. Benjamin was the second of eight children (second son) of Sir Elkanah Armitage, a textile manufacturer of Salford, also a British industrialist and Liberal politician.

Sir Elkanah, the third of six sons of a farmer and linen weaver of Failsworth, Lancashire[6], who was also named Elkanah, left school at age eight to work in the cotton industry. Diligent and shrewd in business, he and two brothers established factories that wove sailcloth, ginghams and checks. The first, with James Thompson in 1829, employed twenty-nine workers and sold cloth in Manchester. By 1848, they'd extended their business to the Pendleton New Mills with 600 workers. The Armitages took over the Nassau Mills in neighboring Patricroft in 1867.

Sir Elkanah, always active in politics, signed the Manchester petition of 1806 to abolish the Slave Trade. He became an alderman in 1841 and served as Mayor of Manchester from 1846 to 1848, during which time he helped divert a crisis regarding the Chartist Movement, the first working class labor movement. This service led to Queen Victoria creating him a Knight Bachelor.

Elkanah unsuccessfully stood for Parliament in 1857, but was appointed High Sheriff of Lancashire in 1866. He died at age eighty-two in 1876, leaving an estate of £200,000 (about fourteen million pounds in today's currency). "His funeral procession was half a mile long and made up of a hundred carriages."

An "x" on the spot where the Armitage vault is located on the map

---

6. Failsworth is very close to Manchester.

indicates Eileen's ashes were buried smack dab in the center of the cemetery. Kathryn added that when she told her father, who was born and brought up in Salford, about her project, he mentioned that part of the lower end of the cemetery was bombed during the Second World War. German pilots were flying toward Salford Docks and dropped the bombs too early. A lot of the gravestones were destroyed and many still bear shrapnel damage. Had that "too early" moment been a few seconds later or earlier, I might have spent the rest of my life looking for a grave that no longer existed.

Gram Eileen and Grandpa Prynce, you are up there pulling strings. I just know it.

Eileen Maud Armitage
18 November 1933

Acknowledgements

Thank you to all my dear English cousins for your help, love and openness: Camilla, Rodney, Cynthia, Ann, James, Harriett, Jon, Candida, Philippa, Lionel, Jason, Michael and Veronica. Thank you to their children: Tom, Hattie, Ellie, Josh, Georgia, Charlie, Laura, Bex, Sophie, Sorrel, Fleurie, Helier and Zephir for tolerating their American relative; to significant others Catherine, Tim, Peter and Thomas for their bits.

Thank you to my English stepfamily: Paul, Judy, Gabrielle, Carolyn, Tim, Jessica and Verity.

Thank you to my mother's friends. All contributed information. Mary Faulkner and Dorothy Colodny helped edit. Rosemary Davies and her husband, Graham, sheltered me and made me feel at home.

Thank you to my mother's siblings: Peter, Jennifer and David, who shared tales and information and gave me moral support. Jennifer, a marvelous writer herself, and who owns the rights to my grandfather's writing, agreed I could publish her father's/my grandfather's story about his life with Eileen as long as I left the story about *her* parents to her.

I can't leave out Jenny X, Oliver and Dr. Ronald Koegler.

Thank you, Michael Struck for recording *La Golandrina*.

Thank you to my sort-of-cousin Jim Baker for his marvelous editing and to my gracious professional editors Wendy Werris, Ana Manwaring and Jane Merryman. Thank you Peter Humphries for your input.

Thank you to the members of my critique group: Karen, Nancy, Lindsay and Don.

Thank you to super detective/genealogist Kathryn Stout. Without her final help, this book would have been shelved as an unfinished manuscript.

Thank you to the staffs of so many libraries: The Family History Centers in San Francisco and Oakland, the New England Historic and Genealogical Society, Sutro Library in San Francisco, the California Room of the San Rafael Library, the British Newspapers Library, The National British Archives in Kew and the Family Records Center in London. There were probably more I've forgotten.

Thank you to my children for putting up with my obsession for genealogy even though you've banned me from discussing it during meals.

And if your spirit can read this somehow, thank you, dear Mom.

Resources

- Genealogist in Manchester: Kathryn Stout
  http://www.rootsfamilyhistoryservice.co.uk/
- Information on the Armitage Family:
  www.en.wilkipedia.org/wiki/elkanah-armitage
- Family History Centers for the Church of Latter-day Saints:
  www.familysearch.org
- British National Archives of England, Wales, and the United Kingdom:
  www.nationalarchives.gov.uk
- Apartment Rentals in London:
  www.LondonChoice.com
- Hampstead Cemetery:
  Fortune Green Road, London NW6 1DR. The burial registers are located at the Cemetery; 0207-435-6142. The registers are accessible via the Islington and Camden Cemetery Services email.
- Camden Centre:
  www.camden.gov.uk/localstudies
- Highgate Cemetery:
  Swains Lane, London N6 6PJ. The burial registers are located at Camden Local Studies Library, Holborn Library, 32-38 Theobald Road, London, WC1X 8PA; 0207-974-6342.
- St. Pancras Cemetery:
  High Road, East Finchley, London N2 9AG. Burial registers located at cemetery; 0208-883-1231.
- Phone number for Information in England: 118247
- Wolverhampton, Staffordshire, England:

www.wolverhampton.gov.uk

- Weaste Cemetery: www.salford.gov.uk/cemeteryheritagetrail.htm

Family History Web Sites

Recommended by the British National Archives (August 2008)

Census:

- www.nationalarchives.gov.uk/census
- www.scotlandspeople.gov.uk (1841-1901 Scotish census)
- www.freecen.org.uk (UK 1841-1891)

Birth, Marriage and Death:

- www.gro.gov.uk (General Register Office web site for ordering your certificates)
- www.scotlandspeople.gov.uk
- www.freebmd.org.uk (General Register Offices indexes, incomplete)
- www.ukbmd.org.uk (civil registration sites and more) http://isys.llgc.org.uk (index of applications for marriage licensces in Wales 1616-1837)
- www.bcarchives.gov.bc.ca/textual/governmt/vstats/v_events.htm (British Colombia births, marriages and deaths)
- www.nmm.ac.uk/memorials (memorials to seafarers and victims of maritime disasters)
- www.bereavement-services.org (information on UK burial grounds, cemeteries and crematoria)

If you type the following into the search field, Google will connect you to a zillion web sites from which you can download lists of useful sites for genealogical research: "useful web sites for family history, pdf, national archives"

CPSIA information can be obtained at www.ICGtesting.com
Printed in the USA
BVOW041558300812

299223BV00002B/3/P

9 780985 053017